Modern Historical
and Social Philosophies

Modern Historical
and Social Philosophies

(formerly titled: Social Philosophies of an Age of Crisis)

by

PITIRIM A. SOROKIN

DOVER PUBLICATIONS, INC., NEW YORK

This Dover edition, first published in 1963, is an unabridged and unaltered republication of the work first published by the Beacon Press, Boston, in 1950 under the former title: *Social Philosophies of an Age of Crisis*.

Standard Book Number: 486-21146-0
Library of Congress Catalog Card Number: 63-20255

Manufactured in the United States of America
Dover Publications, Inc.
180 Varick Street
New York, N.Y. 10014

TO
ELI LILLY

Preface to the Dover Edition

After its original edition in 1950, this work appeared in its British edition in 1952, in German translation under the title *Kulturkrise und Gesellschafts-Philosophie* in 1953, in Spanish translation under the title *Las Filosofías Sociales de Nuestra Época de Crisis* in 1954, and in 1963-64 is scheduled to be published in Portuguese and Hindi translations. It is now reissued in its original text. The only change this original text needs concerns my analysis and criticism of A. J. Toynbee's theory of history. In the twelfth volume of his *Study of History: Reconsiderations,* published in 1961, this eminent historian and philosopher of history introduced several important changes of his theory of history as it was developed in the first six volumes of his monumental work. Among these changes, particularly important is the replacement of his theory of the univariant life-cycle of all civilizations by that of a multivariant life-course of different civilizations. He states: " I have been at fault in having been content to operate with the Hellenic model only. Though this particular key has opened many doors, it has not proved omnicompetent. For example, it has not opened the door to understanding of the structure of Egyptian history." Accordingly, his univariant model of the life-cycle of all civilizations is replaced now by at least three different models of the life-course of civilizations exemplified by the Hellenic, the Chinese, and the Jewish civilizations. In its present form Toynbee's theory of historical uniformities recurring in the life-course of the *Hochkulturen* is in greater agreement with my own theory of change of cultural and social systems and also with the theories of A. Kroeber and F. S. C. Northrop, analyzed in this volume, and with the philosophies of history expounded by J. Ortega y Gasset, F. R. Cowell and others.

With the exception of this change the book hardly needs any revision or reconsideration of its analyses, evaluations, criticisms and conclusions.

Winchester, Mass.   Pitirim A. Sorokin
1963

Acknowledgments

This book is an enlarged version of my Cole Lectures on "Recent Philosophies of History," presented in April, 1950, at the seventy-fifth anniversary of Vanderbilt University. For the privilege of giving the Cole Lectures, I am indebted to the faculty of the School of Religion at Vanderbilt University, and to its Chancellor, Harvie Branscomb, and its Dean, John Keith Benton. I am also grateful to my audience for its generous response to these lectures.

I wish to thank the following publishing firms for their kind permission to quote several passages from works published by them:

Alfred A. Knopf, Inc., for the quotations from *Decline of the West* by Oswald Spengler, Volume I copyright 1926 by Alfred A. Knopf, Inc.; Volume II copyright 1928 by Alfred A. Knopf, Inc.

The Macmillan Company for the quotations from *The Philosophy of Civilization* by Albert Schweitzer, copyright 1949 by the Macmillan Company; and from *The Meeting of East and West* by F. S. C. Northrop, copyright 1946 by The Macmillan Company.

The Oxford University Press for the quotations from *A Study of History* by Arnold J. Toynbee, 6 volumes, issued under the auspices of the Royal Institute of International Affairs, copyright 1934–1936 by Oxford University Press; and from *Civilization on Trial* by Arnold J. Toynbee, copyright 1948 by Oxford University Press.

The University of California Press for the quotations from *Configurations of Culture Growth* by Alfred L. Kroeber, copyright 1944 by the University of California Press.

The dedication is a token of my respect for, and gratitude to, Eli Lilly and the Lilly Endowment, Inc., to whose initiative and financial support the Harvard Research Center in Altruistic Integration and Creativity largely owes its establishment.

PITIRIM A. SOROKIN

Harvard University
Cambridge, Massachusetts

Contents

PART ONE

OUTLINE OF MODERN SOCIAL PHILOSOPHIES

I

Man's Reflection on Man's Destiny in an Age of Crisis

Even in normal times, cogitation about man's destiny—on the whence and whither, the how and why, of a given society —is now and then carried on by at least a few thinkers or scholars. In times of serious crisis these problems suddenly assume exceptional importance, theoretical as well as practical; for thinkers as well as for plain folk. An enormous part of the population finds itself uprooted, ruined, mutilated, and annihilated by the crisis. People's routine of life is entirely upset; their habitual adjustments are broken; and large groups of human beings are turned into a flotsam of displaced and disadjusted persons. Even the ordinary man in the street cannot help asking: How has all this come about? what does it all mean? who is responsible for it? what are its causes? is there any way out? where do we go from here? and what is going to happen to me and my family, my friends and my country? In a serious crisis these questions press still more intensely upon the thinkers, leaders, and scholars in a society. Many of them do not pay much attention to their sociocultural "shoes" until they begin to pinch. When, however, the "pinching" of the hardships of the crisis becomes unbearable, they are forced to begin to ponder on the how and why of the crisis and on all the other problems of a painful transitional situation.

This means that in times of crisis one should expect an upsurge of cogitation on and study of the how and why, the whence and whither, of man, society, and humanity. This expectation is corroborated by the relevant facts. Most of the significant "philosophies of history," most of the "intelligible interpretations of historical events," and most of the important generalizations about sociocultural processes have indeed appeared either in the periods of serious crisis, catastrophe, and transitional disintegration, or immediately before and after such periods. Thus in ancient Egypt, the earliest "philosophies of history," represented by such documents as *The Admonitions of an Egyptian Sage* (Ipuwer), *The Complaint of Khekheperre-sonbu, The Prophecy of Neferrohu, The Dialogue of a Misanthrope with His Soul, The Song Which is in the House of King Intef,* all date from the periods of catastrophic crisis in the life-history of Egypt, from the interim period between the Old and the Middle Kingdoms, and then between the Middle Kingdom and the New Empire.[1]

Likewise, there is the elementary germ of a philosophy of history in a surviving document from the thirteenth century B.C. of the Hittite culture; and in somewhat similar Babylonian documents, including the Babylonian "Book of Job." These documents date from the periods of the profound crises in the history of these countries.[2]

In China both the Confucian theory of three stages through which mankind passes, the stages of "the Disorderly, the Small Tranquility, and the Great Similarity," and the corresponding philosophy of history,[3] as well as the Taoist mystical and sociopolitical interpretations of sociocultural processes, both appeared in times of a prolonged crisis and profound disorders. Most of the subsequent neo-Confucian and neo-Taoist, neo-Buddhist and positivist, individualistic and collectivistic, economico-materialistic and idealistic interpretations of history by Chinese thinkers appeared in times of troubles and calamity.

Likewise in India the detailed theory of the great and small cycles through which the world and mankind pass, beginning with the longest cycle of the "elemental" dissolution of the world of some 311,040,000,000,000 mortal years, and ending with the "occasional" dissolution recurring at the end of each Kalpa of 4,320,000 mortal years with its four stages, the Krita-Yuga, the Treta-Yuga, the Dwapara-Yuga, and the Kali-Yuga—these theories and corresponding philosophies of history seem also to have emerged mainly in times of crisis: the theories themselves state that since about the fourteenth century B.C. mankind has been in the stage of decline and crisis, the Kali-Yuga stage that lasts 432,000 years. During it all the great institutions, beginning with religion and caste and ending with the family and marriage, are destroyed; the governments become "of churlish spirit, violent temper, and addicted to falsehood and wickedness. They inflict death on women and children . . . they seize the property of their subjects," and so on.[4]

In the Bible the germs of the Jewish philosophies of history are given mainly in the prophetic and Messianic theories of the prophets and of the author of Ecclesiastes. And all these works (except possibly Ecclesiastes) appeared in the time of the greatest catastrophe for the Jewish nation—after the loss of its independence in Babylonian and other captivities.

In Greece the elements of historico-philosophical thinking found in the works of Hesiod and Theognis, the later interpretations of history by Plato, Aristotle, Thucydides, Polybius, and in Rome by Lucretius, Cicero, Varro, Philo, Apollonius of Tyana, Plutarchos, Apuleius, and the authors of the *Hermetica,* then by the rhetoricians like Censorinus, by the early Church Fathers, up to St. Augustine's *City of God* and Orosius' *Seven Books of History*—they all were created in the periods of either an acute and profound trouble and catastrophe (like the plundering of Rome by Attila) or of a most serious prolonged crisis.

In the Middle Ages, the most significant interpretations of history, like Joachim of Floris' *Eternal Gospel,* appeared in the twelfth century—the century of the great transition from the dying Medieval Ideational culture to the different Idealistic culture of the thirteenth and the fourteenth centuries.

Similarly, one of the greatest philosophies of history ever written, Ibn-Khaldun's *Historical Prolegomena,* was created in the fourteenth century, when profound crisis and decay overtook Arabic culture. Ibn-Khaldun himself eloquently describes this critical period and his own troubles in his *History of Berberes, Autobiography,* and *Prolegomena.*

The list can be prolonged by Machiavelli's *Prince, Discourses,* and *History of Florence,* by Giambattista Vico's *New Science,* Hobbes' *Leviathan,* Locke's socio-philosophical treatises, by certain works of Voltaire, Rousseau, De Maistre, De Bonald, and by dozens and dozens of other significant works in the field studied. They all were conceived and born in the conditions of crisis of the society in which the thinkers lived and often in the course of a crisis in the personal life of the author. Theognis or Hesiod, Plato or Aristotle, Cicero or Ibn-Khaldun, Dante or Joachim of Floris, Machiavelli or Hobbes, Rousseau or De Maistre, up to Karl Marx and Lenin: these and from seventy to eighty per cent of the eminent "philosophers of history" and social thinkers were either imprisoned or banished, had to flee to save their lives or underwent other critical troubles.

These cases, a few out of many, demonstrate the concurrence of an upsurge of interest in, inquiry into, and discussion of the historical jig-saw puzzle with a time of crisis. They explain also the fact of such an upsurge in our own century, especially after the First World War. Being a period of possibly the greatest crisis in the whole history of humanity, the twentieth century has already produced a multitude of philosophies of history. More, some of the books propounding these philosophies have become either bestsellers, like Spengler's or Toynbee's volumes, or, as some other "readings of historical events" have done, reached tens of thousands of lay readers. These facts mean an enormous increase in the efforts in the direction of an intelligible interpretation of historical processes on the part of the intellectuals and a notable diffusion of these quests among laymen. Passively and actively, the problems of the whence and whither, the how and why of oneself, of one's family, people and nation, of mankind and culture, are pulsating in the minds of millions of people today. These problems are indeed on the agenda of history.

Another thing to be noted is the kind of philosophy of history that appears in critical times. Elsewhere I have shown that *there is a close correspondence between the dominant type of culture and the type of social philosophy prevalent in it.*

Thus, generally, *in a Sensate culture, Sensate theories and philosophies dominate; in an Ideational culture, Ideational ideologies; in a preponderantly Eclectic culture, Eclectic theories.* When one dominant type of culture ends and another is coming in, these philosophies, ideologies, and theories change correspondingly: those connected with the crumbling type of culture decline and those that are in harmony with the rising type of culture take root and blossom.[5]

As to philosophies of history, I have also shown [6] that in the predominantly Sensate cultures similar to the culture in the West for the last four centuries, the progressively linear theories of the evolution of humanity tend to dominate. In such a culture the whole historical process is viewed as a sort of progressive advance along the highway, with some deviations and little detours, from "the caveman to superman," from "barbarism to civilization," from "stupidity to wisdom and genius," from "bestiality to semi-divinity," from war and struggle for existence to peace, harmony, and mutual aid—and so on. In hundreds of variations this progressively linear theory of human history tends to be dominant in Sensate culture, especially in the course of its rise and at its zenith.

In predominantly Ideational cultures a variety of non-mechanistic but divinely guided, cyclical or eschatological or trendlessly undulating philosophies of history tend to dominate. Purely mechanistic theories of the cyclical or oscillating interpretation of historical processes and Apocalyptic-Messianic conceptions of man's destiny, with the catastrophic end of the world and human history, tend to proliferate at the declining stages of Sensate and, to a lesser degree, of Ideational culture.

Since Western culture has during the last four centuries been mainly Sensate, the dominant philosophies of history and theories of social evolution of that period must have been chiefly, according to the above rules, progressively linear. As is shown in Chapter XIV, they have indeed been such. The theories of progress-evolution by Kant and Fichte, Herder and Lessing, Hegel and Adam Smith, Auguste Comte and Herbert Spencer, Karl Marx and John Fiske, the Darwinian and biological theories of evolution—these are the typical representatives of historical processes, trends, laws of evolution of that Sensate period of Western culture.

Since the twentieth century is the period of the greatest crisis, the end of the Sensate era and a catastrophic transition to a new culture, the hitherto dominant linear conceptions of history must be expected, according to the foregoing rules, to be on the decline; and the rising philosophies of history, to be either cyclical, creatively recurrent, eschatological, or of an Apocalyptic and Messianic type.

The facts confirm this expectation. The twentieth century has, in the whole field of the social and humanistic disciplines, hardly produced any original or significant theory of linear progress or evolution. All the numerous linear theories of the twentieth century have been but midget variations of Hegelian, Comtian, Spencerian, or Marxian conceptions of progress-evolution.

On the other hand, as we shall see in this book, practically all the significant philosophies of history of our critical age reject the progressively linear interpretations of historical process and assume either a cyclical, creatively rhythmical, eschatological, or Messianic form. Besides the revolt against the linear interpretations of history, these social philosophies display many other shifts in the dominant social theories. They proclaim utterly inadequate the hitherto dominant "positivistic" and "empiricistic" methods of understanding social phenomena; the empiricistic theory of cognition and truth; the hitherto prevalent techniques of investigation of sociocultural phenomena; and most of the beliefs and notions described as "naturalistic," "scientific," "mechanistic," "operational," "instrumental," or "quantitative" social and humanistic disciplines. Almost all of the new theories contend that at best these methods, techniques, and beliefs can give a cognition of only one aspect of sociocultural phenomena: their dead shells. In no way do they give an adequate cognition of especially the living and creative aspects of sociocultural processes. In brief, the rising philosophies of history of our critical age represent a sharp rupture with the dominantly progressive, positivistic, empiricistic philosophies of the dying Sensate era. Insofar the contrast once more confirms the rules given above.

Subsequent chapters outline, criticize, and assess most of the significant and typical philosophies of history in our critical age. I do not endeavor to survey all the "readings of historical events" of the twentieth century. An enormous part of these "readings" have been trivial or incompetent, unintelligible or epigonic. As such they hardly deserve to be discussed and criticized. On the other hand, the interpretations of history discussed in the following pages appear to be the most symptomatic, original, and influential for our age. They are an expression of its crisis and anxiety; its eschatology and Messianic hopes; its disillusionment in the old, and its quest for a new, deeper and more valid understanding of man and his destiny.

Our analysis begins with the "aesthetic" philosophies of history derived from investigations of art-phenomena. Recent studies of art-types and especially of art-dynamics have led many a scholar to a sort of philosophy of history that foreshadowed and "scooped" most of the subsequent, general theories of historical process. Often neglected, these "aesthetic readings of history" should be given due credit.

Subsequent chapters deal with a group of theories advanced by Danilevsky, Spengler, Toynbee, Schubart, and Berdyaev. Though Danilevsky's *Russia and Europe* was first published in 1869, he is included in this group because he was a true predecessor of Spengler, Toynbee, Schubart, and Berdyaev.

Later chapters are devoted to an outline of the theories of Northrop, Kroeber, and Schweitzer. Each of these theories is important in itself and represents many other "interpretations" of our time.

Part Two is devoted to a criticism of the main shortcomings of all these theories.

Part Three is an attempt to sum up the main points of agreement in all these theories and to indicate their valid contributions.

The volume as a whole is a supplement to its companion volume, *Contemporary Sociological Theories*.

II

Aesthetic Interpretations of History

I

THEORIES OF W. M. F. PETRIE, PAUL LIGETI, AND OTHERS

One of the earliest and most stimulating currents in the recent upsurge of "intelligible readings of historical events" appeared in works dealing with art-phenomena. Either earlier than most of the subsequent philosophers of history (except Danilevsky) or simultaneously with them, a number of thoughtful investigators of art-phenomena discovered several uniformities in the change, development, and cycles of art-phenomena, and of sociocultural processes in general. A considerable fraction of these generalizations "scooped" many formulations made later by various philosophers of history. These aesthetic interpretations of historical events on the basis of—or through the window of—art-phenomena continue with an undiminished vigor up to the present. A concise survey and criticism of these theories is dictated not only by their significance but also by reason of the fact that they serve as a good introduction to the subsequent comprehensible readings of the historical jig-saw puzzle. Of many theories of this sort only a few, the most typical and important, are outlined and critically dealt with here. References to a few others are made only in the Notes.[1] The theories chosen give a fairly good idea, how-

---

[1] See pages 323 ff.

ever, of the kind of aesthetic philosophies of history enunciated in these works.

We shall begin our analysis with those that attempt to explain uniform sequences in development and florescence of art-phenomena and—through those—uniform sequences in the change of sociocultural phenomena generally. Is there any uniform sequence in the blossoming of the several forms of art in various cultures? For instance, is it architecture or music or painting or sculpture or literature or drama that uniformly blossoms first, and one of the other arts second, third, fourth, and so on? If there is such a uniform order of development and florescence of these arts in all cultures, what is it? If such a uniformity exists, what is the position of art-phenomena generally in the time-order of change and blossoming of other sociocultural phenomena—science and philosophy, religion and law, economics and politics?

Of several recent works which deal with these questions on the basis of art-phenomena, two representative volumes are *The Revolutions of Civilization*,[2] by Sir Flinders Petrie (whose contentions were more recently reiterated in his article "History in Art,"[3]), and Paul Ligeti's *Der Weg aus dem Chaos*.[4] According to Petrie not all forms of art in a given culture, or in its great period, blossom simultaneously. Some branches of art always reach the stage of liberation from the archaic and advance into free and finer forms earlier than others. Generally, a uniform and regular sequence is established: the turning point appears first in architecture and sculpture:

. . . next comes Painting, then Literature, Music, Mechanics, Theoretic Science, and lastly Wealth. When there is no survival of useful abilities, then the race is doomed, and only lives on its prestige and savings, until its wealth attracts a more vigorous people. Mene, Tekel, Upharsin may be seen written on every full-blown civilization.[5]

Having studied from this standpoint the eight periods of Egyptian culture and several periods of the Graeco-Roman and European civilizations, he finds that this order has been uniformly recurrent. For instance, for the European period corresponding to the eighth in his classification, he gives the following dates for the turning of the various branches of art and other kinds of creative activity from "archaic" form to "freedom":

European sculpture	in	1240 A.D.
European painting	in	1400
European literature	in	1600
European music	in	1790
European mechanics	in	1890
European science	after	1910
European wealth	after	1910 [6]

Thus in this great cultural period, if we take the advance in sculpture (and architecture) as the standard of comparison, the turning point from archaism to freedom, which is near the culmination point, lagged in painting by about 160 years, in literature by about 360 years, in music by 550 years, and in science and wealth by some 650 years.

A similar uniformity of sequence is shown, according to Petrie, in the development of all civilizations. The sequence is always the same. The lag may vary, however, tending to become longer as time advances.[7]

The theory of the eminent Egyptologist is undoubtedly stimulating and suggestive. Is it, however, valid? I am afraid that Petrie, like many others,[8] ascribes to social and historical processes a uniformity they do not have.

Let us examine his evidence. His sequence is based upon the "turning point from archaism to freedom" of each of the above cultural categories. Is the meaning of "turning point" clear enough and sufficiently definite so that such a point may be located and fixed? I am afraid not. And since the meaning is neither clear nor definite, it is not possible to locate the "turning point" objectively, whether in art, literature, music, or science; hence, any attempt to make such a location for each class of cultural phenomena must of necessity remain questionable, and the entire sequence remains subjective.

A slight examination of Petrie's proof is sufficient to establish the validity of this criticism. Let us take one of his best cases, his Period VIII (European). He writes:

In European sculpture the turning point has been here set at A.D. 1240, mainly on the strength of the well-dated Bamberg sculpture.

. . . In architecture [which "goes closely together with sculpture in all ages"] Salisbury Cathedral stands for the perfect acquirement of freedom.[9]

This is practically the only basis upon which he makes the year 1240 A.D. the turning point in European sculpture and architecture from archaism to freedom. So far as architecture is concerned one wonders why only one cathedral is taken and even this one not necessarily the best. No less remarkable cathedrals as "free" as the Salisbury were built: the marvelous Abbey Church at Jumièges c. 1048, cathedrals at Noyon c.1140–1170, St. Denis c. 1144, Sens 1144–1168, Notre Dame at Senlis 1155–1185, Paris Cathedral 1162–1182, Chartres c. 1172, Reims 1211, Amiens 1215, Beauvais 1225, Canterbury 1174, and Notre Dame at Paris, completed about the middle of the thirteenth century. It is clear, without extending this list, that the "turning point" can be fixed one or two centuries earlier than the year 1240, and there is as much reason for such a date as for the one chosen by Sir Flinders Petrie. The same can be said of sculpture. The turning point had already become apparent about the middle of the twelfth century in the royal portal at Chartres c. 1145, and in portals of other churches.[10] It is true that at about the middle of the thirteenth century both Gothic architecture and sculpture reached their climax, but the climax is not the turning point. If it were, then again one would wonder why the climax of European sculpture is put at 1240 and not at the period of the great Renaissance masters. One can admire the sculpture of the thirteenth century but cannot easily dispose of the sculpture of the Renaissance as inferior. Many specialists would rate it as superior to that of the thirteenth century. Thus if we mean by the turning point in European sculpture and architecture the beginning of a new form, then it had already appeared by the twelfth century. If we mean by the turning point the climax in their achievement, then the date 1240 A.D. is no better than several others which are earlier or later by several centuries.

Sir Flinders Petrie's claim with regard to sculpture and architecture is not nearly so open to question, however, as that for other cultural phenomena, such as music, literature, mechanics, and science. He puts the turning point of music at around 1790, for the following reasons:

> Perhaps we may say that Haydn was still archaic in most of his life [?], but steps freely for the first time in his great symphonies of 1790; while Beethoven only shows some memories of archaism rarely in his earlier symphonies, from 1796 onwards. Hence, perhaps, 1790 may be accepted as the turning point.[11]

That is the only argument for 1790 as the turning point in music from archaism to freedom. Thus all the Flemish, French, Italian, and English Polyphonic schools of the fourteenth, fifteenth, sixteenth, and seventeenth centuries, and all the great and very different creators of music, like Dufay, J. Okeghem, Josquin Deprès, Palestrina, C. Festa, da Vittoria, Orlando di Lasso, Gesualdo, W. Byrd, A. and D. Scarlatti, Lully, Rameau, Monteverde, J. S. Bach, G. F. Handel, Gluck, and Mozart, not to mention many others, represent, according to Petrie, one archaic stage of music! And only with Haydn (not Bach!) does music enter the stage of "freedom." I am afraid such dating is quite subjective and will fail of support by the majority of musicians.

Still more questionable are Petrie's turning points for mechanics and science, fixed at 1890 and 1910 respectively. From the standpoint of either the number or the importance of scientific discoveries or inventions, these dates are arbitrary.[12]

The data show that there is no foundation for regarding the periods before 1890 and 1910 as "archaic" in mechanics and natural science, respectively, and the periods since 1890 and 1910 as "free." The whole of Petrie's claim that there are these turning points in the various cultural phenomena and that they follow the sequence he describes remains subjective and has no objective basis in empirical facts.[13] Still less warranted is his contention that the sequence is uniform for all cultures.

Let us now turn to a theory of Paul Ligeti, recently set forth in his interesting and impressive *Der Weg aus dem Chaos*. In contradistinction to Petrie he does not think that "Sculpture and Architecture go closely together in all ages," [14] but that in all cultures architecture always blossoms before sculpture. The essence of Ligeti's theory of the art sequence is as follows: in any great culture, architecture is the first and earliest form of art to flower; then, when the culture reaches the point of maturity, sculpture flowers; finally, as the culture begins to decline, painting reaches a high level of art. This order is invariable and uniform in the development of all great cultures. In European culture the Middle Ages are marked by the greatest development of architecture, sculpture and painting remaining primitive. The Renaissance is the period that sees the triumph of sculpture, as the synthesis of architecture and painting. Finally, in the present modern age nothing remarkable has been achieved in sculpture or architecture, but in painting an incomparable level has been reached. Similarly, the first centuries of Greek art produced architectural triumphs; the sculptural or plastic age, represented by the statues of Harmodius and Aristogiton (*c.* 510 B.C.), culminates in the art of the Age of Pericles and ends about 390 B.C. with the work of Myron, Phidias, Polycleitus, and others. After 390 B.C. came the age of painting, the *malerisch* age. Likewise in Egypt the art of the Old Kingdom was architectonic, and its greatest achievement was in architecture; the art of the Middle Kingdom was plastic; the New Kingdom was marked predominantly by great achievement in the field of painting. We find the same sequence in the history of China, Japan, and other countries. Ligeti writes:

Behind the rhythm of these arts there is a law, or the uniformity which operates everywhere that human culture is given. . . . Each culture begins with the architectonic period and ends with the period of painting.[15]

Side by side with these long waves, on which Ligeti's "law of the three states" in the development of art and culture is based, are waves of a still longer duration, as well as other, shorter waves. Thus, with regard to the longer waves, not only does every culture pass through these three states enumerated by Ligeti, but all cultures, considered together, show the same uniformity in their time sequence: the great ancient cultures, like the Egyptian, are predominately architectural; later cultures, like those of Greece and Rome, are predominantly plastic; modern cultures, like the European, are predominantly *malerisch*. Such is the long rhythm of the development of human art generally and human culture as a whole.[16]

As to the shorter waves, there are periods about one hundred and thirty years long, in which the same architecture-sculpture-painting sequence occurs. In the history of Western culture there are seven waves of this kind.[17] These shorter waves are analogous to surface ripplings upon the longer waves of the ocean, and the longer movements are similar to surface waves upon the tidal ebb and flow of the whole of human culture. Such, according to Ligeti, is the main sequence of art development.

We shall later enter into a discussion of the ingenious, sometimes profound, and always interesting interpretations by Ligeti of the meaning of this sequence, the reasons for its occurrence, and its social correlations with other forms of culture. For the present we shall merely inquire whether the existence of the sequence has been established conclusively from the standpoint of the facts. Ligeti evidently believes that in each culture architecture reaches its highest development first, sculpture next, and painting last.

It goes without saying that such a construction involves an estimation of what is the highest achievement in each of these arts, and as is the case with all such evaluation, it contains an element of subjectivity. For one investigator the highest achievement in a given art may be of one kind; for another, a different kind. The periods of highest accomplishment would be correspondingly different for each investigator. If, however, an investigator claims to have discovered a uniform law, the least his theory must do is to agree in general terms with the timing of the highest points established by many competent investigators. When we consider Ligeti's statements in the light of the timing indicated by other authorities, Ligeti's "uniform law" does not appear to be uniform at all, and thus ceases to be a general law.

If we take the cultures of Egypt, India, China, Japan,

France, Italy, Germany, England, Greece, and Rome, the time sequence in which the specified arts reached their highest expression and the periods marking this zenith appear, according to several historians of the respective art of each country, as on the next page.[18] It is granted that the periods of the climax for each art here indicated are only approximate and that in this timing some elements of subjectivity are involved; for some countries other specialists have in some cases chosen for the blossoming of one of the arts a period different from that which is given in this list. Nevertheless, it is not possible to regard these estimates as less valid than the claims and estimates of Ligeti. Under such circumstances it becomes clear at once that Ligeti has elevated into a uniform law a fact which occurs only in a limited number of cases: in only three cultures out of the ten considered—that is, in Greece, Germany, and France —does his sequence occur. In the other seven cultures the sequence is either the reverse of or quite different from his "law of lag" and his sequence—once again a case in which "an ugly fact kills a beautiful theory."

Postponing for a moment a description of the subsequent part of Ligeti's theory, let us review briefly some other theories of the uniform sequence of the development of various arts in various cultures or, what is the same, theories which claim that in all cultures certain arts always lead in the change of style while other arts always lag. Such a theory of a uniform lag is but the theory of uniform sequence of change in various arts. In either a systematic or an unsystematic way such contentions had been set forth many times before Ligeti and Petrie. For instance, V. de Laprade developed a theory [19] that the art of the Orient (India, Egypt, Persia, China) was predominantly architectural; the art of Greece and Rome, predominantly sculptural; of Christian medieval Europe, mainly *malerisch;* and of the present time, essentially musical. "Architecture responds to God; sculpture and painting, to an ideal or real man; music, to the external sensate world." [20]

The theories of Ligeti and Laprade, as well as several others of this type, are possibly influenced by the theory of Hegel's *Aesthetik.* In any case, there are several resemblances

SEQUENCE OF BLOSSOMING OF THE MAIN ARTS IN TEN GREAT CULTURES

Egypt

1. Literature   2000–1225 B.C.
2. Sculpture   1580–1350
3. Architecture 1580–1250
4. Music   1411–1284
5. Painting   750–525

India

1. Literature   400 B.C.–100 A.D.
2. Sculpture   500–725
3. Architecture 1489–1706
4. Music   1600–1771
5. Painting   1615–1800

China

1. Literature   479–300 B.C.
2. Sculpture   618–960 A.D.
3. Painting   960–1200
4. Architecture 1400–1500
5. Music   1400–1500

Japan

1. Literature   700–1142 A.D.
2. Music   806–1146
3. Sculpture   1000–1137
4. Painting   1350–1500
5. Architecture 1350–1583

Greece

1. Music   750–600 B.C.
2. Literature   524–450
3. Architecture   500–430
4. Sculpture   450–350
5. Painting   430–350

Rome

1. Literature   86–25 B.C.
2. Sculpture   30 B.C.–69 A.D.
3. Painting   50–108
4. Architecture   60–138
5. Music   466–495

Germany

1. Architecture 1130–1260 A.D.
2. Sculpture   1400–1500
3. Painting   1491–1559
4. Music   1720–1880
5. Literature   1756–1850

England

1. Architecture 1272–1377 A.D.
2. Literature   1573–1618
3. Music   1600–1675
4. Painting   1717–1763
5. Sculpture   1758–1787

Italy

1. Literature   1290–1333 A.D.
2. Architecture 1444–1564
3. Painting   1472–1548
4. Sculpture   1500–1600
5. Music   1560–1800

France

1. Architecture 1150–1350 A.D.
2. Sculpture   1200–1250
3. Music   1652–1700
4. Painting   1760–1853
5. Literature   1779–1895

between Hegelian theories and the theories of these men. The essentials of that aspect of Hegel's theory which is relevant to this problem are as follows. In conformity with the chief principle of his philosophy, Hegel views the evolution of art as the process of self-realization in the course of time, or of an unfolding of the Idea or Spirit.[21] In this process of unfolding there are three stages (*Hauptstufen*), each with its characteristic type of art: the *symbolic,* the *classical,* and the *romantic.*[22] In the symbolic stage and type of art,

. . . the idea is still seeking for its true artistic expression, because it is here still essentially abstract and undetermined, and consequently has not mastered for itself the external appearance adequate to its own substance.[23]

Here matter dominates the Idea, and the Idea does not find an adequate expression in Sensate forms.

. . . The second type of art, the classical, is based upon an absolutely homogeneous unity of content and form.[24]

Here there is an adequate harmony between the Idea and its expression.

Finally,

. . . the romantic type of art annuls the completed union of the Idea and its reality.

As "Mind is the infinite subjectivity of Idea," it does not find a quite perfect expression even in the finite classical art.

To escape from such a condition the romantic type of art once more cancels that inseparable unity of the classical type, by securing a content which passes beyond the classical state and its mode of expression.[25]

Thus in the symbolic state and type of art the Idea is inadequately expressed and is dominated by external form; in the romantic stage the balance is again disrupted, because here the Idea, being infinite, strives to be free from the finite forms of external sensate expression, and therefore soars in all its infiniteness, as a result demoting the external form to a place of secondary importance.

Such are the main types, and at the same time the stages, of art evolution.

Hegel develops these principles further, showing that the most adequate objectivization of the symbolic stage and type is architecture; of the classical type and stage, sculpture; of the romantic, painting and, especially, music and poetry.[26] This is not all. Each of the arts, in the process of its evolution, passes through these three stages; for instance, architecture evolves through symbolic, classical, and romantic periods. The same is true of sculpture, painting, music, poetry.

In the progression from architecture to poetry and, within each art-form, from the symbolic to the romantic stage, we have, then, a complex scale of progression from the very least to the fullest unfolding of Spirit. Viewed from the standpoint of the Hegelian classifications, the art of the Orient has remained almost exclusively at the symbolic, the art of Greece and Rome at the classical stage. The only art to reach the romantic stage has been the European, especially in modern times.[27]

From this outline one can see the points of similarity between the Hegelian conception and that of Ligeti.

Since my whole *Dynamics* is a refutation of linear conceptions of sociocultural processes, there is no need at this point to make a special criticism of the Hegelian theory. As far as its factual side is concerned the foregoing data are sufficient to show its inadequacies and blunders.

A further theory to be discussed is that of J. Combarieu, according to whom music, in the change of its style, uniformly lags behind the other arts.

> Music almost always lags in social evolution. Schütz, Bach, Handel should be pushed back a century if one is to find a social mentality corresponding to their artistic mentality. In their sonatas Mozart and Beethoven express the charming conception of life which existed much earlier. The Germans had their musical romanticism about two generations later than their literary romanticism. Even Weber, in the songs of his *Freischütz* (1821), was lagging behind Herder and Burger.[28]

The same lagging of music in comparison with other arts occurred in the Middle Ages, in the time of the Renaissance and later.

At the dawn of the nineteenth century, music was again lagging behind the other arts, though but slightly at this time. Literary romanticism had already appeared at the end of the eighteenth century. Goethe's *Werther* appeared in 1776, MacPherson's *Ossian* about the same time, Chateaubriand's *René* in 1802, Delacroix's *La Barque du Dante* in 1822, and Victor Hugo's *Odes,* Byron's romantic poems, and Lamartine's *Meditations* and *Harmonies* all not later than 1830. Here again,

. . . music was not the first voice of the romantic soul. It could not immediately assimilate the poetry which was diffused around it, and which seems to have solicited such an assimilation. Music was reluctant to abandon its carillons, official rhetoric, theatrical pomp, and . . . its aesthetics of the *petits riens*. It is true that musicians like Lesueur, Cherubini, Spontini show in some of their works that they are at the threshold of a new world; but it is necessary to go to the *Symphonie phantastique* (1830) and the *Robert le Diable* (1831) in order to get the first impressions of the clear change. The *Freischütz* of Weber (1821) was an isolated case, of a specific nature, and without any influence upon French art. Only somewhat later music took its full revenge with Berlioz, Chopin, Liszt, and R. Schumann.[29]

Such is the essence of this theory of lagging, formulated by one of the most competent historians of music.[30]

My previous remarks and the data show this generalization to be also invalid. In another part of his excellent work Combarieu repudiates his own theory, by saying:

We had occasion to say that in the conquest of the Beautiful, music sometimes lags behind the art of painting. . . . But here in J. S. Bach music achieved marvels . . . and by its science of construction and of expression it infinitely surpassed the contemporary art of architecture and painting. Who now knows the names of German architects and painters in 1729? [31]

What is this but the refutation of his own claim? It is easy to bring out many other exceptions to the theory. For instance, in Greece, the "classical" period of music, if we accept the music of Terpander and his contemporaries as representative, preceded by about two centuries the classical age of literature and sculpture; or it was at least not later than the classical age of literature and sculpture, if we consider as representative of it the choral lyrics of Simonides, Pindar, and Bacchylides and the tragedies of Aeschylus, Sophocles, and Euripides. Likewise the classical music of medieval culture, the Gregorian chant, was already in existence in the sixth century, preceding by many centuries the classic age of medieval architecture as represented by the Romanesque and the Gothic styles, of thirteenth-century medieval sculpture, of medieval philosophy, in the writings of Albertus Magnus and St. Thomas, who mark the climax of Scholasticism in the thirteenth century, or of medieval literature. Furthermore, the music of Palestrina, Orlando di Lasso, and their contemporaries was in one sense far behind the other arts, but in another considerably in advance of them. The later classical age in music, the period of Bach, Handel, Mozart, Haydn, Beethoven, was either earlier than, or at least contemporaneous with, the classical age in German literature—the period of Lessing, Schiller, Goethe, and Kant. Even the recent Romanticism in music could hardly be said to be behind that in literature or painting. We must not forget that Beethoven, in several of his later works, had a strong romantic vein, that Weber was contemporaneous with Delacroix, that Schumann, Mendelssohn, and Berlioz were contemporaneous with, or even earlier than, Heine, Hegel, and Schopenhauer. It is also a matter of doubt whether medieval painting and sculpture were "realistic" or whether medieval music "was lost in abstract doctrines."

In brief, there are so many exceptions to the rule of Combarieu, D'Indy, and others that there remains no rule at all. Only by disregarding the extensive array of contradictory facts can one insist upon it.

The same may be said of many other theories concerning the existence of a universal and uniform lag of certain arts when compared with others. Even more inadequate are the views of writers like De Sanctis or Brunetière, who offer another variety of the theory of lag in their claim that literature usually leads in the change and that the other arts, of which music is the latest "because it is the most superficial," [32] usually lag.

Having given these samples of uniformist theories and having indicated their shortcomings, we return now to a discussion of other aspects of Ligeti's theories.

Since the sequential uniformity postulated by Ligeti and others is not a universal law at all, the bottom drops out of their sociological generalizations, and the validity of these now becomes highly questionable. Let us look more closely at Ligeti's sociological correlations. If they are not always accurate, yet they are for the most part suggestive and ingenious. The chief generalizations may be summed up briefly as follows.

1. Any culture (or great period in a culture or even the whole history of mankind) passes through three main stages: architectural, plastic, and *malerisch*.[33]

2. At each of these stages the culture is characterized by several important traits, common to all cultures at the same stage of development.[34] In a concise form these traits may be charted as on page 24.

These represent the chief sociological correlations between the predominant art and other aspects of a culture. If we ask why these correlations occur, the answer of Ligeti is interesting. Like almost all investigators of art, he rightly says that art is one of the best barometers of culture.[35] What are the reasons for this association? They become comprehensible if we study the culture in which a given painting, piece of sculpture, or specimen of architecture was produced. We must consider to whom these objects were addressed and for whom they were created, and we must inquire into the very essence of architecture, sculpture, and painting. A painting is usually the work of one man and of one lifetime. A great building is always the work of many men, of a collectivity, and sometimes of several generations as, for example, most of the cathedrals of the Middle Ages. He who is an individualist and wants to create alone is attracted by painting; those who want to create great things together, in a co-operative association, turn to architecture. "A picture is the message of one man, a building is that of many." [36] Hence the connection of the *malerisch* stage with individualism and freedom, and the architectural stage with cordial, familistic collectivism and collective discipline.

Further, a painter addresses only a few people through his painting, and sometimes he paints for only one person. Pictures are always secluded in a building, and are accessible only to a few. Architecture addresses itself to the masses, because any great architectural creation, whether it be cathedral, pyramid, castle, palace, public hall, or government seat, is

CULTURE CHARACTERISTICS

Architectural	*Plastic*	*Malerisch*
1. The beginning of an upswing of culture. It is virile and stern. It is marked by a collective state of mind and discipline.	Intermediate between the characteristics of the architectural and *malerisch* stages: their harmonious synthesis.	1. Decline of the culture or a great cultural period. It is stamped by femininity, Sensate mentality, and individualism.
2. It is a culture of volition and strong determination to achieve an ideal.	"	2. It is a culture of enjoyment of what has already been achieved before, a culture of waste and sensual indulgence.
3. It is stamped by strong ethical idealism and morality (anti-sensate, anti-hedonistic, anti-utilitarian).	"	3. Such terms as materialistic, skeptical, critical, "scientific," erotic, Epicurean, utilitarian, characterize such a culture.
4. It is dominated by religion, by belief, faith, and religious dogmatism. Its leaders are great religious and moral teachers.	"	4. There is a predominance of reason over belief. Intellectualism and the "scientific" attitude come to the fore.
5. Order and stability predominate over dynamic progress and change.	"	5. Freedom and progress predominate instead of order. There is variety, revolution, disorder, and mobility.
6. Its aristocracy is theocratic, noble because of its religious, moral, and social achievements, but not because of wealth.	"	6. Bureaucrats, moneymakers, imperialists, and "liberal" thinkers are the leaders.
7. There is a predominance of agriculture and handicraft.	"	7. There is a predominance of commerce, manufacture, "business," and machinery.
8. There is a mobilization and integration of mentality and an awakening of the spiritual *Geist*.	"	8. There is a disintegration of mentality and decline of spiritual *Geist*.

seen and can be seen by many, by unlimited masses of people. "Painting can always be properly seen only from one point, by one eye. It is a message of a few, or even of one to the few, or even to one. Architecture is a message of many to many." Architecture is unwieldy, heavy, immobile, but always real. Its material is hard and rough: earth, stone, steel, and the like. It is little suited to express lightness, movement, change, anything merely showy. It is an expression of will, determination, and the demands of effort. There is nothing deceitful about it. It is the reality of the three dimensions, and it creates that reality itself. It is by nature somewhat ascetic and idealistic. It is the *Sein*, Existence, Being (in contradistinction to Becoming). Painting, on the contrary, is Show, Illusion, Deceit, mere Appearance. Its essence is the representation of three-dimensional reality upon a two-dimensional surface, through light and shadow. Thus in its inner nature it is a show, deceit, appearance of the third dimension, which does not exist in fact. It is *Schein*, not *Sein*. In this sense it is not real. For the same reason it is inherently an imitation. Architecture does not imitate nature but creates its own reality; painting imitates the things painted and gives us their illusory appearance. Therefore, painting is especially suited to catching glimpses of the ever-changing shadows of things; it is apt to depict the dynamic, ever-changing, ever-moving, momentary play of light and shadow, color and contour. It is mobile, "progressive," and dynamic by its nature. Architecture must obey the laws and regularities of the realities on which it builds. It is and must be objective because it is reality; painting is and must be subjective and impressionistic because it is and gives a mere show and appearance. Architecture must be orderly, disciplined, systematic and free from mere fancifulness or whim, because otherwise it cannot produce anything lasting. It is Order, System, Effort, Law, and Discipline. Painting can be and is fanciful, individualistic, impressionistic, irregular, anarchistic, free, liberating, because it deals with the world of shadows, passing and momentary impressions. Here the artist is not forced by his materials to obey the laws of the physical, objective world. It does not require a disciplined order, system, effort. It is Fancifulness, Freedom, Life, and Accidental impression of the moment.

When these properties of architecture and painting are considered, it becomes at once comprehensible why a culture at the architectural stage has the characteristics of order and stability, and at its *malerisch* stage is stamped by individualism, freedom, intellectualism, impressionism, light-mindedness, momentary Epicureanism, a *Carpe diem* attitude, irreligiosity, revolution, disorder, and other such traits. It is stamped by these not because of painting, but because painting is the form of art which is best suited for such a cultural *Gestalt*. It is structurally, logically, and causally a part, a symptom, and a quality of such cultural status.

The more "architectural" the inner life of a given culture, the more architectural are its sculpture and painting; and vice versa, the more *malerisch* and showy the inner life of the culture, the more *malerisch* are its architecture and sculpture. The Middle Ages had painting and sculpture as well as architecture, but there was no perspective in the painting, no attempt to represent three-dimensional reality by two-dimensional surface: there was no Show, no Appearance. It depicted things as they were in the mind of the painter, in their eternal essence and idea, regardless of how they looked, how they appeared to the artist's eye. Painting itself, then, was expressionistic, ideational, not visual, not impressionistic. In modern times, especially since the advent of baroque and rococo, at the *malerisch* stage of our culture architecture has become *malerisch,* full of movement, dynamic, purely impressionistic, illusionistic, a mere show for the sake of show. One is almost tempted to call it "Hollywoody." As to modern painting and sculpture, they have become purely impressionistic or visual. They depict, or try to depict, not the eternal essence of the phenomena or objects depicted, not their idea, but their purely visual appearance, even without reference to the other organs of sense. As the visual appearance of things incessantly changes, such artists grasp only the momentary show, give us purely visual snapshots of things, not their durable essence. Hence, impressionism in the arts of a culture at its *malerisch* period is in closest harmony with the organically impressionistic nature of all cultural life at this stage: it is constantly in turmoil and change; it becomes "progressive"; it is showy (providing in our own age, for example, motion pictures and advertising); it is momentary (*Carpe diem,* "Wine, Women, and Song," jazz madness, crooning, and so on); it is individualistic, fanciful, disorderly.

Such is the explanation of the association of the predominant form of art with other important aspects of a culture.

Though many of these ideas are not new and had been presented many times before Ligeti, these pages of his work nevertheless appear to be very suggestive and even profound. Rejecting his main theory that a uniform sequence exists in the development of art and, consequently, his main sociological conclusions about the future of our culture or other cultures, one must nevertheless agree that his discussion contains a great deal that is valid—if not universally, then at least for some cultures and some periods. Ligeti has shown beyond the possibility of doubt that there does exist a close connection between the whole of a culture and the forms of its art.

The evidence presented in this chapter permits us to draw the following conclusions. Of the several theories under discussion which try to establish a definite and universal sequence in the development of various arts in all cultures and civilizations, we are obliged by the facts to adjudge their claim as, at best, only partially valid. They elevate one of the typical cases into a universal rule.

2

THEORIES OF WALDEMAR DEONNA, FRANK CHAMBERS, CHARLES LALO, AND OTHERS

Another group of studies of art-phenomena tries to establish to what extent the development of art generally and of a specific art particularly is uniform in various cultures, what are the uniform stages of the life-course of art-phenomena in different civilizations, how these curves of art develop-ment are connected with the evolution and fluctuation of sociocultural processes, and to what extent the fine art serves as a sensitive barometer of a society and culture. In an at-tempt to answer these questions, several generalizations have been made regarding art-change and the dynamics of socio-cultural processes at large. These theories are a variety of in-terpretations of history through the prism of art. Our critical survey of these interpretations would begin with the most general theories of a uniformity of art development in various cultures. Here are a few examples.

> The arts are subject to a beginning, progression, completion, and termination, a growth, a blooming, and a decay. . . .
> Like all the human institutions, arts originate, grow, and prosper or decay according to certain laws. . . .
> Among all peoples of a high culture the arts pass the periods of in-fancy, youth, maturity, and decadence. . . .
> These periods of origin, splendor, and decline of arts exhibit certain common traits among the majority of peoples. . . .[37]

The first claim of these theories is that any art system is finite in its existence: it appears, blossoms, and declines. I agree with this view, because not only art but, as Plato says, "everything [on this earth] which has a beginning has also an end," and therefore not only art but any empirical system "will in time perish and come to dissolution." There is no reason to insist upon this platitude in special reference to art. There is little in such formulas to inform us about the real nature of the curve of art development.

The second claim advanced is that the art systems of var-ious cultures have the same or similar curves of develop-ment: origin, growth, zenith, and decline; or childhood, ma-turity, and senility. If the theories can show what are the essen-tial characteristics of art at each of these phases and that these phases, each with its special characteristics, are similar in the art systems of various cultures, then their contention becomes quite important.

Do the theories discussed meet these requirements? Unfortunately they do not. Therefore they are of no scientific value. Merely to say that each art system passes through the stages of childhood, maturity, and senility is meaningless, if no concrete data are produced to show what exactly are the characteristics of art childhood, art maturity, and art senility; when and where one stage ends and the next begins; how long is the duration of each stage; and so on. Is the Gothic style the style of childhood, maturity, or senility, and why? If it is one of these three "phases," does it occur in all cultures, in all its essential traits? It is enough to ask these questions to make clear the falsity of such analogies, when they are not followed by the exact suggested specifications. Without such specifications they do not and cannot prove anything concerning either the uniformity or the non-uniformity of art evolution in various cultures, nor can they give us any real knowledge of the phases of development in art.

The same can be said of several other formulas when they are not substantiated and specified along the foregoing lines. Take, for instance, the formula stating that all art systems go through the archaic, classical, and decadent stages. Without factual substantiation it, also, is meaningless and can be dismissed without further consideration.

The situation is different with all the theories of uniform development in art which are supported by factual substantiation and corroboration. Such theories exist, and some of them are very impressive. Often they throw an interesting light on the dynamics of art phenomena. As our first example we shall take the theory of a distinguished historian of art, Waldemar Deonna, brilliantly developed in his several works, especially in the three large volumes of his *L'archéologie, sa valeur, ses méthodes.*[38]

Deonna takes four great art systems in sculpture and, in part, painting—the paleolithic, the neolithic, the Graeco-Roman, and the Christian—and tries to show that each of these systems has passed through similar fundamental periods of archaism, classicism, and finally decadence. In each of these phases the traits and style of all four systems of art are strikingly homogeneous. The similarity is so great that the statues of early medieval Europe (before the twelfth century) can easily be mistaken for those of archaic Greece (before the sixth century B.C.), and vice versa. Likewise, comparing the Aurora of Michelangelo with the Niobe of Rome; the Nymphs of the Fountain by Jean Goujon (sixteenth century A.D.) with the Dancing Woman figure of Pergamum (third–second century B.C.); geometric statues of the archaic paleolithic with those of the archaic neolithic period, and with archaic Greek, archaic medieval, and so on—one cannot fail to see a striking similarity between them, even though they be separated from one another by centuries, even by thousands of years. Some of the statues of the Acropolis were pronounced by many specialists to be remarkably similar to the works of Mino da Fiesole, Francia, and Desiderio da Settignano; some of the sculptures of the Scopas school in Greece (fourth century B.C.), to the sculptures of Francia; some of the works of Praxiteles and Lysippus, to those of Ghiberti and Donatello; and some of the Greek and Pompeian vase paintings, to the paintings of Mantegna, Roger van der Weyden, and Titian; some other works of ancient Greece and Rome, to those of Michelangelo, Velasquez, and Bernini; [39] and so on. Analyzing systematically the art objects of the four art systems, Deonna comes to the conclusion that, in essentials, each of them has passed through the same main stages, and when the art of the same phase in each of the four systems is taken separately it exhibits a remarkable similarity in all the systems. For instance, the art of Greece (mainly sculpture) before the sixth century is similar to that of Europe before the twelfth century; the art of Greece of the fifth century is a replica of the art of Europe of the thirteenth century. The Creto-Mycenaean art, considered by Deonna to be the last phase of neolithic art, is similar to Graeco-Roman art of the Hellenistic period and to European art of the fifteenth and eighteenth centuries. [40] Volumes II and III of Deonna's work are devoted to the factual substantiation of this proposition. On the basis of an enormous amount of material, he proceeds to demonstrate the similarity of the phases in all four systems and the likeness of the art of the four in corresponding phases. He deals not only with the general style of the art but also with a series of details, such as the form of eye, ear, mouth; smile, frontality, nudity, composition of dress, posture; idealism or realism; emotionality or lack of emotion; the presence or absence of landscape, portraiture, genre of a certain kind. His conclusions run as follows:

> To sum up, we can consider art as developing according to a definite rhythm which leads to a recurrence of similar, if not identical, tendencies and forms separated by the intervals of centuries; using an image which is not quite exact but gives an idea of this regular course of art evolution, we can say that the evolution of the history of art can be compared to a spiral, where each curl superimposes over the lower one without touching it, as each period superimposes upon the anterior period. . . . That is what I plan to demonstrate.[41]

Further on, Deonna shows that each of these four systems of art starts, mainly because of inexperience and a lack of skill in the artists, with the archaic form. Then each progresses, becomes perfected and reaches its climax, or classical period, after which each begins to decline.

> Each of these art systems, starting from a similar point of departure, develops with the same logical rhythm and in the course of its evolution produces analogical forms of art.[42]

The archaic phase of the art of the paleolithic, neolithic, Graeco-Roman (up to the sixth century B.C.) and the early medieval (up to the twelfth century A.D.) periods exhibits the same primitive technique, frontality, "horror of emptiness," lack of perspective or perspective by superposition of planes, lack of unity in the composition, triangular heads, "archaic smile," low foreheads, and a similar composition of ears, nose, hair, beard, and other parts of the human body.[43] Likewise, when the classical phase in these four art systems is considered, particularly the Greek art of the fifth century B.C. and the Christian art of the thirteenth century, one finds a complete similarity between them. The technique becomes perfect, the statues begin to live, frontality disappears, and there is present the simplicity of perfection. Idealism becomes supreme, and art now reproduces either the positively valuable and ideal object only, or idealizes natural objects: mortals are made to appear like young gods; human beings are shown as eternally young and always perfect. Nothing prosaic, ugly, defective, or low finds a place in this art. Even the postures of the human figures are idealized. Order, inner calm and peace, lack of passion and emotion are characteristic; perfect balance and harmony reign supreme. Idealization does not admit realistic portraiture. Nothing pathetic, macabre, or passionate is shown. Eternally young and perfect human beings, with serenity on their faces—even in the funerary statues of the dead, calm and immortal, these are the types of the classical period. Neglect of landscape, of prosaic and realistic genre, and of profane historical scenes is a further characteristic of the Greek as well as of the Christian art of this period. Both of these arts are profoundly religious. Both are essentially anonymous, and the artists retreat before the community; both are local in detail but universal in topic; both incorporate the unity of mind of their entire society and are the work of the entire society; both are rationalistic, meditatively speculative and free from any sensuality.[44]

If we then take the period of "overripeness," in the Mycenaean, the Hellenistic, and the modern European arts—the end of the classical period and the beginning of the period of decline—we again find, in all of them, a series of striking resemblances. In spite of being separated by great intervals of time, they show the same style, the same spirit, and similar forms and content. We find skilled technique which can reproduce anything but, having no strong "soul" of its own, it mixes all kinds of styles incongruously and conscientiously imitates the "primitive" style. Not idealism but sensory or visual naturalism is now supreme. Art is down to earth. Where the idealistic art deified mortals, this naturalistic art makes the immortals mortal. It imitates sensate nature and empirical reality. It has a particular inclination to the reproduction of the negative, the macabre, the pathetic, the passionate, the prosaic, the picturesque, and the ugly phenomena of life. The old man is reproduced now with all the ugliness and misery of old age, and the prosaic scenes of life with all their drab reality. Calm serenity is gone, and instead we have distorted figures, suffering, ugliness. Women, who figure little in the classical art, are one of the favorite subjects in this phase. They now are depicted "realistically," in terms of voluptuousness, sensuality, sexuality, seductiveness, and "prettiness." The spirit of a purely sensate Epicureanism is conspicuous. Men are also represented "naturalistically," often as effeminate, and usually smooth-shaven. Masses and crowds, impressionistic portraiture, the genre of daily life and especially of the lower classes and picturesque urchins, are also favorite subjects of the period. Lack of proportion and symmetry, fugitive and dynamic aspects of empirical reality, violent motion, incoherence and mixture of styles, "colossalism," urbanity, sophistication, and suavity are dominant. In brief, these "over-ripe" phases exhibit the same characteristics in all the three systems of art.[45]

The outline shows that Deonna was not content merely with vague generalizations, but presented a vast amount of factual material for substantiation and verification. Whether or not the main claims of his theory are valid, we shall determine after further investigation. For the present let us take some other theories of the same type. A theory set forth by Frank Chambers will serve as a good example.

Frank Chambers also tries to prove that the curve of art evolution and its essential stages are very similar in Ancient Greece and in Europe. Making use of literature and literary criticism as the main body of his material, he comes to the conclusion that both arts have passed through two similar stages. The first stage is characterized by a non-aesthetic estimation of beauty and the fine arts. In this stage all the great art creations are produced, not for art's or beauty's sake, but for the sake of religion, morals, patriotism, civic virtue, and other non-aesthetic ends. The fine arts as such, and beauty as beauty, are viewed negatively and resisted. However, this does not hinder the creation of the greatest art values. Such was the stage in Greece up to the fourth century B.C., and in

Europe up to the Renaissance and the fall of classicism—
i.e., the Academies. In the second stage there appears an
appreciation of the fine arts for arts' sake, and beauty for
beauty's sake. At this stage the arts become free from their
duties as the handmaid of religion or of other non-aesthetic
values. "Aestheticism," art collecting, the connoisseur, art
education, art criticism, and so on, now make their appearance. In spite of this, the art of the second stage hardly achieves
the summits that were reached during the first stage, and it
is soon destined to disintegration and decline.

> Both ancient and modern, both the Pagan and Christian eras, seem
> to have had a parallel aesthetic history. In both eras two aesthetic states
> of mind have existed successively. The first state of mind was that
> which, say, deified the sun and prayed to it; the second poetised self-
> consciously and said: "How beautiful!" It was the first state which
> caused the Parthenon to be built; it is the second state which now
> ponders its ruins, argues about its reconstruction, and sees passionate
> and romantic visions. The like of Homer, the Lyric poets, Herodotus,
> Thucydides, belong to the first state; the like of Strabo, Plutarch,
> Lucian, Athenaeus, Plotinus, to the second; Aristotle and, to a less
> extent, Plato are the links between the two.[46]

In his later work,[47] where he analyzes the development of
European art, Chambers repeats the same conclusions in a
somewhat modified form. At this hour we live in a latter-
day world, not unlike that of Lucian, Philostratus, Athenaeus,
and Plotinus, and in a few generations our civilization and its
art will have run its appointed course.[48]

While the theories of Deonna and Chambers deal mainly
with the fields of sculpture and painting, other theories, making similar contentions concerning the uniformity of the main
phases of art in various cultures, try to establish their claim
with regard to literature and music. The theory of Bovet may
be taken as an example for literature, and that of Charles Lalo
for music. Both of these theories, however, go further than
those of Deonna and Chambers and insist not only on the
uniformity of the stages of the evolution of these arts in various cultures, but also on the recurrence of these stages (or
cycles) in time in the same cultures: when one cycle ends,

another, in a different concrete form but with similar stages, begins and, having run its course, is again succeeded by a new cycle with the same stages, and so on.

Bovet [49] develops a theory propounded by Victor Hugo in his *Cromwell*. In the preface to his work Hugo says that the literature of every people passes through three consecutive stages: lyric, epic, and dramatic.

Poetry has three stages each of which corresponds to an epoch of a society. The primitive times are lyrical, the antique times are epical, while the modern time is dramatic. The ode chants the eternity, epic solemnizes history, drama paints life. . . . In primitive times man chants: when he is young he is lyrical. Prayer is his whole religion; the ode is his whole poetry.

When larger groups and empires appear, battles and other heroic deeds occur, "man becomes epical" and tells of great deeds and events. Then, with the complication of social life, there appear drama, reflection, disappointment, and pity. Then poetry becomes dramatic. This universal law, according to Victor Hugo, is valid, whether we take the course of poetry in time, regardless of nations (the Bible is lyric, Homer epic, and Shakespeare dramatic) or within any great nation and great literature. The Book of Genesis in the Bible is lyrical; Kings, epic; Job, dramatic. In France, Malherbe came before Chapelain, and Chapelain before Corneille; in Greece, Orpheus came before Homer, and Homer before Aeschylus. Such is the essence of Hugo's generalization. With some reservations Bovet developed it further. In his interpretation, the lyric-epic-dramatic sequence is valid with regard to the development of the literature of all nations if it is not hindered by purely exterior circumstances, which in some cases may break its natural course. It is also valid in the sense that it recurs in this order several times in the history of a great literature. In other words, it recurs in social space as well as in social time.

For corroboration of this "law" Bovet makes special use of the course of French literature:

In the course of one thousand years the French literature three times has passed the stages: lyric-epic-dramatic. This universal law has not, however, manifested itself so clearly and so regularly in any other literature. There is a reason for this. It is the interference of external conditions which may cause—and has caused—deviation in the course of some of the literatures from the above natural sequence.[50]

Such is the essence of the Hugo-Bovet law. As we see, Bovet, contending for its universality, admits at the same time that external conditions may break the sequence. Therefore, he himself regards it as non-rigid and approximate. As a matter of fact, it is not universal at all. Even in regard to French literature, Bovet's periods and sequences are to a considerable extent artificial. In regard to other literatures his "law" has so many exceptions that it can hardly pretend to be even an approximate rule.

Turning to Charles Lalo's theory,[51] we find that, like Bovet, he claims the uniform sequence of the phases of development of music which he gives to be valid in social space as well as in time. Any fundamental musical system runs through the same stages during its life cycle. If in the history of a given culture several musical systems have followed one another, each of them has run through the same stages. The number of stages, their character and sequence, may be observed in the following table, which gives all the essentials of the theory.[52]

SUCCESSION OF THE THREE PHASES IN THE HISTORY OF OCCIDENTAL MUSIC

A. Greek Music
  (1) *Preclassical Phase*
      (a) Primitives
          Greeks of Asia Minor: mythical personalities (?)
      (b) Predecessors
          Authors of the names taken by the classics: epical personalities (?)
  (2) *Classical Phase*
      (a) Great Classics
          Terpander of Sparta (end of eighth and beginning of seventh centuries B.C.)
      (b) Pseudo-Classics
          Thaletas and the Doric musical instruments (middle of the seventh and beginning of sixth centuries B.C.)
  (3) *Postclassical Phase*
      (a) Romantics

Phyrius, Timothy, the dithyramb, and tragedy in Athens (fifth century B.C.)
- (b) Decadents
  Alexandrian, Roman, and Hellenistic cosmopolitanism (since fourth century B.C.)

B. Christian Melody
- (1) *Preclassical Phase*
  - (a) Primitives
    First Oriental and Roman hymns (second to third centuries A.D.)
  - (b) Predecessors
    Ambrosian chant of Milan (fourth century A.D.)
- (2) *Classical Phase*
  - (a) Gregorian chant of Rome (sixth or seventh [?] century A.D.)
- (3) *Postclassical Phase*
  - (a) Romantics
    Tropes and sequences of Rhenish countries (ninth century A.D.)
  - (b) Decadents
    Plain song (chant) in savant's language, then as dead, finally as liturgical (since eleventh century A.D.)

C. Polyphony of the Middle Ages
- (1) *Preclassical Phase*
  - (a) Primitives
    Organum and counterpoint of Northern France (from tenth [?] to fourteenth centuries)
  - (b) Predecessors
    Gallo-Belgian and Flemish schools (fifteenth and beginning of sixteenth centuries)
- (2) *Classical Phase*
  - (a) Grand Classics
    Palestrina's school in Rome (middle of sixteenth century)
  - (b) Pseudo-Classics
    Dramatic madrigal (end of sixteenth century)
- (3) *Postclassical Phase*
  - (a) Romantics
    Dramatic and eclectic polyphony of Bach and Handel (beginning of the eighteenth century)
  - (b) Decadents
    Counterpoint and fugue of the school of the savant language, already almost liturgical (since eighteenth century)

D. Modern Harmony
  (1) *Preclassical Phase*
    (a) Primitives
        Singers on lute; Florentine opera (beginning of seventeenth century)
    (b) Predecessors
        International dramatic music: France, Italy, Germany (end of seventeenth and beginning of eighteenth centuries)
  (2) *Classical Phase*
    (a) Grand Classics
        German symphony: Haydn, Mozart, Beethoven (end of eighteenth century)
    (b) Pseudo-Classics
        Chopin, Mendelssohn, Schumann (beginning of nineteenth century)
  (3) *Postclassical Phase*
    (a) Romantics
        German and French symphonic drama and poem: Wagner and Berlioz (middle of nineteenth century)
    (b) Decadents
        Archaism, exoticism, symbolism, contemporary eclecticism

In all these systems the preclassical phase is characterized by an indeterminate confusion, incoherence, and complexity (contrary to Herbert Spencer's formulas of evolution), poor technique and impure mixture. In the predecessor phase, the technique improves, and the confusion and mixture begin to decrease. The classical phase is marked by simplicity, pure internal harmony, and an organic unity of music with perfect technique. It puts an end to the incoherent complexity and unbalanced confusion of the preceding phase. The characteristics of the classical phase exist in the pseudo-classical phase of the period, but an admixture of romantic and other complexities begins to creep in. Finally, in the postclassical phase senility and sickness are found. It is marked by an increase of non-equilibrated complexities, by a lack of balance, by romanticism and patheticism, by eclecticism of styles, by "colossalism," by a growing attempt to find "new ways" and "new methods," which results in ever-increasing incoherence. Very notably there comes a desire to imitate the preclassical, particularly the primitive, music. Various extreme modernisms and radicalisms abound. Music loses its organic unity and becomes more and more difficult. Instead of a free creation of genius it tends increasingly to become the result of painful research, difficult calculation, scientifically computed excess. It turns into an impurity and becomes the product of the manipulation of savant prestidigitators and researchers.[53] In this way it gradually degenerates and finally dies, to give place to a new system which will run through similar phases during the course of its existence.

To complete the characterizations of the theories of Deonna, Chambers, Bovet, Lalo, and many others with similar views, it is necessary to add that almost all these authors view the likenesses in different art systems as the result not so much, if at all, of diffusion and imitation, as of independent invention free from imitation and copying. It is due partly to the similarity of human nature, partly to identical technical conditions (for instance, a lack of skill in archaic periods), partly to similar cultural configurations, and partly to the inner immanent logic of each art, the organization of which tends to create its own inner milieu in which, being isolated from the rest of the world, it lives its own life according to its own nature.[54]

These theories do not, of course, exhaust the list. There are numerous other theories of the uniform development of art among various peoples and cultures.[55] Such are, for instance, the theories which claim that among all peoples art passes from the "physioplastic" to the "ideoplastic" style (Max Verworn); from the expressionistic to the impressionistic (Schafer and, in part, Riegl and Schmarsow); from the architectural, through the sculptural, to the *malerisch* style (Victor de Laprade, Ligeti, and others). Other theories claim that the art of all cultures passes, in the course of its development, through the decorative, plastic, architectural, and *malerisch* stages in conformity with a corresponding *Weltbegriff* (Coellen), and so on. Many theories claim a sort of endless alternation of a number of styles or rhythmical processes in art-phenomena: hardening a form of poetry and literature into a convention and a revolt against the hardened conventional form on the part of a new style which in turn becomes convention and provokes a revolt against it, and so on; [56] an alternation of the linear and *malerisch* styles in painting, sculpture, architecture; [57] of the Gothic and the Greek styles; [58] of the *haptisch* and *optisch* (Riegl); *plastisch* and *malerisch* (Schmarsow); *Seinstil* and *Formstil* (Panofsky); cubistic and organic (Coellen); *tektonisch* and *kontratektonisch* (Cohn-Wiener); mechanical and organic (Scheltemas); alternation of the styles of *Abstraktion* and *Einfuhlung* (Worringer); of idealism and naturalism (Dvořak); of classicism and romanticism; and others. [59] We pass now to a brief examination of the validity of these theories.

It can hardly be questioned that between the art systems of various cultures there exist many similarities in both small and great matters. Whether they are due to diffusion or to independent and spontaneous creation, or to both factors, such recurrences of similarities in space and time are readily observable. Whether we take the so-called geometric style or geometric ornamentation, or the physioplastic or ideoplastic style; or whether we consider the essentials of technique or subject matter, or the manner of their presentation, or other factors, the existence in the arts of divers peoples and cultures of an enormous number of similarities in these respects —similarities sometimes of a striking character—is beyond doubt. And other conditions being equal, the nearer to each other the general characters of the whole culture of the peoples compared, the greater the similarity in their arts. The art forms of all *nomadic hunters* who have lived in quite different parts of the world seem to exhibit more similarities than can be found when the cultures of nomadic hunters are compared with those of industrialized and urbanized peoples. The same is to be said of the art forms of all *agricultural* peoples, even though isolated from one another, and of the comparison between the arts of agricultural and non-agricultural peoples. [60] Similarities exist, are numerous and often essential. [61] Thus far the theories concerned are valid and cannot be rejected.

Quite different, however, is the claim that the main stages of the life history of all art systems are the same, that there exists a uniform sequence of these stages, and that therefore the life curve of all art systems has practically the same configuration, with its zenith in the classic period and a decline in the direction of the initial (archaic) and the final (post-classic) periods. These claims appear to me to be questionable. There is a large body of material to support this doubt. Here, in the way of criticism, I shall limit my task to the formulation of brief statements sufficient to expose the weak aspects of the "uniformist" theories.

The life curve of the art systems of various cultures cannot be said to be the same. Some art systems among so-called primitive peoples do not go beyond the archaic phase, in spite of the existence of their culture and art over periods of centuries. The life curve of such systems remains, so to speak, on the same primitive level, without rising to the level of classicism.[62] On the other hand, as far as factual data are concerned, the art of the paleolithic peoples—this "miracle," as it is styled by many specialists—appears as already "mature" and far above the archaic phase. It shows skill in drawing, artistic perfection, ripeness.[63] It is true that Deonna foresees this objection and tries to obviate it by the assumption that the known perfected forms of the paleolithic art constitute the classical phase of its development, a phase which of necessity had been preceded by the archaic. This assumption sounds probable but remains a mere guess, uncorroborated by data, and thus not convincing. Similarly, the known art of Crete and Mycenae belongs, in the main, to the "overripe" phase of Deonna's curve. He again assumes that it was, of necessity, preceded by the archaic and classical stages of this art, but in its surviving examples there is little to support the assumption. For this reason, the life curve of such art systems lacks its first part, a line rising from the low level of the archaic to that of the classical stage. It thus differs from the uniform curve assumed in the theories discussed.

If we take such art systems as the Egyptian, the Chinese, or the Christian-European, we are again confronted with a curve very different from the one postulated. Indeed, the history of Egyptian art shows that it had not one parabolic "top," but several "tops" and several "bottoms." In other words, it follows a curve consisting of several waves rather than a single wave with one archaic, one classical, one declining phase. So far as sculpture is concerned, there was a classical period in the Old Kingdom, during the Second to Fourth dynasties, another in the Middle Kingdom, in the Eleventh and Twelfth dynasties, another in the New Kingdom, in the Eighteenth and Nineteenth dynasties; and later on, in sculpture as well as in architecture and painting, there were several more "ups and downs." [64] Any reasonable standard of judgment will disclose these ups and downs. To reduce this many-wave curve, with its several crests and troughs, to a single wave is impossible. Therefore, the form of the life curve of Egyptian art most sharply deviates from the uniform curve assumed in the theories under discussion. The same may be said of Chinese art.[65] Its beginning is observed to have either a very short archaic stage or none at all.

It may be said of Chinese painting, as well as of other forms of early Chinese art, that it appears from the beginning almost full-fledged. The earliest specimen known today reveals an art which has reached a high degree of independence and maturity.[66]

We reach the same conclusion if we take the history of European art. The impossibility of reducing its life curve to the postulated uniformity may be seen in the work of Deonna himself. His table runs as follows.[67]

PARALLELISM OF GREEK AND EUROPEAN ART

Art		Century				
Greek	Before VI B.C.	VI	V	IV	Hellenistic art	
European	Before XII A.D.	XII	XIII	XIV	XV	XVIII

This table shows that somehow he was not able to find the Greek counterpart to the European art of the sixteenth and seventeenth centuries: he had to place this art outside his scheme. Moreover, he did not put the art of the nineteenth and twentieth centuries into his table.[68] Without bringing forward further points for discussion, one can see that the life curve of European art is not identical with that of Greek art and deviates greatly from the alleged uniform curve. Like paleolithic painting, the literatures of many cultures cannot be plotted on a parabolic curve, because the greatest literary creations in such cultures appear "miraculously" almost at the initial stages of their life history and are not excelled in the later stages. In Greek literature, Homer's *Iliad* and *Odyssey,* in the Hindu literature *Mahabharata* and *Ramayana,* in the Finnish literature *Kalevala,* in the Assyro-Babylonian literature *Gilgamesh,* and in the Hebrew literature a part of the Bible, are cases in point. In such cultures the top, the most classical of all the classics, appears at an early—at almost the initial—stage but not at a later one. Something similar may be observed in the history of music in certain cultures. However limited our knowledge of Greek music may be, the existing evidences suggest that its great period, that of Terpander, was reached sometime in the eighth century B.C. during the archaic stage of Greek culture.

This conclusion is valid not only in regard to the general form of the curve of art development and its phases, but also in regard to many, if not all, of the most important changes in the style of an art. Their character and sequence are different in the art systems of various cultures. Here are a few instances.

(1) In some cultures the earliest art style is predominantly ideational, symbolic or ideoplastic (Max Verworn), or expressionistic (H. Schafer); in other cultures it is predominantly visual, impressionistic, perspectivistic, illusionistic, or naturalistic; in still others both styles are found simultaneously.

(2) The alternation of these styles from the standpoint of the length of domination, of the frequency of alternations, of the intensity of the shifts from one to another, and so on, are again considerably different in various cultures.

(3) The art of some cultures (e.g. the Hindu) remains predominantly ideational throughout its history, whereas the art of other cultures (e.g. the paleolithic, the Creto-Mycenaean) remains predominantly visual or naturalistic.

(4) The same propositions can be made with regard to the idealistic (not to be confused with ideational) and impressionistic (as the extreme form of the visual styles), their presence or absence, their alternations, and so on.

(5) The same propositions hold true for the linear and the *malerisch* styles—in the sense that these terms are used by H. Wolfflin, and for classicism and romanticism.

(6) Other differences, implying a lack of universal uniformity, occur in the arts of various cultures among many other important characteristics, such as: (a) the proportion of the religious and secular subjects of the art, and its changes in the course of the existence of a given art in a given culture; (b) the proportion and intensity of the ascetic, of the Sensate (with the sexual as a form of this) mentality embodied in the art systems of various cultures at various stages of their existence; (c) the relative place occupied by such classes of painting and sculpture as portrait, *paysage,* genre of various types, historical, mythological, and others; by such musical works as oratorio, sonata, opera, symphony; by various forms of poetry and prose; (d) the relative predominance of the spirit of individualism and of collectivity; (e) the proportion of "pure" art or "art for art's sake" (which has never existed in the literal sense of the word) and of art not divorced from other cultural values, like religion, morals, patriotism, and so on. In all of these and in many other respects the art systems of various cultures offer a considerable diversity and exhibit lack of rigid uniformity. If we grant that this is really the situation, then the laws of the uniform development of art in various cultures, of the uniform lagging of certain arts behind the others, of uniform curves of the quantitative and qualitative rhythms of the arts—all these and similar claims so dear to the linearists, cyclicists, evolutionists, and uniform-

ists, in the social sciences of the nineteenth and twentieth centuries, are at best only somewhat prevalent or approximate rules.

(7) When such rules are not overstated, however, they have a highly important cognitive value. To a considerable degree they make intelligible an otherwise incomprehensible jungle of chaotic historical events. Without these approximate generalizations we are entirely lost in the jungle and its endless facts make little sense in their how and why. With the modicum of the main rules we have several roads crossing the jungle and orienting us in its unmapped darkness. Such is the cognitive role of these limited, approximate prevalent rules and uniformities. There is no doubt that several of the above generalizations are roughly valid, when they are not overextended beyond their legitimate boundary. Taken within the necessary limitations, Ligeti's, Deonna's, Lalo's, Chambers' and many other generalizations make comprehensible a large portion of the jungle of art-phenomena, art-types, art-rhythms, art-dynamics, and through art-phenomena their formulas make sense of thousands of incomprehensible facts of the historical process itself.

3

Sensate, Ideational, Idealistic, and Eclectic Art

Such also is the cognitive value of four main types of art-phenomena and of their fluctuations, discussed in my *Dynamics*. The theory presented there is not irreconcilable with other theories mentioned above. In a number of points it agrees with the best of other theories; in the points where it deviates, the difference is largely due to the different goals of various investigations of art-phenomena.

There is no need to outline here my rather extensive study of the painting, sculpture, architecture, music, literature, and drama of the Graeco-Roman and Western cultures, or my much more cursory study of paleolithic, neolithic, primitive, Chinese, Hindu, and ancient Egyptian art forms.[69] But some of the most general conclusions may be briefly mentioned.

First, from the standpoint of art's inner content, external style, and objective or functions, all art-phenomena easily fall into four main types. (1) *Sensate* art chooses sensory topics (housewife, plant, portrait, animal, fight, kiss, etc.); the style is naturalistic or realistic, and the main purpose is to give sensory enjoyment and pleasure. (2) *Ideational* art has for topics the supersensory and superrational (the Kingdom of God, angels, soul, devils, mysteries of Salvation, Redemption, etc.); its style is necessarily symbolic—"a visible sign of the invisible world"—because supersensory phenomena do not have any sensory forms; and its objective is to bring the human soul closer to God or to itself or to Tao, Nirvana, Brahman, etc. (3) *Idealistic* art has for its topics partly the supersensory, partly the noblest sensory phenomena; the style is partly idealized naturalism, partly symbolic and allegoric; and the objective is an ennoblement and beautification of the sensory world and man and the bringing of man's soul closer to the Highest Value, i.e. God, Tao, Nirvana, etc. (4) *Unintegrated Eclectic* art shows no unity of topic, style, and objective. It is an incoherent potpourri or hash of all sorts of topics, styles, objectives.

Second, though all four forms of art are found virtually in all cultures and at all periods of the same culture, one of these different forms of art is often dominant in a given culture at a given period and the dominant forms are often different in different civilizations. Thus the Hindu, the ancient Egyptian, or the Taoist-Chinese art has been preponderantly Ideational; the known Creto-Minoan and Creto-Mycenaean arts were predominantly Sensate. The dominant art of some pre-literate tribes and paleolithic art are Sensate; neolithic art and that of other tribes is mainly Ideational or Idealistic. Finally, the art of many groups and cultures has been predominantly eclectic and incoherent.

Third, in practically all great cultures the dominance shifts from one art form to another in the course of time. For instance, the dominant art of Greece between the ninth and the sixth centuries B.C. was Ideational but in the fifth and fourth centuries B.C. became Idealistic; from the fourth century B.C. to the fourth century A.D. Graeco-Roman art was predominantly Sensate; from the fifth to the twelfth centuries A.D., Ideational form dominated Western art; in the thirteenth and fourteenth centuries the Idealistic art-form was dominant in Europe; from the fifteenth to the twentieth centuries Western art has been Sensate. At the present time, this Sensate art is disintegrating and Western art is in a transitional, eclectic, incoherent state, manifested in so-called "modernism," cubism, futurism, pointillism, dadaism, surrealism, etc.

Though not so sharp, somewhat similar dominant waves can be observed in the art of India, ancient Egypt, China, and several other countries.

Fourth, each form of art expresses a certain mentality or "soul" and is inseparably connected in each instance with a specific type of personality and culture. Cultures as well as types of personalities display the same four forms: Sensate, Ideational, Idealistic (plus "Integral"), and Eclectic. (See their brief characterization below, in Chapter XI.) Sensate art occurs with a predominantly Sensate culture and in a society made up of mainly Sensate personalities; Ideational art in a predominantly Ideational culture and society; and so on. When a culture or civilization passes from one dominant type to another its art undergoes a similar change. When the Medieval European culture, dominated by an Ideational supersystem, passed after the fourteenth century into a predominantly Sensate form, what had been predominantly Ideational Medieval art became predominantly Sensate. In other words, a given type of dominant art does not exist and change by itself, independent of the culture and the type of human personality that predominates in the society in which it appears and functions. Art is flesh of the flesh; it is one with the society, culture, and prevalent type of personality which has produced it. Each type of art emerges, grows, changes, and declines with the emergence, growth, change, and decline of the given type of culture, society, and personality.

Fifth, at the present time, the Sensate culture, society, and personality that have been dominant for the last five centuries in the West are disintegrating; crumbling also is the Sensate Western art that has been dominant for these five centuries.

Sixth, when studied in detail these patterns of the fluctuations of art do not fundamentally disagree with what some of the forementioned theorists have had to say about types of art and their cycles or rhythms.

Such in brief are the most general conclusions concerning art-phenomena reached in the course of an investigation of the main types of culture and of their dynamics.

4

CONCLUSION

The foregoing outlines the main types of the aesthetic philosophies of history, their real contributions and their weaknesses. It shows that many general theories of culture or civilization have (as we shall see) been preceded by similar theories about the types and dynamics of art-phenomena. The total contribution of these art-theories to the recent "intelligible reading of historical events" is enormous.

This is the reason why in the discussion of recent interpretations of historical events the aesthetic philosophies of history had to be mentioned, outlined, and given due credit. In addition they serve well as an introduction to the more general philosophies of history. Now we may turn to an outline and an analysis of these philosophies.

III

Nikolai Danilevsky

Nikolai Iakovlevitch Danilevsky (1822–1885) studied at
the University of St. Petersburg, receiving a *magister* degree
in Botany in 1849. Soon after, suspected of being mixed up
in the Petrashevsky political affair, he was imprisoned for
one hundred days in the Petropavlovskaya fortress—a Russian Bastille. In contrast to Dostoievsky and others involved
in that affair who were condemned to hard labor in Siberia,
Danilevsky was acquitted and soon appointed by the government to the staff of the governor of Vologda and later
of the Samara provinces. Thereafter his career was that of a
government official in charge of fairly diverse functions, now
an economist or engineer in the Ministry of Agriculture, now
a special governmental representative to this or that governmental body or committee. His main official position, however, one he held between 1853 and 1885, was as a specialist
in fisheries; he finally became head of the Russian Commission
on Fisheries.

The diversity of his official functions and a certain amount
of leisure afforded him from official duties explain the variety
and number of Danilevsky's publications. Besides many special publications in the field of fishery, he published a two-
volume work on *Darwinism,* two substantial works in economics called *Devaluation of the Russian Rouble,* two works
in political science called *General European Interests* (1878)
and *Russia and the Question of the Orient* (1879), a historical monograph on the *Route Followed by the Magyars,* a
work in the field of linguistics (on the *Dictionary of the Grand
Russian Language*), and a number of papers on various topics
of current interest.[1]

Erudition, plus a spark of real talent, enabled him to write his *Russia and Europe*—a work which required and displays his wide range of interests and knowledge. *Russia and Europe: A Viewpoint on the Political Relations Between the Slavic and Germano-Romanic Worlds* was first published in 1869 as a series of articles in a Russian magazine, *Zaria* (Dawn). Its first edition in book form appeared in 1871, and seventeen years were required to sell out the first and second editions. But the third edition in 1888 sold out in a few months—a very rare event in Russia at that time for this type of book— and called for a fourth edition in 1889.

From its first appearance, the work attracted a great deal of attention among Russian thinkers, writers, and statesmen. It was enthusiastically praised by Slavophils and conservatives and bitterly assailed by Russian "Westerners," liberals, and partisans of "Progress." Together with his other works, it made Danilevsky one of the leading proponents of Slavophilism and later of Panslavism in Russia. After its fourth edition the work began slowly to diffuse throughout Europe. In 1890 an abbreviated French translation appeared (J. J. Skupiewski, *La Doctrine Panslaviste d'après N. J. Danilewski,* Bucarest, 1890) and in 1920 a German translation was published (N. Danilevskii, *Russland und Europa,* tr. by K. Nötzell, Berlin, 1920). The publication of Spengler's *Decline of the West* greatly increased interest in Danilevsky's work and augmented the considerable literature about it that already existed. Thus we have here an example of a work whose vitality has increased rather than decreased in the course of time, for two reasons: the character of Danilevsky's philosophy of history in general, and the contemporary tension between Europe and Russia that makes Danilevsky's views startlingly up to date. His *Russia and Europe* is more alive today than it was eighty years ago.

Danilevsky's theory of the structure and dynamics of "historico-cultural types" is set forth by him not so much for its own sake as for the sake of explaining the much narrower and more temporary problem of *why Europe remains perennially inimical to Russia.*

Europe does not consider Russia as its own part. Europe sees in Russia and in Slavs generally something quite alien to itself and at the same time something that cannot be used as mere material to be exploited for Europe's profit, as Europe exploits China and India, Africa and the greater part of the Americas, a material which Europe can fashion and shape in its own image and pattern. . . . Europe sees in Russia and in Slavhood not only foreign, but an inimical, force [principle].

No matter how great the sacrifices that Russia makes for Europe, Danilevsky goes on to say, or how great the services she renders either to Europe's conservative or liberal factions, Europe persists in its hatred of Russia.[2] "The more sincerely and unselfishly we have accepted any European standpoint, the deeper Europe has hated us. It has not believed our sincerity and has seen some aggressive-imperialistic plans where there has been only the most sincere devotion to European interests." The history of Russo-European relations, and especially the Crimean war, he adds, has shown that

. . . Russia and Slavhood have been hated not by some single European party or faction, but by all European parties. . . . No matter what interests divide Europe, all its parties unite together in their animosity towards Russia. In this animosity European clericals shake hands with liberals, Catholics with Protestants, conservatives with progressives, aristocrats with democrats, monarchists with anarchists, the reds with the whites, the legitimists and the Orleanists with the Bonapartists.[3]

Danilevsky briefly surveys the history of Russia and points out that Europe has no rational basis for her animosity towards Russia. Russia has not threatened Europe. Russia has grown more peacefully than most European countries and in growing has expanded mainly over non-occupied areas or areas occupied by a few pre-literate tribes, and only in a few instances over areas inhabited by European Germano-Romanic peoples. It is not Russia that has regularly invaded Europe, but Europe that has invaded Russia many times and forced Russia to defend herself and expel her invaders.

Thus the composition of the Russian state, the wars which it carried on, the objectives it pursued, and especially the most favorable situations, so often repeated, which Russia could use for its aggrandizement and did not, all go to show that Russia is not an ambitious power bent on conquest. In the recent period especially, Russia sacrificed many of her obvious, most just and legitimate interests in favor of European interests, often acting intentionally and dutifully not as a self-sufficient organism, having itself a justification for all its strivings and actions, but as a mere instrument of European interests. Whence then, and what for, I ask, does this distrust of, injustice toward, and hatred for, Russia exist on the part of all governments and public opinions of Europe? [4]

However long we search for the reasons of this hatred of Europe towards Russia we cannot find them either in this or that action of Russia, or in other rationally comprehensible facts. There is nothing conscious in this hatred for which Europe can account rationally. The real cause lies deeper. It lies in those unfathomed depths of tribal sympathies and antipathies which are a sort of historical instinct of peoples and lead them (regardless of, though not contrary to, their will and consciousness) towards a goal unknown to them. For, in the main, historical process does not proceed according to arbitrary human plans, which determine only its secondary patterns, but according to unconscious historical instincts. This unconscious tendency, this historical instinct, is responsible for Europe's hatred towards Russia. . . . It also explains why the Germanic tribes easily blended with the Romance tribes, and likewise the Slavic tribes with the Finnish; and why, on the contrary, the Germanic and Slavic tribes were mutually repellent and antagonistic, and when one succeeded the other it had to exterminate that other, as did the Germans with the Polabian Slavic tribes and with the Baltic Slavs.[5]

To sum up: The antagonism between Russia and Europe is unquestionable, and certain too are its deep roots—unconscious historical instinct or drive reinforced by conscious considerations and historical conflicts. This raises the question of why and how this antagonism between the Russian and Teutonic-Romanic tribes appeared, why and how it has persisted, and whether it is a sort of temporary misunderstanding destined to disappear in the future, or is something perennial that is going to persist. These questions led Danilevsky to his "philosophy of history." [6]

Whether Europe is right or wrong in viewing Russia as something alien to itself depends on Europe's characteristics as a genus, and on whether Russia is one of its species. In analyzing this problem Danilevsky states that Europe is not a geographic unit because there are no natural geographic boundaries that clearly divide Europe from Asia. Geographically Europe is but the Western peninsula of Asia, much less clearly designated than many other peninsulas or areas of Asia.

Europe is not a geographic, but a *culture-historical sort of unit*. It is *"an area of the Germano-Romanic civilization or . . . Europe is the Germano-Romanic civilization itself. These two terms are synonymous."*

Europe or Germano-Romanic civilization is not universal human civilization. It is only one of many civilizations. Even Greek and Roman civilizations were Mediterranean and not European. Their areas lay partly on European, partly on Asiatic and African shores of the Mediterranean. Homer was seemingly born in Asia Minor; there, too, began poetry, philosophy (Thales), history (Herodotus), medicine (Hippocrates), and the sculpture of Greece. From there Greek culture crossed the Aegean sea and was planted on its European shore; Athens became its center, and from there it spread to Alexandria.

Thus in the course of its development ancient Hellenic culture diffused and acted on all three continents: Asia, Europe, and Africa. In no way was it the exclusive property of Europe. Graeco-Roman culture neither originated nor ended in Europe. The Greeks and Romans, in projecting their civilization to barbarian countries, equally included the European, Asiatic, and African shores of the Mediterranean in the civilized area, and they regarded the rest of the world, including the greater part of Europe, as barbarian, in the same manner in which the Germano-Romanic people confront Europe—the area of their historical activity—to the rest of the world.[7]

Similarly, "Russia, fortunately or unfortunately, also does not belong to Europe or to the Germano-Romanic civilization." Russia did not nourish herself on any roots of European culture. She did not form a part of the supernational, truly European Holy Roman Empire of Charlemagne and his successors; she did not have, nor did she participate in, a supranational and generally European feudal system, nor did she take part in its liquidation for the sake of civic and political freedom. Neither did Russia accept either Catholicism or Protestantism. Russia did not experience the oppression of scholasticism, nor did she know the freedom of thought that created modern science. In brief, Russia has not participated in European good or in European evil. Her life and activities have been entirely segregated from those of Europe.

Russia does not belong to Europe either by birthright or by right of adoption, "affiliation," or "apparentation" as an adopted child of Europe. The whole history of Europe's policies towards Russia does not indicate any parental attitudes or feelings. Europe does not even allow Russia to play the role of an agent of European civilization in the Orient or anywhere else. As soon as Russia tries to play this role—whether it be in Turkey, Persia, the Caucasus, India, China, or wherever—Europe at once vetoes such an action and begins a cold or hot war against Russia in alliance with blatantly non-European and non-Christian nations like Turkey, Persia, and China, or even with pre-literate groups and savages.[8]

The widespread idea that the European or Germano-Romanic civilization is identical with the universal human civilization is based on several fallacious principles, such as a vague and untenable conception of a cultural system or of the unit of historical study, a linear theory of progress, or a belief that only European civilization is progressive, whereas all others are static and uncreative, etc. The generally accepted division of historical events into the Ancient, Middle, and Modern periods is an example and result of these wrong assumptions. It takes the downfall of the Roman Empire as the boundary event which separates the Ancient from the Medieval period, and the discovery of America or a similar event in European history as the landmark between "Middle" and "Modern" History. Thus some event in Graeco-Roman and European history is taken as the landmark to divide the whole process of human history into three periods. Logically as well as factually, this periodization is entirely fallacious. It is only a slight improvement over the division of all of history into the following periods: "Before I was born" (ancient), "At the time of my graduation" (middle), and "After I was married" (modern). The utter inadequacy of this sort of periodization is perfectly obvious. Meanwhile the commonly accepted periodization is not much better. If its downfall was an important event for the Roman Empire, it was of no concern to China, India, or many Arab tribes. If 476 A.D. marked the end of the Western Roman Empire, this same year and the decades at the end of the fifth century did not signal any radical change in the life history of an incomparably greater part of humanity. Consequently, these dates are inapplicable and meaningless to all but those whom they concerned directly.

Why, then, did the downfall of the Roman Empire unite into one group of events, referred to as "Ancient history," (by contrast to another group, the Medieval period) the already defunct destinies of ancient Egypt and Greece and those of India and China, which continued their life-course undisturbed as though there were no Roman Empire? . . . Generally speaking, there is no single event which could reasonably divide the destiny of all of mankind into periods applicable to all humanity, for there never has been and hardly ever will be any event that will synchronously mean the same and be of the same importance for all of humanity. . . . Even Christianity—the event of the greatest importance to mankind—becomes a historical boundary line of the destiny of different peoples at different times. If we take Christianity to be the main historical dividing landmark, then the history of the Roman nation would be split into two parts, whereas in fact the post-Christian period was an indivisible continuation of Rome's pre-Christian period. . . . Ancient history is but a replica of the artificial Linnaean classification of plants (which puts mushrooms and ferns into the same class because both have no flowers) whereby Greeks, Egyptians, and Chinese are lumped together simply because they all lived before the downfall of the Roman Empire.[9] While Egypt, India, China, Babylon, Assyria, Iran, Greece, and Rome, each of which passed through several different stages of development, are placed in one and the same group of Ancient history, the stages of development of the Germano-Romanic peoples are divided into the "Medieval and the Modern periods" which represent one and the same group of phenomena, for Europe's Modern history is either a development of what was started in the Middle Ages or its rejection carried on in the same civilization.[10]

As a result of this senseless periodization, Cato, Constantine the Great, Solomon, Ramses, Pericles, and the Gracchi are united into one group and one period, while Rudolf Hapsburg, the Emperor Maximilian, Philip the Fair, Louis XI, Richelieu, even the Sultans Bayaset and Soleiman, who did the same work and plowed the field of history with the same plow, are separated from each other and put into two different groups, stages and periods (the Medieval and Modern). "Such a classification is identical to that which puts a crow and an oyster into the same species because both of them do not have four legs."

The whole matter of this periodization is due also to the historians' faulty perspective: the close time proximity of European events and the fact that they are a part of European civilization, makes the differences between the European Medieval and Modern periods appear so great to historians that they regard the numerous preceding centuries of the history of the rest of mankind as a mere background which they dump into one unit. The closer the object, the bigger it looms before us; therefore the more easily we lose the correct perspective. And this is exactly what happened to historians and their untenable periodization.

Strictly speaking, Rome, Greece, India, Egypt, and all historical peoples each had its own Ancient, Mediaeval, and Modern periods; like any organism each of these had its own phases of development, though the number of these phases is not necessarily three, no less and no more.

Just as botany and zoology gave up the artificial unilinear classification of plants and animals and replaced it by natural classification into a number of different types (genera and species) of organisms, each of which represents not a step in a unilinear hierarchic development on the ladder of gradual perfection of organisms, but rather entirely different plans of organization, each perfect in its own way; just as there are not one but many great architectural styles each of which is perfect in its own manner; so also there are not one but many civilizations or historico-cultural types, each perfect in its own way and all together manifesting the infinitely rich creative genius of humanity. Only within the life-history of each of these types of civilization can one talk of its ancient, middle and modern phases of development.

Thus we arrive at the view that there are several different historico-cultural types or civilizations, that the total history of mankind is not a linear movement following one trend, one direction, and increasingly exhibiting only one kind of cultural achievement, but is in fact composed of multi-directional movements, developing along different lines, and exhibiting diverse aspects or values through several different types of civilizations. Each civilization emerges, develops its own morphological form, its own values, thus enriching the total treasury of human cultural achievement, and then passes away without being continued in its *specific* and *essential* form by any other civilization. In contrast to the artificial historical system "the natural system of history consists in distinguishing different culture-historical *types* of development as the main basis of history's divisions." [11]

Having reached this conclusion, Danilevsky proceeds to classify naturally the main culture-historical types or great original civilizations. In chronological order they are as follows:

(1) Egyptian, (2) Chinese, (3) Assyro-Babylonian-Phoenician-Chaldean or Ancient-Semitic, (4) Hindu, (5) Iranian, (6) Hebrew, (7) Greek, (8) Roman, (9) Neo-Semitic or Arabian, (10) Germano-Romanic or European.

To these may be added two American types, the Mexican and Peruvian, that perished by violent death and did not complete their life-course. Only the peoples of these culture-historical types were positive agents in the history of mankind. Each of these peoples developed in its own way the creative potential inherent in the particulars of their spiritual nature as well as in the specific conditions of their environment, and thus enriched the common treasury of humanity. Among these types we must further distinguish between the *solitary* types or civilizations and *successive* or *transmittable* civilizations or types whose fruits of activity were transmitted from one to another as material for nourishment or as fertilizer (for enrichment and assimilation) for the soil on which the successive civilization would develop. The Egyptian, Assyro-Babylonian-Phoenician, Greek, Roman, Hebrew, and Germano-Romanic or European civilizations are examples of such transmittable types. Since not one of these types is endowed with the privilege of endless progress, and since every people is eventually worn out and exhausted creatively, it is comprehensible that the achievements of these five civilizations that successively replaced one another, together with the supernatural gift of Christianity, greatly excels the *solitary* achievements of the Chinese or Indian civilizations, despite the fact that the longevity of these equals that of all five civilizations taken together. Herein lies the simple explanation of so-called Western progress and Oriental stagnation. However, these solitary historico-cultural types developed such aspects of sociocultural life which were not present to the same degree among their luckier "successive competitors," and thereby these solitary civilizations contributed greatly to the unfolding of the many-sided manifestations of the creative human spirit, which in itself constitutes true progress.[12]

In further developing his theory, Danilevsky continues:

These positive historico-cultural types—successive and solitary—do not, however, exhaust all the agencies of history. In a solar system, side by side with the planets, there appear from time to time comets which come and then disappear for many centuries into the darkness of space. Falling meteors, stars, and zodiacal light are other forms of the manifestation of cosmic matter. Similarly, besides the above positive cultural types or civilizations, there are in the human universe intermittent temporary agencies like the Huns, the Mongols, and the Turks who, having performed their destructive mission, having helped dying civilizations to die and then scattering their remains, return to their previous nothingness and disappear. We can call them the *negative agencies* of history. Sometimes, however, constructive as well as destructive missions are performed by the same tribe, as for instance, by the Germans and the Arabs. Finally, there are tribes or peoples whose creative *élan* is, for some reason, *arrested* at an early stage and who are therefore destined to be neither constructive nor destructive, neither positive nor negative agencies of history. They represent only *ethnographic material,* a sort of inorganic matter entering the historical organisms, the historico-cultural types. Undoubtedly these tribes increase the variety and richness of the historical types, but in themselves they do not achieve any historical individuality. The Finns, and to a greater degree, most of the tribes of mankind, are examples of this.[13]

Sometimes the dead and decayed civilizations disintegrate to the level of this ethnographic material until a new formative (creative) principle unites their elements with a mixture of other elements into a new historical organism, until this principle calls them to an independent historical life in the form of a new historico-cultural type. The peoples that made up the Western Roman Empire serve as an example of this. They became ethnographic material after the disintegration of the Empire and re-emerged in a new form, known as the Romanic peoples, after experiencing the influence of the Germanic formative principle.

To sum up: The historical role of a tribe or people is three-fold: it is either the positive creative role of a historico-cultural type (civilization), or the destructive role—the so-called whips of God that render the *coup de grace* to senile, agonizing civilizations, or the role of serving the purposes of others as ethnographic material. [14]

Such is Danilevsky's morphologic-dynamic classification of all human tribes and populations into three classes and the historical role of each class on the incessantly changing stage of history. In a schematic way it can be summed up as follows:

Main Historical Types

I. Positive (creative) civilizations or historico-cultural types

(1) Egyptian, (2) Assyro-Babylonian-Phoenician-Chaldean or Ancient-Semitic, (3) Chinese, (4) Hindu, (5) Iranian, (6) Hebrew, (7) Greek, (8) Roman, (9) Neo-Semitic or Arabian, (10) Germano-Romanic or European. In addition two civilizations, one Mexican, one Peruvian, met violent death at an early stage.

II. Negative (destructive) peoples and tribes: those who render the *coup de grace* to senile and dying civilizations

Mongols, Huns, Turks, and others.

III. Ethnographic material

Most of the tribes that do not reach the level of historical individuality as civilizations; that do not act like a historical tornado, destroying decaying civilizations; that serve as mere material which the positive or negative types use for their activity and achievement. Besides most pre-literate types and "non-historical" peoples, the remnants of disintegrated civilizations also play this role.

Having arrived at this stage, Danilevsky proceeds to study these types in detail and then to formulate the basic uniformities or laws of their development and dynamics. Here too, as in the preceding part, his ideas are clearly formulated, his logic is consistent, and his special knowledge as a natural scientist is evident in the manner of his thinking and of the exposition and demonstration of his propositions. In a sense his whole theory bears the marks of natural science and is, perhaps, one of the very best applications of the classificatory and other principles of natural science, particularly botany and zoology, to social and historical phenomena.

In Danilevsky's own words, the following are the main laws or uniformities of development and change that apply to his historico-cultural types or civilizations, to the destructive types, and to the ethnographic material in their relationship to one another:

Law 1. Every tribe or family of peoples identified by a language or by a group of languages whose resemblance is perceived directly, without deep philological explorations, constitutes an original historico-cultural type if it is mentally or spiritually capable of historical development and has already outgrown its childhood.

Law 2. It is necessary that a people enjoy political independence if its potential civilization is to be actually born and developed.

Law 3. The basic principles of a civilization of one historico-cultural type are not transmissible to the peoples of another historico-cultural type. Each type creates its own civilization under the greater or lesser influence of alien—preceding or synchronous—civilizations.

Law 4. A civilization of a given historico-cultural type reaches its fullness, variety, and richness only when its "ethnographic material" is diverse and when these ethnographic elements are not swallowed by one body politic, but enjoy independence and make up a federation or political system of states.

Law 5. The course of development of historico-cultural types is similar to the life-course of those perennials whose period of growth lasts indefinitely, but whose period of blossoming and fruitbearing is relatively short and exhausts them once and for all.[15]

I shall mention a few points of Danilevsky's fairly detailed comments on these laws.

In the case of the first and second laws, he points out that of the ten great historico-cultural types whose development makes up the contents of human history, the Chinese and Egyptian each had its own language. Of the other civilizations, three were Semitic, each with its own language belonging to the Semitic group: Chaldean, Hebrew, Arabic; five were Aryan, each with its own language belonging to the Aryan family of languages: Hindu (Sanskrit), Iranian, Greek, Roman, and Teutonic. Of the two other main branches of Aryan languages, the Slavic peoples are now becoming the eleventh great historico-cultural type, while the Celts did not make their own great civilization because they were conquered by the Romans and lost their political independence at an early stage in their development.

No civilization has been conceived and developed without political independence, though after it has reached maturity a civilization can live for a limited amount of time after it has lost its independence, as is shown by the case of Greece. In the same manner as the development of personality is hindered in a state of slavery, so also the development of peoples who live in a state of political dependence is obstructed, for in both cases the person and the people are rendered a mere instrumentality serving the purposes of others.

Thus the second law explains the exception of the Celts, despite their conforming to the first law. In accordance with the second law, conquest and subjugation, together with extremely unfavorable geographic and social conditions, account for the inability of an overwhelming majority of tribes to reach the level of civilization and to create their own historico-cultural type.[16]

The third law seems to be clearly confirmed by history. Even the little known Egyptian and Hindu civilizations seem to have diffused only among the peoples of Egyptian and Hindu (Sanskrit) origin. Neither civilization was transmitted in its entirety to peoples alien to these "language" groups. Similarly, the Ancient Semitic (Assyro-Babylonian-Phoenician-Chaldean) civilization spread only among the peoples of this common origin and could not be transmitted to the aborigines of Africa; the Chinese civilization diffused only among the Chinese and Japanese (who were probably migrants from China); the Hebrew culture-type could not be transmitted to any of the peoples that surrounded the Hebrew people.

The numerous efforts to spread Greek civilization among non-Aryan or Oriental peoples—even by means of Alexander the Great's conquests—all failed. Some seventy or eighty years after Alexander's conquest the planted Hellenic civilization disintegrated, and the Iranian civilization was restored in the Eastern part of the Alexandrian empire. In its Western part, particularly in Egypt, Greek civilization seems to have blossomed for a longer time, although this blossoming was carried on not by Egyptians or other non-Greek aborigines from Asia Minor, Syria, etc., but by persons and groups of Greek origin and Greek migrants, such as Greek kings and queens, philosophers, scientists, architects, merchants, artisans, and workers. These Greeks all spoke and wrote Greek instead of Egyptian, and established and operated famous libraries, museums, and academies in Alexandria. Learned Alexandria was but a Greek colony. Despite all the efforts of the Greeks, Greek civilization could not be transmitted to Egypt and the Orient.

Today we can observe a similar failure by the English to transmit European civilization to India. The English established many educational, scientific and cultural institutions in India; they have made many commendable efforts to "europeanize" India. And yet, these efforts have in the main borne no fruit, for India remains a Hindu, and not a European, type of civilization.

The transmission of a civilization to another people evidently means that this people must absorb all cultural elements—religious, political, social, aesthetic, scientific, ethical folkways and mores—of the transmitting people, must become permeated by these elements to a degree equivalent to that of the transmitting people, with whom they can compete, and whose transmitted civilization they will continue.[17]

From this standpoint even the most successful case of the transmission of a civilization—that of the Greeks to the Romans—is not an exception to the rule. Despite the Hellenization of Rome, the Romans proved themselves great creators only in those instances when they remained Romans, such as in creating a great political empire and the greatest system of law—fields in which the Greek genius was uncreative—and in specific forms of original (not imitative) Roman architecture, poetry, and history (Tacitus). In the fields of culture taken from Greece—in philosophy, ethics, many forms of fine arts, drama, epos, etc.—the Roman nation remained uncreative, a mere third-class imitator. In these fields the diffusion of Greek culture only poisoned and killed the promising possibilities of the early Italic or Etruscan civilization.

Similarly, the somewhat coercive imposition of Roman civilization on all conquered peoples remained ineffective. It only suppressed the promising development of the original cultures of several conquered peoples.

Such is Danilevsky's main thesis in his third law. Obviously this thesis sharply contradicts the prevalent theories of "acculturation" and "imitation."

Does this mean that Danilevsky denies that one civilization has any influence on another? that he denies any "interpenetration" of the elements of one civilization into another? No, for his third law applies only to the civilization taken as a *whole*, in all its essential individuality. This law does not apply to the *elements* of a civilization. These can be transmitted and can penetrate from one civilization into another.

We pointed out that the *successive* historico-cultural types have advantages over the *solitary* types. How, then, does this succession go on? It does not proceed by way of transmission (which is impossible) but by several specific ways. . . . The simplest way of diffusing a civilization is by transplanting it from one area to another, by *colonization*. In this way the Phoenicians handed their civilization to Carthage, the Greeks to Southern Italy and Sicily, and the English to North America and Australia.

The second way of diffusing a civilization is by *grafting*.

The prevalent understanding of this second method of diffusion is fallacious; it forgets that the grafted scion or shoot and the plant into which it is inserted still remain what they were before the grafting took place. By grafting we only turn the plant into a means for the scion; the scion remains an alien body in the plant which it exploits parasitically, from which it gets its nourishment, and which is cut and trimmed for the sake of the scion. The grafted scion does not at all benefit the plant into which it is grafted. Hellenic Alexandria, for instance, was such a cultural scion on the Egyptian tree, and so was Roman culture on the Celtic trunk. Grafting, then, occurs, but it usually suppresses the native culture and turns it and its people into a mere means for the grafted cultural scion.[18]

The third way in which one civilization is influenced by another is through *fertilization or mutual cross-fertilization.* A given original culture enriches itself by using the material of another civilization as a sort of fertilizer or nourishment in building its own pattern or type. It can borrow the achieved results of another civilization, especially in the fields of science and technology, which are practical techniques not confined to any specific civilization. These neutral elements do not affect the specific individuality of any given civilization and do not threaten to erase or deface its type. Other, non-neutral elements of an alien civilization—such as religious, philosophical, social, humanistic, ethical, and artistic systems—can also be ingested, but only as fertilizing material that will be patterned according to the type of the borrowing culture. Any original civilization is thus a highly selective organism: it takes only that which fits it and rejects all that does not harmonize with it.[19]

Thus, *colonization, grafting,* and *fertilization* (borrowing) are the main ways in which civilization is diffused.

The fourth law stresses the importance of the richness and variety of "ethnographic material" patterned and built into a growing civilization, and the autonomy of the political units that build the civilization. This richness, variety, and political autonomy of linguistically related peoples or states are necessary conditions if a civilization is to become truly great and historical. The absence of these constitutes one of the important reasons why many tribes and their "ethnographic cultures" cannot grow into historico-cultural types. "The richest and fullest civilizations so far have been Greek and European," precisely because of the variety of their "ethnographic material" and the autonomy of the several political units (states) that have been the human builders and bearers of these civilizations.[20]

All the Greek states—Sparta, Athens, etc.—were human bearers of one and the same Greek civilization; therefore this Greek civilization, and not Athens or Sparta or any other

Greek state, is the real unit of historical study. Outside of the context of this Greek civilization no special history of Athens or Sparta is possible. They are so interdependent that they cannot be studied or understood as separate histories; only as aspects of the same Greek civilization do they become comprehensible. Similarly, "we can hardly talk of a separate history of France, Italy or Germany; there is no such history. Instead we have the history of Europe from the French, Italian, German, or English standpoints with special attention being paid to the events in each of these countries." As soon as we pass beyond the boundaries of each culture-historical type, a common history of these different types becomes impossible because their histories have little in common, are non-synchronous, and remain quite different time-series of events hardly related to one another. Except for wars, the histories of Greece and Persia remain separate, as the historical series of Europe and Russia also remain separate.[21]

Finally, the fifth law states that the period of blossoming or the "phase of civilization" of each culture-historical type is comparatively short; it exhausts all its forces and does not repeat itself a second time. By the "phase of civilization" Danilevsky means the last period of development of a culture-historical type. Its first or ancient period ends with its emergence from a merely ethnographic form of existence into a patterned form; its second or "middle" period consists in building its cultural and political independence, this independence assuming the form of a state or a loose federation of states; finally, its third "civilization" or modern period fully develops all its creative potentialities and achieves a practical realization of its ideals of justice, freedom, and social and individual well-being.[22] This period ends when the creative powers of the peoples of this type of historical culture are exhausted. After that some nations, like China, either become petrified and begin to rest on their laurels while they senilely age in an apathy of self-satisfaction and view the traditions of the past as the eternal ideal of the future, or they reach the state of insoluble contradictions, conflicts and disillusion. They fall into an apathy of despair. Rome, during the period of the diffusion of

Christianity, serves as such an example. The case of Byzantium shows that this second form cannot last long and reverts to the first form (from the apathy of despair to that of self-satisfaction and petrifaction).[23]

This period of blossoming or of "civilization" lasts on an average of four hundred to six hundred years, in contradistinction to the first, preparatory, or ancient period which is measured by millennia, and the medieval period which likewise is long (though the number of these periods is not necessarily three). The first two periods are those of accumulation and organization of the creative forces of a given culture-historical type. In the third or blossoming period these forces are magnificently spent. Like all spending, this proceeds rapidly and leads to the exhaustion of the respective peoples, followed by the decline and disintegration of the civilization in question. This decline is inevitable. One of the main reasons for it is that each great culture-historical type develops and realizes only one or a few of the great creative values—none is encyclopedic. Thus, Greek civilization realized *beauty* to an extent unexcelled and hardly rivaled by any other civilization. The main contribution of European civilization is a realization of science; of the Semitic civilizations, religion; of the Roman civilization, law and political organization of an empire; of the Chinese, the practically useful; of the Indian, imagination and fantasy, together with some mysticism.[24] The unfolding of any single value has its limit; when this is reached the civilization has achieved its task and is bound to die.

There is nothing more absurd than the idea of one endless linear progress. Real progress consists not of a linear movement in one and the same direction in the course of time, but of multi-linear and multi-directional movements that cover the whole field of humanity's historical activities. And that is exactly what is being done by the totality of great civilizations, each of which crosses the whole field in one direction (creating one sort of value) and all of which together cover the field in all its main directions. Therefore not one of the great civilizations can boast that it is better than the preceding ones in all aspects of development or progress.[25] Nobody can say that the head of Cuvier was better than that of Aristotle; that Laplace was more intelligent than Archimedes; that Kant thought better than Plato; that Napoleon was a greater military genius than Caesar or Hannibal; or that Canova understood beauty better than Phidias or Praxiteles.

Each of the great civilizations contributes its main value in its full form, which is unexcelled by subsequent civilizations. "The task of mankind consists in an unfolding of and realization, by different peoples at different periods, of all the aspects and forms of creativity that virtually or potentially underlie all humanity." [26]

The stage of decline and disintegration comes after the period of blossoming, and *it sets in somewhat earlier than is observable.* The reason for that is the same as that which we know to hold true for many natural processes:

[In Europe] the time of summer when the sun is at its highest and the day is longest, is June; but the results of this position of the sun, in so far as they concern the highest temperature, only appear in July and August. Still later, in autumn, its results appear in so far as they affect fruitbearing: as a fulfillment of the promise of spring, the above results occur when the days are already much shorter and the sun rises much lower on the horizon. [In the daily cycle] the highest culmination point of the sun is at noon, but its heat results continue to rise some two or three hours after the cause of them has begun already to go down. [Similarly] an individual reaches a full development of his physical and moral forces when he is about thirty years of age. Meanwhile the results of this development fully manifest themselves only after forty years of age.[27]

[Generally] the moment of the highest development of the forces or causes that produce a certain series of effects does not coincide with the moment of the maximum abundance of the effects, which follows from a gradual development of these forces: the moment when these effects are at their highest point ordinarily comes considerably later than the moment of the highest development of the causes.[28]

For these reasons the time of decay of a civilization already sets in when the civilization blooms and appears to be at its zenith. The decline is due not to the external conditions but to the inner causes of the civilization. What these are we do not exactly know, just as we do not know about the causes of aging and senility in the life of an individual.

Such are the main laws of dynamics of sociocultural types or civilizations.

There is neither time nor space to follow in detail the development of these laws and of many other of Danilevsky's ideas. Briefly, however, I can mention a few of his theories.

(1) A nation or a group of linguistically related nations that create the same type of civilization are the main instrumentalities through which the creative mission of humanity is carried on. From this standpoint each creative nation or group of nations definitely patterns science, philosophy, the fine arts, and generally all the main forms of creativity.

(2) This leads Danilevsky to an outline of a *sociology of knowledge* and of a *comparative psychology of nations.* Not only are religion, philosophy, the fine arts, and social and humanistic disciplines stamped with the characteristics of a creative nation, but even science and technology, which are supposed to be identical for all nations, bear the marks of a respective civilization and its nation(s). In this sense we can speak of the national character of science. This national character manifests itself in: (a) the sort of predisposition which each nation shows to certain branches of science; (b) the point of view with which each nation approaches a scientific study of the reality; (c) the kind of subjective peculiarities it mixes with the objective truth. Thus the three basic English theories of Thomas Hobbes, Adam Smith, and Charles Darwin all manifest the central trait of the English nation: the ethos and pathos of free competition and struggle. This central value of the English nation shows itself in the Hobbesian theory of *bellum omnium contra omnes,* in Adam Smith's theory of free competition in the economic field, and in Darwin's theory of the struggle for existence.

Since beauty and aesthetic value is the central trait of Greek civilization and nations, this trait manifests itself in the Greek preference for "geometric, instead of analytical, method" in their thought and creativity. Danilevsky goes into considerable detail and supplies factual evidence to show that each of the leading nations has its own peculiarities and that even science and technology are greatly conditioned by, and stamped with, the national traits and values. Here again many of the characteristics which Spengler and Toynbee ascribed to several of the main historical civilizations are but a reiteration of Danilevsky's ideas (possibly without a knowledge of his theories). Likewise, several recent sociologies of knowledge, like those of Karl Mannheim and, in part, myself, are somewhat similar to the ideas of Danilevsky in a number of points.[29]

(3) There are several uniformities of a *lead and lag*. (a) The period of decline of a civilization sets in earlier than is apparent, or the moment of the manifest consequences of the decline-cause lags from the moment when these causes start their work; (b) the political unification and independence of the peoples that are the agencies of a great civilization precede the cultural blossoming or "civilizational" period of a given culture-historical type; (c) the development and blossoming of the fine arts precedes those of science in the same civilization.[30]

(4) Finally, Danilevsky, in answering his initial question, why Europe hates Russia, delineates in detail the nature, interrelationship, and the future of the European and Slavic culture-historical types. Europe hates Russia and Slavhood because the European and Slavic civilizations are different types and because Europe has already entered the period of decline, whereas Slavic civilization is just about to enter its blossoming and most creative period. Not able to turn the Russian-Slavic peoples and culture into mere ethnographic material for its own use, and intuiting its own old age and coming dissolution, Europe cannot help being envious of and inimical towards Russia and Slavhood. The European or Germano-Romanic civilization is a double civilization that creates mainly in the political and scientific-technological-aesthetic fields. In Danilevsky's analysis, the emerging Russian-Slavic civilization tends to be a triple or even quadruple type of civilization that creates in all the four main fields of culture: religious, scientific-aesthetic-technological, political, and economic, but mainly in

the socio-economic field through the building of a new and just socio-economic order; [31] in other words, the Slavic culture-historical type is turning into the first civilization that synthesizes in itself all four fields of cultural creativity.

Because of this basic difference in the European and Slavic types of civilizations, they have hardly ever understood each other and each has been unsuccessful when trying to interfere in the affairs of the other. Except for such "neutral" elements of culture as science and technology, all efforts (both European and Russian) to europeanize Russia and Slavhood have failed, remaining either ineffective or distorting the original Russian institutions and values. Slavic Poland, which allowed herself to be "europeanized," did not get European values, but rather lost Slavic ones, and presents a deplorable example of a distorted and unbalanced cultural "mongrel." On the other hand, when Russia, chiefly for altruistic motives, wanted to help Europe and took an active part in European affairs, the results were deplorable for Russia as well as for Europe.

The European civilization is some five hundred years older than the Slavic-Russian civilization. This Russian type is just now passing from its second into the third stage—the phase of maximal blooming or "civilization." The European culture-historical type is at the end of its blossoming period. As a matter of fact, its decline started in the seventeenth century, but because of the lag between the moment of the apparent and that of the real decline, the first symptoms of European decay have begun to appear only in recent decades. This decline manifests itself in many forms: in a weakening of European creativity; in the growing cynicism of Europe; in her de-Christianization; and especially in Europe's insatiable lust for power and world domination, not only in the political and economic spheres, but also in the cultural sphere. [32] The weaker become the creative forces of Europe, the stronger grows its lust for world domination. Such domination by any single civilization would mortally endanger humanity: it would forever impose one type of culture on all humanity, would preclude the emergence and growth of a new type of civilization, and would put an end to the creative mission of mankind. For this reason alone real friendship cannot exist between this aged European civilization that tends to dominate, and the fresh and youthful Slav civilization; for it is this civilization's great historical mission to oppose and to limit Europe's lust for world domination. This is an additional reason why Europe cannot help hating Russia and why the war between Europe and Russia (the war with Slavhood) is inevitable.

Only united Slavhood can fight the united Europe. This united Slavhood does not threaten world domination but, on the contrary, it is the only possible guarantee for preserving world equilibrium and the only protection against the world domination of Europe. . . . As soon as Europe settles its own affairs, it will invade Russia under the first handy pretext, as was the case in the Crimean War.[33]

However, federated Slavhood and its own emerging civilization will be able to withstand any onslaught by semi-senile Europe, will take up the torch of world creative leadership from the exhausted European civilization, and will carry it on in the future until the Slavic civilization itself begins to decline or to merge with the world civilization.

Such are the essentials of Danilevsky's work. Begun as a political pamphlet of the highest grade, it demonstrated its political contentions to such a degree that it became a brilliant treatise on the philosophy of history and cultural sociology, and ended up by being an unusually shrewd and essentially correct piece of political prognostication and prophecy. In reading its political sections, one cannot fail to see a remarkable similarity between Danilevsky's views on the Russo-European relationships and prospects, and those of the Soviet government on this same subject. If one removes the Marxist terminology and a few other insignificant details from the policies and political propaganda of the Soviet government, Danilevsky's and the Soviet leaders' ideologies regarding Russo-European relations are essentially similar. Thus, in this respect, a most conservative Slavophil and the Communist Politbureau and International shake hands with each other. One can hardly imagine stranger bedfellows!

IV

Oswald Spengler

Oswald Spengler was born at Blakenburg, Germany, on May 29, 1880; he died on May 8, 1936. After studying mathematics, natural history, history, and art at the Universities of Halle, Munich, and Berlin, he became a high-school teacher (*Oberlehrer*) at Düsseldorf, Hamburg, and Munich. Practically unaided, he worked alone for three years from 1911 to 1914 on the first version of his main work, *Der Untergang des Abendlandes* (*Decline of the West*). Its first version was completed in 1914 but the explosion of the First World War, among other things, prevented its publication. By the spring of 1917 he had redrafted the manuscript and it was finally published in July of the following year. Of the thinkers who influenced his philosophy of history, Spengler in the preface to the revised edition of 1922 specifically mentioned Goethe and Nietzsche, "those to whom I owe practically everything. . . . Goethe gave me method, Nietzsche the questioning faculty."

Despite the fact that the author was unknown both to the public and to the learned world and notwithstanding the difficult and pessimistic character of his philosophy of history, Spengler's work had a sensational success, sold more than ninety thousand copies in a few years, evoked a vast literature, and was translated into several languages. *Decline of the West* has proved to be one of the most influential, controversial, and durable masterpieces of the first half of the twentieth century in the fields of social science, philosophy of history, and German philosophy. It catapulted an unknown high-school teacher into the ranks of the century's most influential social thinkers.

Besides his main work, Spengler published several others, but all these are either variations on the themes of his masterpiece or elaborations of some of its detailed points. The titles of these works are *Preussentum und Sozialismus* (1920), *Pessimismus* (1921), *Politische Pflichten der Deutschen Jugend* (1924), *Neubau des Deutschen Reiches* (1924), *Der Mensch und die Technik* (1931), and *Jahre der Entscheidung*. Of these *Decline of the West, Hour of Decision,* and *Man and Technics* have been translated into English by Charles Francis Atkinson and published in the United States by Alfred A. Knopf. The American edition of these books has been successful; all of them have had from a few to fourteen reprintings and are in constant demand up to this time.

Though Spengler's type of thinking and writing and the total character of *Decline of the West* are quite different from Danilevsky's work, the skeleton of Spengler's philosophy of history resembles Danilevsky's in all its basic points.[1] Like Danilevsky he finds that the "current West European scheme of history," divided into "Ancient-Medieval-Modern" periods from the standpoint of Western culture, is "an incredibly jejune and meaningless scheme." It is a sort of "Ptolemaic system of history" that concentrates on Western history; its "simple rectilinear progression and meaningless proportions become more and more preposterous with each century." "Of course," he ironically remarks, "the nineteenth century A.D. appears to us incomparably more important than the nineteenth century B.C.; but the moon, too, looks much bigger than Jupiter or Saturn! The natural scientist freed himself from this illusion of a relative distance long ago; the historian still remains its victim." [2] He replaces it by the "Copernican viewpoint" in history, which admits no privileged position to the Western or Classical culture as against the other High Cultures of India, Babylon, Mexico, China, Egypt, or of the Arabs, and which considers each High Culture equally as important in the scheme of history as Western or Classical culture.[3]

The main philosophical presupposition of this Copernican system of history consists in a dualistic division of reality, or "existence," or cosmic energy, into two main aspects: the World-as-Nature and the World-as-History. Nature is the "shape" (image) in which the man of higher culture synthesizes and interprets the impressions of his *senses*. History is the "image" which he intuitively, instinctively, and then rationally creates in order to comprehend the world in relation to his own life.[4] These aspects of existence differ from each other along many lines and lead to entirely different methods of cognition of the World-as-Nature and the World-as-History. Here are the most important characteristics of both "worlds" and of the historical and natural science disciplines that deal with each of these aspects:

Existence (Reality) as:

The World-as-History	*The World-as-Nature*
It is a living potentiality (life, soul) in a state of incessant becoming, that fulfills its unique life-course or Destiny in the Time-process, never reversing its Direction, and flowing from the past through the present to the future.	It is a realized actuality, the thing become or fulfilled, static and dead, existing in space or extension with timeless invariable relationships among the things become.
It has Destiny as an organic necessity of potentiality passing into actuality.	It has Causality as a mechanical, repeated necessity of cause and effect in the relationships of the things become.
Consciousness as the servant of Being.	Consciousness as the master of Being.
It follows the logic of time.	It follows the logic of space.
It has rhythm in its becoming, full-blooded individuality, form, physiognomy, and unique events or facts.	It has only quantitative, timeless, mechanical uniformity in the interrelationships of its "variables," and formless, colorless formulas or generalized laws.
"Destiny-men."	"Causality-men."

These two aspects of existence or reality manifest themselves also in two different types of consciousness—historical and natural scientific—in two different "world-images," and lead to two different morphologies of the historical and the natural science disciplines. The specific traits of the historical "physiognomic" and the naturalistic "systematic" (as Spengler designates these two consciousnesses, ways of cognition, and disciplines) may be summed up as follows:

Historical "Physiognomic"	Naturalistic "Systematic"
It is based upon immediate, intuitive, instinctive apprehension of the living potentiality (or life and soul) through the "method of living into (*erfühlen*) the object as opposed to dissecting it," or through aesthetic identification of the cognizing subject with the cognized object. "The Destiny idea demands life-experience and not scientific experience." "Organic logic, and instinctive dream, sure logic of all existence." It cannot be taught without living, intuitive experience. The means of imparting historical grasp are: analogy, picture, symbol. "A Becoming can only be experienced by living, felt with a deep wordless understanding." [5]	It is based upon observation and dissection of the (dead) thing become from outside, never living into the object, never "entering into it" and identifying the cognizing subject with the cognized object. Scientific method of cognition. It is learned and one can be trained in it. The means of imparting it are: concept, causal formula, law, scheme. It results in abstract conceptual systems, timeless, lifeless, ever-valid "truths."
"The means whereby to understand living forms is analogy."	"The means whereby to identify dead forms is mathematical law."
"Chronological number and idea of Destiny."	"Mathematical number and the principle of Causality." Scientific method.
Logic of Time. Contemplation.	Logic of Space. [6]
Inward (immanent) necessity of Destiny. Constructive action becoming Destiny.	Mechanical timeless necessity of ever-repeated cause and effect. Hypothesis, religious dogma, cult and technique.
History is art (not science); it is neither "true" nor "false" (as science) but "deep" or "shallow."	Natural "systematic" science is "true" or "false." [7]

Such are the two orders of the phenomenal world. "Both orders, each on its own account, cover the *whole* world" (or existence), or "cosmic energy," which is the fountainhead of historical events. "The difference lies only in the eyes by which and through which this world is realized." [8]

Such are Spengler's essential philosophical presuppositions. In addition to Goethe's ideas, one can easily recognize in this dualistic division of the whole existence or phenomenal world a variation of the Hegelian dialectical "Idea in itself" (the World-as-History) and "the Idea in its otherness" (the World-as-Nature), Rickert's and Wildenband's division of the sciences into the ideographic (historical) and nomographic (natural science), Bergson's theory of intuition and intellect, of full-blooded and "bleached" time, and several other philosophies and presuppositions that were formulated by some of Spengler's predecessors.

With Spengler's philosophy and epistemology in mind, we can now turn to his "Copernican" philosophy of history, or the "historical physiognomic."

I pointed out above that Spengler, like Danilevsky, rejects and ridicules the linear history of mankind, derived from the Ptolemaic standpoint of recent Western culture, with its empty division into "Ancient-Medieval-Modern" periods, and with its linear theory of

. . . the progress of painting from the Egyptians (or the cavemen) to the Impressionists, or of music from Homer to Bayreuth and beyond, or of social organization from the Lake Dwellings to Socialism, as the case may be, presented as a linear graph which steadily rises in conformity with the author's values. . . .

"Mankind" has no aim, no idea, no plan. . . . "Mankind" is a zoological expression, or an empty word. . . . I see, in place of that empty figment of *one* linear history . . . the drama of a number of mighty Cultures, each springing with primitive strength from the soil of a mother-region to which it remains firmly bound throughout its whole life-cycle; each stamping its material, its mankind, in its *own* image; each having its *own* idea, its *own* passion, its *own* life, will and feeling, its *own* death. . . . Here the Cultures, peoples, languages, truths, gods, colors, lights, movements, bloom and age like the oaks grow and age—but there is no aging "Mankind." . . .

Each Culture has its own new possibilities of self-expression which arise, ripen, decay, and never return. There is not *one* sculpture, *one* painting, *one* mathematics, *one* physics, but many, each of which is different from the others, limited in duration and self-contained.

The Cultures, in the same manner as the flowers, grow with a superb aimlessness. World history presents a picture of the endless formations and transformations of these cultures as organic forms.[9]

"The prime phenomenon" of history or, as Toynbee puts it, the primary unit of historical study, is that of the High or Great Cultures.

"Cultures are organisms, and world history is their collective biography." They emerge, grow, and having fulfilled their destiny, die:

A Culture is born in the moment when a great soul awakens out of the proto-spirituality of ever childish humanity, detaches itself, and becomes a form from the formless, a bounded and mortal thing from the boundless and enduring. It blooms. . . . It dies when this soul has actualized the full sum of its possibilities in the shape of peoples, languages, dogmas, arts, states, sciences, and reverts into the proto-soul. . . . The aim once attained—the idea, the entire content of inner possibilities, fulfilled and made externally actual—the Culture suddenly hardens, it mortifies, its blood congeals, its (creative) force breaks down, and it becomes Civilization.

"Every Culture passes through the age phases of the individual man. Each has its childhood, youth, manhood and old age." At childhood "it is a young and trembling soul, heavy with misgivings." As it approaches its noon-culmination it becomes progressively virile, austere, controlled, and clear in its individual lineaments, and self-assured in its power. At that phase "every individual trait of expression is deliberate, strict, measured, marvelous in its ease and self-confidence."

Finally, when the fire in the Culture's soul dies down, it enters its last phase—that of Civilization. "Every Culture has its own Civilization. The Civilization is the inevitable destiny of the Culture." Civilizations are the last, the most external and artificial states of Cultures:

They are a conclusion, the thing become succeeding the thing becoming, death following life, rigidity following expansion, intellectual age and the stone-built, petrifying world-city following mother-earth and the spiritual childhood of Doric and Gothic. They are an end, irrevocable, yet by inward necessity reached again and again. . . . They may, like a worn-out giant of the primeval forest, thrust their decaying branches towards the sky for hundreds or thousands of years, as we see in China, in India, in the Islamic world.

In this "petrified form" they may even distort a newly emerging young culture (so-called pseudomorphosis).[10]

This stage of Civilization is marked by several characteristics quite different from those of the childhood, youth, and noon of a certain culture. The following are the general characteristics of the Civilization phase of each High Culture: cosmopolitanism and the megalopolis vs. "home," "race," "blood group," and "fatherland"; scientific irreligion or abstract dead metaphysics instead of the religion of the heart; "cold matter-of-factness" vs. reverence and tradition and respect for age; international "society" instead of "my country" and state (nation); "natural rights" in place of hard-earned rights; money and abstract value in lieu of fruitful earth and real (living) values; "mass" instead of "folk"; sex in lieu of motherhood; *panem et circences* in place of religious and spontaneous folk-festivals; imperialistic expansion, urbanization, internationalization, the outward direction of Civilization-man's energy instead of the inward direction of the Culture-man; the cult of bigness, syncretism, lust for power, class struggle instead of quality and unity; and so on. In this late stage several imitative attempts to revive the values, patterns, and spirit of the earlier phase of Culture appear, but all remain fruitless. In the stage of Culture all struggles, even the bloodiest ones, are the actualization of an idea into a living historical fact. In the stage of Civilization all that remains is the struggle for mere power, for animal advantage as such. A Civilization can last for hundreds and thousands of years in such a petrified state—witness the case of China, India, and the Islamic world. In this stage some Civilizations have an "Indian summer." Their dwindling creative powers rise once more in a half-successful effort and "produce the Classicism, common to all dying Cultures."

"Finally, weary, reluctant, cold, it [Culture at the phase of Civilization] loses its desire to be, and, as in Imperial Rome, wishes itself out of the overlong daylight and back in the darkness of proto-mysticism, in the womb of the mother, in the grave." It begins to disintegrate and reverts, in Danilevsky's terms, to "a mere ethnographic material"—historyless and formless. Before its death, however, the Culture-Civilization experiences "the spell of second religiosity," the fever of a new religious movement, a wave of mysticism or gnosticism, such as the spread of the cult of Mithra, of Isis, of the Sun, or, in ancient Rome, of Christianity. (This last point should be stressed for reasons indicated further on.) This "spell of second religiosity" marks the end of the life-course of the Culture-Civilization, its death, and possibly the emergence of a new Culture. Such are the essentials of Spengler's life-cycle of Culture-Civilization.[11] Behind this life-cycle there is the mysterious "cosmic energy" that drives us, that vitalizes the Culture and determines its life-cycle.[12]

The foregoing shows that Danilevsky's and Spengler's theories are similar in a number of basic points. This similarity does not, however, preclude Spengler's originality in the development and analysis of these points.

Instead of Danilevsky's ten great cultures, Spengler mentions only eight: the Egyptian, Babylonian, Indian, Chinese, Classical or Apollinian (Graeco-Roman), Arabian or Magian, Mexican, and Western or Faustian (which emerged around 1000 A.D.). He mentions the Russian as the next possibility. Of these nine Cultures the Mexican died by violent death; the Magian and the Russian underwent a "pseudomorphosis" at an early age, a partial suppression or distortion under the all-powerful influence of the older alien Civilizations, which prevented their full and specific development.[13] Factually, however, Spengler deals only with six of these Cultures, and in detail he treats mainly the Classical or Apollinian, Arabian or Magian (a designation including Arabic, Islamic, Iranian, Jewish, Syrian, Byzantine, Manichean, and early Christian Cultures), and the Western [14] or Faustian. All these great Cultures have passed through the described life-cycle of the

High Cultures and are now either dead or in the phase of their late Civilization.

Each great Culture is based upon *its own major premise* or "prime symbol," which differs entirely for each Culture. "The choice of prime symbol in the moment of the Culture-soul's awakening into self-consciousness on its own soil . . . decides all." *This major premise or prime symbol determines the essential characteristics of the given Culture: the character of its science and philosophy, of its mentality, of its arts and beliefs, of its way of thinking, living, and acting.*[15] A given great Culture articulates its prime symbol in all its main compartments.

There is not one concept of numbers or mathematics, not one concept of the soul or scientific psychology, not one pattern of philosophy or religion, or of the fine arts, but instead many, and exactly as many as there are different Cultures with their different prime symbols. The idea that there is, or can be, only one mathematics, one psychology, one physics, one biology, or one sociology is a mere myth, denied by "physiognomic-historical" as well as "natural-science" evidence. Spengler develops this thesis much more fully than Danilevsky, and the bulk of Spengler's work is devoted to unfolding and demonstrating these propositions.

Let us briefly outline Spengler's treatment of these problems, beginning with the prime symbols of the great Cultures. The prime symbol of the Classical or Apollinian Culture is "the sensuously present individual body as the ideal type of the extended." "Pure and limitless space" is the prime symbol of the Western or Faustian Culture. Correspondingly, "the nude statue is Apollinian, the art of the fugue Faustian. Apollinian are: mechanical statics, the sensuous cult of the Olympian gods, the politically individual city-states of Greece, the doom of Oedipus and the phallus symbol. Faustian are: Galilean dynamics, Catholic and Protestant dogmatics, . . . the Baroque's great dynasties, the destiny of Lear and the Madonna-ideal from Dante's Beatrice to the last line of *Faust II.* . . .The painting that defines the individual body by contours is Apollinian, that which forms space by means of light and shade is Faustian" (the difference between the fresco of

Polygnotus and the painting of Rembrandt). The Apollinian Greek describes his ego as *soma* (body) having no history and inner development. Faustian man sees his ego as something infinite, inner, introspective. Faustian "space" is a spiritual something, rigidly distinct from the momentary sense-present. This sort of "space" is indescribable and incomprehensible to the Apollinian man.[16]

The Doric and Etruscan temple, firmly rooted in the ground, with mere inter-space between its columns, its separate bodies of sculpture, and its relief, is Apollinian; a Gothic cathedral or an impressionistic painting, which completely disembody the world, is Faustian. Olympus of the Classical gods is a real body on Greek soil. Valhalla, devoid of all sensory traits, floating in limitless space that contains unharmonious and lonely heroes, is Faustian. So is the solitude of the Faustian soul in limitless space. Siegfried, Parsifal, Tristan, Hamlet, and Faust are the loneliest heroes in all the Cultures. A hero who is at odds with himself and with God, who is a lonely pilgrim in the infinite universe, is a Faustian man. This solitude is equally felt in Rembrandt's color and in Beethoven's instrumentation. The Cosmos of the Classical Culture is the plurality of separate bodies represented by the antique polytheism of corporeal gods. Apollo and Athens have no souls. The Faustian God is an Infinite All that can be best expressed symbolically in the storm of an organ fugue or music that speaks of the *universalia ante rem*. No wonder that even Faustian modern physics dissolved the material world into bodyless energy in the limitless, void, and swaying indefiniteness of space-time.[17]

This gives some idea of the Spenglerian treatment of the prime symbol of a great Culture and of its articulation through a multitude of important traits in all main compartments of the Culture discussed.

"Stone" is the prime symbol of the Egyptian Culture. "Stone is the emblem of the Timeless Become; space and death seem bound up in it." Stone marks the burial place. The dead strive no more. They are no longer Time, but only static, unstriving space. The Egyptians' life-course is like that of a traveler moving in one unchanging direction to the trial court of the judges of the dead. This one-directional *way,* quite definitely circumscribed and enclosed by *stone* masonry of progressively narrowing passages, courts, and pillared rooms winding up in the chamber of the dead, *is the prime symbol of Egyptian Culture.*[18]

The "cavernous, eternal, vaulted space" and the "Cavern feeling" expressed by the dome, the cupola, barrel-vaulting, and rib-vaulting are the prime symbol of the Magian (Arabic, Iranian, Islamic, Syrian, Jewish, Early Christian, Byzantine) Culture. The "plane without limit" is the prime symbol of Russian Culture. Tao—an indefinable, indeterminate, multilinear, wandering *way*—is the symbol of Chinese Culture.[19]

The foregoing illustrates the kind of connections Spengler draws between the prime symbol of each Culture and its various traits as they manifest themselves in the Culture's different compartments. In conformity with its prime symbol each great Culture is unique and through all compartments speaks its own language—incomprehensible to other cultures. Like Danilevsky, Spengler throughout his work tries to show how each Culture shapes its own type of personality and gives its own *meaning* and its own *style* to science, philosophy, religion, fine arts, and to practically all classes of cultural and social phenomena. Viewed from this standpoint, Spengler's whole work is a systematic demonstration of the cultural determination or conditioning of practically all mental productions from numbers and mathematics to the notion of souls, the style of art and art-meaning. Since all Cultures and their prime symbols differ, there is neither one universally identical mathematics, nor one science, nor one philosophy, nor any one important belief, pattern, or value that is equally accepted, similarly understood, and identically interpreted by all great Cultures.

In accordance with its prime symbol, the Classical Culture and man, for instance, "possessed no memory, no organ of history in this sense." The past and the future are drowned in the present, and the present fills the Classical life with an extraordinary intensity. The Doric column, and even the "histories" of Herodotus and Thucydides, show this negation of time and direction. The Indian Culture and man display in a different way "a perfectly ahistoric soul." Nirvana is a perfect symbol of this. The Indian man forgot everything in his history and life. The Egyptian Culture and man, on the contrary, forgot nothing, remembered everything. But Western Culture and man are uniquely "historical," with an unlimited projection into the past and future. The mechanical clock invented by the West—the dread symbol of the flow of time—and countless clocks on our towers chiming day and night, are the most marvelous expressions of the historical world-feeling of Western man. We men of Western Culture have this exceptional historical sense, and "the world-history" we construct is *our* world-picture and not all mankind's.

These fragmentary remarks on the type of personality created by each Culture give a very imperfect rendering of Spengler's cultural typology of human mentality and personality.[20]

Even such seemingly precise and comparatively invariable notions as number and mathematics have quite different meanings in each of the great Cultures:

> There is not, and cannot be, number as such. There are several number-worlds, as there are several Cultures. We find an Indian, an Arabian, a Classical, a Western type of mathematical thought and a type of number. . . . Consequently, there are more mathematics than one. For the inner structure of the Euclidean geometry is something quite different from that of the Cartesian, the analysis of Archimedes is something other than the analysis of Gauss, not merely in matters of form, intuition and method, but above all in essence, in the intrinsic and obligatory meaning of number. . . . The style of any mathematic which comes into being depends wholly on the Culture in which it is rooted, the sort of mankind it is that ponders it.[21]

In Apollinian Culture, in accordance with its prime symbol, "number is the essence of all things *perceptible to the senses.*" It is a measure of something near and corporeal. It is a thought process dealing not with spatial relations but with visibly limitable and tangible units—with bodies.

In Western Culture, in accordance with its prime symbol, "numbers are images of the perfectly desensualized understanding, of pure thought, and contain their abstract validity within themselves." The Arabian indeterminateness of number is again something quite different from the Apollinian and the Western number.[22]

Spengler proceeds to develop these ideas in considerable detail by analyzing the development of Classical, Arabic, and Western mathematics. He connects their development with the character of the fine arts of each of these cultures. Finally, he shows that Classical mathematics, enunciated by Pythagoras, and Western mathematics, initiated by Descartes, "reached their maturity one hundred years later; and both, after flourishing for three centuries, completed the structure of their ideas at the same moment," when each Culture passed into its phase of Civilization. This means that the time of great mathematicians in Western Culture is also over: only clever detail work, similar to that of the Alexandrian mathematicians of late Hellenism, can be expected in the future.

A historical paradigm demonstrates this point:

Classical Mathematics	*Western Mathematics*

1. Conception of a new number:

About 540 B.C.	About 1630 A.D.
Number as magnitude (Pythagoreans)	Number as relation (Descartes, Pascal, Fermat; Newton, Leibnitz, 1670)
(About 470 B.C., sculpture prevails over fresco painting)	(About 1670, music prevails over oil painting)

2. Zenith of systematic development:

450–350 B.C.	1750–1800
Plato, Archytas, Eudoxus (Phidias, Praxiteles)	Euler, Lagrange, Laplace (Gluck, Haydn, Mozart)

3. Inward completion and conclusion of the figure-world:

300–250 B.C.	After 1800
Euclid, Apollonius, Archimedes (Lysippus, Leochares)	Gauss, Cauchy, Riemann (Beethoven) [23]

Still more glaring is the cultural determination of the notion of the soul and of the psychological discipline of a given Culture, in accordance with its prime symbol.

First, Spengler states that so-called scientific psychology studies not a living soul, or consciousness, or mind, but instead the dead mechanism of these, which has nothing in common with the ineffable, inexpressible, ever-becoming pure experience covered by these terms. "Associations, apperceptions, affections, motives, thought, feeling, will—all are dead mechanisms, the mere topography of which constitutes the insignificant total of our 'soul-science.' One looked for Life and one found an ornamental pattern of notions." [24]

When we take this dead "imaginary soul-body" which each Culture possesses, we can see that it differs in different Cultures, and that each Culture creates its own image. "Each Culture possesses its own style of knowledge of men and experience of Life." In accordance with the prime symbol of Classical Culture, the "Apollinian man looked upon his soul as a Cosmos ordered in a group of excellent parts. The soul of Plato or Aristotle is a well-ordered sum of tangible or bodily things in contrast to a space that was felt nonexistent. This Classical soul does not have any Will." It is missing there for the same reason that space is missing in the Classical mathematics and force in the Classical physics.

In contrast to this *bodily* ordering of the Classical soul, the Faustian soul is *functional* through and through. Thinking, feeling, and willing are functions and forces, not bodies, of which no Western psychologist can get rid. Associations, apperceptions, will-processes are types of mathematical functions $(y = f(x))$, radically un-Classical even in their very form. Directional energy, the Will, denied in the Classical and Indian soul-images, is particularly characteristic of the Western soul-image. Dynamic *voluntas superior intellectu,* the "I," Ego, the Will, with the corresponding individualism and enormous activity, are the specific traits of the Faustian Culture. It is a Will-Culture *par excellence,* with historic distance—becoming projected into the future and the boundless world horizon in its achievements (in the things become). As opposed to it, the Russian soul is "will-less, having the limitless *plane* as its prime symbol. It seeks to grow up— serving, anonymous, self-oblivious—in the brother-world of the plane." It is not the soul and culture of the "I," the Ego, nor of individualism, but of the "we," of collectivity, of all, in the positive and negative traits of each person. It condemns "I" as a sin.

"The hall-mark of the Magian soul-image is a strict *dualism of two mysterious substances, Spirit and Soul.* Their relationship is neither static as in the Classical, nor dynamic-functional, as in the Western soul-image, but specifically 'magian,' mystic." Soul is the individual substance permeating the body; Spirit is the divine substance (self) that falls from the world-cavern into humanity. Man *has* a soul, and man *participates* in the Spirit. "Spirit" is that which evokes the highest world, the divine, and which triumphs over mere life, flesh, nature, and even the individual soul. This soul-image is expressed in St. John's Gospel, in the writings of the Gnostics, by the early Church Fathers (Spengler views Christianity from the first to the ninth centuries as the manifestation of the Magian Culture and not the Western Culture, which, after the tenth century, developed a new religion and new soul-image, also calling it Christianity), by the Neo-Platonists, the Manichaeans, the dogmatic texts of the Talmud, the Avesta, by St. Paul, Origen, Plotinus, and others. The schools of Baghdad and Basra developed this concept still further, as did the psychology of Alfarabi and Alkindi, and the late representatives of this Magian soul-image, such as Spinoza and Schirazi.

The foregoing gives an inkling of Spengler's typology of the soul-image, of the psychology and philosophy of the great Cultures.[25]

In a similar manner he shows that the fine arts, architecture, sculpture, painting, music—in their character, their predominance, their composition, even in the prevalent colors used or in the kind of portraiture practised—are each different in the different great Cultures, each Culture creating its fine arts in its own image as an articulation of its prime symbol, or of its own soul. On the other hand, the fine arts of each Culture pass through the same main phases in about the same number of decades or centuries, and congeal or become quantitative, technical, imitative, repetitive, childish, and petrified at the phase of Civilization. The Western fine arts have also entered this phase. "What is practiced as art today is impotence and falsehood. . . . We go through all the exhibitions, the concerts, the theaters, and find only industrious cobblers and noisy fools, who delight to produce something for the market," something that will "catch up" with a public for whom true art has long ceased to be a spiritual necessity. (What we have and are going to have in the field of art can well be seen from Alexandrian art in about the year 200 B.C.) Today there is faked music, filled with artificial noises of gigantic orchestras; faked painting, full of idiotic, exotic, and sensational effects, which concocts a "new style" every decade; lying plastic that steals from the styles of Assyria, Egypt, China, or Mexico. This is the so-called art of the "man of the world." In the Civilization phase this pseudo-art may last for millennia in a state of vacuous eclecticism and sterile imitativeness of the patterns of the art which prevailed in the Culture's childhood, youth, and maturity. The Civilization art of Egyptian, Indian, Arabic-Persian, and Chinese Cultures serves as an example of such an "endless industrious repetition of a stock of fixed forms" that continued for centuries and even millennia. This has held true for the "last act" in all Cultures; and the same is occurring with Western Culture-Civilization today.[26]

As with the fine arts, "there is *no general morale of humanity*." Instead "each Culture has its own standards, the validity of which begins and ends with it." The Classical ethics are ethics of attitude, whereas the Faustian ethics are those of deed. The Western ethics are those of the Will, of the moral imperative, of the "thou shall," of the claim to power. Other ethics are the ethics of compassion, of catharsis, of purgation, and of complete liberation from any ego, any will, any individuality in the "empty Nirvana" or "divine nothing" or Brahman.[27]

Similarly, each Culture has *its own mode of spiritual extinction* that occurs in its Civilization phase. The specific forms of this extinction through which all great Cultures pass in their Civilization phase is irreligion: mainly ethical Nirvana, for the Indian and Buddhist Culture; the Stoic form for the Classical Culture; or the Faustian Socialist variety for the Western Culture.[28]

Finally, *each Culture has its own Nature-Knowledge*. Not one but many physics or chemistries have existed, each patterned on the respective Culture's own image. From the prime symbol of the Classical Culture—the individual nude body —grew the Greek *static of bodies*, a *physics of the near*, the Classical *atom as a miniature body*, and many other characteristics of the Apollinian natural science. The Arabian Culture's prime symbol—the "cavern" or vault—was the origin of *alchemy* with its mysterious "philosophical mercury" and elixir of life. From the prime symbol of the Faustian Culture emerged the idea of Nature as a *dynamics of unlimited space*, a *physics of the distant*, of *the minimal quanta of energy*. Thus, the idea of *matter and form* belongs to the Classical, the idea of *substances* with visible or secret *attributes* is the creation of the Magian, and the physics of *force, mass, of quanta of energy* belong to the Faustian Nature-Conception. Consequently it is a myth that physics and chemistry are the most objective sciences, for each is created by Culture in its own image. The Western physics of quanta is but an expression of the Will-to-Power of the soul of the Faustian Culture.[29]

In analyzing its evolution during the last three hundred years, Spengler comes to the conclusion that an increase of the role of statistics in physical sciences, which have replaced necessity by probability and chance, the emergence of the theory of relativity, the elimination of mass, abandonment of the absolute time and space, replacement of the atom by the complex universe of intra-atomic forces, the principle of indeterminacy, especially the notion of entropy, and so on, all indicate the beginning of the dissolution of Faustian physics and Nature-Knowledge. These new notions of modern physics and mechanics contradict "the Galilean-Newtonian" physics and mechanics. "Becoming and Become, and Destiny and Causality, historical and natural science elements, are beginning to be confused. Formulae of life, growth, age, direction, and death are crowding up." Modern physics deviates increasingly from its "classical systematic" and tends to become more and more "historical physiognomic." In this way the Alexandrian-Civilizational phase of Western physics unfolds to an ever greater extent, becomes increasingly confused, then skeptical, and finally gives way to "the second religiousness" of the Faustian Culture. Men dispense with proof, desire only to believe, and not to dissect.[30] Thus the physical science which emerges from religion at the youthful phase of each Culture returns to its initial spiritual home—religion.

Such are the main High Cultures, their unique prime symbols, and the soul, science, art, philosophy, religion, and other important characteristics of each.

After analyzing the life-cycle of the High Cultures and showing wherein and how they differ from one another, Spengler gives a concise synoptic summary of the main stages of the life-cycle of several Cultures, indicating the "contemporary" epochs in "spiritual," expressive, and social forms through which they passed. An abbreviated summary of Spengler's tables is given on pages 90–92.

This picture is supplemented by a similar table (pages 93–95) of "contemporaneous" stages in the cycle of the "fine-art forms" in the life-cycle of the Egyptian, Classical, Arabian, and Western Cultures. Parallel with these forms unfold the respective forms of mentality or "spirituality" and of social organization of each of these Cultures. All are aspects of one living organism or a system, and all change in togetherness and in the same direction.

Contemporary Spiritual Epochs

	Indian (from 1500 B.C.)	Classical (from 1100 B.C.)	Arabic (from 0)	Western (from 900 A.D.)
	I. Birth of a Myth of the Grand Style, Expressing a New God-Feeling, World-Fear, World-Longing			
SPRING	1500–1200 Vedic religion	1100–800 Hellenic-Italian	0–300 Primitive Christianity	900–1200 German Catholicism
Rural-intuitive; great creation of the newly awakened dream-heavy Soul; superpersonal unity and fullness	Aryan hero tales	"Mother-earth" religion of the people; Homer; Heracles and Theseus legends	Mandaeans, Marcion, Gnosis, Synchretism; Mythras, Baal; Gospels, Apocalypses; Christian, Mazdaist, and pagan heroic legends	Edda, Bernard of Clairvaux, Joachim of Floris, Francis of Assisi; popular epos (Siegfried); legends of the Western saints
	II. Earliest Mystical-Metaphysical Shaping of the New World-Outlook: Zenith of Scholasticism			
	Preserved in oldest parts of the Vedas	Oldest Orphic, Etruscan discipline; after-effect: Hesiod, cosmogonies	Origen, Plotinus, Mani, Iamblichus; Avesta, Talmud; Patristic literature	Thomas Aquinas, Duns Scotus, Dante, Eckhardt; mysticism, scholasticism, 1200–1330
	III. Reformation: Internal Popular Opposition to the Great Springtime Forms			
SUMMER	Brahmanas; oldest Upanishads, 10th and 9th centuries	Orphic Movement, Dionysiac religion; "Numa" religion (7th century)	Augustine, Nestorians, Monophysites, Mazdak (400–500)	Nicolaus Cusanus, John Hus, Savonarola, Kalstadt, Luther, Calvin (1300–1600)
Ripening consciousness; early urban and critical stirrings				

AUTUMN

Intelligence of the city; zenith of strict intellectual creativeness

IV. Beginning of a Philosophical Form of the World-Feeling: Opposition of Idealistic and Realistic Systems

Upanishads	Pre-Socratics (6th and 5th centuries)	Byzantine, Jewish, Syrian, Coptic, Persian literature of 6th and 7th centuries	Galileo, Bacon, Descartes, Bruno, Boehme, Leibnitz; 16th and 17th centuries

V. Formation of a New Mathematic Conception of Number as Copy and Content of World-Form

(lost)	Number as magnitude (proportion); geometry, arithmetic; Pythagoreans (from 540)	The indefinite number (algebra), development little studied	Number as function (analysis); Descartes, Pascal, Fermat (c. 1630); Newton, Leibnitz (c. 1670)

VI. Puritanism: Rationalistic-Mystic Impoverishment of Religion

(lost)	Pythagorean society (from 540)	Mohammed (622); Paulicians and Iconoclasts (from 650)	English Puritans (from 1620); French Jansenists (from 1640); Port Royal

VII. "Enlightenment": Belief in Almightiness of Reason; Cult of Nature; Rational Religion

Sutras; Sankhya; Buddha; late Upanishads	Sophists of 5th century; Socrates; Democritus	Mutazilites; Sufism; Nazzam, Alkindi (c. 830)	English Rationalists (Locke); French Encyclopedists; Voltaire, Rousseau

VIII. Zenith of Mathematical Thought: Elucidation of the Form-World of Numbers

(lost)	Archytas, Plato (conic sections)	Not investigated (theory of number; spherical trigonometry)	Euler, Lagrange, Laplace (infinitesimal problem)

Contemporary Spiritual Epochs

WINTER

Dawn of megalopolitan civilization; extinction of spiritual creative force; life itself becomes problematical; ethical-practical tendencies of an irreligious and unmetaphysical cosmopolitanism

	Indian (from 1500 B.C.)	Classical (from 1100 B.C.)	Arabic (from 0)	Western (from 900 A.D.)
IX. *The Great Conclusive Systems*	Idealism: Yoga, Vedanta; epistemology: Valcashika; logic: Nyaya	Plato, Aristotle	Alfarabi (d. 950); Avicenna (d. c. 1000)	Goethe (Schelling) Kant (Hegel, Fichte)
X. *Materialistic World-Outlook: Cult of Science, Utility, and Prosperity*	Sankhya, Tscharvaka, Lokoyata	Cynics, Cyrenaics, last Sophists (Pyrrhon)	Communistic, atheistic, epicurean sects of Abbassid times; "Brethren of Sincerity"	Bentham, Comte, Darwin, Spencer, Stirner, Marx, Feuerbach
XI. *Ethical-Social Ideals of Life: "Non-Mathematical Philosophy," Skepsis*	Tendencies in Buddha's time	Hellenism, Epicurus, Zeno	Movements in Islam	Schopenhauer, Nietzsche, Hebbel, socialism, Wagner, anarchism, Ibsen
XII. *Inner Completion of the Mathematical Form-World: The Concluding Thought*	(*lost*)	Euclid, Apollonius, Archimedes (c. 250 B.C.)	Alchwarismi (800), Ibn Kurra (850), Alkarchi	Gauss, Cauchy, Riemann (c. 1850–70)
XIII. *Degradation of Abstract Thinking into Professional Lecture-Room Philosophy: Compendium Literature*	"Six Classical Systems"	Academy, Peripatos, Stoics, Epicureans	Schools of Baghdad and Basra	Kantians, "Logicians," and "Psychologists"
XIV. *Spread of a Final World-Sentiment*	Indian Buddhism	Hellenistic-Roman Stoicism (from 200)	Practical fatalism in Islam after 1000	Ethical socialism from 1900

Contemporary Cycles of Fine-Art Forms

	Egyptian	Classical	Arabian	Western
Pre-cultural Period:	*Chaos of Primitive Expression Forms: Mystical Symbolism and Naïve Imitation*			
	Thinite period (3400–3000)	Mycenaean age, Minoan (c. 1600 on)	Persian-Seleucid period (500–0); late Hellenistic; and Indo-Iranian	Merovingian-Carolingian era (500–900)
CULTURE I. Early Period	*A Style Formative of the Entire Inner-Being: Form-Language of Deepest Symbolic Necessity*			
	Old Kingdom (2900–2400)	Doric (1100–500)	Early Arabian form-world: Sassanid, Byzantine, Syrian, Sabaean, Armenian, Early Christian (0–500)	Gothic (900–1500)
	1. Birth and rise: Forms sprung from the land, unconsciously shaped			
	2930–2625: geometrical temple; pyramid temples; ranked plant column; rows of flat relief; tomb statues	11th to 9th centuries: timber buildings; Doric column; architrave; geometric style; burial urns	1st to 3rd centuries: basilica, cupola; cult interiors; Pantheon as mosque; column-and-arch; sarcophagus	11th to 13th centuries: Romanesque and Early Gothic cathedrals; flying buttress; glass-painting; cathedral sculpture
	2. Completion of the early form-language: Exhaustion of possibilities; contradiction			
	VI Dynasty (2625–2574): extinction of pyramid style and epic-idyllic style; *floraison* of archaic portrait—plastic	8th and 7th centuries: end of Doric-Etruscan Archaic style; proto-Corinthian-early-Attic vase painting	4th–5th centuries: end of Syrian, Persian, and Coptic pictorial art; rise of mosaic picturing and arabesque	14th–15th centuries: Late Gothic and Renaissance; from Giotto (Gothic) to Michelangelo (Baroque); from Van Eyck to Holbein; counterpoint and oil painting.

	Egyptian	*Classical*	*Arabian*	*Western*
II. *Late Period*	Middle Kingdom (2150–1800)	Ionic (650–350)	Late Arabian form-world (Persian-Nestorian, Byzantine-Armenian, Islamic-Moorish) (500–800)	Baroque (1500–1800)

3. *Formation of a mature artistry*

	XIth Dynasty	Ionic column; fresco painting until Polygnotus; plastic in the round	Completion of the mosque interior (Hagia Sophia); zenith of mosaic painting	Pictorial style in architecture from Michelangelo to Bernini; reign of oil painting from Titian to Rembrandt; music from Orlando di Lasso to H. Schütz (d. 1672)

4. *Perfection of an intellectualized form-language*

	XIIth Dynasty; pylon temple, labyrinth; character statuary	Acropolis of Athens (480–350); sculpture from Myron to Phidias; end of fresco painting (Zeuxis)	Ommayads (7th–8th cent.); victory of featureless arabesque over architecture	Rococo; reign of classical music (Bach to Mozart); end of classical oil painting (Watteau to Goya)

5. *End of strict creativeness: Dissolution of grand form; end of the style; "Classicism and Romanticism"*

	Confusion of forms after about 1750	The age of Alexander: Corinthian column; Lysippus and Apelles	"Haroun-al-Rachid" (c. 800); "Moorish art"	Empire and Biedermeier; classicist taste in architecture; Beethoven, Delacroix

CIVILIZATION

Existence without Inner Form: Megalopolitan Art as a Commonplace: Luxury, Sport, Nerve-Excitement: Rapidly Changing Fashions in Art (Revivals, Imitations, Borrowings, Pseudo-Discoveries)

1. *"Modern art"; "art problems"; portraying and exciting the megalopolitan mind; transformation of music, architecture, and painting into mere craft-arts*

Hyksos period	Hellenic and Pergamene art: theatricality, bizarreness, subjectivity, "art exhibitions"	Sultan dynasties of 9th–10th centuries: prime of Spanish-Sicilian art; Samarra	19th–20th centuries: Liszt, Berlioz, Wagner; Impressionism from Constable to Manet; American architecture

2. *End of form-development: Meaningless, empty, artificial, pretentious architecture and ornament; imitation of archaic and exotic motives*

XVIIIth Dynasty: rock temple of Dehr-el-Bahri; Memnon-Colossi; art and Cnossos and Amarna	Roman period (100–0–100): indiscriminate piling of all three orders; fora, Colosseum, triumphal arches	Seljuks (from 1050): "Oriental art" of Crusade period	From 2000

3. *Finale: Formation of a fixed stock of forms; "bigger and better"; provincial craft-art*

XIXth Dynasty (1350–1205): gigantic buildings of Luxor, Karnak, and Abydos; small art (textiles, beast plastic, arms)	Trajan to Aurelian: gigantic fora, thermae, colonnades, triumphal arches; Roman provincial art (ceramic, statuary, arms)	Mongol period (from 1250); gigantic buildings (e.g. in India), Oriental craft-art (rugs, arms, implements)	From 2000

Spengler's analysis of the life-cycle of social forms is less systematic than that of the forms of Culture, but nevertheless the essential points are clear. Herewith follows a concise outline of Spengler's dynamics of social forms, or forms of social organization, which succeed one another as the Culture passes from its emergence, to its early period, up to its last, Civilization epoch.

PRE-CULTURAL STAGE

Pre-cultural, early man is a carnivorous ranging animal, nomad, keen, and anxious in his senses, a beast of prey, unsettled and fighting the elements of hostile Nature. With the advent of agriculture a radical change takes place. Man becomes a peasant, a plant, settled and rooted in the earth; the peasant soul discovers a soul in nature and in the countryside. Nature becomes *Mother* Earth. These stages are historyless. The peasant is historyless. The village is not a part of world-history. The peasant is the eternal man, independent of every Culture. He precedes it, he outlives it, a wise and dumb creature propagating himself from generation to generation, a mystical soul, dry and shrewd, the eternal source of the blood that makes world-history in the cities. Mistrustful of everything urban, he looks on urban life indifferently, accepts the city products, from religion to the latest gadget, and remains the same as he was in Charlemagne's day. His piety is older than Christianity; his ethic and metaphysic lie outside the realm of all religious and spiritual history—in fact, they have no history at all.

In this pre-history or pre-Culture stage there are no politics, no classes, no mass, no state even. There are only the blood-related nomadic and agricultural tribes with their chiefs, with their own proto-mystical "soul," serving as a sort of ethnographic material for outsiders. This pre-Cultural stage existed in Egyptian Culture about 3400–3000 B.C. (Thinite period, Menes), in Classical Culture about 1600–1100 B.C. (Mycenaean age, "Agamemnon"), in Chinese Culture around 1700–1300 B.C. (Shang period), and in Western Culture from 500 to 900 A.D. (Frankish period, Charlemagne).[31]

EARLY PERIOD OF CULTURE

This period consists of two phases: feudalism and the aristocratic state.

(1) *Feudalism*. The beginning of world-history, the emergence and early period of Culture, are marked by two epoch-making phenomena: the emergence of the *city* and of the *primary classes of nobility and priesthood*. With the advent of the city and these classes begins an organic articulation of political existence. The pre-cultural tribes and folk begin to organize into a feudal nation and a feudal state. The castle and the temple or cathedral appear on the countryside landscape. Along with the city and the priesthood there emerges the intellect, in the forms of religious-chivalric ideas, idealism, and values. The whole organization, however, remains feudal and agricultural. The city is still only a market, or a stronghold, or a religious center. The political life consists largely of the struggles of the vassals and feudal lords with one another or with an overlord. The prevalent spirit and values, economic and social, are still purely agrarian.

(2) *Emergence of the aristocratic state*. Feudal, patriarchal forms, politics, blood ties and relationships, feudal economics and values undergo a crisis and dissolve. Instead there emerges a sort of nation, headed by an aristocracy and organized into an aristocratic state. The role of the city and of the intellect increases. The early period of the Culture begins to pass into its late period. In the four Cultures these phases of the early period occurred as shown in the table on page 98.

LATE PERIOD OF CULTURE

In this period the idea of the state and national government is realized in its mature and full form. A third class—the bourgeoisie—emerges and grows. The city grows quantitatively and qualitatively. It begins to dominate the countryside politically, economically, technically, and intellectually. Urban values replace agricultural values. Money emerges victorious

Early Period of Culture

	Egyptian	Classical	Chinese	Western
1. Feudal	Old Kingdom (2900–2400): Dynasties I to V	Doric period (1100–650): the Homeric kingship	Early Chou period (1300–800): feudal nobility	Gothic period (900–1500): Roman-German imperial period; crusading nobility; papacy
2. Crisis and emergence of aristocratic state	VI to VIII Dynasties: interregnum	Aristocratic synoecism; dissolution of kingship into offices; oligarchy	934–904; I-Wang; interregnum	Territorial princes; Renaissance town; Lancaster and York; 1254: interregnum

over landed property and values. The city begins to exploit the countryside. Blood ties become unimportant. The bourgeoisie elevates its position and grows in influence.

This late period can be divided into three fairly clear phases: (1) Structuralization of states and their forms, with the *Frondes* bickering with the dominant state power. (2) Climax of the state form and its absolutization; absolute monarchies; unity of town and country; co-ordination of "three estates" (nobility, clergy, and bourgeoisie); "unified nation." (3) Break-up of the absolute state form and "absolutism"; revolution and Napoleonism; victory of the city over the countryside, urbanization over agriculturalism, of "the people" over the privileged, of the intelligentsia over tradition, of money over property and most of the traditional values.

The actual centuries in which these phases of the late period took place in the four Cultures are tabulated on page 100.

THE PERIOD OF CIVILIZATION

At this last stage of a great Culture the body of the people, now essentially urban in constitution, dissolves into formless mass. The state, the nation, the social estates, tend to disintegrate. The city grows into a pathological megalopolis, artificial, inorganic, cosmopolitan. With it there emerges the "fourth estate"—the "masses." In the process of revolutions and anarchy "Caesarism" emerges, a tyrannical dictatorship of various "upstarts." Just as in the late period of Culture money became victorious over the policy of *"noblesse oblige,"* so now a rude force-politics triumphs over money and the money-policies, including the bourgeoisie.

The period of Civilization can also be subdivided into three phases. The timing of these phases in the four Cultures studied is given by the table on page 101.

This cut-and-dried presentation serves only as a lifeless skeleton for Spengler's rich, colorful, often brilliant, and always thoughtful picture of the development of the social, economic, and political organization forms at various periods of

Late Period of Culture

	Egyptian	Classical	Chinese	Western
1. Crystallization of the state form	Middle Kingdom (2150–1800), XIth Dynasty: centralized bureaucratic state	Ionic period (650–300); first tyrannis; the city-state	Late Chou period (800–500): period of "Protectors," and congresses of princes	Baroque period (1500–1800): dynastic family power and *Fronde* (Richelieu, Wallenstein, Cromwell), c. 1630
2. Climax of state absolutism	XIIth Dynasty: strictest centralization; court and finance nobility	The pure Polis (absolutism of Demos); rise of the tribunate; Themistocles, Pericles	Chun-Chiu period (590–480): Seven Powers; perception of state forms	*Ancien Régime*; rococo; court nobility; Habsburg, Bourbon, Louis XIV, and Frederick the Great
3. Break-up of the state form (revolution and Napoleonism)	1788–1680: revolution and military government; decay of the realm; small upstart potentates	4th century: social revolution and second tyrannis; Alexander the Great	480: beginning of Chan-Kwo period; 441: fall of Chou dynasty; revolution and civil wars	End of 18th century: revolution in America and France (Washington, Mirabeau, Robespierre); Napoleon

Period of Civilization

	Egyptian	Classical	Chinese	Western
1. Domination of money ("democracy"); economic powers dominating the political forms and authorities	1680–1580: Hyksos period; decline; after 1600 the rulers of Thebes	300–100: political Hellenism; from Alexander to Scipio; from Cleomenes III and Flaminius to C. Marius and radical demagogues	480–230: period of the "contending states"; the imperial title and incorporation of the last states into empire	1800–2000: from Napoleon to the World War; the system of the "Great Powers"; annihilation wars; imperialism; upstart dictators
2. Formation of Caesarism; victory of force over money; increasing primitiveness of political forms; decline and disorganization of nations into formless populations; increasing crudity of despotism of upstart Caesars	1580–1350: XVIIIth Dynasty; Thuthmosis III	100–0–100: Sulla to Domitian; Caesar, Tiberius	250–0–26: house of Wang-Cheng; Western Han Dynasty. 221: Augustus-title (Shi) of Emperor Hwang-ti 140–180. Wu-ti	2000–2200
3. Private and family policies of Caesars and upstarts; the world as spoil; petrified Egypticism, Mandarinism, Byzantinism; "barbarians" and young peoples assailing the "civilized nation" and imperial machinery; primitivization of the civilized ways of life	1350–1205: XIXth Dynasty / Sethos I / Rameses II	100–300: Trajan to Aurelian / Trajan, Septimius Severus	25–220 A.D. Eastern Han Dynasty / 58–71: Ming-ti	After 2200

the great Cultures. A few comments on the Civilizational social structures may give an inkling of this.

At the Civilizational phase there arises the world city, the monstrous symbol and vessel of the completely sophisticated intellect, the megalopolis in which the life-cycle of the Culture ends by winding itself up. A handful of such world centers devalues the entire motherland and turns the rest into inferior and insignificant "provinces." Babylon, Thebes, Alexandria, Rome, Constantinople, Pataliputra, Baghdad, Uxmal are examples of the early world cities. Paris, London, Berlin, and especially New York, are recent examples. "And the rise of New York to the rank of the world city may prove to have been the most pregnant event of the nineteenth century."

These cities are "wholly intellect." They aim at the chessboard form—the symbol of soullessness. They are not "home." The birth of these cities entails their death by their growth and their contrast of riches and poverty, by their artificial stimulation and their *toedium vitae,* and finally by the increasing sterility of the megalopolitan man. The world city displays a metaphysical turn towards death. The man of a megalopolis no longer wants to live. The peasant woman is first of all and most of all a *mother*. The megalopolis woman is a childless Ibsen woman, Nora or Nana, whether in Paris or New York, in Lao-tzu China or Charvaka India.

At this level all Civilizations enter the stage of depopulation which can last for centuries:

> The whole pyramid of cultural man vanishes. It crumbles from the summit, first the world cities, then the "provinces," then the land itself whose best blood has poured into the city and exhausted itself. At the last, only the primitive blood remains, alive, but robbed of its best elements. This residue is the Fellah type, dull, dumb, semi-serf, semi-free peasant-laborer.[32]

In today's Western world cities, with their machine technics, we are the observers and actors in the last act of a great Culture's tragedy. The lord of the world, the Nordic man, is becoming the slave of the machine. The mechanization of the world has entered a phase of highly dangerous over-tension. All organic things are dying in the grip of this megalopolitan machine organization. It begins to contradict even its economic practice. The machine in the end defeats its own purpose. In the great cities the motor car has, by its numbers, destroyed its own value: one moves faster on foot. In the stone-steel cage of the world cities the Faustian man begins to be sick of machines and civilization, and starts returning to simpler forms of life, nearer to Nature. Occultism and Spiritualism, Hindu philosophies and metaphysical gnosticism in Christian or other forms, are reviving. Second religiosity is already under way. The born leader's flight from the machine has begun. The exploited colonial peoples are rising against the megalopolitan white man. This machine technics is beginning to destroy itself and one day

. . . will lie in fragments, forgotten, our railways and steamships as dead as the Roman roads and Chinese wall, our giant cities and skyscrapers in ruins like old Memphis and Babylon. The history of the megalopolitan machine technics is fast drawing to its inevitable close. It will be eaten up from *within,* like the grand forms of any and every Culture. When, and in what manner, we know not.[33]

In a similar way money and "democracy" undermine themselves and are "eaten up from within," giving way to the victorious policy of undisguised forces and Caesarism. In the early period of Culture the governing powers are pre-established, God-given, and unquestioned. They are represented by the aristocracy among the nobility and clergy. The policy of that period is the policy of these estates, and not the policy of the party.

With the rise of the city the intellect, money, and the bourgeoisie take over the leading role. In place of the estate there appears the party. The prime party is that of money and mind, the liberal, the megalopolitan. Aristocracy in the completed Culture, and democracy in the insipient cosmopolitan Civilization, stand opposed until both are submerged in Caesarism. The forms of the governing minority develop steadily from the stage of the estate, through that of the party, towards the following of the dictatorial individual (Caesar). The estate has instincts, the party has a program, but the following has a master.

Democracy's passage into Caesarism—the government representing in its inward self a return to thorough formlessness, to dictatorial arbitrariness—is marked by the following steps. At the outset of democracy the field belongs to the responsible, noble, and pure intellect alone. It introduces the bill of rights and equality under the law. Soon, however, it turns out that one can make use of constitutional rights only if one has money. The leadership passes from the idealist intellect to the shrewd money-maker, the bourgeois. It begins to control the vote and the voters through its political machinery. The press, as a powerful propaganda weapon, becomes one of the most influential and insidious parts of this machinery. Democracy through its newspaper and mass magazine expels the book from the people's mental life. Through the press, "mass education," and mass propaganda, it teaches the people to think less and less for themselves and to accept more and more what is offered by the press (and radio and television). The book world, with its profusion of standpoints that compelled individual thought to select and criticize, is now the possession of only a few. The people read the *one* paper, "their" paper, which spellbinds the intellect from morning to night, drives serious books into oblivion, promotes the books it wants, and kills the books it disapproves of.

What is truth (under democracy)? That which the press wills. Its commands evoke, transform, and interchange truths. Three weeks of press work and the "truth" is acknowledged by everybody. Mass education tends to shepherd the masses into the newspaper's power area. Of course, there is freedom of speech in democracy, but the press is free to take, or not to take, notice of what the "citizen" says. It can condemn any "truth" to death by simply passing it by in silence, by not communicating it to the world. In lieu of the stake and faggot there is the great silence.

Such a press and such mass education pave the way for the Caesars. The dictature of party leaders supports itself upon that of the press. The leaders strive to train the bulk of their followers by whipping their souls with articles, telegrams, and pictures that are more effective than a physical whip or military service, until the masses clamor for weapons and seemingly force their leaders to an eventual dictatorship, which these leaders have carefully prepared. "This is the end of Democracy. If in the world of truth it is *proof* that decides all, in that of facts it is *success*. Success means that one being triumphs over the others." Through the press and other means, the masses, their minds, and their actions are kept under the iron discipline of the parties, which in turn are the retinue of the few bosses. Parliaments, congresses, and elections are a sort of preconcerted game, a farce, staged in the name of popular self-determination.

"Through money, democracy becomes its own destroyer, after money has destroyed intellect." Noble intellectual and moral leaders of the beginning of democracy are now replaced by unscrupulous and non-intellectual politicians. One boss is overthrown by another. Fights, disturbances, and insecurity become chronic. As a result men become tired and disgusted with money values, with all this bickering, and begin to hope for salvation from somewhere or other, from a revival of old values, unselfishness, honor, inward nobility, to the arrival of a new Savior.

In this way Caesarism grows on the soil of degenerated democracy and sooner or later conquers it. It establishes money economics and a purely political will-to-order. Caesarism is thus the final act of the Civilization in the field of social, economic, and political organization. Eventually barbarization sets in, and the Culture's social form steadily disintegrates. It ends with the "second religiosity" and with the forms which it—and its church—impose upon the remnants of the Culture's life-cycle. Its social history is ended.[34]

Such, in bare outline, is the core of Spengler's philosophy of history. A few of the many important points of this grand conception must be briefly mentioned.

(1) *How and why does the High Culture originate?*

Why did only a few great Cultures emerge from the multitude of "pre-cultural" elements and materials inherent in the pre-historic tribes and groups? What are the factors that de-

termine the emergence of a High Culture's soul? In accordance
with his principle of Destiny and the World-as-History Spengler seems to find it impossible to apply the principle of causality
and causal factors to these phenomena. Consistent to his major
philosophical presupposition, he simply states that the whole
matter (like his Destiny) is a mystery "that is not to be explained by any why and wherefore and yet is of inward necessity" (grasped by intuition). The same is true of the difference
between Destiny and incident in the whole historical process.
"In the endless, self-repeating flows for evermore the Same
. . . all the straining, all the striving is eternal peace of
God." [35] Any causal conceptions are applicable only to the
World-as-Nature and are an outrage and unmitigated blunder
when they are applied to the World-as-History. Here the inward necessity of Direction or Destiny—incapable of being
grasped through conceptual approaches—reigns supreme and
is an explanation in itself. "For only youth has a future, and *is*
Future, that enigmatic synonym of Destiny. Destiny is always
young." He who replaces it by a mere cause-and-effect chain
simply makes the non-realized future into a past, the young into
old; he kills the living destiny and eliminates direction. [36] Factually, the origin of life and any new living form—whether plant
or animal—are mysteries: they "appear suddenly and at once
in their definite shape," as Goethe and H. de Vries rightly indicated in their mutation theory.

These sudden and profound changes, like the advent of the
glacial age, are of a cosmic nature, originating beyond the
earth's boundary and incomprehensible in causal terms.

The situation in regard to the Cultures is similar. "We observe that swift and deep changes assert themselves in the
history of great Cultures, without assignable causes, influences,
or purposes of any kind." The pre-cultural world of humanity,
of which we know little and understand still less (the anthropologist's collection of the fragments of this primitive culture
possesses only a few dead shreds of what was alive long ago)
was something quite different from the High Cultures. The
sudden emergence in this ocean of "primitive culture" of the
High Culture of Egypt and Babylon (c. 3000 B.C.), or Sumer,

is an unforeseen incident. Its emergence in the form of a "single huge organism" is also a mystery from a causal standpoint. It is not due to specific geographic, racial, or other "causal factors" because it is not a given tribe or race that selects the Culture; but rather it is the suddenly emerging Culture which makes not only of custom, myth, technique, and art, but of the very peoples, races, and classes that it incorporates, the vessels or instrumentalities of one single form-language and one single history. The choice is made by cosmic forces. They determine which of the primitive cultures becomes a High Culture. Just as in the history of the Coniferae or other species we cannot prophesy whether and when a new species will arise, so in cultural history we cannot say whether and when a new Culture shall come into existence. However, as soon as it is conceived we do know the inner form of this new life-course. The intuitive life-experience opens to us a Culture's logic of Destiny and its life-course.

The actual number of High Cultures and the place and the time of their appearance are also an incident whose roots are concealed in the cosmic universe beyond our causal understanding. But the destiny-course of these Cultures is known to us by way of the instinctive, intuitional, historical logic of Destiny.[37]

Such is Spengler's answer to these problems—an answer consistent with his philosophical premises and quite different from that of A. J. Toynbee and many others influenced by Spengler.

(2) *Destiny as immanent theory of sociocultural change*

After its emergence, the whole life-cycle of a High Culture, with all the numerous changes involved, is immanently determined by the Culture itself. Like an organism immanently passing from childhood to old age, the Cultures go through their spring-summer-autumn-winter stages by virtue of their own natures. Even their death is due to their own nature and is not caused by external conditions. It is the Culture's natural death.

The role of external factors consists essentially in favoring or hindering, accelerating or retarding the immanent unfolding of the life-cycle of the Culture; now and then the external conditions can distort and, in exceptional cases, kill the Culture's organism. But they cannot pattern the Culture's form, or the stages of its life-cycle, or change its essential traits. The Arabian and the Russian Cultures' full unfolding of their potentiality has been distorted, hindered, and partly suppressed by the alien, more powerful, and older Cultures. However, this distortion and inhibition has not been able to change basic, inherent traits of these Cultures. The external forces can distort and hinder the development of a given Culture, but they cannot transform, say, the Classical into the Egyptian, or the Arabian into the Western Culture, just as the external conditions cannot change a bird into a cow, though they can mutilate and even kill it. Of all the High Cultures only the Mexican died a violent death inflicted by the Western Culture —a Culture alien to it.

Besides these functions of the external factors, the Culture's life-course, after its emergence, is self-determined.

(3) *The problem of diffusion and transmissibility of one culture to another*

On this point Spengler's and Danilevsky's views are again essentially similar. Each Culture is unique and can only be understood by men of this Culture. As such it cannot be transmitted and diffused in an alien cultural world.

If one Culture borrows another's material or pattern or element, it is as though J. S. Bach or another creator were writing a fugue on an alien theme. The element of the other culture serves as mere material for the self-expression of a given Culture. Even when one Culture seemingly takes a whole cultural system from another, be it Plato's philosophy, Roman Law, Christianity, architectural form, sculpture, or what not, it is only the borrowing that is apparent. The Western interpretations of Plato are mainly misinterpretations. The Roman law taken by continental Europe is, in fact, fundamentally different from the real Roman law; in addition, different European countries adhere to several different Roman laws. Christianity

(Spengler ascribes its creation to the Arabian or Magiau, and not to the Classical or the Western, Cultures) of the Western World after the eleventh century, with its dogmas, ritual, hierarchy, and spirit, would be rejected by St. Paul or St. Augustine; it is basically different from the Magian Christianity of the first centuries of our era. Similarly, when the Italian Renaissance supposedly revived "the Classical Culture," it in fact created its own Culture for which it used some material from the Classical world: the sculpture of Phidias or Praxiteles has nothing in common with that of Michelangelo or Donatello. Frequently such "borrowing" is but a "deliberate misunderstanding."

It is true that with the exception of the Egyptian, the Chinese, and the Mexican, all Cultures have grown under the influence of some alien, older Cultures. Each Culture shows some alien features. Most Cultures are thus interrelated, "affiliated," or "apparented." However, all such alien traits, borrowings, and influences are absorbed mainly as material patterned in the "borrowing" Culture's image, or the material is given a quite different meaning from that which it had in its original Culture. All is transformed in the "borrowing" Culture. In brief, in all such cases (except when, as discussed above, a younger Culture is killed or distorted by an older one) a great Culture writes a fugue of its own on a foreign theme.

To sum up, each Culture is closed to all who are alien to it, and is fully comprehensible only to itself and to its own human members.[38] The same is true of different nations.

(4) *The problem of leadership in the Culture phase and the Civilization phase*

In the early, and to some extent in the late, period of a High Culture the leadership belongs to the creative minority— the nobility and the priesthood, the castle and the cathedral. One symbolizes the World-as-History; the other, the World-as-Nature. Their "plantwise and racewise" leadership is sure-footed and creative; in politics it is childlike, for "the best diplomats are the children." They act intuitively, and in their feeling of self-vocation and inward obligation there is indeed something noble. Therefore, at this stage of a Culture their actions, even those that seemingly involve an animal struggle, are an actualization of something spiritual, the translation of a creative idea into a living historical form, whether in the struggle between art forms such as Gothic and Renaissance, or philosophies like Stoicism and Epicureanism, or political forms like oligarchy and tyranny, or economic forms like land economy and abstract money economy.

At the end of the late period of a Culture and at the stage of a Civilization, this creative leadership is gradually replaced by the epigoni of the nobility and priesthood—by the bureaucracy of the state government, by party leaders, by the captains of industry and finance, and by various intellectuals, scientists, and scholars. The group of scholars and scientists descends from the group of the priesthood, while the state bureaucrats, party leaders, and captains of industry and finance are the epigoni of the nobility. Eventually the progressively sterile leadership of these epigoni is replaced by that of the Caesars and their henchmen, who lead the inchoate urban "masses" and their "parties," "unions," "cliques," and an unorganized "public." Such a leadership becomes increasingly uncreative, in spite of intellectual rationality, developed science, rational planning, and other devices of intellectuality. In contrast to the early period of a Culture, this Civilization period is devoid of the actualization of a creative idea in the concrete historical form. "Whereas previously power, even when to all appearance destitute of any inspiration, was always serving the Idea somehow or other, in the late Civilization even the most convincing illusion of an idea is only the mask for purely zoological strivings." Even the noblest ideas of peace, brotherhood, love, and so on, remain powerless at that stage and serve mainly as a hypocritical screen for animal and selfish drives.[39] This "uncreative minority" is one of the symptoms of the Civilization, and its decline parallels the disintegration and petrifaction of the Civilization.

(5) *Second religiosity*

As has been mentioned before, this appears at the end of the Civilization phase of all great Cultures. Weary and disillusioned, insecure and uncertain, uncreative and tired, the "masses" begin to look for salvation and peace of mind in a revived old, or in a new, form of religiosity—mysticism, theosophy, gnosticism, astrology, and various (domestic and foreign) religious cults, sects, and movements, with their "Saviors" and "Messiahs." Parallel with this there arises a wave of purified—old or new—ethical gospels, teachings, and movements (of love, brotherhood, pacifism, etc.). These anti-intellectual and anti-civilizational, anti-urban, anti-technological, anti-economic ideologies and movements grow rapidly and sweep away the civilizational ideologies and cults of utilitarianism, happiness and prosperity, scientism and technology, urbanism and machine progress, intellectualism and rationality. This second religiosity serves as the "Finis" of the Culture and sometimes as a harbinger of a new, awakening Culture. These Spenglerian ideas will be developed by Toynbee into his theory of the "Universal Church" as a bridge between the old and the new Culture-Civilization, or as the supreme goal of any great Culture.[40]

(6) *The life-cycles of Cultures*

Spengler contends that all Cultures pass through similar stages in their life-cycles; and that each of them passes from one stage to another in about the same length of time. In connection with this, he claims that there are 50, 100, 300, and 600 year periodicities in historical processes. "Every one of the Culture's intrinsically necessary stages and periods has a definite duration, always the same, always recurring with the emphasis of a symbol." [41]

(7) *Other Spenglerian ideas*

Among other Spenglerian ideas we may note the following: (a) *The development of the fine arts follows the temporal order: architecture-sculpture-painting-music.*[42]   (b)   David

Hume and Adam Smith are the creators of the Faustian economic world-picture.[43] (c) The psychology and soul of different nations are quite different and even more impenetrable than the souls of different Cultures: Athenian and Spartan spirits were quite distinct; German, French and English modes of philosophical thinking are quite distinct not merely in Bacon, Descartes, and Leibniz, but as early as the age of Scholasticism. Even in today's modern physics, chemistry, and scientific method, the choice of topics, hypotheses, types of experiments differ markedly in these nations. German and French piety, English and Spanish social ethics, the German and English ways of life, are again quite distinct from one another. When different nations begin really to understand one another, then humanity ceases to live in nations, given nations cease to be individual organisms, and therefore cease to be historic.[44]

In Spengler's extraordinarily rich and idea-laden work there are many other theories worth mentioning; but the limitations of time and space prevent this and force me to limit the characterization of his masterwork to the above outline. Later I shall point out which of Spengler's ideas may be considered valid and which may not.

V

Arnold J. Toynbee

Born in London in 1889, Arnold J. Toynbee studied at Winchester and at Balliol College, Oxford, where he was given an "old-fashioned education in Greek and Latin classics." During a year spent as a student in the British Archaeological School in Athens he "walked over Greece and became aware of current international affairs through hearing talk in cafes about 'the foreign policy of Sir Edward Grey.' " In 1912 he returned to Balliol as a Fellow and Tutor, and taught Ancient History until 1915, when he entered the government service, working on Turkish affairs in the Political Intelligence Department of the Foreign Office and later at the Paris Peace Conference. From 1919 to 1924 he was Professor of Modern Greek and Byzantine Studies at King's College, University of London, spending a year of that time traveling in Greece as war correspondent for the *Manchester Guardian*. Since 1925 he has served as Director of Studies at the Royal Institute of International Affairs. From 1939 to 1946 he devoted all of his time to government service as Director of the Research Department of the Foreign Office.

During the spring of 1947, Toynbee came to the United States to deliver the annual Mary Flexner Lectures at Bryn Mawr College. While in this country, he lectured widely. Publication of the abridgment of *A Study of History* was timed to take place during his stay. He returned to this country again in February, 1948, at the invitation of the Institute for Advanced Study in Princeton, to work on the final three volumes of the monumental nine-volume *A Study of History*.

He is the author of a number of books. With his wife,

Veronica M. Boulter, he is also co-editor of the continuing series *A Survey of International Affairs*.

The six volumes of his main work, *A Study of History*, were published in the years 1934–1939 by the Oxford University Press. Its abridged, one-volume version was prepared by D. C. Somervell and published in 1947. A series of Toynbee's essays related to his main work was published in 1948 under the title of *Civilization on Trial*. As mentioned above, three additional volumes of *A Study of History* are still to come.

The ideas of *A Study of History* became widely diffused after the publication of Somervell's abridged volume, which became a bestseller in the United States. A considerable literature has appeared about and around his main work.

Toynbee begins with the thesis that the proper field of historical study is neither a description of singularistic happenings contiguous in space or time nor a history of the states and bodies politic or of mankind as a "unity":

> The "intelligible fields of historical study" . . . are societies which have a greater extension, in both Space and Time, than national states or city-states, or any other political communities. . . . Societies, not states, are "the social atoms" with which students of history have to deal.[1]

Combining religious characteristics and territorial and partly political traits, he perceives "civilization" as the proper object of historical study, in which a "civilization" is a "species of society."[2] Of such civilizations, he takes twenty-one (later on, twenty-six) "related and unrelated" species: the Western, two Orthodox Christian (in Russia and the Near East), the Iranic, the Arabic, the Hindu, two Far Eastern, the Hellenic, the Syriac, the Indic, the Sinic, the Minoan, the Sumeric, the Hittite, the Babylonic, the Andean, the Mexic, the Yucatec, the Mayan, the Egyptiac, plus five "arrested civilizations": Polynesian, Eskimo, Nomadic, Ottoman, and Spartan.[3]

Toynbee attacks, first, the problem of genesis of civilizations: Why do some of the societies, like many primitive groups, become static at an early stage of their existence and fail to emerge as civilizations, whereas other societies do reach this level? His answer is that the genesis of civilization is due neither to the race factor nor to geographic environment as such but to a specific combination of two conditions: the presence of a creative minority in a given society and of an environment which is neither too unfavorable nor too favorable. The groups which had these conditions emerged as civilizations; the groups which did not have them remained on the sub-civilization level. The mechanism of the birth of civilization in these conditions is formulated as an interplay of Challenge-and-Response. The environment of the foregoing type incessantly challenges the society; and the society, through its creative minority, successfully responds to the challenge and solves the need. A new challenge follows, and a new response successfully ensues; and so the process continues incessantly. In these conditions no possibility of rest exists, the society is on the move all the time, and such a move brings it, sooner or later, to the stage of civilization. Surveying the conditions in which his twenty-one civilizations were born, he finds that they emerged exactly in the foregoing circumstances.[4]

The next problem of the study is why and how, out of twenty-six civilizations, four (Far Western Christian, Far Eastern Christian, Scandinavian, and Syriac) miscarried and proved abortive; five (Polynesian, Eskimo, Nomadic, Spartan, and Ottoman) were arrested in their growth at an early stage; whereas the remaining civilizations grew "through an *élan* that carried them from challenge through response to further challenge and from differentiation through integration to differentiation again?" [5]

The answer evidently depends upon the meaning of growth and its symptoms. In Toynbee's opinion the growth of civilization is not, and is not due to, a geographic expansion of the society. If anything, the geographic expansion of a society is positively associated with retardation and disintegration but not with growth.[6] Likewise, the growth of civilization does not consist in, and is not due to, technological progress and to the society's increasing mastery over the physical environment: "there is no correlation between progress in technique and progress in civilization." [7] The growth of civilization consists in "a progressive and cumulative inward self-determination or self-articulation" of the civilization; in a progressive and cumulative "etherialization" of the society's values and "simplification of the civilization's apparatus and technique." [8] Viewed from the standpoint of intra-social and inter-individual relationships, growth is an incessant creative "withdrawal and return" of the charismatic minority of the society in the process of the ever new successful responses to ever new challenges of the environment.[9] A growing civilization is a unity. Its society consists of the creative minority freely imitated and followed by the majority—the Internal Proletariat of the society and the External Proletariat of its barbarian neighbors. In such a society there is no fratricidal struggle, no hard and fast division. It is a solidary body. A growing civilization unfolds its dominant potentialities, which are different in different civilizations: aesthetic in the Hellenic civilization; religious in the Indic and Hindu; scientifically machinistic in the Western; and so on.[10] As a result, the process of growth represents a progressive integration and self-determination of the growing civilization and a differentiation between the different civilizations in growth. Such is the solution of the problem of growth of civilization.

The third main problem of the study is how and why civilizations break down, disintegrate, and dissolve. They evidently do so, for, of some thirty species of civilizations, "only four have miscarried as against twenty-six that have been born alive," and "no less than sixteen out of these twenty-six are by now dead and buried" (the Egyptiac, the Andean, the Sinic, the Minoan, the Sumeric, the Mayan, the Indic, the Hittite, the Syriac, the Hellenic, the Babylonic, the Mexic, the Arabic, the Yucatec, the Spartan, and the Ottoman). Of the remaining ten civilizations living,

. . . the Polynesian and the Nomadic civilizations are now in their last agonies and seven out of eight others are all, in different degrees, under threat of either annihilation or assimilation by our own civilization of the West. Moreover, no less than six out of these seven civilizations . . . bear marks of having broken down and gone into disintegration.[11]

The main difference between the process of growth and the process of disintegration is that in the growth phase the civilization successfully responds to a series of ever new challenges, while in the disintegration stage it fails to give such a response to a given challenge. It tries to answer it again and again, but recurrently fails. In growth the challenges, as well as responses, constantly vary; in disintegration, the responses vary, but the challenge remains unanswered and unremoved. The author's verdict is that civilizations perish through suicide but not by murder.[12] In Toynbee's formulation, "the nature of the breakdowns of civilizations can be summed up in three points: a failure of creative power in the minority, an answering withdrawal of mimesis on the part of the majority, and a consequent loss of social unity in the society as a whole."

In an expanded form this formula runs as follows:

When in the history of any society a Creative Minority degenerates into a mere Dominant Minority which attempts to retain by force a position which it has ceased to merit, this fatal change in the character of the ruling element provokes, on the other hand, the secession of a Proletariat (the majority) which no longer spontaneously admires or freely imitates the ruling element, and which revolts against being reduced to the status of an unwilling "underdog." This Proletariat, when it asserts itself, is divided from the outset into two distinct parts. There is an "Internal Proletariat" (the majority of the members) and . . . an "External Proletariat" of barbarians beyond the pale who now violently resist incorporation. And thus the breakdown of a civilization gives rise to a class-war within the body social of a society which was neither divided against itself by hard-and-fast divisions nor sundered from its neighbors by unbridgeable gulfs so long as it was in growth.[13]

This declining phase consists of three sub-phases: (a) the breakdown of the civilization, (b) its disintegration, and (c) its dissolution. The breakdown and dissolution are often separated by centuries, even thousands of years, from one another. For instance, the breakdown of the Egyptiac civilization occurred in the sixteenth century B.C., and its dissolution only in the fifth century A.D. For two thousand years between breakdown and dissolution it existed in a "petrified life in death." In a similar "petrified" state up to the present time the

Far Eastern civilization continues in China after its breakdown in the ninth century A.D. About 1000 and 800 years, respectively, elapsed between these points in the history of the Sumeric and Hellenic civilizations; [14] and so on. Like a petrified tree trunk, such a society can linger in that stage of life-in-death for centuries, even thousands of years. Nevertheless, the destiny of most, if not of all, civilizations, seems to be to come to final dissolution sooner or later. As to the Western society, though it seems to have had all the symptoms of breakdown and disintegration, the author is noncommittal. He still leaves a hope for a miracle: "We may and must pray that a reprieve which God has granted to our society once will not be refused if we ask for it again in a contrite spirit and with a broken heart." [15]

Such being the general nature of the decline of civilizations, a most detailed analysis of its uniformities, symptoms, and phases is developed in Volumes IV, V, and VI. Only a few of these uniformities can be touched on here. While in the growth period the Creative Minority gives a series of successful responses to ever new challenges, in the disintegration period it fails to do so. Instead, intoxicated by victory, it begins to "rest on its oars," to "idolize" the relative values as absolute, loses its charismatic attraction and is not imitated and followed by the majority. Therefore, it must increasingly use force to control the Internal and the External Proletariat. In this process it creates a Universal State, like the Roman Empire created by the Hellenic Dominant Minority, as a means to keep itself and the civilization alive; it engages in war, becomes a slave of intractable institutions, and works its own and its civilization's ruin.

The Internal Proletariat now secedes from the Minority, becomes dissatisfied and disgruntled, and often creates a Universal Church—for instance, Christianity or Buddhism—as its own creed and institution. Whereas the Universal State of the Dominant Minority is doomed, the Universal Church of the Inner Proletariat (for instance, Christianity) serves as a bridge and foundation for a new civilization ("apparented" by and) affiliated with the old one.

In his *Civilization on Trial*, however, Toynbee somewhat

changes his position. Instead of making religion a bridge between falling and rising civilizations, he now makes successive rises and falls of civilizations into a mere subsidiary means for the growth of religion. Now the successive civilizations become sort of "stepping stones to higher things on the religious plane." [16]

The External Proletariat now organizes itself and begins to attack the declining civilization, instead of striving to be incorporated by it. In this way Schism enters the Body and Soul of civilization. It results in an increase of strife and fratricidal wars that lead to ruin. The Schism in the Soul manifests itself in the profound change of the mentality and behavior of the members of the disintegrating society. It leads to an emergence of four types of personality and "Saviors": Archaist, Futurist (Saviors by Sword), detached and indifferent Stoic, and—finally—Transfigured Religious Saviors, posited in the supersensory world of God. The sense of Drift, of Sin, begins to grow; Promiscuity and Syncretism become dominant. Vulgarization and "Proletarization" invade arts and sciences, philosophy and language, religion and ethics, manners and institutions.

But all in vain. With the exception of Transfiguration, all these efforts and "Saviors" do not halt the disintegration. At best the civilization can become "fossilized," and in this form of "life-in-death" can linger for centuries and even thousands of years, but its dissolution, as a rule, finally comes. The only fruitful way turns out to be the way of Transfiguration, the way of transfer of the goal and values to the supersensory Kingdom of God. It may not stop the disintegration of the given civilization, but it may serve as a seed for emergence and development of a new affiliated civilization; and through that, it is a step forward to the eternal process of elevation of Man to Superman, of "the City of Man to City of God," as the ultimate terminal point of Man and Civilization. The volumes close with an almost apocalyptic note: "The aim of Transfiguration is to give light to them that sit in darkness . . . it is pursued by seeking the Kingdom of God in order to bring its life . . . into action. . . . The goal of Transfiguration is thus the Kingdom of God." [17]

The whole human history or the total civilizational process thus turns into a Creative Theodicy: through separate civilizations and their uniform, but concretely different, rhythms, the reality unfolds its richness and leads from "under-Man" and "under-Civilization," to Man and Civilization, and finally to Superman and Transfigured Ethereal Super-Civilization of the Kingdom of God:

The work of the Spirit of the Earth, as he weaves and draws his threads on the Loom of Time, is the temporal history of man as this manifests itself in the geneses and growths and breakdowns and disintegrations of human societies; and in all this welter of life . . . we can hear the beat of an elemental rhythm . . . of Challenge-and-Response and Withdrawal-and-Return and Rout-and-Rally and Apparentation-and-Affiliation and Schism-and-Palingenesia. This elemental rhythm is the alternating beat of Yin and Yang. . . . The Perpetual turning of a wheel is not a vain repetition if, at each revolution, it is carrying a vehicle that much nearer to its goal; and if "palingenesia" signifies the birth of something new . . . then the Wheel of Existence is not just a devilish device for inflicting an everlasting torment on a damned Ixion. The music that the rhythm of Yin and Yang beats out is the song of creation. . . . Creation would not be creative if it did not swallow up in itself all things in Heaven and Earth, including its own antitheses.[18]

In *Civilization on Trial* Toynbee contends that the movement of civilizations may be cyclic and recurrent, while the movement of religion may be on a single continuous upward level. "It may be served and promoted in its Heavenwardly progress by the cycles of birth and death of civilizations." Christianity appears to be the final goal of human history and the highest measure of man's greatest good on Earth. The whole historical process thus becomes Theodicy—a progressive realization, in this world "to come to know God better and come to love Him more nearly in His own way." [19]

Such is the general framework of Toynbee's philosophy of history. He clothes it in a rich and full-blooded body of facts, empirical verification, and a large number of sub-propositions. The main theses, as well as the sub-propositions, are painstakingly tested by the known empirical facts of the history of the twenty-one civilizations studied. The work as a whole is a real contribution to the field of historical synthesis.

VI

Walter Schubart

In any discussion of the recent "rhythmic" philosophies of history, which are concerned with the present state and interrelationship of the European and Russian cultures, Walter Schubart's *Europa und die Seele des Ostens* should be mentioned. Its author is a German philosopher and historian who spent a considerable amount of time in Russia (before and during the Revolution), and who is well versed in Russian history, literature, philosophy, politics, art, and the Russian way of living and thinking. Its publication in Switzerland in 1938 was little noticed at the time. A few years later it appeared in an abbreviated Russian translation (outside of Soviet Russia); and recently in French and English translations. Greater attention has been paid to it and to his *Dostojewski und Nietzsche* (1939) and *Geistige Wandlung* (1940) in the last few years. Like Danilevsky's work, Schubart's centers around the problem of the present and future status of Russian and European cultures. Schubart's general philosophy of history is presented as a means to unravel the East-West problem. Therefore *Europe and the Soul of the East* contains a sketch, rather than a fully developed theory, of social and cultural change. But the sketch is clearly outlined and well applied to the interpretation of the East-West problem. Its similarities and dissimilarities to other theories discussed are also interesting. Of these theories, Schubart knows well Danilevsky's, Spengler's, and Berdyaev's—not to mention many others—and is notably influenced by them.

The essential points of Schubart's philosophy of history are as follows:

(1) Historical processes are rhythmic. The old Hindu, Persian, Jewish (the book of Daniel), Mexican, Empedoclian, Heraclitian, and more recently Goethe's, Nietzsche's, and Spengler's "cyclic" interpretations of sociocultural processes are essentially correct in their central ideas.[1]

(2) The most important historical rhythm consists in a succession of four aeonic prototypes of culture and of personality. The unfolding of each prototype in the course of time and its struggle against its predecessors and its successors constitutes the central process of cultural history, endows it with epochal rhythm, tension, and conflict.

(3) Each aeonic prototype of culture transcends the boundaries of a nation or a race. Its area may cover the whole continent. Often it is difficult to define clearly the boundaries of its diffusion and domination. But within its domination-area each cultural prototype permeates the whole culture and every human being in the area with its specific character. Without losing his moral freedom, each person is forced to reckon with the dominant cultural prototype, either actualizing it or opposing it, but never ignoring it. After all, opposition is but a form of recognition.

(4) Each time mankind is "fertilized" by a new prototype, a great creative process repeats itself anew. The feeling of youthfulness sweeps over the respective culture. All that preceded the new prototype appears "antiquated" and obsolete. The new prototype is experienced as the supreme value, the end toward which all preceding history has been a mere preparation. The "new epoch" or the "modern period" begins. The emerged prototype in time unfolds itself and the values it was pregnant with are created and delivered. Having exhausted its creative mission, it ages and in its turn gives way to a new prototype. Thus the epochal rhythm continues:

Behind this change of the prototypes some unknown law is probably hidden—the law according to which the divine creative forces now pour themselves into the given empirical world of things, now withdraw from it. Not being able to explain them rationally in all their details, we can only guess at these uniformities; we can either intuit them silently or hint at them by parables and symbols.

(5) There are four main prototypes of culture and personality, or "soul," that replace one another in the course of time: (a) Harmonious, (b) Heroic, (c) Ascetic, and (d) Messianic.

The *Harmonious* culture-mentality and Harmonious man experience the Cosmos as animated by inner harmony, as perfect, not requiring any human leadership or reconstruction. The idea of evolution or progress does not exist in such a cosmos because Harmonious man regards the *purpose of history as achieved*. The cosmos, being perfect, is viewed as eternally static and not dynamic. The Harmonious person lives peacefully in and with the whole world, as an inseparable part of it. The Homeric Greeks, the Confucian Chinese, and the Gothic Christians of the West from the eleventh to the sixteenth centuries are examples of this Harmonious prototype. Permeated by the feeling of eternity, the Gothic Christian trustfully looked up to heaven. His temples piously surged higher and higher into the sky. The earthly landscape was largely forgotten and Gothic man busied himself mainly with the salvation of his soul, the grace of God and *requiem eternam* in God's kingdom.

The *Heroic* culture-mentality and man view the world as a chaos which they must put in order by their organizational effort. The Heroic man does not live peacefully with the world but is set against it in its existing form. He is full of self-confidence, self-pride, and lust for power. He looks at the world as at a slave; he wants to master and mold it according to his own plans. The world is given the purposes determined by the Heroic man. He does not look up to heaven reverently; instead, being full of lust for power and pride, he looks down at earth with inimical and jealous eyes. He goes progressively farther away from God and sinks deeper and deeper into the world of empirical things. Secularization is his destiny; heroism, his main life-feeling; tragedy, his end.

In such a world, especially in such a culture and man, everything is dynamic. Nothing is static in the heroic universe. Like Prometheus, the Heroic man challenges any power and any God. He is active, tense, and maximally energetic. Accordingly, the Heroic or Promethean epochs are especially dynamic, mobile, and active. The Roman world at the zenith of Roman power felt itself to be thus, and in the Germano-Romanic West after the sixteenth century this prototype has also been dominant. The Promethean Western culture and man of the last four centuries are a good sample of this prototype.

The *Ascetic* culture-mentality and man experience the empirical existence as an error, the sensory world as a mirage and evil temptation. They run away from both into the mystic realm of supra-essence or supra-reality. The Ascetic person leaves the sensory world without regret. He has neither desire nor hope for its improvement. He does not try to change it at all. Therefore the epochs of the Ascetic prototype's domination are even more static than those of the Harmonious culture and man.

The Hindu of Hinduism and Buddhism, the Neo-Platonists, and most of the truly ascetic groups and sects are examples of the Ascetic prototype of culture-mentality and man.

Finally, the *Messianic* culture-mentality and man feel themselves called upon to establish on earth the supreme divine order, whose idea they ineffably bear in themselves. The Messianic man wants to re-establish around himself the harmony which he feels in himself. He does not accept the world as it is. Like the Heroic man, he too wants to change it, not for his own self-will or self-satisfaction, but in order to fulfill the mission assigned to him by God. Like the Harmonious man he also loves the world—not as it is, but as it ought to be. The goal of the Harmonious man is reached; that of the Messianic man is far away, in the future. In contrast to the Ascetic man, however, he firmly believes that this goal can be reached. The Messianic man is inspired not by the lust for power, but by the mood of reconciliation and love. He does not divide in order to rule, but looks for the divided in order to unite it into one whole. He is not moved by suspicion and hate, but by deep trust in the true reality. He sees brothers, not enemies, in human beings. He views the world not as booty to be grabbed, but as rough stuff in need of enlightenment, ennoblement, and consecration. He is possessed by a sort of cosmic passion to unify what is separated, to harmonize what is discordant, to make visible on this planet the Kingdom of God or his highest ideal. He works for a realization of this highest ideal here on earth.

Like the Heroic man he is full of energy, activity, and dynamism. Accordingly, the Messianic epochs are dynamic too. The early Christians and most of the Slavs are examples of this prototype.

These four prototypes can be summed up by the following mottoes: consonance with the world (Harmonious); domination over the world (Heroic); running away from the world (Ascetic); and consecration of the world (Messianic).[2]

(6) Like Danilevsky, Spengler, and Toynbee, Schubart rejects the linear interpretation of historical process and the "justification" of all history by some future and final goal of progress. He states, as do all partisans of the rhythmical conception of sociocultural change, that "before God all times are equal," even the Heroic epochs, which do not care for God at all. Each aeonic epoch contains its own value and justification, as great as those of any other epoch. Like a pause in a melody, even the Godless periods have their own *raison d'être*. An incessant unfolding of the creative, divine forces occurs in each time-moment; therefore each moment bears in itself the justifying reason of its existence, for otherwise no future goal can justify any past moment of history.

(7) Especially breath-taking are the periods when one prototype dies out and a new one begins to emerge. These periods are the intermediary, apocalyptic moments of humanity. In such periods people feel that everything is crumbling and the end of the world is coming. In fact, such moments have been repeated many times and will be repeated many times in the future.

(8) The twentieth century is one of these intermediary, apocalyptic periods. For several decades now, a few seers have foreseen that something important was ending: the post-

Atlantis humanity, according to Merejkovsky; Christianity, according to Unamuno; the thousand-year-long Western Culture, according to Spengler; capitalism, according to Marx; the epoch of the Renaissance, according to N. Berdyaev. It is precisely this transitory character of our age that makes it so dynamic and so self-contradictory. It is full of sadness and full of hope, of dark forebodings and of cheerful prospects. Before our eyes, accompanied by explosions and catastrophes, we see dying not a single race or nation, nor a single culture, but a whole preceding cultural epoch. Which epoch?

(9) During the last thousand years two epochal prototypes have grown on European soil: the Harmonious-Gothic and the Heroic-Promethean. The Gothic prototype was born of the catastrophes of the eleventh century and lasted up to the sixteenth century. It was a Harmonious culture with all its earmarks. It was creative and fruitful in its own way. However, between 1450 and 1550 a transition from the Gothic-Harmonious to the Heroic-Promethean prototype took place. This Promethean-Western man cared little for God or the salvation of his soul, and much for the conquest of the world. He wanted to be the master of the Earth. His ambition was such that he was ready to challenge any God and any power above himself. In the course of some five hundred years the Promethean man, through his most intense activities, has indeed succeeded in changing the surface of the earth and in pushing his ambitious plans far and high. He has indeed created a new sociocultural world in his own image.

After five hundred years of the Heroic-Promethean epoch we are now at the threshold of a new epoch. The heavy clouds of Destiny are hanging over the Promethean culture. Lightnings and deadly tornadoes are sweeping over it. Europe is fatally sliding into her most bloody catastrophe; she is approaching her end which was inherent in the birth of her Promethean culture. Nothing can stop its death. On the horizon, however, the dawn of a new epochal prototype, the *Messianic-Johannian* (St. John of the Gospel), is beginning to loom. This Messianic-Johannian epoch will be congenial to the Gothic-Harmonious. While the Promethean man and culture hated and disdained the Gothic culture and man, the coming Messianic culture and man will admire them and love the Middle Ages of Europe. This Johannian epoch will be animated by the spirit of solidarity, reconciliation, love, and unity. The realization of a truly creative and friendly one world will be the chief mission of the Johannian man.

(10) Which human groups will be the leaders or instrumentalities of the new prototype, and which are going to oppose it, depends upon the specific characteristics of these groups at the moment of the emergence of the prototype. The point is that at any *given* moment various contemporaneous human groups differ from one another in their racial (blood), national or vital, mental, and moral traits. These differences are caused by the different geographic environments or different "landscape atmospheres," or different "territorial spirits," in which these groups live. These geographic differences are responsible for so-called racial and national differences in human groups. Contrary to prevalent opinion, racial and national traits are not constant but are derivatives of geographic conditions, changing with a changing "landscape atmosphere." However, insofar as the geographic conditions change very slowly, and insofar as most of the human groups used to live each amidst the same "landscape spirit" for a long time, the racial and national traits are comparatively constant, and change much more slowly than the traits stamped by the change of the cultural prototypes. Thus the "landscape atmosphere" determines the group differences in space, while the cultural prototype causes the differences in time. The combination of these two factors—the relatively constant geographic environment and the ever dynamic change of the prototypes—determines the essentials of historical process and the "physiognomy" of each group, including the racial and national groups, at any moment of history.

(11) When these relatively constant national traits coincide with, or are congenial to, the emerging cultural prototype, the nation in question becomes the leader in the rising culture

and reaches the zenith of its cultural creativity, which may or may not coincide with the zenith of its political power. The congeniality of the "landscape spirit" of a given nation with the spirit of the new prototype reinforces both, while their antagonism leads to conflict between the new prototype of culture and the adverse national group with an uncongenial "landscape spirit." For this reason the *arena* of the main historical processes and the national groups, as the main actors in the new epochal drama, also change when the prototypes change. A shift of the prototypes results in a shifting of the territorial stages and the main actors in the new historical tragedy. The role of "stars" falls to those national groups which, in their "landscape spirit," have best developed the national traits necessary for a full realization of the new prototype. Thus, with the emergence of the Western Promethean man and culture, Prussia and the Prussians became the leaders among the Germans and the German states because their ethnic-national traits were most congenial to those of the Promethean prototype. Among the European nations the Prussians and the Anglo-Saxons became the leaders and the examples of this epoch. For the same reason the Jews have become increasingly influential during the last 150 years; their relatively constant traits happened to be congenial to those of the Promethean man.

While the preceding Gothic-Harmonious epoch created the spiritual unity of Europe, the succeeding Promethean epoch, according to its *divide et impera,* developed centrifugal, dividing forces, beginning with the division of Europe by the Renaissance and then by the Reformation, followed by the political division which Frederic II of Prussia carried out. With the development of the Promethean culture the initiative progressively comes from the North and the main historical stage shifts to the North. The leadership of the sixteenth century belonged to the Italians and the Spaniards, of the seventeenth century to the French, passing in subsequent centuries to the Prussians, then to the Anglo-Saxons and the Scandinavians. The Lower-Germans (*Niederdeutsche*), the Anglo-Saxons, the Prussians, and the Puritans (Americans)

—these are the titans of the Promethean technological epoch. Parallel with this change in leadership the main arena of the Promethean culture has also shifted northward, from Italy-Spain to Northern Germany, England, and North America.

(12) In the emerging Johannian-Messianic epoch the central stage of history again shifts and the leadership passes from the Promethean nations to those whose national character is best suited to the Johannian prototype:

The most important event in the making is the rise of the Slavs as the emerging cultural leader. However unpleasant this is for many, such is historical destiny; nobody can stop it; the next centuries belong to the Slavs. The Nordic Promethean culture is dying; its place is being taken by an Oriental Culture. Johannian epoch is Slavic aeon.[3]

(13) Having reached this conclusion Schubart passes on to an analysis of the West-East conflict as a *cultural* problem. His conclusion, as well as his analysis of the Russian-European relationships, is notably similar to Danilevsky's main propositions. Schubart reminds us that Goethe and Leibnitz, Schopenhauer and Herder, not to mention Von Baader, Von Humboldt, Von Hartmann, Rückert, Neumann, and others, understood the one-sidedness of Promethean Western culture and man, their coming decay, the necessity of supplementing them with Eastern culture and man, beginning with the Hindu and Chinese and ending with the Russian; and they saw the synthesis of the East and West as the only solution of the problem. Unfortunately Europe did not pay much attention to these warnings and, if anything, through increasing pride and superiority, continued to exploit, disdain, and neglect, sometimes to fear and hate, the East, especially Russia, as the "backward" country and people. The First World War and a series of subsequent events and catastrophes served as a rude awakening from this double illusion of Western superiority and Russian and Eastern inferiority. The West was forced to reconsider its illusion and to become aware of its astounding ignorance of Russia. With a better understanding of Russia it becomes clearer why and how Russia is going to be the leader in the emerging Johannian-Messianic prototype:

The Promethean West enriched humanity through the most perfect forms of technics, statehood and communication, but it deprived mankind of its soul. Russia's mission consists of returning this soul to humanity. Russia possesses exactly those spiritual forces which Europe either lost or destroyed. Russia is a part of Asia, and at the same time a member of the Christian Commonwealth of nations. She is a Christian part of Asia. In this lies the specific peculiarity of Russia and the uniqueness of her mission. India and China are isolated from the Western man; Russia is accessible through the ways and channels of a common Christian religion. Only Russia can spiritualize a humanity that is drowned in the swamp of material things and spoiled by the lust for power; and this in spite of the Bolshevist agony that Russia is experiencing at the present time. The horrors of the Communist regime will pass, just as the night of the Tartar yoke passed, and the old motto, *"Ex oriente lux,"* will come through. By this I do not want to say that the European nations will lose their importance; they will only lose the spiritual leadership. They would no longer represent the dominant human type, and this would be a real blessing for humanity. An enormous multitude, and especially many of the finest minds, long for the end of the worn-out Promethean culture. They feel its present poverty and look for a new possibility. However reckless it may sound to many, it should be stated definitely that Russia is the only country which can and will free Europe, because Russia's position in regard to all the vital problems is opposite to that of the European nations. From the unfathomed depths of her own crucifixion Russia is obtaining the deepest understanding of human beings and of their life values, in order to communicate it to all nations of the earth. The Russian nation has the necessary spiritual qualities for this mission. In its present form the West-East cultural problem appears as the problem of renovating mankind, as a possible spiritualization of the West by the East, as an indication to splintered humanity to re-unite again in its primeval unity, as a mission to accomplish the creation of a perfect man.[4]

(14) The realization of this goal will not be achieved peacefully, according to Schubart. Politically, the West-East problem signifies conflict and war. Some five hundred years would be required for its solution, a period similar to the one that was necessary to achieve a balance between the Germanic peoples and ancient Rome. One of the main functions of war is to bring the warring nations together and, contrary to their desire, interpenetrate one another—culturally and mentally. War is not only a great destroyer, but also a great cross-fertilizer. Hate can pass into respect and sympathy, but not

into indifference. A grand reconciliation is often preceded by intensive political and military conflicts.

Viewed in this light, the Russian-European relationship has grown increasingly tense. Though Europe invaded Russia several times before the twentieth century, was repulsed and (by way of Russian self-defense) invaded by Russia, these conflicts were few, sporadic, and "incidental." But beginning with the Napoleonic-European invasion of Russia in 1812, the political conflicts with Europe have become increasingly important. The Western Promethean man began to be more and more attracted by the East, and the Eastern—particularly the Russian—Messianic man became ever more closely involved in the West's affairs. In this way the process of increasing mutual interpenetration and equalization of Russian-Western souls and cultures has been under way. The most pregnant consequence of the French Revolution and the Napoleonic wars was not the execution of Louis XVI, but the conflagration of Moscow and the awakening of the Slavs. In this manner the Russian East entered the history of Europe once and for all. Since that time "Europe has been worried mainly by two things: Revolution and Russia," as a great Russian poet, Tutchev, said long ago.

This "mutually interpenetrating" political conflict between Russia and the West has continued *crescendo* since 1812. Europe has incessantly tried to weaken, stop, suppress, and crush Russia economically, culturally, diplomatically, and militarily. Besides invasion by separate European states, Europe as a whole invaded Russia in 1854 (the Crimean War), threatened to do so several times later on, and then invaded again in 1914. After being repulsed and answered by the Russian Revolution, the West once more, in 1918, sent its combined expeditionary forces to crush the Revolution, suffocate Russia by the *cordon sanitaire,* and destroy Russia by shearing from her as many of her Asiatic, Caucasian, Pre-Baltic, Western, and Eastern parts as it could. Failing in this, the West organized the Fascist, Nazi, and other anti-Russian forces and created a new gigantic military power for a new invasion. (Schubart's book was published in 1938, before the Second World War.) In brief, the war of 1914 opened a new "Hundred-Year War" between the Promethean West and Russia, or rather the East organized and led by Russia. The historical destiny of Russia is to revolt against the Promethean West and possibly to take the lead in unifying all humanity in the emerging Messianic culture. This Russian role, predicted by Napoleon in 1816, Danilevsky in 1869, and Spengler in 1918, is unfolding before our eyes. The center of history is increasingly shifting towards the Orient and moving deeper and deeper into the East. All these tragic conflicts and various bizarre events, like Russian Communism or German Nazism, are but appearances through which and under which the basic process of interpenetration, harmonization, and unification of humanity in a new Messianic universal culture, based upon love, is progressively growing. Such is the meaning of the Eastern-Western—or the Russian-Western— problem as a *political* conflict.

(15) In a subsequent part of his book Schubart gives a comparative history of the Promethean and Russian souls, and outlines the comparative psychology of various Western nations, specifically the German, French, Anglo-Saxon, and Spanish. The following are some of the traits he ascribes to the national soul of Russia, compared with the Promethean soul of the West.

The *Harmonious* soul represents the national soul of Russia before it was somewhat weakened, distorted, and temporarily suppressed by the Western Promethean and other alien influences. These transformed it into the Messianic Soul of the later period. The Harmonious soul is manifested by the ancient Russian Orthodox religion. It is tolerant and it extols and practices humility, peace of mind, spiritual soberness, love, spiritual courage, moral nobility, and total inner harmony. These traits can be seen in the collective, spontaneous, and brotherly organization of the ancient Russian Church; in its teachings and practices; in its icons, music, and architecture. The same Harmonious soul shines through the persistent and dominant Russian philosophy and ethics; through the free democratic organizational forms of life and of social institutions of ancient Russia; through the federated union of Russian communities (*Mir, obschina, bratstva*), "city-states," and "free principalities"; through the absence of any racial or ethnic persecutions; through the population's spontaneous enactment of customary laws and moral norms; through the absence of any privileged knightly aristocracy, kings, monarchs, and czars in pre-Mongolian Russia; through the domination of the noblest moral values over the formal legalistic statutes of the official "lawyers' law"; through the congeniality between the Russian soul and Plato, in contrast to that of the Western soul and Aristotle; through the Russian-Orthodox teaching of "Man-Godness" of Christ and Christ as a real "brother" in contrast to the Western "autocratic God-Father"; finally, it shines through the greatest Russian poet, Pushkin, whose poetry is a hundred times more harmonious than even Goethe's.

It is true that this Harmonious soul of ancient Russia has often been distorted, "jammed," and "suppressed" by Byzantine influences that imposed on the Russian soul the ideas of an Autocratic Panto-creator God, a centralized and autocratic organization of the Church, the idea of an Empire, and so on; by the Mongolian yoke, lasting some 250 years, which greatly disfigured the Harmonious soul and culture of the pre-Mongolian period; by the Germanic-European invasions of the thirteenth and subsequent centuries; later by the waves of Westernization started by Peter the Great; during the last three centuries by the world-outlook of the Promethean soul and culture which is incessantly passing over Russia; finally, by Marxism, Communism, and materialism, which are the products of the Promethean soul and not the creations of the Russian soul. All these influences greatly changed and distorted the Russian soul, culture and institutions. In Spengler's terminology, they called forth a "pseudomorphosis" of Russia.

Along with producing disordered and ascetic souls in Russia, the pseudomorphosis consisted mainly of a transformation of the initial Russian *Harmonious* soul into a *Messianic* one.

The religious, ethical, political, and socio-economic Messianism of recent centuries is the dominant form of the transformed Russian soul's reaction to all manifestations of the Promethean culture. This Messianism permeates the great Russian literature of the nineteenth and the twentieth century, especially that of Gogol, Dostoievsky, Tolstoi, and others, up to Andreiev, Gorki, Chekhov, and even the Soviet writers; the dominant Russian philosophy and metaphysics, represented by Skovoroda, Soloviev, up to Berdyaev, Boulgakov, Lossky, and others. In a distorted form the Russian Messianic soul even shows herself in the Soviet-Communist policies: being Promethean in its nature, Russian Communism displays the most intense Messianic enthusiasm for a fundamental reconstruction of the World. Schubart lists a long series of facts corroborating his thesis.[5]

The Western soul and culture are those of the *moderate middle,* those of Russia are of the *extreme poles.* The European only wants to somewhat improve the world, which is in most respects all right; the Russian wants to spiritualize it from the bottom to the top.

The Western soul and culture are permeated by primeval *fear and anguish;* the Russian by primeval *confidence and trust* in the inner, transcendental forces of the world.

The Western prototype considers *order* as the basic value; accordingly it is legalistic and formal. The Russian prototype builds on the principles of *spontaneity* and *devotion;* he values little the formal and legalistic norms. The Western culture is the culture of law norms; the Russian is that of superlegal, moral, and free efforts and ideals. The Western culture can easily degenerate into *soulless formality,* ossification, and suffocation of life and virtue in the deadly norms of legality; the Russian culture can easily fall into the chaos of *normless anarchy,* spiritual nihilism, and hysteria.

The rational soul of the West thinks *purposefully* in its utilitarian and hedonistic nature; the Russian Messianic soul thinks *expressively.* The Western ethics is that of the *imperative;* the Russian is the ethics of *spontaneity* and of *impulse.*

The Western soul is *egoistic, self-centered, and individualistic;* the Russian is *"brotherly," "we-centered," and collectivistic.* The Western soul is permeated by *competition,* the Russian by *co-operation.* The Western Promethean Christianity is an imperialistic cult of the *sword, power,* and *conquest:* as such it represents an utter distortion of the early Christianity. Russian Christianity remains faithful to the *Christianity of Christ:* even under the Soviets there have been more Christians in Russia who humbly preferred to die as martyrs than in any country of the West. The Russian Church remains free from the elements of Promethean Caesarism while the main Western denominations—from the Roman Catholic to some Protestant—are Caesarian political machineries, permeated by the spirit of *conquest and imperialism.* The Russian Christ, so well presented by Dostoievsky, is free from any element of Caesarism, Imperialism, or Domination in any form whatever.

The Russian prototype is *"eternally feminine"* while the Promethean prototype is essentially *"masculine."*

While the English national idea since Cromwell has been that of a *chosen nation,* the French idea that of *intellectual leadership,* and that of Germany something in between these ideas, the national idea of Russia has been the *liberation and unification of humanity.*[6]

(16) Schubart concludes his book by reiterating that the Promethean prototype of the West is coming to an end and a new Messianic soul is being born in Russia. This Messianic man is not simply the man of 1917 or of 1789, but a new man with an oriental soul that has passed through the tragic test of fiery martyrdom. Though he is a real Russian, this man is at the same time heir to all the immortal values of the West. This man is in the stage of being born; his maturity and creative life are still in the future. But this future belongs to his leadership:

The coming Russia is that refreshing wine which will revitalize the dried up life-stream of today's humanity. The West is that strong container in which we can keep the wine. Without a strong, holding form the wine will be spilt and lost; without the wine the precious container will only remain an empty and useless toy. Contemporary Europe is a form without life. Russia is the life without form. . . . The Englishman wants to see the world as a factory; the Frenchman, as a *salon;* the German, as a military barrack; the Russian, as a Church. The Englishman seeks for profit; the Frenchman wants glory; the German, power; the Russian, sacrifice. The Russian wants nothing from his neighbor except brotherhood. . . . This is the essence of the Russian brotherhood and of the Gospel of the future. . . . Only the Russian All-Man as the bearer of the new solidarity can free humanity from the superman's individualism as well as from the sub-man's collectivism of the masses. To the autonomous individual—the ideal of the Renaissance—he confronts the soul organically connected with God and the universe; to the coercive unification of men he contrasts the spontaneous, mutually loving union of free souls. In this way he simultaneously creates a new concept and ideal of personality and freedom. . . .

The Promethean man is already marked by the seal of death. Let the Johannian man arise! [7]

VII

Nikolai Berdyaev

Nikolai Berdyaev was born in Russia in 1874 and died in France in 1948. He graduated from Kiev University and attended Wildenband's lectures at Heidelberg University. For a short time, at the beginning of his scientific work, he was one of the first Marxians in Russia, and the Czarist government arrested and banished him to Vologda Province. Eventually he freed himself from all unscientific elements in Marxianism and became one of the notable idealistic Russian thinkers. Among other positions, he occupied the chair of political economy at the University of Moscow and was one of the founders of the Russian Religious-Philosophical Society. In 1922 Berdyaev was arrested and expelled from Russia by the Soviet Government (in the same group in which I was banished).

Berdyaev is the author of many works in philosophy, social science, political economy and ethics: *The Meaning of Creativeness* (1916), *The Meaning of History* (1923), *Philosophy of Inequality* (1922), *The New Middle Ages* (1924), *Christianity and Class Struggle* (1931), *Solitude and Society* (1930), and many others. Most of Berdyaev's books have been translated into several languages.

Omitting the metaphysical part of Berdyaev's philosophy of history, the following empirical points of his reading of historical events should be mentioned.

(1) Methodologically, a mere description of singularistic historical events, persons, and objects only results in a dead corpse of history. "When one reads a scientific book on, say,

ancient peoples, one clearly feels that from the history of cultures of these peoples their soul, their inner life are removed and one gets instead only a sort of external photograph or picture"—which does not in the least explain the why, wherefore, or even the how of all these events and persons. In order to understand these whys and wherefores, the soul and the inner logic of history, it is necessary "not only that the object-matter of history be historical, but also that the cognizing subject of historical study experience and unfold in himself 'the historical.' " It is necessary that the cognizing subject and cognized object of history become one, that the subject himself live history, not merely look on historical events from the outside. On this point Berdyaev, like Spengler and Northrop, insists on a direct intuitional identification of the cognizing subject with the cognized object, without which no adequate understanding of anything, especially of historical and socio-cultural processes, is possible.[1]

(2) Like all the other authors under consideration Berdyaev rejects all forms of the linear interpretation of historical process and all linear theories of progress in its unilinear, oscillating, spiral, and branching varieties.[2] Theories of progress are not tenable either metaphysically, logically, factually, or ethically.

(3) All great cultures are simultaneously mortal and immortal in their existence within the limits of empirical history itself. They contain temporal as well as eternal principles. Each of the cultures experiences moments of emergence, florescence, and ups and downs, and eventually declines as a unity; at the same time, each of the great cultures survives in its perennial, eternal values. Graeco-Roman culture did not disappear entirely at the time of its fall. Its perennial values, such as Roman law, Greek art, Greek philosophy, and so on, did not die; they were incorporated into the culture of the Middle Ages, Arabian culture, and are still living a vigorous life. In other words, the temporal elements or values of a culture die; the perennial ones persist and live as long as human history goes on. Even after its empirical end the transfigured perennial values will, in some transcendental, mysti-

cal way, pass beyond the empirical end of history into the "transcendental great beyond." [3]

Here Berdyaev points, in general terms, to what I call the lasting and dying elements in culture, with their indefinitely long and limited life-durations, a point that has so far been overlooked by social scientists and philosophers of history.[4]

(4) Independently of—and possibly even earlier than— Spengler, Berdyaev regarded the Western culture as already having passed its Barbaric, Medieval-Christian, and modern Humanist-Secular phases. Its Medieval-Christian phase was over in the thirteenth century, and its Humanist phase ended in about the nineteenth century. To Berdyaev the twentieth century is the transitory period from the dying Humanist phase to the emerging phase of the "New Middle Ages."

The main task of the medieval phase of Christian-Western culture, according to Berdyaev, was to discipline, manifoldly develop, and spiritualize man, or an accumulation of the "spiritual fission-forces" in the developed personality and the Western culture. Monkhood and knighthood fulfilled this function by disciplining and spiritualizing man. The images of a monk and a knight are veritably types of a disciplined, integrated, and manifold personality, spiritually free, unafraid of anything external, with enormous concentration on the inward through tense "fission-forces" centered around the Kingdom of God. This medieval phase had to end and did end because it did not supply a sufficient channel for releasing the enormously concentrated forces for a free, creative transformation of the empirical reality. The Middle Ages end with the marvelous Christian mystical Renaissance of the thirteenth century that serves as a bridge to the subsequent Humanist phase. Joachim of Floris, St. Francis of Assisi, Dante, Giotto, and St. Thomas Aquinas are the brilliant stars of this wonderful Renaissance, which is the summit and the end of the Medieval phase.

Then follows the largely non-Christian, even increasingly anti-Christian, phase of Western culture's secular Humanism. Humanism puts man in the center of the universe, makes him the measure of all things and the highest value. Its main function was to release and develop the free, creative forces of man: man's trial and test in freedom, unhampered by anything except man's own sense, reason, and self-control. It was, therefore, the period of man's liberation from all "superhuman" controls, and deconcentration of his concentrated inner forces, the period in which he spent the creative funds accumulated in the medieval period, and abandoned the religious central value of the Middle Ages; the period of secularization and external freedom. These tasks were accomplished in the course of some six centuries. Humanist culture spent most of the funds accumulated in the previous periods and exhausted its creative power. As a result in the nineteenth century this Humanist culture immanently produced the ever-increasing germs of its own destruction. The Medieval-Christian and the Humanist-Modern phases both dialectically led to their own decay.

The Medieval-Christian culture aspired only to the Kingdom of God and denied value to the empirical City of Man. But instead of becoming absorbed in the City of God, it ended —dialectically—by becoming enmeshed in the City of Man. The Christian Church itself grew into the most powerful empirical organization in entire Medieval Europe. Humanist culture aspired to man's glory, power, and creativity, and sought to make him both self-master and master of the empirical world. It finished by utterly demoralizing man, disintegrating the man-made universe and exhausting man's creative forces:

Here the dialectics of history consists of the self-affirmation of man that has led to his self-extermination, and the development of the free play of purely human forces, not connected with the super-human high purpose, that led to the exhaustion of purely human creative resources. . . . The passionate striving towards a creation of beauty and perfection of form, which marks the advent of the Humanist-Renaissance phase, led to the destruction and distortion of the perfection of form. . . . The more proudly Humanist man relied upon himself, and the more he moved away from the Christian, Divine, Medieval foundations of personality, the less creative, less powerful, and less self-controlling he grew progressively.[5]

The Humanist period opens with man full of joy and self-confidence. It ends with a deep disillusion in all the dreams, strivings, and illusions of the Humanist man and culture. None of the great expectations were realized.[6]

The crisis and end of the Humanist phase was already quite apparent in the nineteenth century. The entrance of the machine and technology into man's historical existence dealt a mortal blow to Humanism. Increasing loss of man's control over the human race's machine-made universe, decreasing self-control and mastery of the lower, animal propensities in man, a growing distortion of the very image of a true humanist man in favor of a demoralized human mechanism and human animal so different from humanist man—these are some of the signs that mark the end of the Humanist phase. The emergence and successful growth of anti-Humanist philosophies and ideologies are further signs. Nietzsche's final verdict, "Man is a shame and disgrace; man must be overcome and transcended"—Humanism must be ended in order to open the way for the superman—is one example of this. Marx also sacrifices man and humanism on the altar of the inhuman, superpersonal kingdom of collectivism. Similarly, even the philosophies and ideologies of Kant, Comte, Spencer, right up to Husserl, are anti-humanistic. Likewise, Humanist ethics and aesthetics, politics and economics, either developed into non-humanist forms or else disintegrated into fragmentary atoms, devoid of power, form, and control. Many mystic, explicitly anti-Humanist currents appeared. In the nineteenth century, socialism, anarchism, capitalism, futurism, "modernism" and theosophy all revolted against, and mortally weakened, the Humanist culture. At the present time the Humanist phase is largely over and mankind is entering the "New Middle Ages."

(5) In discussing the reason why all great cultures eventually disintegrate as unities (surviving, however, in their perennial values), and why their creative power eventually declines, Berdyaev makes a highly suggestive generalization. "Culture is not a realization of a new *life,* of a new way of existence, but a

realization of new *values*. All achievements of culture are symbolic rather than realistic."

At its creative period culture creates not for the practical purpose of a utilitarian or hedonistic improvement of the empirical life, but for the sake of the values themselves. It creates truth for the sake of truth and cognition, beauty for the sake of beauty, goodness for the sake of goodness. In all this there is little of "real, practical life," of the passionate "will to live," of the intense desire to organize "life," to enjoy "life." There is little of practical utility.

Having created the values, however, culture immanently changes its direction and passes beyond culture into the Spenglerian "civilization." Created values cannot help entering real life and changing it; with the change the culture itself changes. It now tends towards a practical realization of its power, towards a practical organization of life, towards a diffusion of its applied results. A mere blossoming of the arts and sciences, a deepening and refinement of thought, the highest flare-ups of artistic creativity, the contemplation of the kingdom of God and of genius—all these now cease to be experienced as real life, cease to inspire as the highest goal. Instead, there grows an intense will to live, to enjoy the "full, real life," to master, improve, and transform this life. This lust for "real life" eventually undermines the creative genius of culture. A period of cultural blossoming presupposes a severe limitation of the will to "live"; it demands an unselfish, somewhat ascetic transcendence over the passionate "gluttony for life." When such a "gluttony for life" develops in the masses, then this "life," and not the cultural creativity, becomes the supreme end. Since they are always aristocratic, cultural creativity and culture cease to be the supreme self-values and become mere means for the "practical improvement of life," for "prosperity and happiness." With this degradation of culture and of pure creativity to the level of third class means-values, the will for culture and disinterested creativeness weakens and eventually dies. With it dies the will for creative genius, and genius becomes increasingly scarce. Under these conditions culture cannot stay at its high level;

it is bound to slide down; its quality tends to be replaced by quantity; a sort of social entropy develops and culture turns into an uncreative "civilization." Culture immanently declines and crumbles because it deviates from the purposes and tasks that were born at its creative phase.

This explains why the highest cultural blossoming of Germany at the end of the eighteenth and beginning of the nineteenth centuries—when within a period of a few decades the world saw Lessing, Herder, Goethe, Schiller, Kant, Fichte, Hegel, Schelling, Schleiermacher, Schopenhauer, Novalis, Mozart, Handel, Haydn, Beethoven, and dozens of other first-class "stars"—occurred in the period when the real life of Germany was poor, difficult, depressing, and bourgeois. Similarly, Italy's real life of the Renaissance period was miserable and unenviable. Even the practical life of the great creators themselves—be it Mozart or Beethoven, Leonardo or Michelangelo—was painful and tragic. "Culture has always been a great failure with respect to life." There is a kind of oppositeness between culture and life. When life becomes "civilized," "happy and prosperous," then the creativity of culture declines and culture is replaced by "civilization." "Culture is unselfish and disinterested in its highest achievements; civilization is always utilitarian and interested." Such is the dialectic of the decline of creative culture into uncreative civilizations.

Although it is fairly general, this degradation of culture into civilization is not a creative culture's only destiny. Culture can take another way—the way of religious transfiguration of life, and through that the realization of genuine existence (being). Such was the course that the declining Graeco-Roman culture followed. It resulted in the emergence and growth of Christianity. At its heroic and truly Christian period, Christianity led to the religious transfiguration of life and the creation of a great Christian Medieval culture. Eventually Christianity ceased to be truly religious and became largely verbal, ritualistic, an economic and political machinery; as such it lost its transfiguring power. It is possible that the West's transitional culture will choose this religious way of transfiguring life in order to perpetuate its perennial values and bring humanity closer to a genuine creative life.

Russia may play an important role in this pilgrimage of culture; however, this role still remains problematic and uncertain. Berdyaev is much less complimentary towards Russia than are Schubart, Danilevsky, and Spengler. "The traditions of culture have always been weak in Russia. We have built a rather ugly civilization. Barbarian forces have always been strong with us. Even our will towards a religious transfiguration of life has been infected by a sort of sickly day-dreaming." Under these conditions only Russia's potential religiosity, together with the most intense suffering and a consciousness of the epochal crisis, may help Russia find the way of religious transfiguration of life instead of decaying into an uncreative civilization or barbarism.[7]

VIII

F. S. C. Northrop

F. S. C. Northrop is a descendant of the Joseph Northrop who in 1638 came to New Haven and in the following year founded Milford. Born in Wisconsin in 1893, he graduated from Beloit College in 1915, received his master's degrees from Yale and Harvard and his Ph.D. degree from Harvard in 1924. He also studied at the University of Freiburg in Germany, at Trinity College in Cambridge, and at the Imperial College of Science and Technology in London, England, later traveling extensively and studying in China, Mexico, Great Britain, and the Continent. The outbreak of the First World War found him in social work. Rising from the ranks, he was at the war's end a commander of a tank corps. In 1923 he again returned to teaching, finally becoming Sterling Professor of Philosophy and Law at Yale University. He is author of *Science and First Principles* (1931), *The Meeting of East and West* (1946), and *The Logic of the Sciences and Humanities* (1947). The volume entitled *Ideological Differences and World Order* appeared under his editorship in 1949.

Of all Northrop's works, *The Meeting of the East and West* is for our purpose the most important, giving as it does a comprehensible account of historical events and of the interrelationship of sociocultural phenomena. In the first place, the work shows convincingly that the *total* culture of any nation, such as the United States, Great Britain, Germany, Soviet Russia, or Mexico, and even the *total* culture of the East and West, is not a mere dumping ground for numberless atomistic sociocultural phenomena, unrelated to one another —not, in fact, a congeries. It consists, chiefly, of one or several large sociocultural systems, each based on certain philosophical principles articulated in all its chief aspects—in its arts and philosophy, religion and law, economics and politics, manners and mores, in the prevalent type of personality and basic social institutions.

Cultures with differing political, economic, aesthetic and religious ideals or values are grounded in differing philosophical conceptions of the nature of man and of the universe. . . . Actually in any culture there are as many different theoretical beliefs as there are different individuals or different opinions of the same individual at different times. Usually, however, certain beliefs capture a majority opinion.

As such, Northrop says, beliefs are articulated by the main components of a certain culture and society and give to them their individuality and specific "physiognomy."[1]

In the last analysis these "philosophical presuppositions" (or "major premises" or "prime symbols") of each cultural system are in turn based upon the state of science or the basic scientific theories existing in a given culture.

Mathematical and natural science, as its facts are made theoretically systematic and articulate, gives rise to [a corresponding] philosophy; and this philosophy . . . gives technical meaning and—since it is scientifically determined—publicly valid empirical justification to the claim of [a corresponding] religion and morality; and these in turn and the science and philosophy from which they stem, when applied, generate the [corresponding] arts of poetry, painting, music, sculpture, architecture, and governmental and ecclesiastical polity in their normative character, as well as engineering and technocracy. . . . In short, philosophy . . . is natural science made articulate with respect to its basic assumptions on the theoretical side.[2]

Several social scientists reached similar conclusions before and simultaneously with Northrop.

The real significance of Northrop's propositions is two-fold. By arriving at these conclusions independently he additionally confirms their validity; he demonstrates this validity admirably, especially in the cases of the Mexican and the United States cultures.

Having taken the *total* culture of Mexico, Northrop convincingly shows that it is made up largely of five co-existing systems of culture, each grounded in its own philosophical principles (and a corresponding state of natural science). At Mexico City, he points out, one meets, within one square mile, shops and parks reminiscent of Paris, Manhattan skyscrapers, the Spanish Hotel Majestic, the colonial Catholic cathedral and National Palace, and the distinctly Mexican Zocalo, whose lawns cover the Aztec ruins:

There they were. All within one square mile. Five distinct and unique cultures: ancient Aztec, Spanish Colonial, positivistic French nineteenth century, Anglo-American economic, and contemporary Mexican. Harmonious, yet competitively diverse.[3]

Subsequently Northrop analyzes in detail the purely Indian, pre-colonial culture of Mexico in all its main variations and manifestations, with its underlying science and philosophy, its "theoretic" and "aesthetic" principles, beginning with the Place of the Gods (Teotihuacán) and Pyramid of the Sun, and ending with the kind of fresco, with its naturalistic colors, recently unearthed behind the Pyramid of the Sun. In a similar manner he analyzes the Spanish-colonial culture brought by the Spaniards, in place of the almost completely destroyed, very high Aztec culture. This Spanish Catholic culture, with its Thomistic philosophy and science, is manifested by the Spanish Baroque cathedrals and other buildings, in the Catholic cult, in the remnants of the hierarchical order of values and social ranks, and in many other details. A careful study of this Spanish-colonial culture, however, shows how it was modified by the impact of the pre-colonial Mexican culture. For instance, the painting of the angel at the Tepotzotlan Jesuit monastery, and especially the beloved patron Saint of Mexico, the Dark Madonna, the Virgin of Guadalupe, as well as the style of some of the chapels, display a distinctly Indian influence. "The native Mexican appreciation of color and form, for their own sake, made of the Catholic churches of Mexico something unique in the history of art." [4] This Spanish-colonial component of the total Mexican culture is something apart from the typical, orthodox Roman Catholicism.

The third cultural system of Mexico is a French, positivistic, and democratic culture which lasted for some sixty years of the nineteenth century and to a large extent supplanted the Spanish-colonial culture. This French culture, based mainly upon the philosophy of Auguste Comte, has manifested in a thousands ways beginning with the nationalization of church property, the secularization of religion, which became positivistic, and ending with democratic and "enlightened" dictatorial political regimes.

The fourth component-system of the total Mexican culture is that manifested by the Anglo-American system of economic and cultural values, which modified the French and other cultural systems and was articulated especially in the forms of economic organization and the material aspects of living. In the colonial period, Mexico was dominated by "the Spanish-Catholic religious passion," in the nineteenth century by the French "political passion," and at the end of that century by the "economic passion" and the "economic democracy" of Bentham, Mill, Jevons, Marshall, Taussig, and others. The period of the Diaz dictatorship was the golden age of American and British capitalists, as well as of industrial progress as the main instrument of social progress.

Finally, the fifth component of the total Mexican culture is the contemporary Mexican culture. It represents a sort of combination of the intuitive (Bergson), phenomenological, and axiological philosophy of Husserl, Max Scheler, and Hartmann—not to mention Mexico's own notable non-positivistic philosophers—with Anglo-American democracy and technology and Soviet Russian and Marxian economic, political and social values. The fusion of these elements into the passionate, thoroughly "aesthetic," deeply religious—and at the same time Marxian—scientific and economic culture is clearly expressed in the frescoes of Orosco and Rivera. This fifth new culture is not quite integrated as yet; it is still in the process of becoming, but it is already the most important component of the total Mexican culture.

This summary gives an idea of how Northrop proceeds in his analysis of culture and how he validates his generalized propositions. Northrop's analysis along these lines is incomparably more factual and convincing than this outline can show.

In a similar manner he analyzes the "free culture" of the United States. Concretely diverse, "the soul of the United States is basically Anglo-American, just as the soul of Mexico is Spanish-American in character." In the total complex and diverse culture of the United States this dominant Anglo-American cultural system is based largely upon the philosophy of John Locke (supplemented by that of David Hume, Bishop Berkeley, and other English empiricists), a philosophy grounded in turn in the science of Galileo, Huygens, and especially Newton's *Principia*. The Declaration of Independence, the Constitution of the United States, the main legal statutes concerning property and other rights, the prevalent conception of the role of government and of the rights of man, all these and many other basic traits and values of the United States culture are almost a verbatim articulation of the principles of Locke's philosophy. So also, essentially, is the economic organization of this country as the "businessman's world." Its economy and ethics are, in a broad sense, the economy of Adam Smith, Malthus, Ricardo and Jevons, in addition to the utilitarian ethics of Jeremy Bentham and John S. Mill, which are a sort of application of Locke's principles to the field of economics and ethics.

Again, the predominant Protestant religion of the country is largely an enunciation of Locke's principles in the realm of religion.

Even such a detail as the policy of this country towards Mexico has consistently been an articulation of Locke's idea that the main function of government is the protection of private property. In accordance with this principle, the United States tried to protect the rights of American corporations that owned almost all of Mexico's oil and other natural resources, by sending a military force into Mexico and protesting against the nationalization of these resources by the Mexican government. The main argument of our Secretaries of State, from the time of Woodrow Wilson's administration through Secretary Cordell Hull, has been that the rights of property are sacred and inviolable, even when such rights rob Mexico's native population of the necessary minimum means of subsistence and of the elementary rights of man and citizen. In brief, the central and largest part of the total culture of the United States has been but a consistent articulation of Galileo's and Newton's mathematics and physics as the foundation of the Lockean philosophy and the philosophical, economic, and ethical principles of other English empiricists, such as David Hume, Bishop Berkeley, Adam Smith, Bentham, J. S. Mill and others.

The elucidation, development, and demonstration of this proposition is brilliantly set forth in one of the very best passages of Northrop's book.

Besides this central cultural system, the total culture of the United States of course contains aspects of several other systems: remnants of Indian pre-colonial culture, the culture of the Aristotelian-Thomist Catholic Church, and the emerging new culture that transcends the Galilean-Newtonian-Lockean culture; it is based on up-to-date natural science and a philosophy grounded in this modern science. So far, however, these have been minor cultural systems, the major one being the Lockean-Protestant-Individualistic-Businessman-Atomistic-Operational cultural system articulated in all compartments of American culture, up to Grant Wood's picture entitled "Daughters of the Revolution," which is an example of Locke's *tabula rasa* of human soul or personality.[5]

In a similar way, though more sketchily, Northrop shows the unique British combination of Richard Hooker's theology and Aristotelian philosophy as to the ends and ideals of government, with John Locke's democracy in relation to the mechanics of government. This "combination of the organic, hierarchical, communal values from the old [medieval order represented by Hooker's theology-philosophy] with the ego-centric, laissez-faire individualistic values from the new [order of Locke and other empiricists] became the accepted practice of the British" and resulted in the typically British "middle course" set by Henry VIII and Elizabeth.[6]

This combination, especially Hooker's old principles, explain the inroads that Marxism and the Labor Party policy have made in recent times, modifying but not radically changing this unique British cultural system.

The philosophy in which Britain [of the war and the post-war period] is believing, notwithstanding the defeat of the Conservative party in 1945, draws more heavily upon Hooker and the Church of England, than upon Locke and the non-Conformists, and incorporates more of Marx and working class socialism than of Bentham and the nineteenth century liberalism. Yet in truth Britain is being guided by both the individualistic and the organic doctrines.[7]

Passing on to German culture, Northrop indicates the basic role played by the German idealistic philosophy of Kant, Fichte, and Hegel in the main cultural system of Germany, in its predominant ethics and mores, in its notion of freedom, in its authoritarian government and in hundreds of other important cultural phenomena.[8]

In the case of Soviet Russia the author shows the decisive role of Marxian philosophy in establishing the basis of contemporary Soviet-Russian culture. "Russia is what it is today not because there was any necessity that it be that way, but largely because, for the reasons indicated [in the analysis], the leaders of the Russian revolution took the speculative philosophical theory of Marx, and by persuasive and forceful means brought others to its acceptance, and built political action and cultural institutions in terms of it." [9] Marxian-Hegelian philosophy (and the natural science in which it is grounded) is the main premise that is now articulated by thousands of ideological, philosophical, religious, political, economic, artistic, and other cultural phenomena of Russia's main cultural system. This Marxian philosophy is the master key to a comprehensive explanation of millions of small and large enigmas of the total Soviet culture.

Besides the cultures of nations, our eminent scholar similarly analyzes the culture of the Roman Catholic Church, especially in the thirteenth and subsequent centuries. In Northrop's analysis the total Roman Catholic culture, in St. Thomas Aquinas' marvelous Christian interpretation, represents the perfect articulation of Greek Aristotelian science and philosophy. St. Thomas succeeded admirably in building the whole, consistent world-view on Aristotle's science (and philosophy) whereas, for instance, John Locke partially failed as the philosopher of Newtonian science and through this failure has been responsible for many subsequent difficulties and perplexities confronting Western culture. The synthesis of St. Thomas also explains the recent revival of Thomism and Neo-Scholastic philosophies in Europe, as well as in the United States and the Americas (through Robert M. Hutchins and others). Thomist and Neo-Catholic philosophy, although antiquated by the enormous progress made by post-Aristotelian natural science, is still more consistent than the philosophy of various epigoni of Lockean and other empiricist philosophies; the latter have failed to give as marvelous a synthesis of Newtonian and post-Newtonian mathematics and science as Aquinas' synthesis of Aristotelian and Greek science. Almost the whole Roman Catholic culture, beginning with its theology and ending with its cult, economics, and politics, is an articulation of the principles of Aristotelian-Thomistic philosophy.

Having shown the existence of comparatively vast cultural systems in the total cultures of separate nations or in the Roman Catholic Church, Northrop goes farther and "unearths" *the two most vast cultural systems or supersystems: one based upon "scientific" or "theoretic," the other upon "aesthetic" or "intuitional," components. The first is dominant in the West's culture; the second in that of the East.*

The aesthetic or intuitional cognition or knowledge is derived from, and refers to, objects directly arrived at through experience, the "pure facts" like "blue" or "love" or any other "pure experience" unmediated by any concepts, and properly knowable only to a person who has such an experience. "Blue" is inaccessible to the blind; the music of Beethoven remains unknown to the deaf; at best they can only have a substitute diagram for these. A person who never experiences love or hate remains ignorant of these emotions. All phenomena belonging to this category of the immediately sensed, perceived, apprehended, experienced phenomena make up the aesthetic continuum or aesthetic component in the nature of things or reality. Any knowledge or notion derived in this direct, intuitive way is the aesthetic or intuitive component in knowledge or cognition. The aesthetic continuum itself has two main forms: (a) the *differentiated*, like "blue," "soft," "lovely," "warm," or "cheerful," when some of the infinite properties of the undifferentiated continuum are specifically distinguished, "picked up," or differentiated by direct intuition as "pure fact"; (b) *undifferentiated* aesthetic continuum, meaning the primeval aesthetic continuum out of which arises any directly sensed differentiation. It pervades all the differentiated "aesthetic phenomena." It is neither *A* nor non-*A*, neither this nor that; at the same time it is the *coincidentia oppositorum* that potentially embraces *A* as well as non-*A*. This undifferentiated aesthetic continuum is the Jen in Confucianism, Tao in Taoism, Nirvana in Buddhism, Brahman, Atman or Chit in Hinduism; the "Divine Nothing" of true mystics, the "Infinite Manifold," the *coincidentia oppositorum* and the Supra-essence of St. Augustine, Pseudo-Dionysius, J. S. Erigena, Nicolas of Cusa, and of all true mystics. It cannot be expressed in words. It cannot be described by any concepts or terms. It is truly ineffable. It can be experienced directly only as a "pure fact" through the specific technique of the Yogi or of the true mystics. It cannot be conceptualized and analyzed scientifically.

In this undifferentiated form the aesthetic aspect of the nature of things has been intuited or immediately apprehended in all its all-embracing indeterminateness, mainly in the Oriental cultures of China, India, and other Buddhist or Jainist cultures. And these cultures have been largely built on this aesthetic—differentiated and undifferentiated—continuum and the aesthetic component of human knowledge.

Theoretic or scientific knowledge, concept, or cognition is indirectly derived from, and refers to, the component in the nature of things that is never presented as "pure experience." It is postulated as an *a priori* hypothesis and is in part and indirectly verified *a posteriori* through experimentally checked deductive consequences. Any scientific theory, according to Northrop, always asserts more than has been obtained through observation and is never verified directly. To be scientific means, paradoxically, to be metaphysical, to transcend the immediately given experience. The theoretic or scientific component in reality or in the nature of things is therefore quite different from the aesthetic component: the theoretic component is never immediately sensed, perceived, intuited, or apprehended, but is always postulated, mathematically designated, and indirectly verified through its experimentally checked deductive consequences. Chairs, tables, or any three-dimensional objects, electrons, molecules, universals—everything up to God the Father—belong to the theoretical component in the nature of things. Not one of them is immediately sensed, perceived, or apprehended.

The two components of the nature of things or of reality are thus quite different from one another, but they are mutually supplementary. Each presents its own "aspect" of the nature of things, quite different from the other, but equally real and mutually supplementary. As a matter of fact, an adequate knowledge of anything requires its "epistemic correlation"—namely, a valid correlation between the aesthetic component and the respective theoretic component. Together they give an adequate knowledge of the nature of things. Separately they give at best only a one-sided comprehension or apprehension of things, either purely "aesthetic" or purely "theoretic." Thus, what is "aesthetically" sensed as "sound" is theoretically a "vibration of air waves"; the "aesthetically perceived" color "blue" is theoretically either a vibration of ether waves of a certain length or of light waves of a certain spectral composition. An electron cannot be immediately observed. It is an *a priori,* postulated hypothesis. However, its reality and postulated properties can be experimentally verified through the Wilson cloud chamber where, on the chamber's fuzzy aesthetic continuum, the electrons appear as "flashes" that follow one another in a certain order deductively calculated from the postulated hypothesis. The correspondence between the actual flashes and the calculated ones is an indirect, experimental confirmation of the theoretically postulated hypothesis of electrons. Aesthetic "flashes" and theoretic "electrons" thus are epistemically correlated and together give a "two-sided," adequate cognition of the nature of electrons.[10]

Having elucidated the aesthetic and theoretic kinds of knowledge and components in the nature of things and their epistemic correlation, Northrop proceeds to show that the Orient's total culture, especially that of China and India, has been dominated mainly by the vast aesthetic cultural supersystem that is based upon aesthetic or intuitional apprehension. On the other hand, the total Western culture has been dominated by the vastest scientific cultural supersystem, based upon the theoretic or scientific (postulational) knowledge. Several theoretic cultural systems have played the role of minor systems in the culture of the East, and several minor aesthetic cultural systems have existed in the West's culture; but they are minor currents in these predominantly aesthetic and theoretic cultures.

The main Oriental religions and ethics, such as Confucianism, Taoism, Hinduism, Jainism, with their absolutely indeterminate "aesthetic continuum" of Jen, Tao, Brahman, or "empty Nirvana"; the Chinese, Hindu, and Buddhist fine arts, especially painting; their psychology, with its indeterminate "perhaps" or "maybe"; the tolerance of these religions and ethics towards other religions and ethics as "differentiations" of the undifferentiated aesthetic continuum; their laws and even many forms of their economic and political processes; these and thousands of other phenomena are but articulations of the basic "aesthetic component" that lies at the foundation of these cultures.

On the other hand, the remarkable progress of Western science and technology; the determinate, theistic, and deistic Catholic and Protestant religions, supplemented by the Jewish and the Mohammedan, all claiming the monopolistic truth and all being theoretically postulated and indirectly rationalized; the Western determinate—rational—ethics and law; the Western fine arts, which are mainly a means to convey some theoretically conceived ideas and values; the predominant Western philosophy—Thomistic Aristotelianism, Cartesian rationalism, Lockean-Humean empiricism, Kantian criticism, Fichtean ethical idealism, Comtian-Spencerian positivism, Hegelian-Marxian dialectic; these and thousands of other cultural phenomena of the West are but the articulations of the theoretic component on which they are based.

Northrop's development and demonstration of this thesis, especially in the field of Western and Eastern fine arts, is brilliant. He does not deny that the total Eastern and the total Western cultures each exhibit enormous diversity and self-evident contrasts. Nevertheless, the more contrasting the various parts of each culture are, the more similar and congenial they are in the basic aesthetic or theoretic components that permeate all parts of each culture.

The purpose of developing these theories is to find out whether diverse cultures are only diverse or mutually contradictory; and, if they are conflicting, what is the scientific way of resolving the conflicts between the Anglo-American and the Latin-American (specifically Mexican) cultures; between the "capitalist" and "communist" societies; between the Lockean liberal, political democracies and the Marxian socio-economic democracies; between Roman Catholicism and Protestantism; and especially, and most of all, between East and West.

Since all the main cultural systems and social institutions are based upon their respective philosophies, which in their turn are grounded in their respective states of science (and/or aesthetic apprehension), the most effective way of solving the conflicts, according to Northrop, is to eliminate the apparent or real contradiction between the mathematical and natural science of conflicting cultures and societies; and then the conflict between the basic philosophies, grounded in the different natural science of the conflicting cultural systems and institutions. When the conflict between these true foundations of the antagonistic cultural systems is removed, these cultures and institutions become mutually compatible and harmonious. Then peaceful coexistence, co-operation and mutual supplementation replace the conflict and struggle between the cultural systems and their human societies. In brief, when the scientific-aesthetic-philosophical foundations of previously incompatible cultural systems become compatible, then the cultural systems, their social institutions, and their human groups also become compatible.

The transcendence of the conflict of the scientific-aesthetic-philosophical principles can be achieved only through removing their merely apparent contradiction or, when they are really incompatible, through new, more adequate, more embracing, scientific-aesthetic-philosophical principles which transcend both the conflicting science and philosophy, being freer from errors and one-sidedness and representing a valid synthesis of the truth and value of both competitors. More specifically, insofar as the conflict of the predominantly aesthetic culture of the East and of the preponderantly theoretic culture of the West is the main conflict of our time, and insofar as the science and philosophy of either of these cultures is one-sided and inadequate, the proposed epistemic correlation of the aesthetic and theoretic components into a mutually supplementing unity is the looked-for solution of the problem. Knowledge and apprehension based upon the correctly correlated aesthetic and theoretic components are obviously more adequate than those based on only one of these principles.

A philosophy and culture built on the epistemic correlation of both components removes the contradiction of East and West, of Soviet Russia and the Lockean democracies, of the United States and the Latin-American cultures. Each culture and society gains immeasurably and enriches itself by being supplemented by the harmoniously infused different cultural values. Thus, for instance, the West can enrich itself enormously by taking in the Eastern aesthetic component as it appears in the Oriental religions, fine arts, the spirit of tolerance, the general aesthetic apprehension, and especially the specific immediate intuition of the undifferentiated aesthetic continuum exemplified in the technical experience of the Yoga, Zen Buddhism, and so on. On the other hand, the East can benefit immeasurably by taking in Western science, technology, and other theoretic values of the predominantly scientific Western culture. The epistemic unification of both components is permitted to both parties and can be achieved without loss of dignity or any real value derived from its present one-sided culture and way of life. In a similar way the basic conflicts of our time can be solved. In each case the knowledge, the apprehension, the philosophy, and finally the cultural system erected upon the foundations of both components are more valid, more adequate, more perfect, beautiful and transcending than those based upon only one of the two components.

The author elucidates these ideas in considerable detail and applies them to the concrete solution of most of the important conflicts of our time.

Such are the leading ideas of Northrop's philosophy of history and sociology of culture. His book contains several other important theories in the field of scientific methodology, philosophy, and epistemology. But since these theories do not directly concern our main problem, we can now pass them by without discussion. Some of these ideas, however, will be mentioned in Part Two.

IX

Alfred L. Kroeber

Born in 1876 at Hoboken, New Jersey, Alfred L. Kroeber received his A.B., A.M., and Ph.D. degrees at Columbia University and an Honorary Sc.D. at Yale University. He taught English and anthropology at Columbia University and participated in several anthropological expeditions. He became a full professor of anthropology at the University of California, where he was also curator and director of the Anthropological Museum. He is the author of several books in the field of anthropology: *Zuni Kin and Clan* (1917), *Peoples of the Philippines* (1919), *Anthropology* (1923), *Handbook of the Indians of California* (1925), *Cultural and Natural Areas of Native North America* (1939), *Peruvian Archeology in 1942* (1944), and *Configurations of Culture Growth* (1944).

For our purposes this last work is the most important. The main task of Kroeber's study is to investigate the manner in which the high-level cultures change. Does their creativity proceed steadily or by bursts, now rising and now declining? Is their creativity manifested simultaneously in all fields of cultural activity or only in some? Do different cultures show themselves creative (or uncreative) in the same, or in different, fields? Do they have only one or several creative growths and declines? What are the durations of the periods of blossoming and of sterility? How and why do the highest levels of cultures develop? Do cultures die? What are the factors that determine the cultures' flowering and aridity? Are these factors inherent in the culture or external to it? Do the peaks of creativity come early or toward the end, or is the growth curve symmetrical? Such, in brief, are the main problems with which the volume deals.

The answers to these questions are sought inductively, through an analysis of the configurations of growth—in time, space, and degree of achievement—of philosophy, science, philology, sculpture, painting, drama, literature, music, and the state organization and power of ancient Egypt, India, China, Japan, Iran and of the Arab-Muslim, Graeco-Roman-Byzantine and Hebrew cultures, and of the separate Western countries—France, Germany, Italy, Spain, England, the Netherlands, Switzerland, the Scandinavian peoples, Russia, Poland, other Slavic peoples, and finally, the United States of America.

This brief enumeration indicates the enormous field covered. The specific procedure used to note and even roughly "measure" the changes in culture patterns for each country is to study the number and rank of men of creative genius. Insofar as an important pattern in any field of culture is most fully expressed through the men of genius, the appearance of a galaxy of creative geniuses of the first rank at one period, and their quantitative and qualitative decline at another period, can be taken as a good index of the flowering and decline of creativity in a given cultural compartment for the periods considered.

"As a quasi-objective mechanism for defining [the time-space configurations of part of the culture-patterns] I have used the roster of genius as generally accepted in dated history: individuals are dealt with, but not as an end: they are no longer personalities, but measures of culture growth." They are viewed merely as "the indicators of realization of coherent growths of cultural value" or as "indicators of cultural phenomena . . . not as agents or even as if they were agents. . . .[1] My rating of genius and values . . . is in the main the currently conventional one: I have followed the books, and their consensus is fairly close."[2]

In accordance with this material and procedure, Kroeber's analysis opens with "philosophy," beginning with the Greeks. Kroeber compiles a list of all the main Greek philosophers, carefully noting the years of their life spans and the place of their births. Accepting the prevalent evaluation of the rank

of the philosophers he sums up the main creative movements
in the life history of Greek philosophy as follows:

> In Greek philosophy, two grand divisions must be distinguished:
> a productive period, little more than three centuries long; and a period
> of essentially non-productive continuation, which is of indefinite dura-
> tion. The productive period . . . runs from 585 to about 270, when
> the Stoic, Epicurean, and Sceptic doctrines had taken shape. The
> culmination is universally set with Plato and Aristotle, and may for
> convenience be put at 350, when both were alive and adult. Within
> fifty years of Aristotle's death, nothing new was any longer being
> produced in Greek philosophy, even by able men. The patterns which
> it had developed were evidently exhausted.

"They merely continued to be refilled, in more or less new
combinations, thereafter" [3] until the last school of philosophy
at Athens was closed by Justinian in 529. Thus we have here
one of the skew curves that are fairly typical for many creative movements: three centuries of rising development followed by eight of decline and final extinction. "An activity
begins, develops, reaches a peak, begins to decline, and there
freezes. Thereafter it may continue indefinitely with imitation, repetition, or reduction" in an institutionalized form, or
otherwise, as long as the culture that produced it survives.[4]

Kroeber goes on to note several details of the whole process,
up to its overlapping with a different "reorientation movement"
of the Neo-Pythagoreans, Gnostics, Neo-Platonists, all eventually merging into a cosmopolitan Christian Medieval philosophy.

The foregoing gives an idea of how this eminent anthropologist proceeds to observe the creative ups and downs,
growths and declines, integrations and disintegrations, stag-
nations and epigonic inertia of the life-movement of Greek
philosophy from its beginning to its end.

In a similar manner he follows the configurations of growth,
fluctuation, and decline of Christian and non-Christian "later
Mediterranean," Arab-Muslim, Occidental—Medieval and
Modern—philosophy (German, French, Italian, English,
Dutch), and of the Indian and Chinese philosophies. At the
end of these explorations he sums up the significant conclu-

sions concerning the configurations of growth and decline of philosophical creativity generally, and its particular forms specifically. Here are some of these conclusions.

The contents of no two philosophic growths are ever the same.

Most of the cultures under consideration have produced their important philosophies in two growths or separate movements. In some of these cultures (the Greek and Chinese, for instance) the first blossoming of philosophy was the greater while in others (the Occidental and Arabic, for instance) the second wave was more creative.

In some cultures philosophy was born and moved within the main religion; in others, philosophy grew up without a close tie with religion or with very loose ties.

Equally diverse is the relation of philosophy to science. In some cultures, for instance the Arabic-Muslim, a philosopher was at the same time a scientist and vice versa; in other cultures, like the Chinese, Indian, and the Medieval Occidental, philosophy emerged and grew without a close tie with science, because science remained as yet undeveloped when important philosophical systems had already appeared. In other words, in some cultures the emergence of important philosophical systems is preceded by the development of science; in others both emerge together; in still others, great philosophical systems emerged and grew before science was developed.[5]

As to the duration of the creative pulse, it also varies, from the most frequent duration of some 300 years to as long as 400 or as short as 150 years.[6]

The culmination of the growth sometimes falls near the end of the growth period, sometimes early in the second half.

The data show the rarity and spottiness of philosophical creativeness, and the spottiness is not random but highly concentrated. Philosophical creativeness in the five main cultures studied flourished during little more than a third of the duration of the civilizations in which it had become established as an activity. And it occurred in only a small fraction of the area of these civilizations: early Chinese philosophy flourished only in northeastern China; the Hindu, in the Ganges Valley and later on in southern India; Greek philosophy was mainly Ionic. Even in these fractions of areas, philosophy was blossoming in one place while it was inactive or quiescent in another. Considering further that many great cultures such as Egypt, Mesopotamia, Persia, Japan, not to mention a multitude of lesser cultures or civilizations, have not produced any truly significant philosophy, the rarity and spottiness of philosophical creativity becomes striking.

It is significant that the great philosophies emerged simultaneously, about 600 B.C., in three of the five cultures—the Chinese, Indian, and Greek. Another moment of philosophical creativity occurred at about the same time, from 1050 to 1200, in three cultures—the Chinese Neo-Confucian, Christian Scholastic, and Arabic.

Why this is so, and what the factors are that determine philosophical creativity, remains an enigma. Negatively we can assert that neither a certain civilization's general flourishing state, nor its political power and economic prosperity, is enough to produce a great philosophy. The same is true of a flourishing condition of religion or science. In a number of cases when the cultures considered passed from lesser to greater economic prosperity, from lesser to greater political power, from a less to a more scientific or religious state, no signs of philosophical creativity are observed. The significant factors are seemingly internal to the respective culture and the philosophy itself. Exactly what they are still remains in the dark. They are superpersonal and somehow related to "cultural energy." But again the nature and the operation of this energy are as yet little known and do not, at present, allow more precise specification.[7]

In a similar way Kroeber proceeds to study the dynamics of creativity in *science* in the same main cultures; then in *philology, sculpture, painting, drama, literature,* and *music.* Finally, he studies separately the movement of creativity in all these classes of cultural phenomena in *each of the nations studied.* This last investigation gives us the dynamics of the intellectual, philosophic, and aesthetic creativity of Egypt, China, Japan, India, Greece, Rome, the Near East, Islam, and the main Western countries, including Russia and Scandinavia, the Jews, and the West as a whole. A study of the cultural growth of nations permits grasping the typical constellations of these classes of cultural phenomena within one nation, and their change in the course of time.[8]

Egyptian civilization uniquely rose and fell at least four times within the same patterned frame before it exhausted itself. This shows, among other things (contrary to Danilevsky, Spengler, and Toynbee), that a given civilization can have more than one period of blossoming and decline. Of 2,790 years, about 64 percent were reasonably successful—prosperous and politically satisfactory. In many cases, creativity paralleled political and economic prosperity in several fields of culture; but this did not always happen, and in the case of science and literature the non-synchronicity of economico-political progress and flare-ups of scientific-literary creativity are fairly conspicuous.

China had two big creative pulses; Japan had four; India, two; the Graeco-Roman-Byzantine culture had several; the Arabic, one big one; France, three; England, three; and Germany, four. In most of these instances, the economico-political prosperity peaks did not notably coincide with the peaks of cultural creativity.[9]

Passing by other conclusions arrived at by Kroeber in this part of the study, we must now sum up the main results of his extensive and scholarly analysis of the hows and whys of change in culture or civilization.

(1) There is no universal uniformity dictating that every culture must develop into the high-level culture with master patterns of this or that cultural value. Only a very limited number of cultures have developed such patterns.

(2) There is not sufficient evidence "of any true law in the phenomena dealt with; nothing cyclical, regularly repetitive, or necessary."

(3) There is no uniformity decreeing that every culture, having once flowered, must wither without chance of revival.

(4) Each major culture displays "the existence of certain fundamental patterns characteristic" to it. The number of such "high-value culture patterns" is very limited. They occur only rarely, in a few cultures only, have a limited life-span, and are concentrated in time and space, with a usually continuous rise and fall of value.[10]

(5) The life-span or duration of these "high-value culture patterns" seems to be shorter than that of "low-grade culture patterns," that can go on with much less change and for a much longer time.[11]

(6) The average duration of the growth and blossoming of these patterns fluctuates greatly, from a few decades to a few centuries, depending upon the class of cultural phenomena and their constellation.

(7) The duration of a vaster (embracing) pattern tends to be longer and more continuous than that of a narrower sub-pattern, a part of the vaster one.[12]

(8) Though all the reasons for this transience of the high-value culture patterns are far from clear, one is patent: it is inherent in or immanent to the pattern. To become and to stay "a high-quality pattern" it has to be selective, choosing among a number of potentialities. It must also specialize, adopting certain values and forms and rejecting others. Having become specialized, the high-value pattern either has to run through the limited number of its variations or engage in a conflict with the rest of the culture, or both. Having run through all its possible variations, the pattern exhausts its potentialities and either dies or becomes aridly repetitive and ossifies. In either case its creative life comes to an end. In other cases the high-value pattern is smashed by the rest of the culture with which it is in conflict. Often the pattern's creative life comes to an end in both ways. In other words, the main reason for the limited life-span of the high-value patterns is inherent in or immanent to them and is due to the limited possibilities of their variation and to their "saturation"

and exhaustion in the course of time. "The pattern can be said to have fulfilled itself when its opportunities or possibilities have been exhausted." [13] In all these cases the pattern disintegrates and its creative career ends.

(9) As a detail, the high-value patterns of contemporary philosophy or fine arts have, since 1880 and more strongly since 1900, displayed signs of creative exhaustion of their possibilities and growing dissolution of their patterns: "jagged rhythms and dissonance in music, free verse in poetry, plotless novels, cubism, abstractionism, and surrealism in sculpture and painting." "Only science and wealth-production probably are holding up their heads." However, until science becomes sterile and wealth-production shrinks, it would be rash to predict the impending death of Western culture.[14] Revolt against the preceding "classical" patterns, whether Kantian philosophy, or Beethoven's music, or Goethe's style of writing, is due to the exhaustion of the possibilities of these patterns. Having been exhausted, their continuation inevitably results in an ever-increasing sterile and epigonic repetitiveness, which is deadly in its uncreativeness. Revolt against such "dead corpses," with an attempt to remove them to the morgue of history and to replace them by some new patterns, is comprehensible and excusable. In other cases these outlived patterns become sterile and quietly die without being overthrown by any revolt.

(10) In the life-course of a high-value pattern there is now only one "pulse" or blossoming, now two, now three, and once in a while even a greater number of "pulses" or flowerings, with periods of "lulls" or creative rests in between. Sometimes the first "pulse" is the greatest creatively, sometimes the second, sometimes even the third. In brief, there is no uniform evidence that all "master patterns" of culture blossom only once, nor that they all have the same number of creative pulses.[15]

(11) The duration of the pattern's growth and blossoming is ordinarily shorter than that of the decline and "petrifac-

tion." Similarly, the total duration of all creative pulses in the total life-history of the pattern is usually shorter than the total duration of all the barren "lulls" in the total existence of the pattern.

(12) The profiles of the patterns' growth curve, as well as the points of culmination, vary: they are sometimes symmetrical, but more frequently asymmetrical, with the culmination peaks at times early, at other times late in the configuration. In other words, there is no "normal form of time-quality curve in florescences." [16]

(13) In studying the life-curve of the pattern, one should distinguish the transformations, pulses, and lulls of the same pattern from those of different patterns often criss-crossing with one another. Sometimes it is difficult to decide whether we deal with the changes of one and the same pattern or with criss-cross pulses and lulls of different patterns. As a rule, all uni-lingual, uni-national patterns and the patterns with one main culmination are the changes within one and the same pattern. Likewise, the patterns with one "basic idea-system" (religious or other) that is only sketchily developed in the first phase and more fully developed in the subsequent phases ordinarily belong to one and the same pattern-system when they have such pulses and lulls. The presence of the "basic idea-system," articulated in all pulses and lulls, is a sufficient guarantee of that. [17]

(14) Practically all national cultures studied are deficient in creativity in one or more fields of culture; none is encyclopedically creative. Thus the cultures of Egypt, Mesopotamia, Rome, Japan, and Renaissance Europe were uncreative in philosophy. So was Arabic civilization in sculpture. Rome, Medieval Europe, Japan (excepting in algebra), and largely China, were uncreative in science. The economic and political blossoming of Greece, Germany, and Italy was absent during most of the cultural florescences of these countries; and so on. [18]

Since cultural florescence occurs in some fields of culture, while creativity in other fields is absent, this means that cultural creativities in two different fields are hardly causally or functionally connected with one another. Such a conclusion openly contradicts the theories of the total integration of each culture, explicitly and implicitly claimed by the so-called "functional sociologists and anthropologists" and "the total integralists" of culture.[19]

(15) Studying the relationship of the florescence of *sculpture* and *painting*—generally considered particularly close to each other—Kroeber finds that, out of thirteen instances, sculpture develops (in the same nation) earlier than painting five times, simultaneously twice, later twice; and four times one or the other is lacking. Similarly, the relationship between *philosophical and scientific florescences* also happens to be far from close. Twice—in China and India—great philosophical systems appeared before any tangible scientific progress was made, and subsequently scientific progress lagged behind that of philosophical creativeness in these cultures. In Greece, and in a few other instances, philosophy and science emerged together, flourished together for some time, and eventually separated from one another and followed different courses in their creative pulsations. In most of these cases the course of scientific creativity happened to be more continuous and of a longer duration than that of philosophical creativity. Generally, where (as in India and Medieval Europe) philosophy develops into religion or is closely connected with it, it is likely somewhat to impede scientific progress; therefore the courses of their "ups and downs" are likely to be non-parallel. Where philosophy is "naturalistic," does not develop into religion, and remains independent of it, there is a closer alliance between philosophy and science and they "step together" more frequently.[20]

(16) A similar lack of close interdependence is shown *between political-economic growth and the florescence of other cultural activities*. First there were nations (the Mongols, Turks, Lithuanians, Macedonians, Achaemenians and Sassanian Iranians—except for the Iranian creativity in religion)

that built powerful empires without either simultaneously or generally contributing much to most fields of culture. They represent what Danilevsky calls "the negative agencies of history." On the other hand several nations, like Germany in its earlier cultural florescences, or Renaissance Italy, or even Greece, had their cultural florescences in a state of political weakness, disintegration or unintegration. Some others showed their cultural creativity in certain fields even after losing their political independence. The pre-Islamic poetry of Arabia; Polish literature and music of the first part of the nineteenth century; Chinese florescence about 200 A.D.; the cultural creativity of Iran after it lost its independence to the Arabs and that of the Jews after they lost their "state"—these are examples. However, such a negative relationship between politico-economic and cultural creativity is less frequent than either a neutral or positive relationship between these variables.[21] In the history of Egypt and Japan, both rise and fall more or less together; in the history of China, India, and most of the Occidental countries, they move together only partially; finally, in the history of Sweden, Germany, Italy, and partly in that of the U.S.A., the relationship is rather negative. Of various cultural activities, scientific florescence seems to go most closely with politico-economic florescences.[22] "After all, peace, population and wealth alone do not produce great achievement; as second century Rome shows. . . . Ethnic or national energy and higher cultural energy tend to be related, but the relationship is not complete."[23]

(17) Other conditions being equal, the richer the item-content of a culture the greater the chance of creating a more important qualitative pattern, or cultural value. Cultures that are poor in content have a lesser chance of such creativity. Hence, the importance of cross-fertilization of one culture by another. If the cross-fertilizing culture (such as Buddhism imported into Chinese culture) is congenial and if the fertilized culture can "digest" and mold the imported elements into its own pattern, such an enrichment usually stimulates creativity. If these conditions are lacking, however,

an increase of the content-items of a given culture may lead instead to cultural "indigestion," to a disintegration and decline of creativity. The same decline or "pseudomorphosis," as Spengler calls it, of culture can take place when the foreign culture is too overwhelming and too rich in its content (as well as in its patterns). This results in a suppression of the native culture or, in Danilevsky's terms, it turns the native culture into a mere means for the grafted foreign culture.[24]

(18) Kroeber does not study religious creativity as he does the fine arts, science, philosophy, and to some extent politico-economic creativities, but in passing he does make several observations. One is that within the same national culture

> . . . It seems normally to be religion which first reaches its chief climax, and then the aesthetic and intellectual (scientific and philosophical) activities as they free themselves from religion. . . . I cannot think of a single people which first evolved a high science, philosophy, or art, and thereafter a religious pattern which was important intrinsically and institutionally; at any rate, not within the bounds of duration of what we customarily consider civilization.[25]

Thus a definite time order of the blossoming of these cultural classes is stated here: first come religious, then aesthetic-scientific-philosophical florescences. This "uniformity" does not preclude the development first of a scientific, aesthetic, or philosophical creativity in the peoples who do not develop any important religion afterwards; such cases, however, are comparatively rare.

Another of Kroeber's observations is that *religion often produces its own philosophy and its own fine arts*. Europe's High Medieval philosophy, architecture, sculpture, and literature, culminating in Dante, are examples of this. Something similar happened in the life-course of India, the Islamic cultures and so on. (Compare my Ideational art and philosophy.)

The third observation is that *a philosophy or art completely dominated by religion is not likely to be the highest or greatest form of philosophical or aesthetic creativity*. Only when these acquire some degree of autonomy from religious control and become secular to a degree, do they seemingly reach the culmination point. "In the Italian Renaissance this process is clearly evident. Raphael, Leonardo, Michelangelo, represent at once the climax and the moment of liberation. So, correspondingly, does Phidias." So also did Western music reach its peak at a similar point, when it became considerably liberated from religious control. The same is true of the culmination points of the pictive art in Japan and China in its relationship to Buddhist control. (Compare my Idealistic art and philosophy.)

However, *when this liberation is complete and the art (or philosophy) becomes completely secular and usually quite profane, the decline of creativity sets forth.* "Room is made for the shallow and the frivolous, for the purely formal and precious, and decline sets in." (Compare my overripe Sensate art and philosophy.)

The same is true of philosophy and, in a few cultures, even of science. Though these often flourish quite independent of religion, now and then these activities begin more or less to decline and this leads, as in the late Graeco-Roman world, to a revival of religious philosophy and then of religion.[26]

(19) As to the *tempo* of the change, or of the progress of growth, contrary to the prevalent opinion of its acceleration, "the data indicate rather conclusively that the rate has not gained in speed." "So far as high quality growths are concerned, they seem to take about as long now as they did one or two thousand years ago." Perhaps in regard to content-items the belief in acceleration is valid—"information material" may now be produced faster—but it is wrong insofar as the high forms or great cultural patterns are concerned.

The extraordinarily long, continuous, and therefore possibly slow tempo of Hindu culture change is to be noted as an additional detail. "In the face of the eternal verities with which the Hindu is preoccupied, time perspective is bound to be a rather trivial consideration." [27]

(20) "Owing to the accidents of where and on whom civilization alights" there have been many areas or peoples uncreative in culture generally, or creative only in regard to the

lesser values, or actually retarded in cultural creativity. From the standpoint of total culture-history all the populations of Europe belong to the retarded group: none of them participated with distinction until less than three thousand years ago; most, except the Greeks and Romans, entered the stage of cultural creativity much later, only from 1500 to 1000 years ago; finally, the marginal peoples of the north and east of Europe began to contribute the highest cultural values only some two or three centuries ago.[28]

(21) The insular cultures of the East Indies, Japan, and Great Britain show some peculiarities of culture growth common to all three cultures. (a) They are all somewhat backward or late in becoming civilized. (b) Their cultures are dependent upon and derived from the continental cultures of India (in the case of the East Indies), China (for Japan), and Europe (for Britain). Only after 1550, possibly, did Britain cease to be backward in Western cultural creativity. (c) The comparatively isolated insular position of the East Indies and Japan (but not of Britain) is possibly responsible for the leveled character of the configuration of their culture-dynamics: it is comparatively free from sharp ups and downs.[29]

(22) By studying the culture growth in space, *its two different types of expansion or diffusion are noticeable; one from the center onward, the other from the periphery toward the center.* The first type is more frequent than the second. The second, originating at the periphery, happens when a geographically marginal part of a given culture is exposed to cross-fertilization or stimulation by another culture. The time precedence of Ionian creativity, compared with that of the Greek mainland, in Greek philosophy, sculpture, painting, literature, and possibly music, is an example. It was only in the fifth century B.C. that the mainland of Greece began to participate in the cultural creativity of Greece, whereas Ionia was already active in the sixth century. This inward diffusion continued up to about 330 B.C. After the Macedonian conquest of the East the opposite process took place: Greek cul-

ture diffused outwards from its center, over the non-Greek countries and peoples. One result was a shift in the leadership in the arts and sciences from Athens to Alexandria, from Sparta or Corinth to Antioch or Pergamum. This diffusion continued through Rome and the Latin populations of Italy. Later on, however, "Italy and the Western provinces, which had entered Graeco-Roman civilization late, were also the first to drop out of it," while it was continued in the East (Byzantium), where the Roman empire as well as the arts and learning were "tolerably maintained" for centuries after the end of the Western Roman empire and Greek arts and learning. By 500 A.D. the shrunken domain of Graeco-Roman civilization was confined to the eastern Mediterranean. Thus, within some thousand years the Greek culture diffused enormously and then shrank enormously. Beginning on a unilingual basis it became bilingual (Graeco-Latin), then multilingual, and then declined again to unilingualism.

In this case we also observe that the territorial expansion of the Classical civilization occurred when the quality of its cultural products was declining. In other words, territorial and political expansion here lagged behind intellectual and aesthetic growth.

In other cases two processes—intellectual and aesthetic growth and politico-territorial expansion—seem to proceed in parallel lines, more or less synchronously. "Normally it would seem, geographical expansion is a symptom of the growth, and contraction, of the decline, of a culture." [30]

(23) Culture as such does not and cannot die. But specific cultures, geographically limited, can and do die, not so much through the death of their populations as through replacement by different cultures. Today there is still a Mohican population, but Mohican culture is already extinct. Language as such does not die; but specific languages do die. Ordinarily the cultures die through being replaced by a "superior" (under the circumstances) culture, regardless whether this superiority is real or apparent. However, it remains unclear why a given culture can resist such smothering by another

culture for a time and then succumb after a certain period. We are equally in the dark about whether cultures can die by themselves, without interference by other cultures. We know that biological organisms die by themselves, though we do not exactly understand why. The destiny of particular cultures may be somewhat similar: they, too, may die by themselves, though this is uncertain and the causes remain still less understandable than in the case of an organism's death.[31]

Kroeber, non-committal on these points, says merely that ". . . cultures do not necessarily either age or progress, but they undergo variations in vigor, originality, and values produced. . . . Fluctuations of cultural vigor are normal." These fluctuations follow from the very nature of the patterned high-grade culture value, with its limited possibilities of variation, with their exhaustion, and with the competitive cultural universe in which they function. However, even on this point he remains non-committal and adds that all these problems "I thus leave unanswered." [32]

(24) Kroeber does not share Spengler's organismic conception of culture with all its parts tightly integrated around the prime symbol, nor does he fully share Spengler's thesis that great cultures can never blend or be transmitted, and that they must die and be superseded by other cultures. Culture material is surely borrowed or transmitted; with it some patterns are also passed from one culture to another. However, in regard to larger master patterns the situation may be different. Without further study of the problem the Spenglerian view can be neither discarded nor accepted.

(25) Kroeber also finds it impossible to accept, without further evidence, the Spenglerian view that all great cultures pass through the same stages.[33] He finds several valid points with which he agrees in the Spenglerian theory, but the above and several other points he finds impossible to accept.

(26) He admits that, as an infrequent phenomenon, a high-value cultural pattern can be and is once in a while fundamentally reconstituted. Having reached a point of saturation

along its previous line of growth, after a pause and through certain efforts, it resumes its growth along somewhat new lines. In other words, it transforms itself into something very different from what it was, without losing its sameness or identity.

Such are Kroeber's main conclusions. They have been intentionally outlined here in some detail for two reasons: to give an adequate idea about the conclusions reached and to show further that an overwhelming majority of these conclusions were also reached—and now and then more precisely formulated—in my own *Social and Cultural Dynamics*. Kroeber and I worked independently at about the same time, as inductively as possible; we had and we have different starting points. The similarity of the conclusions reached reinforces their validity. In subsequent chapters this will be shown more specifically.

X

Albert Schweitzer

Albert Schweitzer was born in Kaisersberg, Alsace, in 1875 and educated at the Universities of Strassburg, Paris, and Berlin. Before 1913 he was curate of St. Nicholas in Strassburg, organist of the Orfeo Catala in Barcelona, and visiting lecturer at several universities. He became a notable theologian, philosopher, and social thinker, as well as one of the greatest authorities on J. S. Bach and a most eminent performer of Bach's organ music. In 1913 he left Europe and founded a hospital at Lambarene in French Equatorial Africa. Since that time, with the exception of a few visits to Europe and one to the United States, he has remained there, working as doctor, missionary, philosopher, thinker, and a foremost ethical leader. Albert Schweitzer is the author of *The Philosophy of Civilization* (1923), *The Quest of the Historical Jesus* (English translation, 1926), *J. S. Bach* (English translation, 1938), *Indian Thought and Its Development* (English translation, 1936), and many other works.

Only a few points of Schweitzer's interpretation of the decay and restoration of civilization or culture (in contrast to Spengler he uses these terms synonymously) directly concern us. The bulk of his books in this field deal with ethics—its nature, its role, and how it is to be realized—rather than strictly with the reasons and ways in which civilizations rise and decline.

(1) Schweitzer's conception of civilization is pre-eminently ethical. "Civilization is twofold in its nature: it realizes itself in the supremacy of reason, first, over the forces of nature, and,

secondly, over the dispositions of men. . ." Moral control over men's dispositions is much more important than control over nature. Mastery over human disposition means ethical mastery in the sense of willing material and spiritual good to mankind, to every individual, even to every living organism. Reverence for life is the essence of this ethical mastery. Such an ethics of unconditional will to live and reverence for life is "the essence of civilization." Its progress is much more important than the material progress of humanity. In its integral sense, civilization means the sum total of all progress in all fields of man's creative activity, insofar as it leads to ethically perfecting the individual and the community.[1] This supremacy of the ethical permeates the whole theory of this eminent moral teacher of humanity.

(2) Understood in this sense, contemporary Western civilization is in a state of deep (though not hopeless) decay. The decline began around the middle of the nineteenth century and has progressed steadily from that time up to the present. In contrast to previous decays of various civilizations, this decay is much more important because "the earth no longer has in reserve, as it had once, gifted peoples as yet unused, who can relieve us and take our place in some distant future as leaders of spiritual life . . . All of them are, like ourselves, diseased, and only as we recover can they recover." In the present crisis it is not just the civilization of this or that people that must be given up as lost, but that of mankind, present and future, if no rebirth takes place within the present civilization.[2]

(3) The main reason for this, as well as for previous decays of civilizations is ethical. "If the ethical foundation is lacking, then civilization collapses, even when in other directions creative and intellectual forces of the strongest nature are at work." [3] More exactly, this ethical foundation is twofold: the ethics itself is based upon the ultimate, directly given, unquestionable will to live as the universal principle, and upon a corresponding *Weltanschauung* or world-view that affirms this universal will to live and interprets the whole world in the light of unconditional reverence for life, whenever and wherever it appears in

whatever form. Correspondingly, the indispensable conditions for the florescence of a civilization are an approximation to the ethics of reverence for life, preached and practised by the respective society, and a corresponding world-philosophy that rationalizes, develops, justifies, demands, and affirms such an ethics in the mentality, behavior, social institutions, and culture of social groups.

Each time in the past when such a world-view and ethics were operative, the society or period flourished. Each time these forces were weak, or were altogether absent, or the world-view was of a wrong kind, the civilization or culture passed through a crisis. Of the past world-philosophies, Taoism, Confucianism, Hinduism, Buddhism in the Orient, and some of the Greek and subsequently European philosophies, only partly met the demand of the ethical world-view; the Stoic philosophy, and especially the rationalist and empirical philosophies of the illuminati and the empirical rationalists of the eighteenth century, met the demand much better than did other world-views. As a result, the Graeco-Roman or Western civilizations of these periods were in comparatively satisfactory shape. Europe of the eighteenth century, permeated by an approximation to the ethics and world-view of life affirmation, was creatively growing and flourishing in almost all fields of Western civilization. Around the middle of the nineteenth century this creative *élan* came to an abrupt end.

The reason for this and for the subsequent "suicide of civilization in progress" was the abandonment of the ethics of life-affirmation and the modern "philosophy's renunciation of her duty." [4] The philosophy of the eighteenth century put forward ethical ideals and tried to embody them in practice by guiding thought and life in general, but in spite of its considerable success this philosophy could not meet acid criticism and succumbed because it too was vulnerable and inadequate. Attempts by Kant, Goethe, Schiller, Fichte, Hegel, and others to provide this tottering building with a new foundation were unsuccessful because their world-views were also vulnerable. As a result "the ethical ideas on which civilization rests have been wandering about the world, poverty stricken and homeless. No theory of the universe has been advanced which can give them a solid foundation. . . . Therefore, instead of being inspired by a profound and powerful spirit of affirmation of the world and life," we are driven hither and thither by fragmentary and superficial ideologies and by fruitless practices. "We have entered a dark journey in a time of darkness." [5]

Several secondary factors, derived from the lack of an ethico-philosophical foundation, have furthered the decay of Western civilization. These are: modern man's fettered economic position; his being overworked and incapable of self-collectedness; an increasing inability to concentrate on meditation; a decrease in creative thinking and an increase in superficial "mob-mindedness," patterned by various "manufacturers of public opinion" (newspapers, etc.); lack of spiritual independence and humanity; development of ethical nihilism and an unethical conception of civilization; [6] greater development of the material, rather than spiritual, part of our civilization; a rapid advance in ethically indifferent knowledge and technology.[7] All these are by-products of the main cause of the decline; but after their emergence they, in their turn, contributed to the suicidal drift of our civilization.

(4) This drift, however, is not absolutely hopeless. It can be stopped and reversed. An accomplishment of that purpose will require building up a new ethico-philosophical foundation for our civilization which can stand any criticism, is "full-proved," logically impeccable, and factually unassailable. Schweitzer's ethics and philosophy of life affirmation is such a foundation.

In surveying the history of ethics and philosophy, beginning with the Taoist, Confucianist, Hinduist and Buddhist "world-views" and ethics, and ending with the modern European-American ones, he finds that all these ethics and world-views were inadequate to different degrees. They all suffered from a dualism between world-view and life-view; between knowing and willing; between the ethical aspirations and the physical world as it is; they all tried to root their ethical values and imperatives in various properties and processes of the external world as it is presented by science. They all failed in this task because "if we take the world as it is, it is impossible to attribute to it a meaning in which the aims and objects of mankind and of individual men have a meaning also. Neither world-and-life-affirmation nor ethics can be founded on what our [scientific] knowledge of the world can tell us about the world." We cannot discover in it anything ethical, any evolution towards ethics, or any value precious for us. Any ascription of such values, ethics, and purposes to the world as it is is just an anthropomorphism based on nothing and rejected by science.[8] The world as it is cannot serve as a basis or support for an ethics of life-affirmation or for any ethics whatsoever. The world as it is is ethically and humanely neutral. Therefore it is hopeless to try building an ethics on the properties of this world, as all preceding ethics and world-views have done. The source of their inadequacy and failure lies in this attempt to bridge the ethics with the external world as it is given by science.

Instead of engaging in this hopeless enterprise, Schweitzer proceeds to build his ethics and world-views from the opposite end. He starts with the most self-evident *will to live* as the ultimate, unquestionable, unmediated, axiomatic experience of everyone living, more axiomatic even than the Cartesian *cogito ergo sum* ("I think, therefore I exist"). On this postulate he builds the whole structure of his ethical and philosophical life-affirmation. "The will to live . . . can feed on the life-forces which it finds in itself." It does not need to know the external world.

The knowledge which I acquire from my will-to-live is richer than that which I win by observation of the world. . . . Why then tune down one's will-to-live to the pitch of one's knowledge of the world, or to undertake the meaningless task of tuning up one's knowledge of the world to the higher pitch of one's will-to-live? The right and obvious course is to let the ideas which are given in our will-to-live be accepted as the higher and decisive kind of knowledge.

Our knowledge of the external world is knowledge from outside, mediated, always incomplete and uncertain. "The knowledge derived from my will-to-live is direct, and takes me back to the mysterious movements of life as it is in itself." The highest knowledge, then, is to know that I must remain true to my will to live, to live life to the full. This will to live and its self-knowledge are dependent on itself alone. Its world-and-life-affirmation carries its meaning in itself and does not depend in any way upon the knowledge of the external world. Even more, the will-to-live, cognizing itself and all the life-forces, penetrates the mysterious, living forces of the universe more easily and reliably than a mere external observation does. In this way the will to live gives us a direct, intuitive understanding of the true reality and builds a more adequate world-view of life-affirmation than does the scientific knowledge of the external world.

"Reverence for life means to be in the grasp of the infinite, inexplicable, forward-urging Will in which all Being is grounded. It rises above all knowledge of things." [9] It leads to a union with the ultimate reality which is "the infinite Being in infinite manifestations." [10]

Thus, this voluntaristic theory starts with a self-evident, voluntaristic will-to-live; from this premise rationally develops the world-and-life-affirmation world-view; and it ends in a non-rational mysticism, because "the rational, when it thinks itself out to a conclusion, passes necessarily over into the non-rational. World-and-life-affirmation and ethics are non-rational." They are not justified (nor can they be justified or rejected) by any knowledge of the nature of the world (from outside). They are perfectly independent of it. "The way to true mysticism leads up through rational thought to deep experience of the world and of our will-to-live. We must all venture once more to be 'thinkers,' so as to reach mysticism, which is the only direct and the only profound world-view. . . ." [11] This world-affirming, ethical, active mysticism has always been hovering as a vision before Western thought, but the latter could never adopt it" because of the wrong way which this thought has always taken at the crucial point. [12]

It is therefore comprehensible why Schweitzer views science and a "scientific philosophy" that studies the world from outside as superfluous for the ethics and philosophy of life-affirmation.

Ethics and aesthetics are not sciences. . . . There is therefore no such thing as a scientific system of ethics; there can only be a thinking one. . . . As to what is good and what is bad . . . no one can speak to his neighbor as an expert. All that one can do is to impart to him so much as one finds in oneself of that which ought to influence everybody, though better thought out perhaps, and stronger and clearer, so that noise has become a musical note. [In ethics] there are only subjective and infinitely various facts to be studied and their mutual connection lies within the mysterious human ego. . . .[13] Ethics have nothing to expect from any theory of knowledge. All attempts to bring ethical and epistemological idealism (or materialism) into connection with one another must be recognized as useless for ethics. Ethics can let space and time go to the devil.[14]

On this point Schweitzer agrees with Spengler, Schubart, Berdyaev, and to some extent Northrop, in stressing the primacy of the living, intuitive, unmediated, direct cognition of the all-pervading infinite Being in its infinite manifestations or "differentiations" versus the mediated, uncertain knowledge from outside where, as in science, the cognizing subject and cognized object are outside one another. On the other hand, he disagrees with Northrop and Kroeber, who consider scientific knowledge and the philosophy grounded in it as the indispensable foundation of civilization and its ethics.

(5) Having cleared the way, Schweitzer, from his axiomatic will to live, deduces the detailed ethics of life-affirmation, life-reverence, love, altruism, and the concrete "imperatives" for ethical conduct and social relationships. He uncompromisingly affirms the ethical protection of any life and any organism, up to the smallest and perhaps even injurious one, resembling the Buddhist ethics in this point.[15]

(6) Since "of all the forces that mould reality, morality is the first and foremost," [16] Schweitzer's "prescription" for a creative rebirth of the civilization of the West and of Mankind consists of elaborating, diffusing, and rooting the ethics and world-view of life-affirmation—grounding it first in individual mentality and conduct and then in social institutions and culture. He does not discuss in detail how the task of interiorizing this ethics and world-view can be successfully accomplished; but he

states categorically that the ethical transfiguration of mankind, individuals, and civilization itself is a condition without which no rebirth is possible. In this point he is the most eminent theoretical, and especially practical, advocate of ethical value as the paramount factor in humanity and civilization. He practices what he preaches. In his total theory of the will to live, he conspicuously exemplifies Spengler's characterization of the Faustian man and culture as voluntaristic par excellence. Moreover, in a sense Schweitzer's whole philosophy is desperately voluntaristic and manifests not only a desperate will to live, but also a desperate will to believe. Finally, Schweitzer's emphasis on the ethical confirms Spengler's view that at the moment of a decay of the civilization, such an emphasis uniformly occurs—the last gasp of the dying civilization.

PART TWO

COMPARATIVE CRITICAL ANALYSIS OF MODERN SOCIAL PHILOSOPHIES

XI

Bases of Criticism: Cultural Systems, Supersystems, and Congeries

I

COMPONENTIAL STRUCTURE OF CULTURAL PHENOMENA

Having outlined the essential propositions of the above theories, we can now subject them to a comparative critical analysis. If this analysis is to be convincing, one must have a fairly clear notion about: (a) the componential structure of cultural phenomena; (b) their ideological, behavioral, and material forms or levels; (c) the main forms of interconnections between cultural phenomena; (d) the difference between cultural congeries and cultural systems; (e) the difference between social and cultural systems; (f) finally, the structure of the total culture of an individual or of a group. These notions must at least be delineated briefly; otherwise no adequate criticism of the above "readings of history" is possible.[1]

In contradistinction to the inorganic phenomena that have only one physico-chemical component, and to organic phenomena that have two components—physical and vital (life) —the cultural or superorganic phenomena have the "immaterial" component of *meaning* (or meaningful value or norm) that is superimposed upon the physical and/or vital components. This component of "meaning" is decisive in determining whether a phenomenon is cultural. Without it there are no cultural phenomena; its presence radically changes the very nature of the inorganic or organic phenomena upon which it is superimposed. Without its meanings, a book—say Plato's *Republic*—simply becomes a physical (paper) object possessed of a certain geometrical form, with certain physical and chemical properties which are noticeable even to mice and which they may nibble now and then. On the other hand, the meaning of Plato's *Republic* can be objectified and "materialized" not only in the paper book, but through quite different physical media, such as phonograph records, or airwaves when it is just read aloud or sung, or other physical "vehicles." Without its meaning the Venus de Milo is just a piece of marble of a certain geometrical form and certain physical properties. Without the component of meaning, there is no difference between *rape, adultery, fornication,* or *lawful sex-relations in marriage,* because the purely physical act of copulation may be identical in all these actions that vary so profoundly in their meaning and sociocultural significance. A physically identical one-thousand-dollar bill handed by *A* to *B* with an identical motion of his hand can socioculturally mean now "a payment of debt," now " a charity contribution," now "bribery," now "investment," now "inducement to murder," and so on. And vice versa, the same meaningful cultural phenomenon can be objectified or externalized through different "material" vehicles or living human agents: hate of *A* for *B* may express itself in thousands of material and organic phenomena, such as annoyance, beating, poisoning, shooting, drowning, frightening, destroying *B's* property, inflicting pain upon his dear ones, etc. Biologically, the organism of a king or dictator may be weaker than that of any of his subjects or victims; socioculturally, the power of an absolute monarch or dictator is incomparably greater than that of his biologically strongest subject. Physically and biologically there are no human organisms that are "kings," "patriarchs," "popes," "generals," "scientists," "laborers," "peasants," "merchants," "prisoners," "criminals," "heroes," "saints," and so on. All these and thousands of other "meanings" are superimposed upon the biological organisms by the sociocultural world or by persons and groups functioning not only as physical objects and biological organisms but mainly as "mindful human personalities," as bearers, creators, and agents of "immaterial" meanings, values, and norms. Thus any phenomenon that is an "incarnation" or "objectification" of mind and meanings superimposed upon its physical and/or biological properties is by definition a sociocultural phenomenon.

Such phenomena are found only in the world of mindful human beings, functioning as meaningful personalities, who meaningfully interact with one another and create, operate, accumulate, and objectify their meanings (or meaningful values and norms) in and through an endless number of "material vehicles"—all physical and biological objects and energies—used for a "materialization" of the "immaterial" meanings, values, and norms of the human mind. Beginning with the simplest tool made, or the simplest path cut in the wilderness, or the simplest hut built, and ending with all the gadgets, machinery, domesticated animals, palaces, cathedrals, universities, museums, all the cities and villages, all the pictures, statues, books, all the energies harnessed by man—beginning with heat and ending with electricity, radio, atomic fission—all this makes the "material culture" of humanity. It is made up of the totality of the bio-physical objects and energies that are used as vehicles for the objectification of meanings, values and norms.

The totality of the "immaterial" meanings-values-norms, not objectified as yet through the material vehicles but known to humanity; the totality of already objectified meanings-values-norms with all their vehicles; finally, the totality of mindful individuals and groups—past and present; these inseparable totalities make up the total sociocultural world, superimposed on mankind's physical and biological worlds.

As has been mentioned before, any meaning that is superimposed on the physical or biological phenomenon radically changes its sociocultural nature. A religious value superimposed on a little stick (*churinga*) transforms it into a sacred totem. When a piece of cloth on a stick becomes a "national flag," it becomes an object for which life is sacrificed. When a sickly organism is declared to be a monarch or "Buddha," it becomes a powerful, sovereign, sacrosanct "Majesty," or "Holiness." When these same monarchs, their organisms remaining unchanged, are stripped of their sociocultural meaning-value, as when they are "deposed" or "overthrown," their power, prestige, functions, social position, and personality change fundamentally; from "Majesty" and "Holiness" they are transformed into despised and hated "outcasts."

Similarly, when an assortment of physical and biological objects, causally unrelated to one another, becomes a vehicle for the same system of meanings-values-norms, *a causal interdependence appears between the physical and biological members of this assortment.* And vice versa: causally connected physical and biological phenomena sometimes become causally unrelated when a meaningful component is superimposed on them. For instance, many persons, ash trays, books, glass flowers, instruments, trucks, buildings, and thousands of other physical objects are not causally connected with one another through their purely physical and biological properties. But when they become the vehicles and agents of a unified system of meanings-values-norms called Harvard University, then a sort of causal interdependence connect them. An important change in one part of Harvard University—the destruction of its main library, for instance, or an important change in its faculty and administration—tangibly influences most of these objects and members. In the case of the destruction of the main library, the enormous expense of restoring it may lead to a notable decrease of the budget for all departments, which in turn may effect a decrease in salaries, in the number and price of ash trays, instruments, paper, books, and diverse objects bought for the departments. When these objects and persons become the agents and vehicles of the same system of meanings and values, then they become causally connected with one another. Otherwise, their causal interdependence, on the basis of purely physical or biological properties, is non-existent. Such, in brief, is the specific componential structure of the sociocultural or superorganic phenomena, clearly distinguishing them from the inorganic and organic phenomena.[2]

2

IDEOLOGICAL, BEHAVIORAL, AND MATERIAL CULTURES OF INDIVIDUALS AND GROUPS

An individual or group can possess a given cultural phenomenon in its *ideological* form only. For instance, an individual or group may well know the ideology—that is the totality of meanings, values, and norms—of Communism or Buddhism without either practicing it or objectifying it through a set of material objects and vehicles, such as a Buddhist Temple with its ritual objects, or a Communist Club with its pictures of Marx, Lenin, and Stalin, and hundreds of other material "vehicles of Communism." Christians who ideologically profess the Sermon on the Mount but do not at all realize it in their behavior or in their material culture are only ideological Christians with respect to the culture enunciated by the Sermon on the Mount. It remains a mere ideology with them and does not penetrate deeper into their behavioral and material culture. The same is true of any cultural phenomenon that functions only on an ideological level without influencing the behavior and the material culture of individuals and groups.

When individuals and groups in their overt actions begin to practice the ideologies of Communism, Christianity, or Buddhism, then the cultures of Communism, Christianity, or Buddhism become *not only ideological but also behavioral.* When the ideologies are also realized through a number of material vehicles that "incarnate" and "objectify" them, Buddhism, Communism, or any other cultural (meaningful) phenomenon assumes "material" form.

Thus *any cultural phenomenon can appear either in a purely ideological form, or in ideological and behavioral, ideological and material, and ideological, behavioral, and material forms.* The purely ideological form is the least strongly rooted and most superficial. When it becomes rooted in the behavior and in the material objects of an individual or group, it becomes more deeply and more strongly grounded than when it remains a mere ideology. As a behavioral and material realization it becomes a factor in molding not only ideas and meanings, but also the overt behavior and the interrelationships of human beings and the physical and biological objects and processes.

To sum up: (1) the totality of meanings, values, norms possessed by individuals or groups makes up their ideological culture; (2) the totality of their meaningful *actions,* through which the pure meanings-values-norms are manifested and realized, makes up their behavioral culture; (3) the totality of all the other vehicles, the material, bio-physical things and energies through which their ideological culture is externalized, solidified and socialized, makes up their "material culture." Thus, the total empirical culture of a person or group is made up of these three cultural levels—the ideological, the behavioral, and the material.[8]

3

Main Forms of Interconnection of Socio-cultural Phenomena

(a) A copy of *Look,* a broken bottle of whiskey, a shoe, and an orange can lie side by side on the pavement, having been brought into close proximity by casual, incidental forces. *Spatial proximity* is the only connection between them. Aside from that, they are not bound together by either a causal or a logical tie. A dumping field near a city exhibits a vast number of various cultural objects lying in close proximity. Since this spatial juxtaposition is the only "connection" between them, one can change—add, take away, break into pieces—some of these objects without changing the rest of the dumped cultural objects. *Any collection of cultural phenomena interrelated only by spatial adjacency (or time adjacency, like many newsreel events) makes the most conspicuous case of cultural congeries.*

(b) A somewhat more tangible connection exists between the phenomena X, Y, Z, each of which is neither causally nor meaningfully related to the others, but each and all of which are causally related to a common factor A, and through A they happen to be connected by an *indirect causal bond*. In my pockets I find a watch, keys, handkerchief, dollar bill, pen, pencil, comb, and something else. None of these cultural objects demand one another either logically or causally. There is no direct causal relationship between the handkerchief, the keys, the dollar bill, and the comb, because ordinarily we find that a handkerchief is not in the company of any of these objects, and none of these objects is accompanied by the others. Likewise, we can tear the handkerchief into pieces without in any way affecting the watch, keys, or the dollar bill. This means that there is no direct causal tie between them, because a causal relationship between A and B means that when A is given B is given (or vice versa), and when one of these is changing the other is changing also.

However, if all these objects are found in my pockets, they are there, in close proximity, because each of them satisfies one of my needs (causal and meaningful ties with *me*). Being directly related to me as their common factor, they become related to one another not only by spatial (and time) proximity, but by *indirect causal relationship*. This ties them together somewhat more closely than a mere spatial (and time) adjacency. The tie is, however, so indirect that they lose it as soon as their common factor disappears. Hence they are still congeries rather than real unities or systems, in which any important change of an important part tangibly influences the other parts and the whole. The sociocultural world is full of numberless collections of two or more cultural objects, phenomena, and processes of this type, lying between congeries and real unities.

(c) Next we shall consider the totality of cultural objects, phenomena, and processes that are bound together into a real unity or system by a *direct causal tie*. They make *causal cultural unities or systems*. The explosion of war or famine or any other great emergency invariably leads to an expansion of governmental regimentation in all societies of a certain kind; and the termination of war, famine, or other emergency regularly leads to a quantitative and qualitative decrease of governmental regimentation. This is an example of two sociocultural phenomena bound into a causal unity by a direct causal tie. Within the limited budget of any nation an increased appropriation for military purposes calls forth a decrease in expenditures for non-military needs. The excessive atomization of ethical and legal values tends to increase criminality. A rigid caste regime is causally connected with a low vertical social mobility in a given population. The shorter days in the winter months cause (in societies equipped with street lights) the street lights to be lit earlier than in the summertime. The northern climate causes fur and heavy cloth coats to be used in the winter months. These are examples of cultural phenomena connected by direct causal ties. The causal unities are real unities or systems.

(d) In contradistinction to congeries or a conglomeration of meanings like "two + Stalin + azalea + water + Jupiter + shoe + Baroque + fish + table" where the meanings are united only by spatial (or time) proximity, any proposition like "*A* is *B*" or "two and two make four" or "*A* is not *B*" is a meaningful little system where the logical subject and predicate are logically united to make one meaningful proposition. *The totality of such propositions united into one meaningfully consistent and comprehensible whole makes up a meaningful system.* Thus, mathematics is a vast meaningful system, eminently consistent from the logical standpoint, for here no important proposition can be changed without introducing inconsistency and making it necessary to change many other mathematical equations and formulas to re-establish its consistency. The same, in a somewhat decreasing degree, is true of physical, biological, and social sciences; the bulk of their propositions is a logically consistent whole (with a few congeries present). It is also true of all great philosophical systems of meanings. The bulk of propositions in Plato's *Republic* or Kant's *Critique of Pure Reason* or St. Thomas' *Summa Contra Gentiles* is mutually consistent (with some congeries here and there). This is no less true of the Christian Credo or the credo of other great religions, of the great ethical systems, even of most of the law codes. Most of their main propositions are mutually consistent and make a *meaningful unity* or *system*. None of their main propositions can be radically changed without affecting the other main propositions and making it necessary to change them also in order to re-establish their consistency.

In aesthetic cultural meanings *the aesthetic consistency of the content and style of the fine-arts phenomena* occupies the place of logical-mathematical consistency. Aesthetic congeries represent a hodge-podge—odds and ends of various disharmonious bits of content and form. A musical composition in which some bars are taken from Bach, some from Stravinsky, from Brahms, from Gershwin, others from Wagner and from jazz, serves as an example of a musical hash. A literary composition written partly in Homeric style and partly in the styles of Dante, Rabelais, Gorki, Shelley, and Gertrude Stein is another example of aesthetic congeries. On the other hand, all the great creations in music and literature, painting and sculpture, architecture and drama display a seamless unity of style and content (with a few "bridges" here and there).

This outlines the profound difference between purely *meaningful congeries* and *meaningful unities or systems*. The parts or the meanings that make a meaningful system are united into one system by the tie of *meaningful (logical or aesthetic) consistency*. Such unities are different from the foregoing purely causal unities. There we find a *causal* interdependence between the parts of the system; here, in meaningful unities, the interdependence is logical or aesthetic, basically different from the causal. This latter is neither logically nor aesthetically consistent; it is simply a relatively constant interdependence of A and B in their co-existence or sequence or concomitant variation.

(e) Finally, when a system of meanings is objectified by material vehicles and becomes not only an ideological but also a behavioral and material system, such a system becomes fully grounded in the empirical sociocultural world. As such it simultaneously becomes a *"causal-meaningful system or unity."* Causal as well as meaningful ties bind together its parts into one ideological-behavioral-material system. This is due to the previously mentioned fact that when diverse persons, material objects, or energies become agents and vehicles of the same system of meanings, the component of the meanings throws a causal net over all such persons and vehicles and introduces a causal dependence where it would otherwise not have existed. For this reason the overwhelming majority of grounded socio-cultural systems are *causal-meaningful unities,* different from purely causal and purely meaningful unities. *The causal-meaningful unities are thus the most integrated kind of sociocultural grounded systems, and the causal-meaningful interconnections between cultural phenomena are the closest possible ties.* Almost all organized groups,[4] beginning with the family or the religious group, and ending with the state (like the United States or Germany), caste, occupational union, political party, and so on, are causal-meaningful social unities. The Constitution of the United States, the Credo of the Roman Catholic Church, the family's set of meanings and values, the charter of a business corporation or a labor union, the platform of a political party, etc., give us the main meanings and values because of which and for the sake of whose realization the group is established and functions as a unified body with a tangible causal interdependence between its members' behavior and the vehicles. No organized group is either purely causal or purely meaningful, but a meaningful-causal social system or unity.

Similarly, all grounded *cultural* systems, whether it be mathematics or science generally, philosophy, religion, law, ethics, music, or the fine arts generally, become meaningful-causal *cultural* systems as soon as they become behavioral and material. Without their system of meanings or "ideology" they simply would not exist: there cannot be any mathematics without the system of mathematical meanings or propositions. When mathematics begins to be "practiced," taught, used for study and practical purposes, it becomes a meaningful-causal system whose ideological, behavioral and material aspects become tangibly interdependent with its human agents and material vehicles. The same is true of practically all other cultural systems grounded in empirical reality.

Thus we find that the interconnections among numberless and immensely diverse grounded sociocultural phenomena are of four different kinds at least: (1) a mere spatial or time adjacency, (2) indirect causal relations, (3) direct causal connections, (4) meaningful-causal ties. Correspondingly all the combinations of two or more sociocultural phenomena give us: (1) *pure sociocultural congeries,* (2) *semi-congeries united by an indirect causal bond,* (3) *causal unities or systems,* (4) *meaningful-causal systems or unities.*[5] Almost all grounded sociocultural systems are meaningful-causal unities.

4

Main Cultural Systems and Supersystems

In the total culture of any population there exists a multitude of congeries and of causal-meaningful systems. These range from the smallest (like *"A is B"*) to ever vaster ones. The "two by two is four" is a little system; the multiplication table is a larger system; arithmetic is a still larger system; all mathematics (arithmetic, algebra, geometry, calculus, etc.) is a yet vaster system; the entire field of science is a still more embracing system. Similarly, we find a wide range of systems, beginning with the smallest and ending with the vastest, in other fields of cultural phenomena.

Among the basic vast cultural systems are language, science, philosophy, religion, the fine arts, ethics, law, and the vast derivative systems of applied technology, economics, and politics. The bulk of the meanings-values-norms of science or of great philosophical, religious, ethical or artistic systems are united into one consistent ideological whole.

This ideological system is, to a tangible degree, realized in all the material vehicles or the material culture, and in the behavior of the bearers, agents, or members of each of these systems. Scientific ideology (of any and all sciences) is objectified in millions of books, manuscripts, instruments, laboratories, libraries, universities, schools, and in practically all gadgets and machinery, from an axe or shovel up to the most complex atomic-radio-electrical-steam machinery, etc., and objects made possible by science. Behaviorally, science is actualized in all educational and research activities of scientists, students, teachers, inventors, scholars, and millions of laborers and farmers, businessmen and technicians who apply scientific discoveries, behave scientifically, and use the utensils and gadgets invented by science. Taken as a whole, the total scientific system—in its ideological, material, and behavioral forms—occupies an enormous portion of the total cultural phenomena of mankind.

Religious ideology likewise is objectified in millions of material objects, beginning with temple and cathedral buildings and ending with millions of religious objects; and then in numberless overt actions by its members—its hierarchy and its ordinary followers—from a simple prayer to millions of ritual actions, moral commandments and charity prescribed by the religious ideology (creed) and to a certain extent practiced by the members of a given religion. Again, taken in all three of its forms—ideological, material and behavioral—the religious system occupies a very large place in the human population's total culture. With a respective modification, the same can be said of the systems of language, fine arts, law and ethics, politics and economics. In their totality these systems cover the greater part of the total culture of almost any population, the rest consisting partly of a multitude of other derivative systems, but mainly of a multitude of cultural congeries. In their totality these vast systems make up the central and the highest portion of any population's culture. Being essentially consistent, they are also a gigantic manifestation of human rational (and partly even superrational) creativity. Their very existence demonstrates the fallacy of all theories that view human beings and human culture as being mainly irrational and non-rational. Congeries testify in favor of this non-rationality or irrationality, but insofar as congeries are a minor part of humanity's total culture, these theories enormously exaggerate human irrationality and non-rationality.

Besides these vast cultural systems there are still vaster cultural unities that can be called *cultural supersystems*.

As in other cultural systems, the ideology of each supersystem is based upon *certain major premises or certain ultimate principles whose development, differentiation, and articulation makes the total ideology of a supersystem*. Since the supersystems' ideologies are the vastest, their major premises or ultimate principles deal with the ultimate and most general truth, proposition, or value. An ultimate or most general truth concerns the nature of the ultimate true reality or the ultimate true value. Three main consistent answers have been given by humanity to the question, "What is the nature of the true, ultimate reality-value?"

One is: "The ultimate, true reality-value is *sensory*. Beyond it there is no other reality nor any other non-sensory value." Such a major premise and the gigantic supersystem built upon it is called *Sensate*.

Another solution to this problem is: "The ultimate, true reality-value is a supersensory and superrational God (Brahma, Tao, 'Divine Nothing,' and other equivalents of God). Sensory and any other reality or value are either a mirage or represent an infinitely more inferior and shadowy pseudo-reality and pseudo-value." Such a major premise and the corresponding cultural system is called *Ideational*.

The third answer to the ultimate question is: "The ultimate, true reality-value is the Manifold Infinity which contains all differentiations and which is infinite qualitatively and quantitatively. The finite human mind cannot grasp it or define it or describe it adequately. This Manifold Infinity is ineffable and unutterable. Only by a very remote approximation can we discern three main aspects in It: the rational or logical, the sensory, and the superrational-supersensory. All three of these aspects harmoniously united in It are real; real also are its superrational-supersensory, rational, and sensory values." It has many names: God, Tao, Nirvana, the Divine Nothing of mystics, the Supra-Essence of Dionysius and Northrop's "undifferentiated aesthetic continuum." This typically mystic conception of the ultimate, true reality and value and the supersystem built upon are described as *Idealistic*.

Each of these three supersystems embraces in itself the corresponding type of the vast systems already described. Thus, the Sensate supersystem is made up of: sensate science, sensate philosophy, sensate religion of a sort, sensate fine arts, sensate ethics, law, economics and politics, along with predominantly sensate types of persons and groups, ways of life and social institutions. Likewise, the Ideational and Idealistic supersystems consist respectively of Ideational and Idealistic types of all these systems. In each of these supersystems the ideological, behavioral, and material elements articulate, in all its parts— in its science and philosophy, fine arts and religion, ethics and law, way of life and social institutions—its major or ultimate premise concerning the nature of the ultimate, true reality-value.

Thus, for instance, in the total Medieval European culture, from the sixth to the end of the twelfth century, we find that the Ideational supersystem was dominant and embraced the main portions of the total Medieval culture. Its major premise was the Christian Credo, with the superrational and super-sensory Trinity, as representing the ultimate true reality and value. This Credo was articulated by the dominant Medieval "science," philosophy, fine arts, law, ethics, economics, and politics. Medieval science was subordinate to theology, which was the queen of the sciences, natural and other sciences being mere handmaids of religion. The supreme truth was the revealed truth of religion. Medieval philosophy was hardly distinguishable from theology and religion. Medieval architecture and sculpture were but the same "Bible in stone," articulating the same Credo. So also were its painting and music, literature and drama. From 85 to 97 per cent of the total great fine arts of the Middle Ages was religious and Christian. Medieval law and ethics were but an articulation of the divine and natural law, formulated in the absolute God-given Ten Commandments and the Sermon on the Mount, with the Canon Law supplementing the secular law. The medieval form of government was theocracy, with the spiritual power supreme over the secular. Even Medieval economics were notably Christian-religious, "non-economical" and "non-utili-tarian." In brief, the major Ideational premise was articulated by all the main compartments of Medieval culture. On the basis of this premise there emerged, grew, and functioned a vast Ideational supersystem, which was the dominant and most characteristic one of Medieval culture. The Sensate and Idealistic systems and congeries were also present, but these were minor systems and congeries.

The total European culture after the sixteenth and on up to the twentieth century presents an entirely different picture. At that period the Sensate rather than the crumbled Ideational supersystem dominated European culture. During the last four centuries the major parts of all the compartments of Euro-pean culture articulated the ultimate premise that "the ulti-mate reality and value are Sensate." All the compartments of this culture became correspondingly secularized. Religion and theology declined in influence and prestige. Religiously indif-ferent, sometimes even irreligious, sensory science became the supreme, objective truth. The real truth was now the truth of the senses, empirically perceived and tested. Sensate philosophy (materialism, empiricism, scepticism, pragmatism, etc.), Sen-sate literature, music, painting, sculpture, architecture, and drama largely replaced the religious medieval fine arts. Sen-sate, utilitarian, hedonistic, relative, man-made law and ethics replaced the Ideational, unconditional, God-revealed law and ethics of the Middle Ages. Material value, wealth, physical comfort, pleasure, power, fame, and popularity became the main values for which modern Sensate men have been fighting and struggling. God and religion went by the board. To-gether with the values of the Kingdom of God they have been given lip service but have ceased to be really important. The predominant type of persons, their way of life, and their insti-tutions also became dominantly Sensate. In brief, the major part of modern Western culture has indeed been dominated by the Sensate supersystem.

If, finally, we take Greek culture of the fifth century B.C., or European culture of the thirteenth century, we find that it was dominated by the Idealistic cultural supersystem. This culture, in all its main compartments, articulated the major Idealistic premise that the true, ultimate reality and value are the Infinite Manifold, partly sensory, partly rational, partly superrational and supersensory.[6] These outlined supersystems are the vastest cultural systems that are known so far.

5

CULTURAL AND SOCIAL SYSTEMS
(OR ORGANIZED GROUPS)

By social system is meant an *organized group* that possesses a set of enforced, obligatory law norms defining in detail the rights, duties, social position and functions, roles, and proper behavior of each and all its members towards one another, outsiders and the world at large; a set of prohibited actions-relations sanctioned by punishment; and a set of recommended non-obligatory norms of conduct. As a result of these norms, this organized group is a clearly differentiated and stratified body, each member of which is assigned a definite position in this differentiated and ranked system, with legal rules that determine a member's promotion and demotion. Such a group has a definite name and symbol of its individuality. It also has some funds and material means necessary for carrying on its functions and making possible the activities of its members. In the human world there are millions of diverse organized groups, beginning with an association, the family, and ending with the state, the nation, the caste, and other groups.[7]

A social system understood in this sense does not coincide with a cultural system. First, because many systems, especially the vast cultural systems like mathematics, biology, medicine, or science generally, enter the total culture of practically all social systems; the family, the business concern, the religious group, the state, the political party, the labor union, all organized groups must use arithmetic or medicine or the rudiments of biological science. The same is true of the language system. There are millions of diverse social groups that speak English. It is likewise true of religious cultural systems. Many social systems have as their religious system either Buddhism or Roman Catholicism or Protestantism or Confucianism. And so on. In all these cases the vast cultural systems are like a vast body of water surrounding a diverse multitude of islands (social groups).

Social and cultural systems also differ from one another in that *the total culture of any organized group,* even of a single person, *consists not of one cultural system but of a multitude of vast and small cultural systems that are partly in harmony, partly out of harmony, with one another, and in addition many congeries of various kinds.* Even *the total culture* of practically any individual is not completely integrated into one cultural system but represents a multitude of co-existing cultural systems and congeries. These systems and congeries are partly consistent with, partly neutral toward, and partly contradictory to, one another. Suppose Mr. X to be a Baptist, Republican, physician, baseball fan, lover of Gershwin music, a man who prefers blondes to brunettes, whiskey to wine (not to mention thousands of X's other cultural traits). The total culture of X thus appears to be partly integrated and partly unintegrated. Neither logically nor causally does his Baptism require him to be Republican, or be a physician, or have any of his cultural traits; meaningfully, Baptism is neutral to the Republican party, to his occupational culture, and his baseball hobby; meaningfully Baptism may even contradict X's preference for jazz, blondes, or whiskey. Causally, all these cultural systems or traits are unrelated. There are many Baptists who are Democrats or do not belong to any party. There are many Republicans who are not baseball fans or do not have a preference for blondes or whiskey; and there are many lovers of whiskey who are neither Baptists, Republicans, nor physicians, and so on. Thus the total culture of an organized group or even of an individual is neither identical nor coterminal with any culture system. *The total culture of even the individual (as the smallest culture-area) is not wholly integrated* into one meaningful-causal system and represents the co-existence of many cultural systems—partly harmonious, partly indifferent, partly contradictory to one another—plus the co-existence of many congeries that have somehow entered the individual's total culture and settled there.[8]

With these concise propositions we can return to our main topic. We shall presently see that this deviation was necessary in order to make comprehensible the subsequent analysis and criticism of the philosophies of history.

XII

Critical Examination of the Theories of Danilevsky, Spengler, and Toynbee

I

ARE CIVILIZATIONS CULTURAL CONGERIES OR UNIFIED SYSTEMS?

Our analysis of the "readings of history" under discussion begins with the following questions: What sort of unity are the civilizational or cultural entities set forth by these theories? Are they just spatial congeries? or indirect causal semi-congeries? or causal unities? or meaningful-causal systems? Though none of the authors has tried to define his unified civilization or culture in terms of these four different categories, they all seem to think that their "entities" are real unities or, in my terms, *causal* or *meaningful-causal* systems. Further, some of them, failing to distinguish the profound difference between social and cultural systems, mix them up and view their "civilization" or "culture" as a kind of *sociocultural unity* in which a certain *social system* (organized group) and a certain *cultural system coincide as something coterminal and identical.* Thus Danilevsky's "culture-historical type" is a loose federation of politically and linguistically related social groups ("Egyptians," "Chinese," "Assyro-Babylonian-Phoenician-Chaldean," etc.) that have one unified cultural system. This system is causally and meaningfully as closely integrated as an organism whose parts are interdependent and dependent upon the whole, and whose whole is interdependent with its parts. Since they are as closely integrated as an organism, the culture-historical unities are born, grow, mature, and die like organisms.

Spengler's High Culture or Civilization has a similar kind of unity. Besides "organically-causal" integration he especially stresses its meaningful unity. The decisive role he ascribes to the "prime symbol" as the major premise upon which each High Culture is built and as the main theme articulated by all its parts, is an explicit accentuation of the meaningful interdependence of the parts of each Culture-Civilization with one another and with the whole. Like Danilevsky, he also identifies his High Culture system with some social group—mainly with a nation—making these two coterminal: the Egyptian nation with Egyptian high culture, the Apollinian with the Graeco-Roman, and so on.

By "civilization" Toynbee means not a mere "field of historical study," but a unified system whose parts are connected with one another by causal and meaningful ties:

Civilizations are wholes whose parts all cohere with one another and all affect one another reciprocally. . . . It is one of the characteristics of civilizations in process of growth that all aspects and activities of their social life are co-ordinated into a single social whole, in which the economic, political, and cultural elements are kept in a nice adjustment with one another by an inner harmony of the growing body social.[1]

Like his predecessors Toynbee, too, identifies his civilization with some kind of social group (see below).

Schubart, Berdyaev, and Schweitzer mention the unity of their "prototypes of culture" or "great cultures" only in the most general way; however, the meaningful unity of these remains certain. Further, they do not identify their cultural system with a social system to as great a degree as do Danilevsky, Spengler, and Toynbee. Though at each historical period a given nation or other social group may be the main bearer of a given cultural prototype, it nevertheless remains something different from its temporary agent—whether a given nation or other group. The very fact that in the course of time a given prototype of culture has been articulated by different groups (nations) at different periods of the prototype's re-emergence is one evidence of the differences between the cultural system and the social system. Berdyaev's statement that the Classical cultural system did not wholly die with the end of the Graeco-Roman nations but survived and is potentially immortal in its eternal cultural values, is further evidence of his distinction between the cultural and social systems.

Finally, Northrop's and Kroeber's cultural unities are either causal or meaningful-causal cultural systems, different from social systems or groups. According to Northrop, the basis of any cultural system is a philosophical presupposition or principle, and the cultural system is but the development and articulation of this presupposition in all its main compartments. Whenever such an unfolded meaningful consistency is lacking, the cultural phenomenon turns into congeries or semi-congeries. The total culture of either Mexico or any other nation is not one integrated whole or one causal-meaningful unity as Danilevsky, Spengler, and Toynbee claim, but is, instead, the co-existence of several vast and small cultural systems and many cultural congeries. Thus, he discerns in the total culture of Mexico at least five vast co-existing cultural systems, not to mention smaller ones and congeries. To sum up: with the exception of his "aesthetic" and "theoretic"—or Eastern and Western—supersystems (see below), Northrop's cultural unities are mainly causal-meaningful cultural systems, different from social systems or organized social groups.

Kroeber, likewise, deals mainly with meaningful-causal systems such as philosophy, philology, sculpture, painting, architecture, music, literature, drama, and religion. Further on, his somewhat vaguely defined "high-value culture patterns" or his "master patterns of culture" also seem to be mainly meaningful-causal systems, insofar as they have the "internal concordance," "interdependence of the parts" and "basic idea-system" and are grounded in empirical reality. These unified cultural systems are quite different from Danilevsky's, Spengler's, or Toynbee's civilization or High Culture. Such a civilization or High Culture, or the *total* culture of any area or nation, is not one unified whole, according to Kroeber and Northrop, but the co-existence of several vast or small cultural systems, partly harmonious, partly neutral, partly contradictory to one another, as well as a multitude of cultural congeries and semi-congeries. Kroeber explicitly refuses to follow Spengler in this point.[2] This does not prevent one cultural system in philosophy or art, in science or ethics, or in any other compartment of culture, from being dominant for a certain period; nor does it hinder the dominance of a sort of cultural supersystem ("master patterns") in the total culture of a population or area. This domination, however, does not mean that only the dominant system or supersystem exists in a given total culture or its compartments. Nor does it mean that the total culture is wholly integrated in and around this dominant system or supersystem. On the contrary, side by side with, say, materialism as the dominant philosophical system, there usually exist minor systems such as idealism and other non-materialistic philosophies, not to mention many congeries. In the total culture of an area there ordinarily co-exist, side by side with the dominant supersystem, many minor cultural systems and many cultural congeries that are partly neutral, partly contradictory to the dominant supersystem or system.

Finally, Northrop's and Kroeber's cultural systems are distinguished from social systems or organized groups.

Most of Northrop's and Kroeber's explicit and implicit conclusions in this point seem to be similar to those reached and systematically developed in my *Social and Cultural Dynamics* and *Society, Culture, and Personality*. Since these conclusions differ considerably from those of Danilevsky, Spengler, and Toynbee, there arises the question of what the shortcomings of Danilevsky's, Spengler's, and Toynbee's views are from the standpoint of my, and possibly Northrop's and Kroeber's, theories.

2

THE FATAL ERROR

The first fatal shortcoming of Danilevsky's, Spengler's, and Toynbee's conceptions on this point consists of their acceptance of their "culture-historical type," High Culture, or "civilization" as a real unity, in the sense of either a causal or a causal-meaningful system. Like the so-called "functional anthropologists" and "totalitarian integrators," they assume that the *total* culture of each of their "prototypes," High Cultures, and "civilizations" is completely integrated and represents one meaningfully consistent and causally unified whole, thus making a sort of cultural supersystem that embraces in itself all the cultural phenomena of the Egyptian, Chinese, Apollinian, Magian, Faustian, or any other culture-civilization they mention.

I have already indicated that even the total culture of a single individual, as the smallest possible "culture-area," is not entirely integrated and represents a dominant system (though many eclectics do not have even any dominant system) that co-exists with many minor systems and a multitude of congeries, partly neutral, partly contradictory to the dominant system or to one another. If such is the structure of the *total culture* of an individual or of the smallest culture area, then the immense and infinitely diverse universe of the *total culture* of Egypt or India, the West or China, consisting of many billions of cultural phenomena, is certainly not, and cannot be, completely integrated into one causal or meaningful-causal system. Assuredly it represents the co-existence of a multitude of cultural systems, of a supersystem (not present in eclectic cultures), and congeries that are partly mutually consistent, partly meaningfully indifferent, and partly contradictory. The whole field of all the cultural phenomena of each of these "cultures," "types," or "civilizations" is a sort of dumping ground where billions of diverse cultural phenomena are thrown together. Only a part of these is causally and causally-meaningfully united with other parts; another part is made up of mere congeries or semi-congeries "tied together" only by spatial proximity or by indirect causal ties. They are not interdependent: a part of these can change without any change taking place in other items in the dumping ground.

None of these authors can indicate any major premise or ultimate principle articulated by all cultural phenomena of Egypt, Babylon, or any of their "cultures" or "civilizations." In this respect, Danilevsky and Toynbee simply state that the Hellenic civilization was predominantly aesthetic, the Indic mainly religious, and the Western machinistic-technological, while others, according to Danilevsky, developed two fields of culture and some nearly all four fields (his "autochthonous" civilizations). Toynbee indicates hardly any specific cultural tendency or "philosophical presupposition" or "prime symbol" for most of his civilizations, except for the three mentioned above. Even in these three instances he mentions only their "aesthetic," "religious," and "technological" specificum most perfunctorily, without any evidence. Later on we shall see that it is generally fallacious to ascribe a specific cultural value that is allegedly inherent in and developed by a given culture during its whole existence. Each of these civilizations has been creative in various fields of culture at various periods of its existence, and all have been creative not in one, but in several fields; all have been "autochthonous." [3]

Moreover, merely to indicate that the Hellenic culture was predominantly aesthetic is insufficient proof that the total Hellenic or Apollinian culture was consistently and causally integrated around a certain aesthetic principle or that in Apollinian culture there was only one instead of several contrasting arts and aesthetic principles. The same is true of the "religiosity" that supposedly pervaded the whole history of the total Hindu civilization, or of the "scientific" principle that permeated the total Western or Faustian culture-civilization. None of these factually wrong propositions can even remotely prove that the total culture of these civilizations was meaningfully-causally integrated in and around these categories. Danilevsky and Toynbee hardly try to prove that their culture-civilization is indeed integrated and that all its parts articulate the same, well-defined principle, premise, prime symbol, or ultimate value. Spengler is the only one of these three thinkers who tries to show that each High Culture is a meaningful-causal system, based upon the prime symbol, and that this prime symbol is articulated by all parts of a certain culture-civilization. In the earlier exposition of Spengler's theory an outline of this point was presented in considerable detail. The prime symbol or major premise of the Apollinian culture is "the sensuous individual body"; that of the Faustian, "pure and limitless space and voluntarism"; that of the Magian, "the cavernous, vaulted eternal space and the cavern-feeling"; of the Egyptian, "stone"; of the Russian, "the limitless plane"; and so on. Spengler tries hard to show that each of these civilizations articulated its prime symbol in all its main parts, thus binding into one consistent and causally interdependent whole all the billions of phenomena that make up the total culture of each High Culture.

I would not deny that in the case of some of his civilizations Spengler's prime symbol serves well as a premise for the meaningful unification of several systems and congeries. But this unified system was only one among many systems and millions of congeries present in the *total* Apollinian, Magian, Faustian, Egyptian, or any other "civilization." His prime symbol serves rather poorly even for a meaningful unification of a few cultural systems (number, mathematics, psychology, architectural order, sculpture, or music): the connections Spengler tries to establish between his prime symbol and some of the cultural phenomena appear in several of his examples very remote, unconvincing and artificial. To claim that the *total* culture of each High Culture is but a consistent articulation of its prime symbol is fantastic. To expect that the billions of cultural phenomena that made up the *total culture* of the Arabic-Islamic-Byzantine-Iranian-Syrian-Jewish   populations ("the Magian culture") are an articulation of the prime symbol of "a cavernous, vaulted, eternal space," is to expect the impossible. Even to try to prove that a connection exists between this prime symbol and the "dualism of Spirit and Soul," as Spengler tries to do, results in unconvincing, and in part fallacious, conclusions. Similarly, to believe that the billions of cultural phenomena of the Faustian culture all articulate the prime symbol of "the pure and limitless space," and that all are meaningfully bound into one unity by this prime symbol, is to believe in a miracle, contradicted at every turn by thousands of facts. At best, Spengler's prime symbol can give us one fairly vast meaningful-causal system in the total cultural field of each civilization-culture. The overwhelming majority of other systems and congeries in the field of the same civilization remain unintegrated in and around the prime symbol or other principle. Spengler's valiant attempt thus fails. The somewhat incidental and vague nature of his prime symbols prevents them from serving as the clearest and most real major premises (like the Ideational, Idealistic, and Sensate) for most embracing cultural supersystems that are much vaster than the ensembles based upon his prime symbols.

The cultural systems based upon his prime symbols, and my Ideational, Idealistic, and Sensate supersystems, are, however, not mutually exclusive: the Hindu Ideational (or Sensate, or Idealistic) cultural supersystem is of a different color from the Greek Ideational supersystem, and both differ in their "local" traits from the Western Ideational supersystem. The bulk of these different colors or local secondary traits of the same type of supersystem may easily be meaningfully integrated around a prime symbol or principle different from the major premises of my supersystems. If, like Spengler, one has an accurate grasp of this "local" prime symbol or premise, one may discover a fairly vast system that by this premise unifies most of the local colors, traits, and patterns of the Egyptian or the Greek or the Hindu or the Western Sensate (or Idealistic or Ideational) local systems. In this sense my supersystems and *Spengler's systems based upon his "prime symbols" are supplementary rather than contradictory.* This reconciliation does not, however, mean that Spengler's prime symbols can and do unify the total culture of his civilizations.

Since it is not a meaningful system, the total culture-civilization of these authors is not a causal system either. If the variables $A, B, C \ldots$ are causally connected, then each time one of these (say A) is given, the other variables (B and C) are also given; and when A changes, B and C also change. Such is the essence of the causal relationship between the variables. If one of the variables is given and the others not, and if one is changing and the others not, this means that *A, B, C are not causally connected and do not make a causal system* in which A, B, C are mutually interdependent. Such a conglomeration of A, B, C is just a congeries of mutually independent phenomena.

Having reminded the reader what the causal connection and system are, I can merely point out that the authors under discussion themselves show convincingly that their civilization-cultures are not causal unities. Toynbee indicates many times that in his civilization its technique and economic life (the variables T and E) often change, while the rest of the civilization (the variables $A, B, C \ldots$) does not change at all; in many other cases the rest of the civilization ($A, B, C \ldots$) changes, while the technique or economics (T or E) remains at rest. In still other cases, the technique changes in one way, economics in another, while the rest of the civilization moves in yet different directions. In a number of additional places his religious element changes without a corresponding change in the arts or politics of the civilization, and so on.[4] Thus, in a convincing manner, Toynbee himself repudiates his basic assumption that "civilizations" are "the whole whose parts all cohere together"; or that they are causal systems.

The sum of the foregoing reasons is sufficient basis for the conclusion that the Danilevsky-Spengler-Toynbee type, High Culture, or civilization is neither a causal, nor a meaningful, nor a causal-meaningful system, but rather a *cultural field where a multitude of vast and small cultural systems and congeries—partly mutually harmonious, partly neutral, partly contradictory—co-exist*. A part of the systems are meaningfully and causally connected to make vaster systems; a part are connected through causal ties only; a part only through indirect causal ties; and a large part are nothing more than spatially adjacent congeries. The totality of all these systems and congeries does not make any unified cultural system, whether Egyptian, Babylonian, Magian, or Mayan "civilization" or "culture-historical type."

This conclusion is further re-enforced by the fact that each of these authors delineates the civilization-cultures in a strikingly different manner. What Danilevsky considers one culture-historical type, as, for instance, his "Assyro-Babylonian-Phoenician-Chaldean or Ancient Semitic Civilization," Toynbee treats as several civilizations (the Babylonic, Hittite, Sumeric, plus possibly the Syriac), all different from one another; Spengler divides it into the Magian and Babylonian civilizations. On the other hand, Spengler's one Magian civilization consists for Danilevsky of two different civilizations—the Iranian and Arabian; whereas Toynbee divides it into at least four civilizations—the Iranic, the Syriac, the Arabic, and the Orthodox-Byzantine. Toynbee's one Hellenic civilization is viewed by Danilevsky as two civilizations—the Greek and the Roman.

Thus, where one of our scholars sees one cultural organism, the others see two or more, and vice versa. This spectacular discrepancy testifies against these "civilizations" being unities. For, if they were such systems, our eminent scholars would hardly have failed to recognize them in a unanimous and identical manner.

Toynbee's pragmatic recipe for the "carving out" of a unified "civilization" from the "cultural field" of humanity does not improve the situation. This pragmatic recipe is as follows:

I mean, by a civilization, the smallest unit of historical study at which one arrives when one tries to understand the history of one's own country: the United States, say, or the United Kingdom. If you were to try to understand the history of the United States by itself, it would be unintelligible. . . .

You have to look beyond it, and take into consideration the history of Western Europe. Beyond it, "you need not look into . . . Eastern Europe or the Islamic world," or even into the Graeco-Roman world. "These limits of time and space give us the intelligible unit of social life of which the United States or Great Britain or France or Holland is a part: call it Western Christendom, Western civilization, Western society, the Western World." [5]

Using this "operational criterion," neither I nor any other competent scholar can understand the most essential what, how, and why of Russia's history without "looking into" the history of Europe as well as that of the greater part of Asia. Without Scandinavian, Balkan, Polish-German history and the history of the Hanseatic League's Europe, a great deal of Russian culture and history before the Tatar invasion is simply incomprehensible. Since the time of Peter the Great almost nothing in Russian history is intelligible unless one first looks into Western Europe. This is still more true in respect to the Byzantine, Iranic, Arabic, Mongol, Turkish, and the Asiatic social and cultural worlds generally. If their influence is not kept in mind, the whole structure and dynamics of Russian culture or civilization—Russian religion, philosophy, fine arts, ethics, law, politics, economics, up to the main forms of social organization and most Russian history—cannot be intelligible. This, according to Toynbee's criterion, means that there is no Russian civilization at all, though he names it among his civilizations. Instead, there is an immense Eurasian civilization that covers practically the whole of Europe and three quarters of Asia.

By consistently applying Toynbee's recipe we cannot arrive at either the Western, the Iranic, the Arabic, the Hellenic, the Egyptian, or most of Toynbee's twenty-one civilizations. The history of Great Britain, Italy, Spain, France, or Western Europe cannot be understood without "looking into" that of the Graeco-Roman, Byzantine, Russian, Arabic, Asiatic, or African world or the American world after Columbus. Neither Western Christianity, nor its law, ethics, fine arts, philosophy, economics and politics, nor the bulk of the histories of the main Western countries, can be intelligible without "looking into" the Asiatic, African, and other cultural continents of this planet. If one simply cancels the consequences of America's discovery or of the West's colonial exploitation of "all four quarters of the world," its post-Columbian history and economic life would be to a notable degree incomprehensible. The history of the Iranic civilization is incomprehensible without that of the Hellenic, Arabic, Egyptian, and several other "civilizations." A whole "Buddhist" portion of Chinese civilization is unintelligible without the Hindu civilization. Even Egyptian civilization becomes in many respects incomprehensible without "looking into" the Babylonian, Iranic, Hellenic, and Minoan civilizations. Any good elementary history textbook shows that it is impossible to carve out Toynbee's twenty-one civilizations on the basis of his criteria. Consistently applied, it would efface the overwhelming majority of his twenty-one civilizations. Toynbee "carves them out" of the field of cultural phenomena not according to his own prescription, but according to some eclectic criteria.

Thus all three scholars make the basic error of taking for a civilizational-cultural system something that is no unity at all. They crown this error by the further one of *mixing up the cultural and social systems (organized groups), and they display an additional inconsistency even in this operation.* After all, the Danilevsky-Spengler-Toynbee classifications are not so much classifications of civilizational or cultural systems as they are of social systems (organized groups). Danilevsky explicitly points out that a loose federation of linguistically related groups is the basis of his culture-historical type. Spengler explicitly states that each great culture-civilization is borne by and is incarnated into a nation in "the uniform of a state." Toynbee regards his civilization as a "species of society," though he does not specifically analyze what sort of an organized group this "species" is. In effect, all three classifications are mainly inconsistent classifications of organized groups and of a few semi-organized social bodies. Not possessing a systematic taxonomy of social groups,[6] these scholars not only mix up social and cultural systems, but they make a class of "civilizations" or "great cultures" out of essentially *different* social groups. In other words, they are writing the equation: Class *A* ("civilization") is equal now to social group *B*, now *C*, now *M*, and so on. Obviously such definitions are faulty in their formal logical structure. Some of their "civilizations" or "cultures" are just *language* groups, such as the Greek or the Arabic, which were hardly ever united into one sovereign state. Their other "civilizations" (or High Cultures) are either pure *state* groups; or *state groups cumulated with a respective language group* (a two-bonded group bound together by common language and common citizenship), like the Iranic, the Russian and Byzantine, the Mexic, the Roman, the Chinese, and the Babylonic. Still others are either *religious* groups, or *religious* plus *territorial*, or plus *language,* or plus *state* groups (two-bonded and three-bonded groups whose members are bound together by religious plus language ties, or religious plus citizenship ties, and so on), like the Hindu, Buddhist China, Egyptian, or Hittite civilizations, and so on. Finally, some of their "civilizations," such as Toynbee's Hellenic, Danilevsky's "Assyro-Babylonian-Phoenician-Chaldean," or Spengler's "Magian," represent a veritable *sociocultural potpourri, made up of several wholes, halves, and quarters of diverse language, state, religious, economic, territorial groups, and unorganized populations.* The heterogeneous nature of these social groups, all identified with one another as belonging to the same class of "civilizations" or "cultural types," displays especially clearly the fallacious nature of these "pseudo-unities." They are not only cultural, but also social, congeries—a medley of entirely heterogeneous, partly organized, partly unorganized groups, all labeled with the term "civilization," "cultural type," or High Culture.

The preceding considerations are sufficient to show Danilevsky's, Spengler's, and Toynbee's fatal error in this basic premise. This error is responsible for a series of other important mistakes they commit in their readings of historical events and sociocultural processes. Some of these mistakes are discussed below—the "sinful progeny" of the fatal "parental" error.

3

WHAT IS NOT INTEGRATED CANNOT DISINTEGRATE; WHAT IS NOT BORN CANNOT GROW AND DIE

If the civilization or culture-type under consideration is not one integrated system, it evidently cannot disintegrate. If it is not a living causal or meaningful-causal unity, it obviously cannot be born, grow, reach maturity, and die. None of these terms is applicable to, and none of these processes takes place in, a cultural dumping ground. The vast pile of cultural congeries (systems and single traits) on such a ground can be mechanically rearranged, increased, or decreased; but it cannot disintegrate, because such a pile has never been integrated. Likewise it cannot die, because it has never been born.

When civilizations or culture-historical types are shown to be neither causal nor meaningful-causal unities, the whole vast superstructure of the civilizations' life-cycle, erected on this foundation, crumbles by itself. The sin of the "parental error" is thus visited upon the children.

The crumbling of the whole life-cycle theory of the civilizations or cultures is enhanced by the choice of an organismic variety of life-cycle in which the civilizations are born, grow, age, disintegrate, and die. Of almost all the theories of the life-course of civilizations or cultures, this ancient organismic variety is certainly one of the least tenable. One can only be sorry that Danilevsky, Spengler, and Toynbee chose this form. Since the earliest historical times the organismic theories of society and civilization have been used by known or anonymous Hindu, Chinese, Egyptian, Persian, Greek, Roman, Arabic, Medieval European, and later thinkers.[7] Besides serving as analogical illustrations, these theories have contributed little to our understanding of historical events and of sociocultural structure and dynamics. Our authors' organismic theories are no exception to this rule. The slightest analysis of what they mean by birth, growth, maturity, breakdown, disintegration and death of their civilizations or culture-historical types at once shows either the meaninglessness of these terms or their conspicuous vagueness and superficiality.

Let us see what they mean by the death of civilizations or cultures.

4

LONGEVITY AND DEATH OF CULTURES OR CIVILIZATIONS

"No less than sixteen out of twenty-six [civilizations] are by now dead and buried." These sixteen dead civilizations include the Egyptian, the Andean, the Sinic, the Minoan, the Sumeric, the Mayan, the Indic, the Hittite, the Syriac, the Hellenic, the Babylonic, the Mexican, the Arabic, the Yucatec, the Spartan, and the Ottoman. Of the remaining ten surviving civilizations—the Western, Christian Near Eastern, Islamic, Christian Russian, Hindu, Far Eastern Chinese, Japanese, Polynesian, Eskimo, and Nomadic—all, except the Western, are "in their last agonies," under the threat of either annihilation or assimilation by our own civilization of the West. Even this Western civilization is in a state of acute crisis.

Such are Toynbee's conclusions about the death of civilizations.[8]

These conclusions are but a variation of similar theories about the death of civilizations (or cultures) proffered by many thinkers of the past and by Danilevsky and Spengler.

Statements of this sort at first appear clear and convincing. When they are closely examined and tested, however, they raise a host of questions as to their exact meaning and their validity. Let us consider the foremost of these questions.

(a) If the foregoing writers mean by the "death of civilizations" that the *total culture of each of these "dead" civilizations*— its language and its political, economic, social, scientific, philosophic, religious, ethical, legal, and other cultural values—no longer exists, is no longer practiced, is not incorporated in living cultural and social institutions, is devoid of influence, or is actually forgotten, no longer constituting a topic of thought or discussion, then their thesis is obviously untenable with respect to virtually all these "civilizations," as well as to the culture or civilization of many pre-literate groups of the past. The greater part of the supposedly "extinct" Graeco-Roman civilization, for instance, is still very much alive: Homer, Hesiod, Sophocles, Aristophanes, and the bulk of its literature; Socrates, Plato, Aristotle, and most of its philosophies; Zeno, Epicurus, and the majority of its ethical systems; its fine arts, especially in its Doric, Ionic, Corinthian, and other "classical" architectural forms; its mathematical and scientific discoveries; the *Corpus Juris Civilis* of Roman law; Graeco-Roman forms of political and economic organizations, including Athenian democracy, Spartan totalitarianism, and Roman imperial organization (in its republican and monarchical forms); its domestic relations laws, even such specific ones as *lex Julia et Papia Poppaea,* and a host of its manners and mores. These and a multitude of other cultural values of Graeco-Roman "civilization" are still imitated, practiced, and incorporated in our civilization, culture, and institutions, in our mentality, conduct, and relationships. They live, function, and influence us, being much more alive than last year's best seller or yesterday's fads and fashions.

With a proper modification the same may be said, in varying degrees, of the other fifteen "dead" civilizations, from the Egyptian to the Ottoman (witness Mohammedanism, certain forms of Ottoman art, and such adopted practices as polo-playing, the wearing of pajamas, and coffee-drinking). More, one may safely contend that many cultural values of pre-literate, nomadic, pastoral, and agricultural tribes are still alive and functioning on a large scale in our culture, embracing such factors as modes of transportation, technology, economics, patterns of taste, art, magical and religious beliefs, and manners and mores. *None of the "great civilizations" is dead in toto.*

(b) If the term "death of civilizations" means the disappearance of *a part of the total culture*—say, its language or religion or an art pattern—the contention is valid insofar as we admit the validity of the definition. As a matter of fact, the phenomenon is incessantly going on in any culture or civilization, constituting a regular sociocultural process. But the disappearance of a *part* of a *total culture* or civilization does not mean its total death. Our fashions and fads vary each season. Our best sellers live on an average only about six months. Types of machinery, tastes, beliefs, political sympathies, popular philosophies, and so forth, change incessantly, emerging, gaining acceptance, and being swiftly consigned to oblivion. But this does not mean that American or European "civilization" is dead and buried. To be sure only a few Egyptologists continue to use the Egyptian language; for the rest of mankind it is extinct. But it does not follow that Egyptian forms of art, political and social organization, or religious and ethical beliefs are necessarily likewise extinct. As a matter of fact, these aspects of Egyptian "civilization" are still vital in two forms: in their original patterns, imitated and reproduced in our contemporary culture, and as the patterns that entered, as an essential ingredient, into the Graeco-Roman, Western, and other civilizations and have thus been preserved to the present day. For example, many a religious and ethical belief of Egypt decisively affected the Hebrew religion and ethics and through Judaism—and even directly, through the cult of Isis, Osiris, etc.—passed into Christianity and thus into contemporary religious and ethical systems. The political organization of Egypt (the "divine right" and unlimited autocracy of the Pharaohs) decisively influenced the Roman monarchical regime and, through it, subsequent Western autocracies and monarchies. With a reasonable degree of certainty one may claim that a substantial percentage of any of the foregoing "dead" civilizations—in some cases a very large percentage—is still very much alive. Hence Danilevsky's, Spengler's, and Toynbee's formulas of the death of civilizations are unduly broad and sweeping and should be replaced by a narrower and more accurate statement, namely, that a *part* of every past civilization or culture has become extinct. Similarly, as we have seen, many features of our own contemporary culture are incessantly becoming obsolete, so that certain cultural traits of today are doomed to go into the discard tomorrow.

(c) If by the "death of a civilization" Danilevsky, Spengler, and Toynbee mean *the disintegration of its unity and individuality,* this proposition is invalid, for we have seen that their civilization and culture are neither causal nor meaningful-causal unities. Since they were not integrated or united, they evidently could not disintegrate. Since they were not born as unified individualities, they could not die. Being conglomerations of a host of meaningful-causal, causal, and spatially adjacent phenomena, some systems in these civilizations disintegrated, while other systems, plus many congeries, did not. For this reason, as we have seen, certain features of these civilizational congeries perished, whereas others survived. If the civilizations had been genuine unities, their disintegration would have been complete instead of partial and "spotty." This "spottiness" is additional evidence that the parts of the civilization were not closely interdependent and united into one whole. Thus the conception of the death of civilizations is also untenable in the sense of the disintegration of a previously integrated civilization.

Their "death of civilizations or cultures" has some simulacrum of meaning only because Danilevsky, Spengler, and Toynbee mixed up their civilization or culture with different social groups. The longevity of social groups is indeed finite. By mixing the civilizational system with the social group, they ascribed the finite life-span of social groups to cultural and civilizational systems. But here again, they made practically no analysis of the life-span of social groups.

The life-span of these groups varies, according to the nature of the group, from a few moments to a few years, decades, or centuries—in rare cases, a few thousands of years. Thus the average life-span of contemporary small economic organizations is about three years; that of bigger business firms, about six years; that of the large business concerns, about twenty-eight years. Small local cultural groups survive, on an average, about two or three years. The longevity of the family ranges from a few days or years to some three hundred years, rarely exceeding this duration, a longevity of from one to three generations being modal. Seventy-seven percent of the existing universities and colleges were founded after 1800, very few, if any, antedating the twelfth century. Of existing cities with a population of 100,000 or over, approximately 40 percent emerged after 1600, 21 percent were founded between the eleventh and the fifteenth century, and only 18 percent antedate the fifth century A.D. The life-span of contemporary small cities is considerably shorter. The duration of states varies from a few weeks and years up to two thousand years or over, most of the existing states (thirty-six) having an age of approximately one hundred years or less. Small religious groups disappear within a few years or decades. The life-span of major religions, such as Hinduism, Taoism, Confucianism, Buddhism, Jainism, Judaism, Christianity, and Mohammedanism, has ranged from approximately 1300 years to 3500 years or more. Similarly, many small language groups have had a life-span of only a few decades. Larger ones have existed for several centuries; a few, for one or two or three thousand years.

All in all, most social groups rarely survive for more than a few centuries.[9] Virtually all organized groups—the state, the family, the language group, the political party, even the religious group—are mortal. After a time they disintegrate and dissolve as social individualities, though this dissolution does not mean either the death of their members or the disappearance of their total culture or civilization. While the group may dissolve, all or a considerable part of its total culture or civilization may be—and usually is—taken over by other groups and often expanded and enriched by them. Although Sparta, Athens, and other Greek states were dissolved long ago, Greek culture or civilization has nevertheless been appropriated, in its greater part, by many other groups and has spread far beyond the confines of Greece and the Hellenic world. The same is true of practically any other great culture that has possessed vital values.

Danilevsky, Spengler, and Toynbee, having mistaken a motley assortment of social groups for civilization, and having observed that social groups are mortal, rashly concluded that both ordinary and major cultures or civilizations die *in toto*. The states of ancient Egypt, Sumeria, Babylonia, and Rome are extinct; so also are many past language, religious, and territorial groups. Nevertheless, a great deal of the total culture or civilization of these groups is still functioning in the contemporary sociocultural world either in its original form or in a disguised and modified form as a part and parcel of our living "civilization." The scientific discoveries of earlier "civilizations," their philosophical and religious systems, their law, ethics, language, literature and fine arts, their forms of political, economic and social organization, their manners and mores— these elements make up the lion's share of today's living "civilization." If, indeed, we were to subtract from Western "civilization" all the values inherited from the "dead civilizations," particularly those of the Graeco-Roman, Arabic, and Jewish worlds (including Christianity), the remainder would be unbelievably meager, as well as incoherent.

Whichever of the foregoing meanings of the term "death of civilizations" we take, the formulas of the "undertakers of civilization" appear to be essentially meaningless.

5

LONGEVITY OF CULTURAL SYSTEMS

Having cleared the ground of encumbering fallacious theories, we may now ask: What is the real situation respecting the longevity, life-span, and mortality of cultural or civilizational systems?

The life-span of empirical sociocultural unities (or systems) seems to be even longer than that of organized social groups. It ranges from almost the zero point to several thousands of years and, for generic systems, to virtually an indefinite period. Petty sociocultural systems—daily utterances of the type *"A is B"* embodied in our conversations, radio talks, newspaper and magazine articles, and the like, trivial songs, drawings, sculpturing, building, playing and even praying—these Lilliputian cultural unities are forgotten almost as soon as they are uttered or created.

When, however, we turn to vast sociocultural systems containing some real and important value—such as a great language, a major religion, a notable philosophical, ethical, juridical, scientific, political, economic, familistic, or kinship system, a significant artistic creation, an important technological invention—we find that they may endure for decades, centuries, or even thousands of years. The foremost of them tend to become virtually immortal, surviving, with ups and downs, for an indefinite period. Such languages as the Chinese, Greek, and Latin have existed for more than two thousand years; other tongues, such as German, French, English, and Russian, for more than a millennium. The same is true of outstanding religious systems, such as Taoism, Confucianism, Hinduism, Buddhism, Judaism, Jainism, and Christianity; of notable philosophical systems, such as those of the Upanishads, of the "six philosophies" of India, of Plato, Aristotle, Plotinus, or Sankara; of scientific and technological systems where the basic discoveries and inventions go far into the past. The overwhelming majority of these discoveries and inventions (with the exception of a few that have been lost and then rediscovered or reinvented) have continued to live up to the present time—that is, for millennia. The same generalization applies to basic ethical and juridical principles or systems, such as the Golden Rule, the Ten Commandments, the ethical systems of love, utilitarianism, hedonism, eudemonism, cynicism, stoicism, and asceticism—all formulated long ago, certainly before our era. Even specific legal codes, such as the *Corpus Juris Civilis*, the laws of Manu and Brichaspati, or the law system of the first books of the Bible, survive not only in books and the writings of scholars but in our contemporary social life, being embodied in law norms actually practiced and enforced. After Roman law was adopted in Italy in the twelfth century, it became the foundation of the law of almost all the countries of continental Europe.

Similar longevity is exhibited by noteworthy aesthetic creations—the Mahabbarata and Ramayana, the works of Homer and Hesiod, Sophocles and Aristophanes, the Gregorian chants, the compositions of Palestrina and Bach, and the architectural systems represented by the Egyptian pyramids and temples, the Hindu temples, the Doric, Ionic and Corinthian orders and Gothic architecture.

Finally, such prehistoric technological inventions and practices as the use of fire, the lever, and the wheel, the domestication of animals, many nomadic, pastoral, and agricultural technologies, and many technologies of the Stone, Copper, Bronze, and early Iron Ages are still very much alive, either as original systems functioning now as auxiliaries, or as elements incorporated in more advanced and comprehensive modern systems.

These examples demonstrate that specific major sociocultural systems survive for thousands of years or even longer. Some of them, to be sure, have perished; others have been mutilated; but the rank and file tend to be immortal. They now display an exuberant vitality and wide diffusion, now undergo an anemic phase marked by a diminution of their influence. But, like an organism passing through alternate periods of low and high vitality, they persist. Now and then some of them, such as many of the Graeco-Roman cultural systems, experience a state of sociocultural "coma" which lasts for years, decades, and even centuries and then suddenly reawakens. The revival or resurrection of certain Graeco-Roman systems during the Italian Renaissance affords a pertinent example.

Finally, if we take not a specific individual form of a major cultural system but its *typical* and *generic* forms, we find these to be virtually immortal. This or that particular language may disappear; but language *per se,* even its principal types, is perennial. This or that specific materialistic or idealistic, rationalistic or empirical philosophical system may perish; but materialistic and idealistic, rationalistic and empirical *types* of philosophies seem to be immortal. The same is true of theistic, pantheistic, and mystical types of religion and of classical and romantic, ideational and sensate forms of art. This or that

scientific theory may decline and be forgotten; but science itself, as a system, even in its basic principles, appears to be
perennial. The same generalization applies to generic and
typical systems of law and ethics and to the fundamental forms
of political, economic, and family organization. Plato's aristocracy, timocracy, oligarchy, democracy, and tyranny are
perennial political systems which, despite their fluctuations and
vicissitudes, never perish.

Finally, even the vastest sociocultural supersystems, such as
the Ideational, Idealistic, and Sensate supersystems, are virtually immortal. Each of their individual forms emerges, flour-
ishes for centuries or even millennia, and then declines, becoming a mere minor element in a given total culture or population and being superseded, as a dominant system, by one of
the other supersystems or by a temporary eclectic congeries.
After centuries of latent existence (in the same or in another
population) it re-emerges, becomes again dominant for a
certain period, then once more declines and eventually re-
appears.[10]

Such, in brief, is the actual situation respecting the life-
span, mortality, and resurrection of sociocultural systems. We
can see that this is very different from our authors' largely
meaningless "death of civilizations."

6

THE BIRTH OF CIVILIZATIONS

Danilevsky's, Spengler's, and Toynbee's basic error is also
responsible for their vague conceptions regarding the birth of
High Cultures, "civilizations," or "culture-historical types."

When is a civilization born? What are the marks of its birth?
What phases, if any, does the birth process consist of? How
long does it take? None of the theories under discussion gives
even a remotely satisfactory answer to these questions. As a
matter of fact, the questions are not even raised. Because of
their confusion of the cultural-civilizational systems with so-

cial groups, our scholars seem to assume that the moment of emergence of this or that political state or national, religious or other organized social group means the birth of a civilization-culture. It has been pointed out above that it is not permissible to identify a cultural system with a social group. It is equally invalid to identify the emergence of a social group with the birth of a High Culture or civilization. The emergence of what state was responsible for the birth of Western civilization? the Merovingian? the Carolingian? the Holy Roman Empire of the German nation? or one of a multitude of European states? Or was this civilization born the moment Christianity became dominant in the West? or at the time of the Carolingian or the thirteenth-century Renaissance? Or was it ushered in by the wave of migrations and the so-called "fall of the Roman Empire"?

Since the civilizations under discussion are not real unities, they are not born, and therefore neither Danilevsky, Spengler, Toynbee, nor anyone else can establish the moment of their birth. On the other hand, both phases of the birth of real, meaningful-causal unities can be established fairly definitely. The birth-process of any such system consists of two phases: the ideological conception of the system, and its objectification in the "material vehicles"—a third phase, that of socialization among other individuals and groups, being necessary for its long life and growth. Any small or great meaningful system— beginning with "two and two make four," "the weather is fine," and ending with the greatest scientific, philosophical, religious, aesthetic, ethical, technological, and other systems conceived by Plato, Newton, Beethoven, Homer, Jesus, and Buddha—is first conceived in the mind of its creator. The moment of the full conception of the system is the moment of the first phase of its birth. Sometimes the creator of a system may be "pregnant" with his ideas for weeks and years before they mature. The second phase of a meaningful-causal system's birth consists of its objectification through material vehicles: writing it on paper, recording it on stone, using sounds (air waves) in the form of speech or music, making a model of an invented gadget, building a house according to a conceived plan, painting a conceived picture, molding such a sculpture, or any of a hundred other ways that objectify the conceived system of meanings, norms, and values. When objectification is completed, the system can be considered as born. When Plato finished writing his *Republic*, Bach his *Mass in B-Minor*, or Isaac Newton his *Principia*, their systems were born. Frequently we even know the exact date when such a completion takes place.

Then, if the born system is destined to live a long time and to grow, it has to undergo the third phase of its grounding in empirical reality—the phase of diffusion, multiplication, or socialization. Its ideological, behavioral, and material forms must be spread among other human beings (besides its author), groups, and cultural systems and congeries. Otherwise it dies with its author. In the cases of the birth of little meaningful-causal systems—such as hundreds of our daily utterances like "*A* is *B*," or "*A* is not *B*"—all these phases are closely "telescoped" into one another and are almost synchronous. When great systems are born, it sometimes requires months and years to complete the ideological conception of the system. Sometimes months and years are necessary to objectify it adequately into material vehicles. Finally, sometimes decades, even a few centuries, are necessary for an objectified system to diffuse widely and to be "recognized" as an important unit in a given total culture.[11]

The theories under discussion are equally vague in elucidating such problems in this field as: Why has only an exceedingly small number of tribes or groups been able to build a great civilization or High Culture? Why has an overwhelming majority of human pre-literate groups remained on a "pre-civilizational" level or on the level of mere "ethnographic material"? What, generally, are the factors of cultural creativity in the sense of discovery and creation of great cultural systems?

We may agree with our authors that the total number of civilizations or cultures that have created great cultural systems and supersystems in the total human history is very small, fluctuating somewhere between nine and forty. The majority of tribes and "peoples" or linguistic groups of human history have remained on pre-literal, pre-civilizational cultural levels. They have not created great cultural systems.

Among our thinkers, Spengler and Schubart practically ignore these questions. They view the whole matter of the emergence and growth of High Culture as resulting from an interference of mysterious cosmic forces in the life of this planet and especially in human affairs. Viewing the earth itself as a particle in an infinitely vast cosmos, they regard each case of emergence of a great culture, and the people who are made its instrument, as determined by the cosmic creative forces which blow where they will and bestow their "grace" in an inscrutable, unforeseen, and unpredictable manner. Such an answer does not help us to understand the why and how, the when, where and who of the emergence of great civilizations. It simply makes a mystery of the whole problem.

Danilevsky and Toynbee try to answer these problems in terms of empirical factors of cultural or civilizational creativity. Danilevsky stresses two factors particularly: first, the political independence of linguistically related groups; second, the diversity and richness of the ethnographic or cultural material accessible to them. Toynbee explains the emergence of a great civilization by triple factors: first, a geographic milieu that is neither too hard nor too comfortable; second, the presence of a creative minority; third, an incessant interplay of challenge and response, withdrawal and return. If the environment is too hard, the development of a great civilization is either arrested or its birth becomes abortive. If the milieu is too soft, there is no strong challenge incessantly stimulating the group's maximum creative effort to meet it successfully. Through the creative minority the group, under the conditions that are neither too soft nor too hard successfully meets the challenge, and by incessantly responding to it ceaselessly develops its creative forces and reaches the level of a prospective great civilization.

Such are the essentials of Danilevsky's and Toynbee's answers to these questions.

Their classification of factors is defective in several respects. It is incomplete. Some of their factors are very doubtful; others are very vague; still others are possibly wrong. Thus, Danilevsky's factor of political independence does not seem to be absolutely essential for a group to be creative in many fields of culture. Sometimes political power and independence can facilitate cultural creativity, at other times they can hinder it, and again they may have no effect. More accurate is the factor of cultural freedom, which allows the creators to create without being suffocated in their creative activities by all sorts of censorship and regimentation arising especially from their political or religious governing powers-that-be. Many politically independent groups do not have this cultural freedom within their groups; and, on the other hand, many groups that are politically subjugated possess this cultural freedom for their creative members. For these reasons the factor of cultural freedom is more instrumental and necessary than Danilevsky's factor of political independence.[12]

Toynbee's factor of a geographical environment that is neither too hard nor too comfortable is vague. Who knows exactly what environment is hard or soft for any given group at any given time? [13] In addition, it is hardly possible to establish that all great civilizations emerged in such an environment. On the other hand, one can state with a reasonable degree of certainty that the environment of hundreds of pre-literate groups has been of a "moderate" kind, neither too severe nor too soft. Yet these groups have not reached the level of Toynbee's civilization. Furthermore, geographic environment changes very slowly and very little. For most groups in the past it has remained about the same over a period of centuries. For centuries many groups remained pre-literate. Then, suddenly, without any notable environmental change, a group begins to evolve into a "civilization." Thus the western Germano-Romanic and other tribes remained for millennia, up to roughly the Carolingian Renaissance, on a pre-civilizational level. It was only after the eighth century that they began to climb into the class of High Cultures. There is no evidence that the geographic environment of Western Europe changed in the seventh or the eighth centuries. If it remained unchanged, then the tribes' rise into the class of great cultures can evidently not be ascribed to the constant factor of geographic environment.

On the other hand, some "breakdowns" and disintegrations of certain "civilizations" occurred without any notable change in their geographic environment. Evidently these declines cannot be attributed to the geographic factor. Further, of several tribes living in the same environment one becomes a civilization while others don't. Such facts again contradict the hypothesis. To sum up: Toynbee's geographic factor is entirely questionable. If its indeterminate, vague nature means something definite, it is neither a necessary nor always a favorable factor of group creativity, nor always responsible for a group's graduation into the class of civilizations.[14]

Also unsatisfactory is Toynbee's factor of a creative minority. He rejects the factor of racial and biological heredity. If we exclude these factors, then whence and how could Toynbee's creative minority appear, and how could it become creative? Unless he follows Spengler's theory of "the cosmic creative grace" choosing in a mysterious way its "elect" and making them a "creative minority," Toynbee's minority remains a complete mystery as to the what, how, whence, and why of its emergence and disappearance. Instead of explaining the creativity of a given group, his postulate itself requires even greater elucidation than the question of why some groups become civilizations while others do not.

Finally, his factors of challenge and response, withdrawal and return, are not very enlightening. As long as *any group* lives, it is incessantly challenged or stimulated by millions of external and internal stimuli and incessantly responds to these challenges. There is no living group or person, including the most uncreative, that is not subject to this factor. Since it is universal, continuous, and common to all living groups and individuals, it evidently cannot be a factor that operates only for creative groups and persons. The same can be said about the factor of withdrawal and return. It, too, is common to creative and uncreative, successful and unsuccessful groups and persons and therefore does not in the least solve the problem under discussion.

Only if Toynbee had specified that what he had in mind was a *special* form of challenge and response, of withdrawal and return, a form found in operation only among creative groups and persons and absent among the uncreative ones, only in such a case would these factors have been helpful. Such a specification was not made by Toynbee; therefore these factors contribute little toward the solution of the problem.[15]

7

FACTORS IN CREATIVITY

On the other hand, Toynbee and Danilevsky do not mention some of the factors that are indispensable for a person's or a group's eminent creativity. Among several as yet little known factors of creativity, the following seem to be indispensable.

(a) *Suprasensory and suprarational genius,* resulting either from "fortunate heredity," of which little is known at the moment, or coming from some other, unknown source. Whatever the source, a suprarational and suprasensory creative genius, different from a mere sensory and rational ability, is an indispensable factor in the discovery or creation of great cultural systems by persons or groups.

(b) The *social need* for a new system, whether scientific, technological, military, religious, ethical, artistic, or other. Without such a need being felt, a given group or person does not set out to do the requisite creative work. The nature of the urgent need also determines the nature of the great cultural system that is to be discovered or created by the creative members of the group. Mountaineers do not try to discover ingenious means for oceanic navigation. Groups not menaced militarily do not invent ingenious military organization and tactics.

(c) *Cross-fertilization of cultural streams,* the factor stressed by Danilevsky.

(d) *Cultural freedom* (discussed above).

(e) *Luck,* a residual factor of an incidental favorable situation or constellation of circumstances that suggests an idea, like the swaying lamp noted by Galileo in the cathedral at Pisa, or the apple falling with a thud in the garden of Isaac Newton.[16]

Each of these factors taken separately is insufficient to account for creativity; taken together, they account for a great deal in the creativity of persons and groups and go far towards explaining why a few groups have been able to create great cultural systems ("civilizations") while many others have remained on the level of "ethnographic material." This classification is possibly somewhat fuller and more adequate than those of Danilevsky, Toynbee, Spengler, and Schubart.

8

GROWTH AND DISINTEGRATION OF CIVILIZATIONS

The foregoing criticism can be applied to the phases of growth, breakdown, disintegration, and dissolution of civilization-cultures as they are outlined in the theories under discussion. The "parental sin" mentioned is responsible for important blunders in these writers' analyses of these problems. Since the civilizations are taken for real systems and since they have to die, according to the organismic scheme, there follows from these false premises the Danilevsky-Spengler-Toynbee postulate of their having been either "abortively born," "arrested," "petrified," "broken down," "disintegrated," or "dead and buried." According to Toynbee, out of twenty-six civilizations, only one—the Western—is still possibly alive at the present time, all the others being either dead or half-dead ("arrested," "petrified," "disintegrating"). According to Danilevsky, Spengler, and Schubart, even this Western civilization is dead until a new one emerges. Since, according to the assumed scheme, civilizations must undergo breakdown, disintegration, and death, these writers must either bury them or consider them "abortive," "arrested," and so forth. Since the scheme demands this and since these thinkers do not have any clear criteria as to what death or disintegration of civilization really is, they willingly assume the role of undertaker to civilizations.

Courageously following the scheme, they are not deterred by the fact that some of the civilizations which, according to their scheme, ought to have been dead a long time ago, survived centuries and longer, and are still very much alive. These writers—especially Toynbee—dispose of the difficulty by the simple device of postulating a "petrified" civilization. Thus China, Egypt, and the Hellenic cultures have been or were "petrified" for thousands of years. All of Roman history was, in Toynbee's scheme, but an incessant disintegration from the very beginning to the end. In such a scheme, civilizations hardly have time to live and grow. If they are not born abortive —as some are—they are arrested. If they are not arrested, they break down almost immediately after they are born and then begin to disintegrate or become a "petrified trunk." Danilevsky explicitly stresses the brevity of the blossoming period. Philosophically, of course, birth is the beginning of death; but one who investigates empirically the life of either an organism or of a civilization can and must be less philosophical and study the process of life itself, before the paralysis or incurable sickness sets in or death occurs. And for most of the organisms and civilizations there is a great distance between the points of birth and death.

The writers under consideration here have given little study to the greater part of the existence of civilizations and have drowned thousands of years of that existence in indulging their penchant for acting as the "undertakers of civilizations." This is not by way of denying the facts of the disintegration or even of the dissolution that real cultural or civilizational systems undergo. Disintegration and dissolution do occur, but with real systems, not with congeries of civilizations. And with the great system they occur not immediately after its "birth" but often after a very long life-span.

The foregoing explains why in Toynbee's work especially, and to a lesser degree in Danilevsky's and Spengler's, little analysis is found of the phase of the growth of civilizations. Only indefinite statements are to be found to the effect that in that phase there is a Creative Minority successfully meeting the challenge, that there is no class war, no inter-society war, and that everything goes well there, moves and becomes more and more "etherialized." That is about all that is said of this phase. Such an "idyllic" characterization of the process of growth of Toynbee's twenty-one civilizations is evidently fantastic. If we have to believe it, we seemingly have to accept that in Greece before 431–403 B.C. (Toynbee's date for the Hellenic breakdown) there were no wars, no revolutions, no class struggle, no slavery, no traditionalism, no uncreative minority, and that all these "plagues" appeared only after the Peloponnesian War. On the other hand, we shall expect that, after this war, creativeness ceased in Greece and Rome, and that there was no Plato, no Aristotle, no Epicurus, no Zeno, no Polybius, no Church Fathers, no Aristophanes, no Lucretius, no scientific discovery. As a matter of fact, the situation in all these respects was very different before and after the breakdown. The "indicators" of war (magnitude measured by war casualties) per million of the population for Greece were 29 for the fifth, 48 for the fourth, and 18 and 3, respectively, for the third and second centuries B.C. "Indicators" of internal disturbances (revolutions) were 149, 468, 320, 259, and 36, respectively, for the centuries from the sixth to the second B.C., inclusive. This shows that the real movement of wars and revolutions in Greece was very different from what Toynbee tells us. The same is true of Rome.[17]

Scientific, philosophical, and religious creativeness likewise reached its peak in and after the fifth century B.C. rather than before that time.[18] In regard to the Western civilization, as mentioned, Toynbee's diagnosis is somewhat ambiguous. In many places he says that its breakdown is already in process; in other places he is non-committal. Whatever his diagnosis, he regards Western civilization before the fifteenth century as in the phase of growth. If this is so, then according to his scheme, no revolutions, serious wars or hard-and-fast class divisions existed in Europe before that century. Factually, however, in the history of Europe the thirteenth and fourteenth are the most revolutionary up to the twentieth century; likewise, serfdom and class divisions were hard and fast, and there were many wars—small and great.[19]

Finally, Medieval Western civilization of the period of growth does not exhibit many of the traits of Toynbee's growing civilizations but displays a mass of traits characteristic of Toynbee's disintegrating civilizations. The same is true of his other civilizations. This means that Toynbee's uniformities of growth and decline of the civilizations are not borne out by the facts. With some modification, this criticism can also be applied to Danilevsky's and Spengler's outlines of this phase.

Further, a large number of the uniformities they claim in connection with their conceptual scheme are also either fallacious or overstated—for instance, Toynbee's uniformity of negative correlation between the geographic expansion of civilization and its growth, between war and growth, and between progress of technique and growth. Granting a particle of truth to his statements, they are at the same time certainly fallacious in this categoric formulation. If Toynbee's twenty-one civilizations had not diffused over large areas and remained just the civilizations of little Sumeric, Greek, Egyptian, or Arabic villages, they could hardly have become "historical." Certainly they would not come to the attention of Toynbee and other historians. All his civilizations are great complexes, spread over vast areas of territory and vast populations. They did not emerge at once in such a vast form, but, beginning with a small area they expanded (in the process of their growth) over vaster and vaster areas and populations and thus became historical. They would not otherwise have been noticed. If Toynbee contends, as in a few places he does, that such a diffusion over vaster areas took place peacefully, through spontaneous submission of the "barbarians" to the charm of the diffusing civilization, such a statement is again inaccurate. All his twenty-one civilizations in their period of growth (according to Toynbee's scheme) expanded not only peacefully but even more by force, coercion, and wars. On the other hand, many of them in the period of disintegration shrank, rather than expanded, and were more peaceful than in what Toynbee calls the period of growth.

Spengler, Toynbee, and in part Danilevsky ascribe specific dominant tendencies to each of their civilizations: aesthetic to the Hellenic, religious to the Indic, machinistic-technological to the Western. (They do not assign such dominant characteristics to most of the remaining eighteen civilizations.) Such a summary characterization is again very doubtful. Western civilization did not show its alleged dominant characteristic up to approximately the thirteenth century A.D. From the sixth to the end of the twelfth centuries the movement of technological inventions and scientific discoveries stood at about zero in this allegedly technological civilization par excellence; and from the sixth to the thirteenth centuries this machinistic civilization was religious through and through, even more religious than the Indic or Hindu civilizations in many periods of their history.[20]

The supposedly aesthetic Hellenistic civilization did not show its aesthetic penchant (in Toynbee's sense) before the sixth century B.C. and displayed quite a boisterous scientific and technological *élan* in the period from 600 to 200 A.D.[21] The Arabic civilization (whose dominant trait Toynbee does not stress) displayed an enormous scientific and technological *élan* in the centuries from the eighth to the thirteenth—much more so than the Western civilization during these centuries.[22]

All this means that the Spenglerian-Toynbee ascription of some specific perennial tendency to this or that civilization, regardless of the period of its history, is misleading and inaccurate. This can also be seen from the subsequent figures about the fields and periods of creativity of various countries. In this respect, Danilevsky's position is somewhat sounder. Side by side with the cultures with one specific tendency, he recognizes at least the autochthonous cultures with many tendencies and the cultures with two, three, and four tendencies. Such a theory is still not quite correct, but it is less fallacious than Toynbee's and Spengler's views.

9

THE FALLACY OF ONE LIFE-AND-CREATIVITY CYCLE OF A CIVILIZATION

Finally, the foregoing criticism shows that the central idea of Danilevsky, Spengler, and Toynbee that each great culture or civilization has only one life-cycle and one cycle of creativity (with a minor "Indian Summer" and "second religiosity") is entirely untenable so far as real cultural systems are concerned. Even in regard to social groups it is tenable only for a small fraction of them. It is not at all tenable as applied to all social systems. If we define clearly the meaning of a quantitative and qualitative growth and decline, of blossoming and deterioration of cultural systems,[23] we can see, as has already been partly shown, that great cultural systems have many quantitative and qualitative ups and downs in their virtually indefinitely long life-span. Even big *social* systems like the Chinese or the Egyptian or the Hindu states and nations have had several ups and downs in their political and social history. So also have many families, religious or economic bodies, political parties and other social groups. In their "success," "creativity," "wealth," "membership" and "power," most of them have several ups and downs in their life-history instead of just one life-cycle and one period of creativity. Subsequent abbreviated figures show that each of the countries (civilizations) has had not one but several creative blossomings and declines in all the fields of creativity the country exhibited. The data show also that, contrary to Toynbee and Spengler, each country (civilization) has been creative not in one but in several fields. (See page 240.)

However approximate, these data leave no doubt that religious, political, scientific, artistic, philosophical, and other cultural systems in all these countries have had not one but two or more flowerings and declines; and the countries themselves (civilizations) as a dumping ground of these cultural systems have had not one but two or more periods of cultural and social creativity.

Periods of creative blossoming in specified fields of culture

Egypt

Religion	c. 3500–3000 B.C., c. 2500–2300 B.C., c. 1580–1490 B.C., c. 1370–1352 B.C.
The State and (to some extent) Economics	2895–2540 B.C., 2000–1785 B.C., 1580–1200 B.C., 663–525 B.C.
Science	c. 4241 B.C., 1900–1500 B.C.
Literature	2000–1225 B.C., 1300–900 B.C.
Sculpture	2840–2575 B.C., 1580–1350 B.C.
Architecture	1580–1250 B.C.
Music	1411–1284 B.C.
Painting	1580–1250 B.C., 750–525 B.C.

India

Religion	c. 1000 B.C., c. 600–400 B.C., c. 272–232 B.C., c. 1–100 A.D., c. 788–860
The State (native, not foreign) and (to some extent) Economics	c. 321–186 B.C., 78–96 A.D., 320–500, c. 606–647, 1350–1600
Philosophy	600–400 B.C., 100–500, 600–1000
Science	700–500 B.C., 400–1150 (Climax c. 500–625)
Literature	400 B.C.–100 A.D., 350–750
Sculpture	c. 150 B.C., 400–725 A.D.
Architecture	1489–1706
Music	1600–1771
Painting	450–750, 1615–1800

Greece

Religion	850–500 B.C., 350–300 B.C.
The State and Economics	750–430 B.C., 500–300 B.C.
Philosophy	585–270 B.C.
Science	585 B.C.–100 A.D.
Music	750–600 B.C., 450–350 B.C.
Literature	800–700 B.C., 550–350 B.C.
Architecture	550–430 B.C.
Sculpture	559–350 B.C.
Painting	450–300 B.C.

France

Religion	Decline after the thirteenth century
The State	1050–1325, 1600–1715, 1800–1815, 1850–1870, 1890–1940
Economics	1100–1325, 1475–1560, 1840–1914
Philosophy	1075–1160, 1300–1350, 1600–1700, 1750–1850
Science	1580–1660, 1750–1870
Architecture	1050–1350
Sculpture	1140–1325, 1450–1550, 1850–1910
Music	1100–1350, 1650–1750, 1850–1910
Painting	1620–1670, 1760–1880
Literature	1070–1300, 1520–1580, 1630–1700, 1780–1900 [24]

10

THE FALLACY OF ONE SPECIFIC CREATIVITY OF A CIVILIZATION

These data show also that each of these countries (civilizations) have had creativity not in one but in several cultural and social fields. The data conclusively demonstrate the fallacy of a specificity of cultural creativeness of each "civilization" or "nation" or "country." Finally, they clearly prove that the field of creativity of a given "nation" or "country" or "civilization" shifts in the course of time. At a given period it may be creative in religion and uncreative in science or the fine arts; at another, it may become creative in these fields and sterile in religion.

11

SHIFT OF CENTERS OF CREATIVITY

Viewed in a broader perspective, this shift of the centers of creativity in various fields of culture is a perennial process. It takes place within a country and among different countries, the leadership in scientific creativity passing from one country

to another. The same is true of the shift of all forms of creativity: religious, philosophical, political, economic, artistic,
legal, ethical, technological.

For instance, in the period from 800 to 1600, Italy made
some 25 to 41 per cent of all the scientific discoveries and
inventions in Europe; in the period from 1726 up to the present
time the Italian share dwindled to from 2 to 4 per cent. The
United States contributed only 1.1 per cent of the total discoveries and inventions in the period 1726–1750, and nothing
before that. This share was increased now to over 30 per cent.
Even the chief center of human history shifts in the course of
time. Before the fourteenth century A.D., it was in Arabic and
Asiatic countries. Later it shifted to Europe. At the present
time it is shifting not so much to Russia (as Danilevsky, Schubart, and in part Spengler, state) but to the Pacific with the
United States, Russia, China, India, and Latin America playing the leading roles in the great historical drama of the next
centuries. Europe will participate in it but only as one of the
actors, in no way as the main star. The European period of
human history is about over.[25]

These considerations and the total body of available evidence testify definitely against the validity of the "organismic"
schemes of Danilevsky, Spengler, and Toynbee. Neither the
real cultural or social systems nor the nations or countries as
a field of cultural systems have a simple and uniform life-cycle
of childhood, maturity, old age, and death. The life-curve of
especially great cultural systems is much more complex, diverse, and less uniform that the organismic life-cycle. A fluctuating curve, with a non-periodic, ever-changing rhythm of ups
and downs, repeating essentially the perennial themes but with
incessant variations, seems to depict the life-course of the great
cultural systems and supersystems more correctly than the
organismic cycle-curve.

In other terms Danilevsky, Spengler, and Toynbee see only
a "three or four beat rhythm" in the life-process of civilizations: the rhythm of childhood-maturity-old age or of spring-
summer-autumn-winter. Meanwhile, in the life-process of cultural and social systems many diverse rhythms co-exist:

two-beat, three-beat, four-beat, and still more complex rhythms, now one kind, then another, becoming dominant in the co-existing multitude of embracing and embraced, short and long rhythms, up to the super-rhythms. Our eminent scholars unduly simplify the richly various rhythms in the life-process of social and cultural systems.[26]

The indicated errors are the basic ones in the theories discussed. Having exposed these, we can pass by, without discussion, a multitude of small mistakes hardly avoidable in works of dimensions as vast as these. As they do not seriously vitiate the central framework of the theories, they require no special criticism here; a few of these inaccuracies will be pointed out below. For the present, we can pass to a criticism of the important shortcomings of other theories and then turn to an appreciation of the sound elements in these "readings of history"—the elements that make an important contribution to our understanding of historical events and of the social and humanistic disciplines.

XIII

Critical Examination of the Theories of Northrop, Kroeber, Schubart, Berdyaev, and Schweitzer

I

NORTHROP'S "THEORETIC" AND "AESTHETIC" CATEGORIES

If my interpretation of the cultural unities of Northrop, Kroeber, Berdyaev, Schubart, and Schweitzer are correct, these unities—being chiefly meaningful-causal systems—are free from the "parental sin" of the civilizational pseudo-unities of Danilevsky, Spengler, and Toynbee. For this reason, my own views on this basic point clash little with the theories of Northrop, Kroeber, and others. My disagreement is mainly on secondary points. In Northrop's philosophy of history the most important of these points are two: first, his "aesthetic-intuitional" cognition, component, and cultural supersystem dominant in the East, and his "theoretic-scientific" knowledge, component, and supersystem, dominant in the West; second, his rigid insistence on the dependence of the philosophical pre-suppositions of cultural systems upon the extant state of science, particularly the mathematico-physical sciences. Let us critically examine these problems.

In Chapter III, we saw that the "aesthetic" and "theoretic" cultural systems are the vastest among Northrop's cultural unities. They can therefore be styled "supersystems," though he does not use this term. We also saw the cardinal importance of the "aesthetic" and "theoretic" components in the nature of things, in ways of cognition, in types of cultural systems, and, finally, in an "epistemic correlation" of these components for an adequate cognition, elimination of conflicts, and pacification of humanity. These two categories cover about the same ground as my own three categories—Ideational, Idealistic, and Sensate (plus Integral and Eclectic).

Let us briefly see how Northrop's "aesthetic-theoretic" dyad differs from my "Ideational-Idealistic-Sensate" triad. Differing from Northrop's two ways of cognition (the "aesthetic-intuitional" and the "theoretic-scientific"), two systems of truth, two main components in (or aspects of) the true reality, and his double "epistemic correlation," I distinguish three—Ideational, Idealistic, Sensate (plus Integral and Eclectic)—ways of cognition, three systems of truth, of science and philosophy, of religion and fine arts, of ethics and law, of economics and politics; three cultural supersystems and three main aspects (or "components") of the "undifferentiated continuum" or of the true reality; finally, triple "epistemic correlation," instead of Northrop's double one.

In brief my ways of cognition and my systems of truth are as follows:

(a) *Sensory cognition and the truth of the senses.* Propositions like "Snow is white and cold," "Sugar is sweet," "The sky is now blue," "He has a fever," "This stone is heavy," are derived from our sense perception, and their validity depends upon the testimony of sense organs. If when glancing at and touching "snow" we do not see its "whiteness" or feel its "coldness," the proposition becomes invalid. If our senses confirm its whiteness and coldness, the proposition becomes true. *All propositions that deal with the sensory aspects of the world, derived from sense perception, and tested by sense organs (in co-operation with rational-syllogistic and mathe-*

matical logic) are sensory; such cognition is sensory; and the truth based upon the testimony of sense organs is Sensate truth. The greater part of contemporary scientific theories consist exactly of such sensory propositions (assisted by and combined with the propositions derived by our reason through syllogistic or mathematical logic). Empiricism with John Locke's motto, *Nihil esse in intellectu quod non fuerit prius in sensu,* is an excellent formulation of this sensory cognition, knowledge, Sensate truth, and sensory-empirical aspect of the "undifferentiated Manifold Infinity."

(b) *Rational cognition and the truth of reason,* obtained through syllogistic and/or mathematical logic is the second fundamental way of cognition, knowledge, and truth; it is concerned with the "rational" aspect of the "undifferentiated true reality." Purely syllogistic conclusions such as "Socrates is mortal," derived deductively from premises and mathematical propositions arrived at through pure "mathematical reasoning" ("mathematical induction" or "abduction"), are the examples of this "rational" or Idealistic way of cognition, knowledge, truth, and of the aspect of the Manifold Infinity. It is fundamentally different from the sensory as well as from the subsequent Ideational cognition, truth, and reality-aspect. This way of cognition, combined with the sensory way and applied to the sense data, gives us contemporary science, scientific method, cognition, truth, and scientific criteria of validity. This "rational" cognition-truth-reality aspect is fairly close to Northrop's "theoretic" or "scientific" cognition-truth component or aspect of the "nature of things."

(c) *Superrational and supersensory cognition and the Ideational truth* is the third form of cognition, truth, and aspect of the Manifold Infinity. It is given by direct "intuition," "grace," "revelation," "mystic experience," by the "enlightenment" or the "zatori" of the Buddhists, the "samadhi" of the Yogi—all and each of these superrational and supersensory ways being basically different from sense perception and sense cognition as well as from the rational, logico-mathematical knowledge and truth. In this cognition the cognizing subject and cognized object become one; it gives the "essence" of the cognized phenomena; and these phenomena are mainly supra-sensory and suprarational (but not supernatural) in their nature. They are unaccessible to, and not cognizable through, senses as well as through rational logic—syllogistic or mathematical. In contrast to purely sensory or rational cognitions which always pick up a point (the object studied) from an infinite ocean of darkness and throw their "pin-point light" only on this speck, the true intuitive cognition sees and grasps not only this speck but also the darkness that surrounds it.

Religious truth and credos concerning the superempirical and superrational world, revealed through sages, prophets, oracles, and seers; the truth and statements of all true mystics about the true reality or the "undifferentiated continuum" or "the Divine Nothing" or "the Supra-essence" or "Tao" or "the Empty Nirvana" or "Jen" or "Chit" or "Brahman-Atman" or "God"—these truths and symbolic signs of the "ineffable" and the "unutterable" are examples of this Ideational cognition, truth, and the suprasensory aspect of the "ineffable."

This way of cognition and creativity functions also in almost all great discoveries, inventions, and the creativity of genius in all fields of culture. A systematic study of how great discoveries, inventions, and creations are made shows that a suprasensory and suprarational "intuition," "enlightening," "inspiration," "grace" or "revelation" plays the most indispensable role at the initial phase of creativeness and in discoveries in science and technology, religion and philosophy, the fine arts and law, ethics and politics.

The Ideational way is, of course, quite different from the Sensate and rational ways.

(d) *Integral cognition and the Integral system of truth.* If sensory cognition gives us a knowledge of the sensory aspect of the ineffable Manifold Infinity, if the rational way tells us about its rational aspect, and if the intuitional cognition enlightens us about its suprasensory and suprarational aspect, then each of the ways gives only a part of truth, and not the whole truth. At best, each puts us in contact with only one of the chief aspects of the "undifferentiated manifold"; separated from the other two ways of cognition, it gives us only partial truth mixed with partial error. Our knowledge and our contact with the true reality become incomparably fuller and more adequate when all three ways of cognition and knowledge are used and unified into one Integral cognition and system of truth in which each of the three ways and truths checks, corrects, supplements, and enriches the others. Such an integration gives us a comprehension of all three main aspects of the true reality instead of only one. It can be called a "triple epistemic correlation" instead of Northrop's double one.

(e) *Eclectic cognition* gives only chaotic bits of information, not organized into any unified or consistent system, self-contradictory in large part.

Such in brief is the triad of Ideational, Sensate, Idealistic (plus the Integral and Eclectic) ways of cognition, truth, and aspects or components of the Manifold Infinity.[1]

In the light of this theory, the main shortcoming of Northrop's dyad is that in his "aesthetic" form he unites two fundamentally different forms of cognition, truth, aspects of the true reality and of the cultural supersystems—Sensate and Ideational. Even in the foregoing brief characterization, the profound difference of these two forms is obvious; in no way can they be identified with each other and treated as one "aesthetic" form.

Northrop seemingly puts them together for the reason that they are both "immediately intuited," "directly sensed," "immediately apprehended," and "immediately perceived." He uses all these terms for the definition of his "aesthetic" cognition and component.[2]

In some places he seems to distinguish the *immediacy of strict sense perception* (of *blue,* for instance) from the direct intuition of a Yogi, a mystic, or a Chinese painter. In one place he differentiates the "concepts by intuition" and the "concepts by inspection." [3] In spite of these distinctions he puts both sensory and suprasensory forms of cognition and components into one class of the *aesthetic, immediate apprehension-perception component.*

Here lies the weak point of Northrop's dyadic division and of a number of conclusions he draws from it. To begin with, the undifferentiated continuum—God, Tao, Chit, Nirvana, Jen, Brahman, Atman—is certainly neither "directly observable" nor "immediately inspected" and "sensed" in the same manner in which we sense, observe, and inspect *blue.* While *blue* is perceived by all (except the blind), the "undifferentiated continuum" is intuited only by a few, and only after a long training, endeavor, and peculiar grace.

Otherwise, everyone would become a yogi or a mystic who reaches union with God, "an enlightened Boddhisatva," a Suffist, a Jewish or Jainist prophet, Greek oracle, or Pithias. Otherwise there would have been none of the millennia-long controversies about these "true realities" between the believers and disbelievers, whose main argument is over an unobservable, unsensed, unperceived character of the undifferentiated continuum or God. Otherwise there would have been no difference between the materialists and the spiritualists, and especially between the empiricists and the mystics. Otherwise, the partisans of the Ideational-Intuitive cognition and truth would not have declared the whole world of sense data to be a Maya or a mirage or a "city of man," or a "mere appearance" or even something negative in comparison with their true reality of Tao, Brahman, Jen, Chit, Atman, the "supra-essence," "the Divine Nothing," "the *Coincidentia Oppositorum,*" the "Ineffable," or God. Otherwise, science would not have been predominantly skeptical in regard to the Ideational cognition, truth, and reality, because science does not question the reality of sense data. Otherwise, there would hardly be any difference between a great genius and an ordinary mind perfectly capable of immediate sense perception, of even good logic, and perfectly incapable of discovering a great verity or of creating a great value.

In brief, an identification of the Sensory with the Ideational cognition, truth, and reality is impossible; they are much more different from each other than even Northrop's "aesthetic" and "theoretic" categories. The probable fallacy of this identification is responsible for several of Northrop's self-contradictory statements in this respect. Thus, in one place he states that the mystic experience and the union with the undifferentiated continuum are accessible to all; in another, that only a few of the select possess it.[4]

In some places we are told that everyone can be a yogi who immediately perceives not only *blue* and other sensory phenomena but also Chit, Nirvana, Tao, Brahman, which lie not only behind and beyond the sensory phenomena but even beyond the rational mind, because this ineffable source of everything and of any differentiation "is not mind; for mind is a limited instrument through which Chit (or Tao or Brahman, etc.) is manifested. It is that which is behind the mind and by which the mind itself is thought. The Brahman is mindless." In several places Northrop says that everyone seemingly can have a mystic union with the "Supra-essence" (of Dionysius the Areopagite) or Tao, etc., that lies far beyond the whole sensory world, even beyond the rational mind and its logic. In other places Northrop denies that everyone can have this mystic (supersensory and superrational) union with the Supra-essence in the same easy way as everyone can immediately sense the sensory-phenomena.[5]

The same error is responsible for the kind of things Northrop puts into each of his two classes, especially into the "aesthetic" category. To the "aesthetic" component belong: all sense data, emotions, pains, and pleasures, Nirvana, Tao, Chit, Jen, Atman, Supra-essence, even the essentials of the Russian Orthodox religion, the frenzy of the Mexican or Spanish soul, practically all the Oriental religions (except Judaism, Mohammedanism, and Shintoism), a yogi in the state of *samadhi,* or a Zen Buddhist in the state of *zatori,* or a Christian mystic who forgets in his state of ecstasy about God the Father and possibly about the whole "theoretic" Christian credo; all the fine art for the sake of art that symbolically and impressionistically conveys to us the undifferentiated continuum, beginning with almost all the art of the East—but not the religious symbolic art of the West—and ending with the pictures of the French Impressionists and the abstract paintings of Georgia O'Keeffe; most of the Eastern cultural phenomena; and a legion of other things that are immediately perceived, apprehended, sensed, intuited, grasped, without any theoretical ideas and concepts by postulation.

To the "theoretic" component belong: almost any theoretical construction beginning with all scientific hypotheses and ending with the theory of the Trinity and God the Father and the Christian, Mohammedan, Shintoist credos and theologies; almost all "rational" philosophies; the bulk of the ideology of the Roman Catholic Church but for some reason not that of the Russian Orthodox Church; all the fine arts— painting, sculpture, music, etc.—that function as a mere means for conveying various conceptual constructions of a theoretical sort, beginning with Christian religious dogmas and ending with philosophical and scientific theories; then all the empirical tables, stoves, three-dimensional objects; then universals, postulational concepts, electrons, molecules, protons; the bulk of the Western cultural phenomena; and all the other things that are not immediately intuited, perceived, sensed, and apprehended.

Without a thorough analysis one can immediately perceive an utterly odd assortment in the contents of each class. For instance, one cannot understand why, according to Northrop, the bulk of Eastern art belongs to the aesthetic and the bulk of Western, to the theoretic category. In both arts, a part has been "art for art's sake" and not a means for communication of this or that "theory." In both arts, a part of the content represents a symbolic communication concerning the undifferentiated as well as the differentiated "aesthetic continuum." A great deal in Western Christian Medieval art represents "a visible and audible sign of the invisible world" of the Kingdom of God in its differentiated and undifferentiated forms. Such also is a large portion of Eastern religious art. It symbolizes not only the "undifferentiated continuum" but no less, and even more, its differentiated forms and respective "theories" and beliefs. Finally, both arts have a secular, Sensate form as a means for hedonistic, eudemonistic, or utilitarian enjoyment, relaxation, happiness, invigoration of the jaded nerves, and just pleasurable time-passing.

Thus a large portion of Confucian art expresses the *differentiated* continuum and theories of the cult of ancestors, filial piety, and a legion of singular deities no less specific than the differentiated forms of the continuum expressed in the religious art of the West in the forms of Mary, Jesus, God the Father, the Holy Ghost, thousands of saints and transcendental mysteries of the Creation, Redemption, Crucifixion, and so on. Similarly, a greater portion of the art of other cultures of the East deals no less with the differentiated forms than with the undifferentiated aesthetic continuum. The symbols of Indra, Vishnu, Kali, Shiva, and of thousands of other Vedic and post-Vedic deities of Hinduism; the endless varieties of buddhisatvas and Buddhas of Buddhism (all as specific as any Christian saint or Greek deity); an endless variety of popular deities of Taoism, Jainism, or Zoroastrianism, with hundreds of very "differentiated" religious beliefs and rituals about each of them and about transcendental mysteries—all this is as "differentiated" and "theoretic" in Eastern art as it is in Western art. On this ground there is no reason to put the bulk of Eastern art into the aesthetic category, and that of Western art into the theoretic.

There is also no reason to put these into different categories on the ground that the art is being used or not used as a means for some other end. Eastern art has been used as a *means* no less than Western. For instance, Confucian fine art was explicitly used as a means for inculcation of filial piety and of various ideas of "propriety" in social conduct and relationship: "To set correctly forth the successes or failures of government, to affect heaven and earth, there is no readier instrument than poetry. . . . For changing people's manners and altering their customs there is nothing better than music." [6] The same can be said of Hindu, Buddhist, and Taoist art.

In brief, by Northrop's own criteria, it is impossible to put most of the art of the East into the aesthetic and most of the art of the West into the theoretic class.

When Eastern, Graeco-Roman, and Western art is carefully studied, these reasonably certain conclusions seem to follow: First, whether it be Eastern or Western art, *its content as well as its form* basically changes in the course of time. Second, in Eastern art we find all the basic patterns of Western art, and vice versa. Third, the proportion of each basic form can, of course, be different in two arts. Fourth, in the East and West, among pre-literate and "historical" cultures, we find, though in different proportion and at different periods, Ideational, Idealistic, Sensate, and Eclectic forms of art. Thus Ideational art—by content dealing with the supersensory and superrational world and by style being necessarily symbolic (since the supersensory phenomena do not have any visible or audible or sensory forms)—we meet in most of the Neolithic cultures, among many recent pre-literate tribes, and in many periods of Egyptian, Hindu, Taoist, Buddhist, Jainist, and Zoroastrian art. We meet it also in Greek art of the ninth to the sixth centuries B.C. and in Western Medieval art, where from the sixth to the twelfth centuries A.D. Ideational art makes up some 80 to 97 per cent of great art. Thus Ideational art was as common and as dominant in the West in the Middle Ages as it has been in any art at any period (except, perhaps, Tibetan art, of which we know little). Similarly, Idealistic art, by content dealing with the supersensory, the rational and the sensory aspects of reality, and by style being a marvelous synthesis of symbolic, allegoric and "naturalistic" styles—this Idealistic art we find again in practically all Eastern arts, specifically in Chinese Confucian art. It is dominant in the Greek art of the fifth century B.C. and in Western art of the thirteenth century A.D. Finally, Sensate art, by content dealing with purely sensory phenomena and by style being "naturalistic," "illusionistic," and trying to render the phenomena as they look or sound or appear to our senses—this art we meet again in the Paleolithic cultures, among many pre-literate tribes, and as the dominant form in the Graeco-Roman art of the third century B.C. to the third century A.D., and in Western art of the last four centuries. There it has become excessively dominant. At the present time this dominant form is disintegrating in the West and giving way to a transitory "Modern Art" in a search for a new integrated form of art. Though in a lesser proportion than in Western art of the last four centuries, Sensate art has also been present in the art of China, India, Japan, Persia, and Arabia, and at some periods it was even a dominant form in Egyptian, Assyro-Babylonian, and Creto-Minoan art. Thus even this supposedly strictly Western form of art has been functioning *urbi et orbi,* in the West as well as in the East, at the earliest Paleolithic stage, and at the latest contemporary period of human history.[7]

The foregoing analysis seems to be sufficient to show the discrepancies in Northrop's interpretations of the phenomena of the fine arts.

Still more odd is Northrop's classification of the cultures of the Catholic, Protestant, Judaist, Mohammedan, and Shinto religions as theoretic, while the cultures of the Russian Orthodox, Confucianist, Taoist, Jainist, Hinduist, and Buddhist religions are placed in the aesthetic category. The reason for this classification is the supposition that the theoretic religions arose from theorizing (through concepts by postulation) about some of the differentiated properties of the undifferentiated continuum, whereas the aesthetic religions are based on an immediate intuition of the undifferentiated continuum (Tao, Brahman, Chit, etc.). Accordingly the theoretic religions make their theories—dogmas and creed, gods and values—monopolistically absolute, intolerant of all other dogmas and deities. As such they are imperialistic in their missionary zeal and belligerent towards all the "damned religions and sinners." The aesthetic religions, on the other hand, are largely free from this absolutization of various *differentia* of the undifferentiated continuum. They assert that the Truth is One but that men call it by different names. As such they regard their own dogmas, deities, and values as relative, among many names pointing to the ineffable Supra-essence. They are free from intolerance, imperialism, missionary zeal, and militancy. Such is Northrop's ingenious generalization.

If taken within the narrow limits of time and space, it certainly contains a grain of truth. In certain centuries most of

Northrop's theoretic religions have indeed been imperialistic, absolutistic, militant, and intolerant. But taken beyond these narrow limits, his division becomes questionable. First, all his theoretic religions, except perhaps Shintoism, certainly contain an undifferentiated continuum—about as much as his aesthetic religions. All the theoretic religions have their mystical aspect, which by its very nature is a suprasensory and suprarational intuition of the Ineffable.

There is a strong mystic current in the Graeco-Roman world (Plato, Xenocrates, Apollonius, Theon, Plotinus, etc.)[8] and in Judaism (Philo, etc.). The Suffist current in Mohammedanism is apparent in the writings of such great mystics as Al Hallaj. An uninterruptedly strong mystic current is apparent in all denominations of the Christian faith. One has only to look into the works of John, Pseudo-Dionysius, Basil, Gregory of Nyssa, Augustine, Maximus the Confessor, Erigena, Anselm, Hugh of St. Victor, Thierry, Joachim of Floris, Francis of Assisi, Nicholas of Cusa, and of the "practical mystics" like John of the Cross, Teresa, Meister Eckhart, Ruysbroeck, and thousands of others. They and their *docta ignorantia* are the Christian "mouthpieces" of the Ineffable, the "Supra-essence," the "Divine Nothing," the *"coincidentia oppositorum."*

Among the main philosophies of the Graeco-Roman culture and of the Western world, mysticism gives an "indicator" of 1039, much stronger than those of fideism (369), scepticism (279), criticism (197), and exceeded only by empiricism (1338), and rationalism (1534). At some periods of Western thought and culture, such as the fourth century B.C., around the beginning of our era, in the second to the fourth centuries A.D., in the twelfth and in the fifteenth centuries, the tide of mysticism was very high in the Graeco-Roman and Christian West. It became low only during the last five centuries of our predominantly Sensate culture. Even more, Ideational truth and cognition, in its religious form similar to the dominant Ideational truth and cognition in the Hindu, Chinese, Mohammedan, and other Asiatic cultures, has also been dominant in Western culture: its index of 1650 is higher than that for the system of truth of rational reason (1292) and the system of truth of the senses (1338), not to mention the index of 476 for scepticism and criticism.[9]

On the other hand, an ideology or theoretical creed based on concepts by postulation is not confined to the Catholic and Protestant branches of Christianity or to Judaism, Mohammedanism, and Shintoism. It is present to hardly a lesser degree in Russian Orthodox and Eastern Christianity generally, in Confucianism and Taoism, and in all denominations of Hinduism. It exists in all Buddhist denominations: the Hinayanic, Mahayanic, Zen and others, as well as in Jainism, Zoroastrianism, and practically all Eastern religions and philosophies. Together with a strictly mystic current, with its "ineffable all in all," these beliefs all exhibit a multitude of "differentiated" dogmas, creeds, philosophies, and ideologies. If the dogma of God the Father makes the Catholic religion "theoretic," why is an identical dogma of the Russian Orthodox Church (differing from the Catholic only in three letters, in *filioque*) "intuitively aesthetic"? Why then do not the dogmas concerning transmigration of soul, karma, Maya, or about Indra, Vishnu, Brahma, or about a long series of the ancestral and "nature" deities of the Taoists, Confucianists, or Jainists, or about the Taoist "magical charms" and "elixir of life"—why does not this multitude of the Eastern "theoretic" dogmas and rituals, often of the most intricate nature, make these religions "theoretic"? Why is "God the Father" considered to be a "theoretic" concept, while Indra, Kali, Shiva, and Brahma are viewed as "aesthetic" concepts? Even such a difference as the alleged absolutism, imperialism, and intolerance of the Jewish, Christian, Mohammedan, and Shinto religions, as opposed to the tolerance and non-imperialism of Buddhism, Taoism, Confucianism, Hinduism, and Jainism, is greatly exaggerated by Northrop. In their long history these "tolerant" religions have also known periods of intense intolerance, missionary zeal, imperialism, and even inter-religious cold and hot wars. Even the absolutization of their "differentiated" deities has hardly been less, especially in the periods of their success, than the absolutization of the theoretic religions.

The predominantly theoretic, scientific, and technological character ascribed to Western culture, in contrast to the preeminently aesthetic, non-scientific culture of the East, also needs serious qualification. Western culture became such only after the thirteenth—or even the fifteenth—century. Before that, the dominant culture of Europe was predominantly Ideational, centered mainly around the supersensory and superrational Kingdom of God, interested little in science and technology and therefore almost sterile in the field of scientific discoveries and technological inventions; certainly it lagged far behind the science and technology of the Eastern cultures of India, the China of Kublai Khan, and of Arabic culture. Here again, instead of a perennial contrast between the allegedly "aesthetic" East and the "theoretic" West, we really have a shifting picture: the West (up to the fifteenth century) lagging behind the East in theoretic science and technology and for the last five centuries leading the East.[10]

To sum up: Northrop's aesthetic and theoretic categories suffer because into the aesthetic category are put two basically different classes—the strictly sensory and the supersensory-superrational. These should not be united in one class; such a unification leads to a series of errors. The two categories being defective, the two cultural supersystems built upon them cannot be and are not real, meaningful-causal unities; correspondingly, the geographical allocation of these supersystems—the aesthetic to the East and the theoretic to the West—is also somewhat incorrect. A translation of Northrop's dyadic statements into the language of my triadic propositions and of Northrop's double "epistemic correlation" into my triple "epistemic correlation," where sensory, rational, and suprasensory cognitions and components mutually check and fruitfully supplement one another, may eliminate most of the shortcomings of Northrop's theory in this respect.

2

AMBIGUITY IN NORTHROP'S VIEW OF DEPENDENCE OF PHILOSOPHY ON SCIENCE

In many passages of his work Northrop states, without reservation, that cultural systems are based upon philosophical presuppositions and that these in turn are determined by mathematical and natural sciences existing in a given culture. In a few instances, however, he implies that philosophical presuppositions can be derived through immediate aesthetic intuition. In such cases the presuppositions and cultural systems based upon them can be fairly independent of the existing mathematical and natural science. Northrop does not make quite clear which of these two positions he holds. If he claims a one-sided dependence of philosophy upon science as a universal and invariable rule, then his theory requires serious reservations. If, according to Northrop himself, philosophical principles can be derived via aesthetic intuition, not touching a scientific road at all, philosophy derived from aesthetic apprehension can be quite independent of science. And cultural systems based upon such intuitional philosophical presuppositions can be little related to the existing body of scientific knowledge.

Further, regardless of the intuitional sources of philosophy, a one-sided dependence of philosophy upon science as a universal and invariable rule can be expected only if human beings and groups are assumed to be perfectly rational, deriving every philosophical principle from the extant scientific knowledge according to all the rules of deductive, inductive, and "abductive" (mathematical) logic. Human beings and groups never have been and probably never will be such perfectly rational creatures. They are partly rational, partly subrational, and partly suprarational. Therefore, they do not always arrive at their philosophical presuppositions according to the demands of perfect rationality. They have beliefs, philosophies, and standards derived from irrational, nonrational, and suprarational sources, independent of and often contradicting scientific theories. As a result, the relationship between science and philosophy in actual human behavior and culture is not so much uniform and one-sided as multiform and two-sided. Now science emerges first and determines the prevalent philosophical presuppositions of cultural systems; now the existing philosophical presuppositions—beliefs, general ideas, philosophies, not to mention other variables—emerge first and determine the state of science. Sometimes these presuppositions can become the foundations of cultural systems in spite of being contradictory to the existing science and can even suppress science or give to its development a different direction from that dictated by science itself. At other times science and philosophy emerge together and mutually condition each other. To sum up: The theory of a one-sided dependence of philosophy or religion or generalizing thought upon physical and mathematical science has to be viewed as a partial and limited case rather than a universal and invariable uniformity.[11]

If, as I hope, Northrop agrees with this position, which logically follows from his two sources of cognition ("intuitional" and "postulationally rational"), my remarks do not concern his theory and are directed to the theories of my eminent teacher, De Roberty, and others who contend a universal and invariable dependence of philosophical or religious ("synthesizing") thought upon the scientific ("analytical").

The foregoing criticisms exhaust the important points of disagreement between Northrop's views and my own. Except for several unimportant details, the rest of our readings of historical events are essentially similar and often supplementary.

3

CRITICISM OF KROEBER'S THEORY

Three shortcomings can be pointed out in Kroeber's theory: first, the vagueness of such of his concepts as the "master pattern," "high-value culture pattern," and the like; second, his use of the number and quality of talented persons as a measure of cultural creativity; third, what might be called a Sensate bias underlying his conception of cultural creativeness.

Anthropologists and sociologists regularly use the term "culture pattern" and its derivatives just as they regularly use the terms "culture integration," "functional system," and their derivatives. Unfortunately, they rarely define these terms clearly. When an attempt is made to clarify the meanings of the terms it becomes apparent that the same term is used to describe the most divergent phenomena and processes, from pure congeries to causal and meaningful systems. An overwhelming majority of "functional" and other "integrating" anthropologists and sociologists have not reached the point of discriminating between congeries and systems as basically different phenomena.[12] Others are just beginning to see the urgent necessity of differentiating congeries from unities and are beginning to define the terms as well as specify the phenomena the terms cover.[13]

Though Kroeber has been careful to distinguish between various combinations of culture traits, his analysis seemingly has not gone far enough to make clear what he means by the terms "culture patterns," "master patterns," and similar descriptive phrases. Do these terms refer to congeries? indirect causal ensembles? causal, meaningful, meaningful-causal systems? Implicitly, and here and there explicitly, he seems to mean something close to my "causal" and "meaningful-causal systems." He does not clarify this point, however.

Like myself, Kroeber uses the number of persons of genius as a measure of cultural creativity. I have also used this method systematically for studying the rise and decline of materialism, idealism, empiricism, rationalism, the movement of discoveries and inventions, and other cultural currents.

For example: For a rough estimate of when, in the period from 600 B.C. to 1920 A.D., the influence of materialistic philosophy was growing and when it was declining, we took all the names of Graeco-Roman and Western philosophers mentioned in the fullest histories of Graeco-Roman and Western philosophy, making a separate listing of all the names of materialistic philosophers. Taking the total number of philosophers (materialistic and non-materialistic) as 100 per cent for each period of 25, 50, and 100 years, we computed for each period the percentage of materialistic philosophers in the total. These percentages of materialistic philosophers gave us a rough measure of the comparative influence of materialistic philosophy in the total philosophy of each period. In one computation of these percentages all listed philosophers were given the value of one. In another, they were rated on a scale from 1 to 12 (according to their magnitude as measured by editions and re-editions of their works, by translations of their works, by the number of monographs about their philosophies, by the size of their followings, and so on). The curve of the percentages of materialist philosophers obtained in this way runs roughly parallel with that based on giving equal value to each philosopher.[14]

This shows that possibly in a more systematic manner, with a fuller list of men and women of genius in each cultural field than the samples used by Kroeber, and with some safeguards taken—like the foregoing two curves of philosophers based on the same value of one and different values from 1 to 12, or the fullest list of scientific discoveries and inventions checked through the list of the names of all known scientists and inventors—in this somewhat fuller and more systematic way, I used a procedure similar to Kroeber's.[15]

If I raise the subsequent questions, I do it not for the sake of criticizing Kroeber but rather to elucidate the danger points in this procedure. To begin with, *this procedure is heavily loaded in favor of all Sensate cultures and periods and against all Ideational cultures and periods*. The point is that Sensate cultures are individualistic and singularistic; Ideational cultures collective and anonymous. In Sensate culture each creative person passionately strives to "immortalize," "glorify," or "publicize" his individual name and achievement. Anything of importance created in such a culture bears the name of its creator and is registered carefully in the annals of its history. In this sense Sensate cultures are "good publicity cultures" for each individual creator, beginning with the greatest and ending sometimes even with mere hucksters.

Ideational culture and man are not interested in advertising the individual creators. Creators in such a culture create for the greater glory of God and not for mortal fame. Creations are done collectively. They remain, as a rule, anonymous. We do not know who created many of the architectural glories of India or Taoist China, or the cathedrals and sculptures of the Medieval cathedrals of Europe. Except for a very few names, nothing is known of their creators. This is even more true of examples of great art on a smaller scale.[16] This difference leads directly to an enormous deflation of Ideational creativity and a great inflation of Sensate creativity when it is measured by the number of individual creators mentioned in Sensate and Ideational cultures or periods. As a matter of fact, the commonly accepted lack of creativity in either our Ideational Middle Ages or the Ideational Hindu or Taoist cultures is largely due to the "deflations" of such cultures. Since Ideational culture is anonymous and collective, it does not care to preserve the names of its creative individuals. Therefore, when creativity is measured by the number of historically preserved individual names, it cannot help appearing uncreative. And vice versa: since the individualistic and "publicity-minded" Sensate culture strives to preserve the names of all the creators, even those who do not deserve fame, the list appears endless and the culture always seems most creative.

Kroeber makes no distinction between Ideational and Sensate cultures and periods. Therefore, the results of his procedure are tangibly biased, calling for correction by a relative increase of the creativity of Ideational cultures and periods and a decrease of Sensate creativity. With such a correction, the creativity curves are likely to be palpably different from Kroeber's curves.

Another shortcoming of this procedure is that it gives a less accurate curve of creativity in a given field than the curve based not on the number of creative persons but on that of the discovered, invented, or created values. In my study of the movement of scientific discoveries and inventions, I made two numerical series: one giving all the known scientific discoveries and inventions and another giving all the names of scientists and inventors mentioned in the *Encyclopaedia Britannica.* Compared with each other, the series of discoveries and inventions is much more complete and accurate than that of the scientists and inventors; in some periods and countries there was a tangible deviation of two series from each other.[17]

The discussion of the biased character of Kroeber's procedure leads us to the point of his study that is most doubtful: the somewhat biased and subjective character of his concept of creativity (or effervescence, blossoming, and other derivatives from creativity) and of the results obtained. By this biased character I mean not only the procedure discussed but the very criteria of what is and what is not creative in a sociocultural field. Kroeber does not distinguish various types of creativity like Ideational, Idealistic, Sensate, "classic and romantic," "religious and secular," or other typological divisions. Instead, without any distinction of the type, he simply takes the names given in a good text in a certain field together with the judgment of the text about the comparative magnitude of some of the names; and in this way he builds his periods of greater or lesser creativity. I have already pointed out how such a procedure inflates the creativity of Sensate and deflates that of Ideational cultures or periods. Now it can be asserted that a non-distinction of Ideational, Sensate, and Idealistic forms of creativity makes these inflations and deflations incomparably greater than the procedure itself does. The point is that what is creative depends upon our criteria. The criteria of great creativity of Ideational and Sensate cultures are strikingly different, often opposite. What is a great creation for an Ideational man and culture (say, a Gregorian chant, a symbolic sculpture or fresco, a "religious" belief, a theological treatise, the life of a saint, a religious ceremony or ritual, an ascetic hermitage, a poor monastic community, meditation and contemplation, etc.) is often mere "dirt, superstition, ignorance, and ugliness" for a Sensate man and culture. And vice versa: most of the great Sensate creations are negative to Ideational man—"devil's temptations, empty, valueless, transitory toys fit for the fools, the sinners, and the condemned." "No one who loves Christ cares for this world." "Lay not up for yourselves treasures upon earth. . . . But lay up for yourselves treasures in heaven. . . . Seek ye first the kingdom of God." These are the typical formulas of Ideational negative appreciation of practically all Sensate values and creations. This polarity of the systems of Ideational and Sensate evaluations of the good or beautiful or creative is present for all values.[18]

In practically all the books used by Kroeber, the criteria of creativity of their authors, which Kroeber accepts, are almost entirely Sensate. An overwhelmingly greater part of the historical books written over the last three centuries have been written by predominantly Sensate historians, with Sensate criteria of what is creative and what is not. The historians have been unaware of their biased Sensate viewpoint and of the fact that this viewpoint is just one of several viewpoints, quite different from Ideational and just as one-sided, subjective, and arbitrary as Ideational, Idealistic, or other standpoints. These authors and Kroeber, who follows them, give to us the movement of creativity of cultures and periods mainly as it appears from the Sensate standpoint. More, Kroeber has omitted practically the whole field of religious and ethical creativity, which are the main areas of Ideational creativity. For this reason, his total creativity of many periods and cultures is inadequate. If the creativity of the same cultures and periods are studied from Ideational or Idealistic positions and religious and ethical creativity are not omitted, the movements of creativity differ greatly from those seen from the Sensate standpoint. This explains why Kroeber's results are one-sided. They appear to be valid only for Sensate man and culture.

From Ideational or Idealistic standpoints they are misleading.

The only way to avoid this one-sidedness is to distinguish Ideational, Idealistic, and Sensate systems of values and types of creativity and, assuming a neutral position for each system, to try to find out what kind of values are created in each of these types of culture. When this is done—as I did in my *Dynamics*—Ideational culture, for instance, will be found to be creative in the field of religion and uncreative in the field of science and technology; it is creative in the field of Ideational music, painting, sculpture, architecture, drama, ethics, and law; and uncreative in the field of Sensate forms of these cultural phenomena. Sensate culture will be found to be creative in the field of science, technology, utilitarian economics, but little creative in the field of religion or Ideational forms of all classes of cultural phenomena.[19]

This explains the inevitably one-sided character of the curves of creativity in Kroeber's work, as well as of the bulk of historical, humanistic, and social-science works of the last three centuries, with their predominantly Sensate standpoint. In this sense, the bulk of these works is still at a Ptolemaic stage, viewing everything from the Sensate standpoint as the only one possible and absolute, not admitting any other standpoint. It is high time that this Ptolemaic standpoint be replaced by at least a Copernican or a contemporary Astrophysical and relativity standpoint. From such a position, Ideational, Idealistic, and Sensate systems and criteria of values and creativity are equally important. A truly scientific standpoint consists not in a one-sided choice of one of these as absolute but in a truly impartial and objective study from the standpoint of each system of values; and from a still higher standpoint transcending and embracing all three systems, the sort of values each cultural type creates and is proud of, when and under what conditions. In this way, one obtains a truly unbiased scientific knowledge of all forms of values and creativity with their why, when, where, and under what conditions. Otherwise, there will be nothing but one-sided, subjective theories, standards, and results, all equally misleading.[20]

The scientific competence and wisdom of Kroeber helped him to avoid this pitfall to a considerable degree. However, he could not escape it completely, and this Sensate bias tangibly vitiates his conclusions and results.

These shortcomings exhaust the main errors in Kroeber's work. With the suggested correction, the bulk of his procedures and results appear to be sound and in essentials coincide with the results of my own study of these problems.

4

CRITICAL REMARKS ON THEORIES OF SCHUBART, BERDYAEV, AND SCHWEITZER

Since none of these authors developed a systematic philosophy of history, criticism of their views can be brief.

Schubart's thesis that the Russian soul and culture are Messianic and are destined to take the leading role in the coming Messianic period of human history remains largely a matter of belief, supported by scant evidence on Schubart's part. It contains only a grain of truth in the sense that the European phase of human history is over and the center of history is now shifting to the region of the Pacific, where besides the Americas, India, and China, Russia will also be playing a leading part. Schubart's prototypes of culture and personality are suggestive but require marked modification. The same is to be said of his contrasting characterization of the Western and Russian personality types; it is impressionistic rather than accurate. However, as we shall see, his as well as Spengler's and Danilevsky's typologies of personality are more penetrating, more real, and therefore more scientific than most of the so-called scientific classifications of personality types. These classifications are mostly an artificial, mechanistic, superficial, and quantitative piling together of several traits of dead human shells rather than of living human personalities.

Since the metaphysical meaning of history in Berdyaev's

philosophy is intentionally omitted in the present work, and since the most doubtful points of his empirical theory were also omitted in the survey given in Chapter VII, the delineated features of his historical interpretations contain only several minor errors rather than big blunders. As such they can be passed by without a special examination.

As to the shortcomings of Schweitzer's philosophy of civilization, the following deficiencies can be noted here. Schweitzer's contentions that each flourishing civilization has a minimum of ethical values vigorously functioning and that a decay of ethical values is part and parcel of the decay of civilization are seemingly correct. However, his theses that the ethical factor is the main foundation of every great civilization and the main factor of its decay are dogmatically asserted rather than adequately proved. In addition, Schweitzer seems to assume that the ethical compartment of a civilization lives and functions by itself, in isolation, depending little upon the civilization's religion and philosophy, fine arts, law, economics, and politics. Such a supposition is somewhat fallacious for at least most of the civilizations. Many a scholarly work, including my own *Dynamics,* has shown rather conclusively that the ethical values of a given culture or cultural supersystem are closely connected with other cultural systems of a certain society. Thus, in a predominantly Ideational culture, the dominant ethics and law are Ideational also; in a predominantly Sensate society, the dominant ethics and law are Sensate. Further, a society's ethical values change along with its other values and in the same direction. Thus, the ethical decay of the contemporary West is but a part of a decline of the whole Sensate supersystem of the West and can be understood only in this context.[21]

The same is to be said of the "world-view" or the *Weltanschauung*. It also does not arise by itself as a *deus ex machina* and does not become dominant in a given society by its own force only, but is tangibly conditioned by the character of the prevailing culture and its dominant supersystem. In a predominantly Ideational society only Ideational world-views can become dominant (mysticism, idealism, religious rationalism, fideism, eternalism, unconditional ethics of love, the sacral law, etc.); in a predominantly Sensate society only Sensate philosophies become dominant (materialism, skepticism, empiricism, positivism, temporalism, man-made relativistic, utilitarian, and hedonistic ethics and law, etc.). When an Ideational supersystem is being replaced by a Sensate, Ideational world-views tend to decline while Sensate philosophies increase at their expense. And vice versa.[22] Schweitzer somehow fails to see this connection between ethics, together with world-views, and the dominant character of a given culture; therefore, he fails to account adequately not only for the decay of Western civilization but even for the rise and decline of ethics generally and the ethics of life-affirmation specifically as well as for the rise and decline of *Weltanschauungen* of different kinds, including the world-view of reverence for life. This failure is strikingly evident when he tries to explain why the comparatively sound ethics and world-view of eighteenth-century Europe suddenly crumbled, opening the door for a rapid downward movement of the Western civilization in the nineteenth century. This decline, as well as a sudden alleged renaissance of ethics and civilization in the seventeenth and the eighteenth centuries, are not at all accounted for in his theory. The same is true of the Stoic ethics and world-view. In other words, Schweitzer contributes little to our understanding of what civilizations really are and why and how they rise, live, and decay. Out of these complex problems he selects only one of many factors or values—the ethical—and asserts that it plays an important role in all these complex processes— an assertion made many times before.

Another serious shortcoming of Schweitzer is his history of the ethical philosophies (world-views). However thoughtful, his interpretations would be questioned as to accuracy by many scholars. Thus his interpretation of the Taoist, Hinduist, Buddhist, and other mystic philosophies of the ultimate reality—of Northrop's "undifferentiated continuum"—as a pure negativity or a pure emptiness would be vigorously criticized as inaccurate by most of the Taoist, Hinduist, Buddhist, and other competent scholars and thinkers. Similar criticism is to be expected in regard to Schweitzer's interpretations of several other philosophies or world-views.

I find especially peculiar Schweitzer's particularly high estimate of the Stoic *Weltanschauungen* and the philosophical, ethical, political, economic, and social theories of the seventeenth and especially the eighteenth centuries—those of Locke, Helvetius, Hume, Bentham, Adam Smith, Condorcet, Herder, Lessing, and others. Schweitzer views these theories and philosophies as especially conducive to the ethical reverence for life, and through that to an invigoration and growth of civilization. He seems to be quite unaware of the shortcomings of these theories so well indicated by Northrop—that most of these theories were Sensate and as such gave rise to, among other things, the relativistic, man-made, utilitarian, and hedonistic ethics which were bound to become increasingly relativistic and hedonistic until in the course of two hundred years or so all these values have been ground into dust and lost most of their binding power and even moral prestige. Ethical values and norms have become a "mere ideological smoke screen," an "opiate of the people's mind," Freudian "rationalizations," Marxian "ideologies," Paretian "derivations," supposedly used by a clever minority to fool and exploit a stupid majority, serving as a beautifying screen for the ugly vested interests of the powers that be.[23]

In other words, Schweitzer extols exactly those Sensate philosophies which, if they did not initiate (because European Sensate ethics and philosophies had already emerged in the fourteenth century), at least gave a great impetus to, an ethical and civilizational decay which became catastrophic, according to Schweitzer, at the middle of the nineteenth century. For me this exceptionally high evaluation of these theories by Schweitzer is entirely incomprehensible. It may be explained only by a great deal of rationalizing and the eighteenth century "enlightenment" that seemingly remains strong in the mentality of Schweitzer; also by a strong individualism that clearly manifests itself in Schweitzer's writings. Otherwise, this particular fondness for the philosophies of the Stoics and the Illuminati cannot be comprehended; nor from a purely scientific standpoint is it correct.

The next important point is Schweitzer's position in regard to *the role of science in the ethical regeneration of civilization.* In contrast to Northrop, who seemingly overvalues this role in regard to philosophy and ethics, religion, and the fine arts, Schweitzer rather greatly underestimates this role. Now and then he explicitly states that

. . . neither world-and-life-affirmation nor ethics can be founded upon what our knowledge of the world can tell us about the world. . . . Our view of life is not dependent on our view of the world . . . it does not originate in knowledge . . . ethics and aesthetics are not sciences . . . there is no science of human willing and doing, and there never can be . . . there is, therefore, no such thing as a scientific system of ethics.[24]

This position is very vulnerable. Here again we meet Schweitzer's separation of *ethical* values and principles from others— in this case, scientific ones. Ethical Goodness (reverence for life) is made independent from, and unrelated to, Truth (and Beauty). On metaphysical as well as empirical bases such a separation is untenable. Metaphysically, Truth (science, religion, philosophy), Beauty (the fine arts) and Goodness (ethics) are three main value-aspects of one Undivided Godhead or the Manifold Infinity. Empirically, each "energy" of this Trinity can be transformed into other two energies: Truth is transformable into Beauty and Goodness, Goodness into Truth and Beauty, and Beauty into Truth and Goodness. Real Truth is beautiful and good; real Beauty is true and good; and real Goodness is true and beautiful. On these grounds Schweitzer's position is untenable.[25]

His position is untenable pragmatically also. We can agree with Schweitzer that the ethical axiom or basic principle is a sort of postulate, independent of science. One can indeed postulate the supreme principle of unconditional reverence for life, as Schweitzer does, or other ethical principles, up to the postulate, "Hate is the supreme ethical value"; and build upon it the ethics of hate exemplified by the ethics of Shakespeare's Timon of Athens. When, however, the postulated ethics are to be built and to become effective in human conduct and social institutions and culture, science enters as the most efficient, necessary, and best expert counselor on the ways and means of grounding of ethics in empirical social reality and a realization of it in the ideological, behavioral, and material culture and population. Without scientific help in these tasks the ethics chosen and postulated have hardly any means of realization. In medicine, the preservation of health and life are also postulated as the main value. But after this postulation has been made, science is the indispensable and best agent for the maintenance and improvement of health and the preservation of life, and it teaches what are the best ways and means for realizing these goals. Even in aesthetics, the relationship between beauty and science is similar. The sort of beauty desired can be postulated. But as soon as we want to realize the postulated beauty, we have to turn to science for real help: the science of painting, sculpture, composition, poetry, and so on.

These considerations show why Schweitzer's position here is untenable and why, among other things, I myself found it necessary to mobilize scientific forces and establish the Harvard Research Center in Altruistic Integration and Creativity for the accomplishment of an ethical task identical with Schweitzer's. If we knew more about how to make human beings and groups, social institutions and culture less egocentric, less selfish, more altruistic, and more creative, the realization of this ethical ideal would be helped along enormously, and future war catastrophes would be eliminated. Without the scientific knowledge provided by these "know-hows," the ethical ideals are doomed to remain unrealized or will be realized incomparably more slowly, fragmentarily, and at an enormous cost in blood and suffering.

Schweitzer's position here explains why he has given us hardly any promising and effective prescription of how to root his "reverence for life" in the sociocultural soil and make it an actual practice in human behavior and interrelationships. The few statements that Schweitzer makes on this point are platitudinous rather than helpful.

Finally, Schweitzer's ethical philosophy itself—the ethics of an unconditional life-affirmation, based on a desperate, somewhat solipsistic, will to live regardless of what the world at large is or is not—is all right and can serve the task of ethical ennoblement of humanity. But, contrary to Schweitzer's claim, his ethics is hardly uniquely better and more adequate than dozens of other ethical systems of love, benevolence, and reverence, of real friendship, of *agape* and *eros,* of Yoga-Karma-Nirvana, of the categorical imperative, and so on. Most of the ethical systems surveyed in Schweitzer's book can serve and have served the task of reverence for life as much, perhaps even more than, Schweitzer's own ethical system. Personally, I regard the ethics of unbounded love, as exemplified in the Sermon on the Mount or in St. Paul's Epistle to the Corinthians, as somewhat more embracing, more universal, more sublime, than Schweitzer's ethics of life-affirmation. The Ethics of Love embraces in itself the whole ethics of life-reverence, but the reverse is not true.

Such are the main shortcomings of the work of this eminent moral teacher. This criticism in no way denies the great services he is rendering humanity by his teaching and especially by his practice. Likewise, we shall see that by stressing the importance of the ethical element in civilization he puts his finger on the most urgent need of humanity at the present time. But these and other virtues of Schweitzer and his work do not override the shortcomings that have been pointed out.

PART THREE

TOWARDS A VALID SOCIAL PHILOSOPHY

XIV

Areas of Agreement among Modern Social Philosophies

In works of such vast dimensions as most of those we have discussed, diverse small inaccuracies and factual errors are to be expected. They do not vitiate the central framework and need not be specifically criticized. Instead, we can now turn to an examination of what these writers offer in the way of a concordant and sound contribution. If in addition to the disagreements outlined, all or some of the theories show concordant conclusions, such agreements are significant and may be roughly valid—for otherwise their authors, so radically different in their basic premises, methodologies, and factual material as well as in personal mentalities and temperaments, could hardly have arrived at concordant results.

I

THE CIVILIZATIONAL OR CULTURAL SUPERSYSTEM

The first basic agreement of the theories discussed is that in the boundless ocean of sociocultural phenomena there exists a kind of vast cultural entity, or cultural system, or civilization, which lives and functions as a real unity. It is not identical with the state or the nation or any other social group. Ordinarily the boundaries of this cultural entity transcend the geographical boundaries of national or political or religious groups. On the other hand, in a nation's total culture two or

more cultural systems sometimes co-exist. Danilevsky calls
these systems the "culture-historical types" or "civilizations";
Spengler calls them the High Cultures which in a later phase
pass into "civilizations"; Toynbee refers to them as the
"civilizations" or the "units and fields of historical study";
Kroeber, as the "high-value culture patterns"; Schubart, as
the "prototypes of culture"; Northrop, as "cultural systems"
or "world cultures"; Berdyaev calls them the "great cultures";
and, finally, I call them the "cultural supersystems," as the
vastest and ultimate ones.

It looks as though all these authors vaguely feel and partly
know that there is a kind of vast cultural entity or deep cultural undercurrent, which largely determines most of the surface ripplings of the sociocultural ocean. The authors try to
grasp its properties, to map its course and area and to clarify
its influence upon the surface of cultural phenomena. They
seem to agree in some points and in others not; but underlying
all discussion is the fundamental agreement that some sort of
vast unified cultural systems live and function in the sociocultural ocean. The preceding critical analysis indicated of
exactly what their differences consist and which of several
variants are comparatively tenable. The point of agreement is
that the ocean of sociocultural phenomena consists of: (a) unintegrated and disintegrated cultural congeries; (b) a multitude of cultural systems or unities mutually co-ordinated, sub-
ordinated, neutral, and mutually contradictory; (c) the vastest
cultural unities or supersystems or civilizations. The terms
"congeries," "systems," "supersystems," are mine; but practically all our interpreters of history admit—explicitly or implicitly—the existence of these classes of sociocultural complexes.

*The second important agreement in regard to the vastest cul-
tural entities is that their total number has in the whole history
of human culture been very small.*

Whatever classification of the basic types of cultural supersystems of non-local or non-national character we adopt, the
number of types can be counted on our fingers. Northrop's
"aesthetic-theoretic," Schubart's four prototypes, my "Idea-

tional-Idealistic-Sensate" are examples. If instead we take other classifications of cultural vast unities, such as "Paleo-lithic-Neolithic-copper-bronze-iron-machine" civilizations (providing that such vast causal-meaningful cultural unities exist indeed), the number of the basic types is again very small. The same can be said of the "civilizations" called variously "hunt-ers-pastoral-agricultural-industrial" or "rural-urban" or any other, based upon either main types of religion, or economy, or the family and kinship system, or the basic forms of government, or forms of solidarity (*Gemeinschaft-Gesellschaft,* the "mechanical-organic"), or any other important criteria. The number of not only the main supersystem types but even of vast special systems (religious, political, economic, artistic, kinship, etc.) is limited. The number of basic types of such supersystems and vast special systems rarely exceeds ten.[1]

Slightly more numerous are the types of local or national civilizations or national cultural supersystems (so far as they are real). But even their number fluctuates among our authors roughly between eight and twenty-six. This means that the boundless cultural ocean reaches the highest integration into the cultural supersystems only in a few of its areas and very rarely at that. Out of thousands of social groups that have existed in human history only very few have been able to create vast cultural prototypes or supersystems. These seemingly are very rare flowers. On this point all our "readers of historical events" agree.

The third point of agreement is that *each of these basic types of cultural prototypes is different from the others:* the Apollinian differs from the Faustian and all the other Spenglerian civilizations; so also the types described by Danilevsky, Schubart, Toynbee, Northrop, and myself.

The fourth similarity consists in either the explicit or the implicit thesis that *each of the vast cultural systems is based upon some "major premise" or "philosophical presupposition" or "prime symbol" or "ultimate value" which the supersystem or civilization articulates, develops, and realizes in all its main compartments, or parts, in the process of its life-career.* Correspondingly, each of the great cultural unities is either *logi-*

cally or aesthetically consistent in the meaningful aspects of its parts and compartments. So far as it is also a manifestation of the supersensory and superrational creative intuition, its inner consistency can reach in some parts even a higher form than a rational one: like the sublime unity of the Sermon on the Mount, or Bach's greatest fugue, or Shakespearean tragedy, the truly immortal parts of a great cultural supersystem are united by a living, superorganic, supralogical consistency of the *coincidentia oppositorum.*

The fifth concordance is that each of these supersystems grounded in empirical reality is a *meaningful-causal unity.* If it were just a bio-physical causal system, devoid of the component of meaning, it would not have been a sociocultural phenomenon at all. If its main parts were not united by causal interdependence, it would have been a vast dumping ground of cultural congeries and not a unified system. The fact that all the authors ascribe to their civilizations unity and meaning ("Apollinian," "Magian," "Messianic," "Ideational," "theoretic-aesthetic," specifically "religious," or "scientific," or "aesthetic," and so on) is evidence of their viewing these unities as meaningful-causal, no matter whether they do or do not use these terms.

The sixth point of agreement concerns the *general characteristics of the supersystem or civilization.* Explicitly or implicitly, all the theories considered ascribe to it the following properties: (a) *reality,* different from that of its parts; (b) *individuality;* (c) *general and differential dependence* of its parts upon one another, upon the whole, and of the whole upon its parts; (d) *preservation of its individuality or its "sameness"* in spite of a change of its parts; (e) *change in togetherness;* (f) *self-directing (immanent) change and self-determination of its life-career* with external forces either accelerating or slowing up, facilitating or hindering the unfolding and realization of the potentialities of the supersystem, sometimes even destroying it, but hardly ever transforming it into something radically different from its inherent potentialities; (g) *selectivity of the supersystem,* which takes in what is congenial to it and rejects what is uncongenial (otherwise it would not be able to preserve its individuality, consistency, and meaningful unity); (h) *limited variability of each supersystem,* which, in spite of its vastness, is a finite phenomenon and as such has limits in its variations; if and when it transcends these limits it loses its individuality and disintegrates.

These general characteristics, systematically studied in my works,[2] are explicitly or implicitly present in all the theories discussed. In the case of a few of these traits the authors differ somewhat as to details; but these minor disagreements do not abridge the major agreement in regard to the characteristics mentioned.

2

REJECTION OF THE LINEAR CONCEPTION OF HISTORICAL PROCESSES

We have seen that practically all the authors reject a linear, "artificial," "Ptolemaic," "pre-Copernican" conception of the historical process and of the life-history of the civilizations, prototypes, and supersystems. They unanimously reject the traditional, linear division of the historical process into the Ancient, the Medieval, and the Modern, viewed from the standpoint of Western civilization. They do not concentrate their energies on discovering the perennial linear trends and tendencies of historical evolution or progress. They often explicitly deny such linear conceptions and state that "before God all moments of history are of equal value." [3] In this respect the theories considered are in line with most of the social-science theories of this century and with the disintegration which our Sensate culture is undergoing. As is shown elsewhere,[4] linear progressive interpretations of history flourish mainly in a dominantly Sensate culture, before its decline. For this reason various linear interpretations were dominant in the seventeenth, eighteenth, and nineteenth centuries in practically all sciences and philosophies of the West, beginning with physics and biology and ending with philosophy, the humanities, and the social sciences. With the sharp decline of the Sensate supersystem in the twentieth century, all varieties of linear interpretations are bound to decline and give place to a cyclical, eschatological, or creatively fluctuating conception of historical processes. Such a replacement of the linear by non-linear theories has indeed occurred. Here is a concise outline of this change or replacement.

The dominant current of the scientific, philosophical, social and humanistic thought of the eighteenth and nineteenth centuries was a firm belief in the existence of perpetual linear trends in the change of sociocultural phenomena. The central content of the historical process of mankind was conceived as an unfolding and ever fuller realization of this "trend of progress and evolution," of steady "historical tendencies" and of the "law of sociocultural development." Some delineated these trends as unilinear, others as "spiral," still others as "oscillating and branching," with minor deviations and temporary regressions; nevertheless in all these varieties the conception of a linear direction of the central sociocultural process remained intact.[5] Consequently the main ambition and central preoccupation of scientific, philosophical, social, and humanistic thinkers in these centuries consisted in the discovery and formulation of these "eternal laws of progress and evolution," and in an elaboration of the main stages or phases through which the trend passes as it comes to fuller realization in the course of time. Discovery, formulation, and corroboration of the existence of such trends and their stages was the focal point of biology and sociology, of the philosophy of history and social philosophy, and of the other nineteenth-century social and humanistic sciences. If in some disciplines like history they did not occupy a very large part in the actual narration of historical events, they served as the guiding stars and referential principles for ordering and interpreting concrete factual material. In this sense, the social thought of the eighteenth and nineteenth centuries was indeed stamped by a faith in linear laws of evolution and progress.

In the *physico-chemical sciences* this faith expressed itself in an emergence and rapid acceptance of the principle of entropy of Carnot-Clausius as a perpetual and irreversible direction of change in any thermodynamic system [6] as well as in the whole universe.

In *biology* the faith expressed itself in an emergence and general acceptance of the "law of evolution," almost unanimously interpreted in the sense of a linear trend (in its unilinear, spiral, branching, oscillating variations) of a progressively growing differentiation and integration; of a passage from the simple to the complex; from "the lower to the higher"; from "the less perfect to the more perfect"; "from the amoeba to man"; "from reflexes and instincts to intelligence and reason"; "from the solitary individual to the family, the tribe, the modern state; and, in spite of narrow-minded and reactionary politicians, we or our descendants will yet see the whole human race brought together into a Society of Nations, a Federation of the World." "Throughout the course of evolution there has been a continual elimination of the least fit and a survival of the fit . . . the elimination of the antisocial and the increase of specialization and co-operation." [7] The linear interpretation of biological (and social) evolution was and still is (though less pronounced now) the main dogma of biology.

The same is true of the dominant conception of sociocultural change in the *philosophy, social philosophy, and philosophy of history* of the eighteenth and nineteenth centuries. The conceptions of Herder, Fichte, Kant, and Hegel are typical in this respect. Herder and Kant both saw the central trend of historical process as a progressive decrease of violence and war, as a steady increase of peace and as a growth of justice, reason, and morality in the course of time.[8]

For Fichte the whole of human history is a sequence of five stages: an ever fuller realization of freedom, truth, justice and beauty. For Hegel the central trend of the historical process consists in a progressive growth of freedom, beginning with freedom for none at the dawn of human history, passing through the stages of freedom for one, then freedom for some, and ending with the stage of freedom for all.[9]

In the *sociology and social philosophy* of the nineteenth century the general concepts of social dynamics held by Turgot,

Condorcet, Burdin, Saint Simon, and Comte and Herbert Spencer's concept of evolution are fully representative. For Comte the whole process of history is but a steady passage from the theological, through the metaphysical, to the positive stage of human mentality, culture, and society. Consequently, Comte's "social dynamics" hardly deals at all with repeated sociocultural processes; it is devoted almost entirely to a formulation and corroboration of his "law of the three stages." Spencer's "social dynamics" is simply an application of his formula of evolution—progress, according to which the whole sociocultural universe passes in the course of time from an indefinite, incoherent homogeneity to a definite, coherent heterogeneity, with a progressively growing differentiation and integration of human personality, culture and society.[10]

Dominated by this linear conception of sociocultural change, most sociologists and social scientists of the nineteenth century reduced their study of the dynamics of sociocultural phenomena, even in purely factual investigations, mainly to a discovery and formulation of various linear trends, successive stages of development, historical tendencies, and laws of evolution of the phenomena investigated. As a result most of the "uniformities of change," they discovered, assumed a linear character.

Here are a few examples out of many.[11] Ferdinand Toennies' theory of the passage of human society in the course of time from the *Gemeinschaft* to the *Gesellschaft* type is a linear theory. So is Emile Durkheim's theory of a gradual change from a state of society based upon the "mechanical" solidarity to one based upon "organic" solidarity, with a subsidiary trend of replacement of "repressive" by "restitutive" law. Similarly linear is the social dynamics of Lester F. Ward which posits a progressively increasing teleological, circuitous, artificial, self-directed, and self-controlled character of human adaptation in the course of time; or H. T. Buckle's dynamics of a "diminishing influence of physical laws and of an increasing influence of mental laws" as time passes; or Herbert Spencer's and Emile Durkheim's laws of the passage of societies from the "simple" to the "compound" ("doubly compound," "triply compound," and so on), in the course of their history. No less linear is Novicow's law of the evolution of the struggle for existence from the earliest form of a bloody "physiological extermination," through a less bloody "economic," then "political" struggle, to a final bloodless form of purely "intellectual" competition. So also the alleged historical trend of a progressive widening of the area of peace and shrinking of the area of war in the course of history, claimed by dozens of social scientists. Novicow's, William F. Ogburn's, and Hornell Hart's law of acceleration of the tempo of change is linear, as is Coste's law of the five stages of evolution of social structures from the "Burg" to the "City," the "Metropolis," the "Capitol" to, finally, a "World Center of Federation." Linear also is Mougeole's "law of altitude" according to which the most densely inhabited areas and the cities descend, in the course of time, from the zones of high altitudes to those of low altitudes; or similar historical trends of the westward, eastward, or northward movement of civilization with the passage of time (according to different authors). Another linear theory is Gobineau's historical trend from the pure and unequal races to the progressively blended and equal ones with the degenerated "human herds, benumbed in their nullity," and the end of human civilization as a terminal point of the trend. Still another is Winiarsky's law of social entropy leading progressively to greater sociocultural equalization of castes, orders, classes, races, and individuals, with the final state a dead sociocultural equilibrium and the end of mankind's history. Linear too is the theory of a perennial trend towards a bigger and better equalitarianism interpreted as the positive trend of history (in contradistinction to its interpretation as a death of society and culture) by a crowd of sociologists, anthropologists, political scientists, ethicists, philosophers, and historians.

Even such social dynamics as those of De Roberty and Karl Marx were not quite free from this linear "obsession" of the nineteenth century. If Marx himself did not give a clear-cut theory of successive stages of social evolution, he nevertheless postulated one eschatological linear trend of history—the trend towards socialism as the final stage of social development of humanity. His followers, from Engels, Bebel, and Kautsky to Cunow and a legion of lesser Marxists, manufactured a series of historical laws in the evolution of economic, political, mental, religious, familial, and other sociocultural phenomena, with appropriate stages of development.

Like Marx, De Roberty and certain others were little concerned with the manufacturing of various eternal trends and stages of development, but even they assumed the growth of conceptual thought in one or more of the four forms as formulated by De Roberty (scientific, philosophical or religious, aesthetic and rationally applied thought) as a central tendency of the historical process. De Greef, together with many political scientists, posited a trend of political evolution from the earliest regimes based upon force to social organization based on free contractual relationships. Ratzenhofer's and Albion Small's trend from the "conquest state" to the "culture state"; or the virtually opposite trend, postulated by Lilienfeld, from the earliest type of decentralized and unregimented political groups to regimes of centralized, autocratic, and regimented political control; or L. T. Hobhouse's trend of social development from a stage of society based upon kinship, through one based on authority, toward a final stage built upon citizenship; or F. H. Giddings' "zoogenic, anthropogenic, ethnogenic and demogenic" stages of sociocultural development (the last stage divided into linear substages: military-religious, liberal-legal, and economic-ethical)—all of these are further varieties of the linear type of trend so extensively manufactured by social scientists of the nineteenth and early twentieth centuries.

To these may be added the dozens of historical trends manufactured by sociology and anthropology, law and history, concerning the evolution of *the family, marriage, and kinship*. All of them were characterized by uniform stages of development: from promiscuous "primitive" sex relationships to the monogamic family (passing through three or four or five stages, according to the fancies of authors like Bachofen, McLennan, Sir John Lubbock, Engels, Bebel, Morgan, and many others); from the patriarchal to the cognatic family based upon equality of the sexes; from the patrilineal to the matrilineal system of descent and kinship, or vice versa; from equality to inequality of the sexes, or vice versa. These and all the other social and humanistic sciences made much of having allegedly "discovered" a host of eternal historical trends with their stages of development: from fetishism or totemism to monotheism and irreligiosity, from religious and magical superstitions to a rational scientific mentality, from ethical savagery to the rational ethical man, from primitive ugliness to a bigger and better beauty, and so on.

Writers in *political science* unhesitatingly formulated a series of various "laws of political progress-evolution" from "autocratic monarchy to democratic republic" or vice versa (depending upon the political sympathies of the scholar), from "direct democracy to representative democracy" or vice versa, from primeval anarchy to centralized government or vice versa, from "government of force" to that of "social service"; all with various intermediary stages definitely following one another in a more or less uniform sequence.

In *economics* likewise a large number of eminent thinkers were busy with trends and stages of economic development through which all peoples were supposed to be passing. Typical examples of this linear "economic dynamics" are: List's barbarian, pastoral, agricultural, and agricultural-manufacturing-commercial stages of economic development; Hildebrand's theory of the three stages that he calls *Naturalwirtschaft, Geldwirtschaft,* and *Creditwirtschaft;* Karl Buecher's three stages of a closed self-sufficing, city, and national economy; and Gustav Schmoller's theory of five stages. The economics of the last century treated in the same linear fashion economic evolution from collective to individual agriculture or vice versa, from primitive collectivism to capitalist individualism or vice versa, and so on, up to the still narrower trends allegedly given in the process of economic change.

Archeology and *history* likewise were dominated by the same linear conceptions of historical change. If in the actual narrative of historical events a discussion of such trends, tendencies, and laws of evolution-progress did not occupy a very large space in factual historical works, such trends and laws (assumed by the archeologists and historians) served as the guiding stars and referential principles for the ordering of chaotic historical material and especially for its interpretation. The archeological and historical "law of technological evolution" with its standardized Paleolithic, Neolithic, copper, bronze, iron, and machine ages is one of these linear laws serving as a fundamental referential and ordering principle. The division of history into Ancient, Medieval, and Modern is another linear conception. The idea of progress itself, interpreted in a linear fashion, is actually still another such principle—an idea which served as the veritable foundation for the bulk of nineteenth-century historical works. Even the explicitly factual histories openly inimical to any "philosophizing" in history did not escape it. The *Cambridge Modern History* provides a typical example of this: in spite of the aversion of its editors and authors to any philosophy of history we read in its opening pages: "We wish to discover the tendencies which are permanent. . . . We are bound to assume, as a scientific hypothesis on which history is to be written, a progress in human affairs. This progress must inevitably be towards some end." [12] It is hardly necessary to add that in other supposedly purely factual narratives, the historians of the nineteenth century, from Mommsen, Von Ranke, Fustel de Coulanges, Guizot, to the authors of the *Cambridge Modern History,* actually formulated a large number of linear laws of evolution, in all fields of social and cultural life.[13]

To sum up: Sociology and the other social, philosophical, and even natural sciences of the nineteenth century viewed the central problem of physical, biological, and sociocultural dynamics in a fairly simple way—the problem was one of discovering and formulating the linear trends believed to be unfolding in the course of time. In the field of sociocultural change the task assumed an almost unbelievably easy character; it simply amounted to drawing a unilinear or oscillating or branching or spiral main line from "primitive" man, society, or culture to the present time. The whole historical process was thought of as a kind of well-ordered college curriculum, with primitive man or society as a freshman, subsequently passing through the sophomore, junior, and senior classes (or others when the classification contained more than four stages), and then graduating either in the class of "positivism" or "freedom for all" or any other final stage suggested by the fancy and taste of the scholar.

In the eighteenth and nineteenth centuries voices were already raised sharply criticizing this dogma and offering different theories of sociocultural dynamics. In the twentieth century these voices finally became dominant. The first result has been an increasing criticism of the assumptions underlying the linear theory of sociocultural change and of the linear laws formulated by the bio-social sciences of the preceding century. These criticisms have been based on logical as well as factual grounds. On the logical side, critics of the linear theories of change have indicated, first, that the linear type of change is only one of many possible types; and, second, that in order for a linear motion or change to be possible, either the changing unit must be in an absolute vacuum, free from interference of external forces, or these forces throughout the whole process of change must remain in such a "miraculous balance" that they mutually and absolutely neutralize one another at any moment and thus permit the changing unit to move forever in the same main direction, whether the movement is rectilinear, spiral, or oscillating. Evidently, both of these suppositions are factually impossible; even the "material point" of mechanics moves neither in absolute vacuum nor amidst forces that incessantly mutually annul one another; even material bodies are under the influence of at least two main forces, inertia and gravitation, which change their rectilinear and uniform motion (owing to the inertia) into a circular or curvilinear motion. This is true of material particles as well as of the heavenly bodies. When we consider that man, society, and culture are much more complex "bodies," that they are subjected to the incessant influence of inorganic, organic, and sociocultural forces, their linear change throughout the whole of historical time becomes still less probable. Add to this the undeniable fact that each of these "units of change" itself incessantly changes in the process of its existence and thus tends to upset the direction of the change, and the assumption of eternal linearity becomes impossible. For these and similar reasons the theories of eternal linear trends have been increasingly rejected and replaced by what can be called the *principle of limit* in the linear direction of change. According to this principle, only some sociocultural phenomena, and these only for a limited period of time (which is different for different sociocultural units), change in a linear direction. Owing to the immanent change of the units themselves and to an incessant interference of countless forces external to them, their temporary linear trends are found to be broken and replaced by "turns and deviations," giving rise to numerous non-linear forms of sociocultural change.[14]

To these and similar logical criticisms of the assumptions and principles of the various linear theories of sociocultural change a heavy weight of factual criticism has been added. It consists of a large collection of relevant data which clearly contradicted the alleged trends and laws. Sociologists, psychologists, philosophers, historians, ethnologists, and others have factually shown that the empirical life-histories of individuals and of various societies and groups do not follow the alleged trends and the alleged stages of development. The factual evidence openly contradicts the assumption that there exists any universal and perpetual linear trend or any universal stages of evolution applicable to the whole of mankind and to all groups and individuals.

As a result of the logical and factual criticism of the linear dynamics of the last two centuries, the enthusiasm for a discovery and formulation of such trends and laws has notably subsided in the twentieth century. Attempts to continue such a dynamics have not entirely disappeared, of course, but they have become increasingly few and more and more restricted to specific societies, to limited periods of time, and to other limits and qualifications.

Having found the linear kind of social dynamics unproductive, the attention of investigators has shifted to a different aspect of sociocultural change—first and foremost to its *constant and repeated features: forces, processes, relationships, and uniformities.*

The concentration on the *constant features* of sociocultural dynamics in twentieth-century sociology and social science has manifested itself in many ways. First, study has been increasingly concentrated on the *constant forces or factors* of sociocultural change and the *constant effects* in sociocultural life and organization.[15]

In the second place, this concentration on the *constant and repeated* features of sociocultural change has manifested itself in an intensive study of the *constant and ever repeated processes in the sociocultural universe.* A large part of twentieth-century sociology is preoccupied with the study of such ever-repeated processes as isolation, contact, interaction, amalgamation, acculturation, invention, imitation, adaptation, conflict, estrangement, differentiation, integration, disintegration, organization, disorganization, diffusion, conversion, migration, mobility, metabolism, etc., on the one hand; and on the other, with an investigation of such repeated processes as they bear on the problems of how social groups emerge, how they become organized, how they recruit and lose their members, how they distribute them within the group, how they change, how they become disorganized, how they die, etc.

The third manifestation of this concentration on the repeated processes has been a most intensive study of the *constant and repeated meaningful-causal-functional* relationships between various cosmo-social, bio-social, and sociocultural variables as they appear in the ever-changing sociocultural world. Though these relationships were investigated in the nineteenth century their study in the present century has been enormously intensified. The main endeavors of the geographic, biological, psychological, sociologistic, and mechanistic schools in twentieth-century sociology have been precisely to discover and formulate the causal-functional or meaningful-causal uniformities of relationship between two or greater number of the variables: between climate and mentality or civilization, between sun spots and business or criminality, between heredity and certain sociocultural variables, between technology and philosophy or the fine arts, between population density and ideologies, between urbanization and criminality, between the forms of the family and the forms of culture, between social division of labor and forms of solidarity, between social *anomie* and suicide, between business conditions and criminality.

Finally, the fourth manifestation of this concentration on the *constant and repeated* aspects of sociocultural change has been a study of *ever-repeated rhythms, oscillations, fluctuations, cycles, and periodicities* in the flow of sociocultural processes. Preoccupied with a discovery of linear trends, nineteenth-century sociology and social science paid little attention to these repeated features of sociocultural change. With certain exceptions (such as Hegel, Tarde, Ferrara, Danilevsky, and a few others), social scientists and sociologists of that century neglected to follow the path marked out by the Chinese and Hindu social thinkers, by Plato, Aristotle, and Polybius, by Ibn-Khaldun and Vico, to mention only a few of the scholars who concentrated their study of dynamics mainly on these repeated cycles, rhythms, oscillations, periodicities, instead of investigating eternal linear trends. The twentieth century has resumed the work of these thinkers and has continued it with an ever-increasing energy.

Among the social and humanitarian disciplines of this present century the earliest and most intensive study of cycles, rhythms, fluctuations, and periodicities appeared in the theory and history of the fine arts and then in economics, with its investigation of business cycles. They have already produced a large body of scientific studies of sociocultural rhythms, cycles, and periodicities in the field of the fine arts and philosophy, ethics and law, economic, political, religious, and other sociocultural processes. A mere summary of the uniformities of rhythm and tempo, of types and periodicities of fluctuations, and of other important results of these studies would occupy several hundred pages.[16] A series of rhythms with two, three, four, and more phases, periodic and non-periodic, short-term and long-term, in narrow and broad, simple and complex sociocultural processes, has been discovered and analysed. In the fine arts this has been done by Petrie, Crawford, Ligeti, Woelfflin, Mentré, Petersen, Wechssler, Pinder, myself, and many others. Joël, myself, and others have done it in philosophy, and a host of economists beginning with M. Tugan-Baranovsky and ending with Wesley Mitchell and Joseph Schumpeter have done it in economics. In political processes, this analysis has been made by O. Lorenz; in fashions, by Kroeber; in the life-history of vast sociocultural systems and supersystems by L. Weber, Alfred Weber, and Smedes, to mention only a few.

Such in brief have been the main changes in the study of social dynamics as we pass from the dominant current of sociocultural thought of the nineteenth to that of the twentieth century.

The foregoing outline shows that the philosophies of history that reject linear interpretations are only a few among "many boats moving in the same direction and making the same trend." And in this they are valid.

As to the differences between these theories, I have already pointed out that a variety of the cyclically organismic conception with which Danilevsky, Spengler, and Toynbee replace the linear theories is untenable so far as these writers view only one, unrepeated "organismic cycle of childhood, maturity, old age, and death" as a universal pattern of the life-course of all civilizations, systems, and supersystems. Some of the cultural systems follow such a cycle. Most do not. Some of the systems for a limited span of time develop along the linear trend. None does it perennially. In both cases the partisans of the neo-cyclical and the neo-linear interpretations elevate a partial and temporary case to a perennial and universal rule. For logical and factual reasons neither conception can be accepted. Both must be replaced by the "creatively recurring and integralist" conception of sociocultural processes and life-courses of cultural systems and supersystems. "Creatively recurring" means incessant variation of the ever-repeated old themes. At each moment the life-course of each system or process is uniquely new and at the same time a recurrence of what has been. At each moment the historical process is ever new and ever old. Therefore, in this integralist, creatively recurring conception of the life-courses of systems we find "links" of the process that are "linear" within a limited duration and system. We also find "links" that are practically cyclical, recurring now and again; and there are also irregular "fluctuations and oscillations." But taken as a whole, the historical processes display an ever-new variation on the old themes and a variety of predominant patterns, directions, rhythms, tempi, and periodicities in the life-courses of different cultural systems or supersystems. Any attempt to reduce this creative variety to one pattern—be it cyclical, linear, "eschatological," "completely and entirely new at each moment," or "wholly old and again and again repeated in the course of time"—any such attempt is certain to be a blunder. In this respect the "organismically cyclical notions" of Danilevsky, Spengler, and Toynbee are untenable.

3

SIMILARITIES BETWEEN "PHASES" OF CIVILIZATION AND PROTOTYPES OR SUPERSYSTEMS OF CULTURE

If we take the periods of growth (childhood), maturity, and breakdown, disintegration, and ossification of Danilevsky's, Spengler's, and Toynbee's civilizations not as periods of the life-course of the same civilization, but as a succession of different cultural supersystems, and if we compare the portraits of these "periods" with the portraits of my Ideational, Idealistic, Sensate supersystems, with Schubart's four prototypes of culture, with Northrop's dyadic types, with Berdyaev's Barbaric, Medieval, and Humanist-Secular phases of culture, we find that these portraits of the "periods" and of the respective prototypes or supersystems are strikingly similar. Most of the main characteristics which Danilevsky, Spengler, and Toynbee ascribe to a given phase of their civilization, the others ascribe to a certain type of culture. The following scheme outlines these concordances.

(a) Most of the traits ascribed by Danilevsky, Spengler, and Toynbee to a "civilization" at the period of its growth (or "spring" or "youth") are ascribed by Schubart to the Ascetic and in part the Messianic types; by me to the Ideational and in part the Idealistic types; by Berdyaev to the "Barbaric" and in part the Medieval types; by Northrop mainly to the aesthetic type; by Kroeber to a religiously dominated culture.[17]

(b) Most of the characteristics ascribed by Danilevsky, Spengler, and Toynbee to the phase of decline of their civilization are found among the characteristics of Schubart's Promethean or Heroic prototype of culture, of Schweitzer's declining civilization, of my late Sensate culture, of Berdyaev's late Humanist-Secular type, of the predominantly theoretic culture of Northrop and of the pre-eminently secular culture of Kroeber.

(c) Finally, most of the traits of the civilization's maturity —its "summer," the beginning of its "breakdown" phase—are found in Schubart's Harmonious prototype, in Berdyaev's fully developed Medieval type, in my Idealistic, and in Northrop's combined "aesthetic-theoretic" form.

At its spring—its period of growth—the civilization of Spengler, Danilevsky, and Toynbee exhibits such characteristics as: intuitional creativity and truth, inner religiosity, "etherialization," predominantly spiritual values, absolutization of these values and a clear-cut differentiation between the positive and negative values; sacral law and ethics; predominantly religious or ideational philosophy and world-outlook generally; religious painting and sculpture, music and literature, architecture and drama; intuitional foundation for almost all the values; undeveloped positivism, empiricism, materialism, relativism and science; absence of almost any purely utilitarian, hedonistic, and "empirical" ethics; predominantly familistic or *Gemeinschaft* relationship among the members of the culture; a preponderantly theocratic-aristocratic creative minority; little urbanization or industrialization or commercialization of the society; strong *esprit de corps;* and so on. The same traits mark Schubart's Ascetic and Messianic prototypes, my Ideational supersystem, in part Berdyaev's "Barbaric" and early "Medieval" types and Northrop's predominantly "aesthetic-intuitional" culture.

The late phase of this civilization is characterized, similarly, by secularism, materialism, utilitarianism, empiricism, hedonism, scientism, development of science and technology, relativisation of values; decay of religiosity and intuitional creativity; secular (Sensate) fine arts; secular ethics and law; increasing replacement of genius by techniques; development of the "bigger and better," of quantity in place of quality; increasing social differentiation, "schism in the soul," internal disturbances, and class struggle; over-developed urbanization, industrialization, and commercialization; replacement of the familistic or *Gemeinschaft* relationship by the contractual or *Gesellschaft,* and eventually by the compulsory ones; replacement of the creative theocratic-aristocratic minority by the creative minority of the middle classes, then by the dominant minority of the rich strata, and eventually by the Caesars, dictators, demagogues, and other unscrupulous leaders of well-armed mobs, cliques, parties. These are also the traits of my late Sensate supersystem, of Schubart's late Heroic-Promethean prototype, of Berdyaev's too ripe "Humanistic-Secular" culture, and, in part, of Northrop's "theoretic" culture.

What Danilevsky, Spengler, and Toynbee call a period or phase in the life-cycle of a civilization, the others call a type or a form of cultural supersystem. What the first three authors consider as the succession of the phases in the life-course of the same civilization, the others view mainly as a succession of different prototypes or supersystems of culture. Thus the real disagreement between the two groups of writers is considerably less than appears on the surface. Their agreement is significant. It suggests that among the great cultural supersystems there are forms somewhat similar to those which Danilevsky, Spengler, and Toynbee outline as the phases in the life-cycle of their civilization ("spring," "summer," "winter," and so on) and which Schubart, I, and, to some extent, Berdyaev and Northrop consider the forms or types of the cultural supersystems.

4

THE TEMPORAL SEQUENCE OF "PHASES" AND PROTOTYPES

The preceding similarity becomes still more significant when we discover that both groups of writers arrive at essentially similar conclusions about the temporal sequence of the "phases" of civilization and of the supersystems of culture. Both groups state that civilization and culture change and in the course of time pass from one "phase" or prototype or supersystem to another. The temporal sequence of the phases of civilization in one group and of the types of cultural supersystems in another is essentially similar.

Temporal Sequence

In the Phases of Civilization	*In Prototypes of Culture or Cultural Supersystems*
1. The growth (or "spring" or "childhood") phase of Danilevsky, Spengler, and Toynbee	1. Sorokin's Ideational, Schubart's Ascetic-Messianic, Kroeber's first "religiously dominated culture," Northrop's dominantly "aesthetic," Berdyaev's "Barbaric-religious" prototypes
2. The maturity (or "summer," etc.) phase	2. Sorokin's Idealistic, Schubart's "Harmonious," Berdyaev's "Mediaeval-Renaissance" types
3. The phase of decline and disintegration ("autumn" and "winter"; Spengler's "civilization-phase")	3. Sorokin's Sensate, Schubart's Heroic or Promethean, Berdyaev's "Humanistic-Secular," Northrop's "theoretic," Kroeber's secular, intellectual-artistic culture, free from religious domination [18]

The similarity does not cease at this point. It goes further. Spengler contends that the last, "civilization" phase of a High Culture is marked by an emergence and growth of the "second religiosity," which serves as a passage to the emergence of a new high culture and its new "spring-phase." Toynbee states that in the last phase of a civilization there emerges the "universal church" and a new religion, which ushers in a new civilization dominated by the new religion in its period of childhood or growth. My study of the succession of the super-systems during some thirty-five centuries of the Creto-Minoan, Creto-Mycenaean, Graeco-Roman, and Western European cultures and in a more cursory way of the Egyptian, Chinese and Hindu cultures has shown likewise that in all observed cases, after the decline of the Sensate supersystem, a new Ideational (religious) supersystem becomes dominant. Spengler's "second religiosity," Toynbee's "universal church" ushering in a new religious phase of a new civilization, Berdyaev's new "Medieval" culture succeeding the declined "Humanistic-Secular," Schubart's new Messianic prototype replacing the decaying Heroic or Promethean prototype—all these concepts are similar. Kroeber also states that often, though not always,

. . . after science and philosophy had run their active course, religion once more becomes important.[19]

Thus even on this point the theories seem to be in an essential agreement as to a new Ideational-Religious supersystem supplanting the declined Sensate, variously referred to as a "second religiosity" or a "new universal church and religion" supplanting the last "civilizational" or "disintegrating" phase of a dying civilization. Though personally I do not claim this sequence as universal and unexceptional,[20] nevertheless it seems to be the prevalent temporal order. In view of this none of the writers considered is surprised at the ever-increasing signs of the growing religiosity in our times and in increasing disillusionment with science, non-religious and anti-religious ideologies, behaviors, and cultures. All this is to be expected in the light of the theories discussed.

Schweitzer, Spengler, Toynbee, Northrop and myself agree also on a *growth and revival of the ethical values, behavior, movements and forces in this transitory period between the decaying and the emergent civilizations or supersystems. This ethical revival goes on hand in hand with the religious revival* mentioned. Schweitzer regards this ethical renaissance as the necessary condition of the renaissance of the civilization itself. Spengler views it as the last gasp of the dying civilization and preparation for the emerging new one: The emergence of the Buddhist reverence for life and ethical Nirvana, of the Stoic ethical upsurge in Greece, the contemporary pacifist, Socialist, and similar ethical movements of the dying Faustian civilization, are examples of this religious-ethical revival at the end of a dying civilization. My studies led to the generalization that in the great crisis of the transition from the declining old to the new emerging supersystem *the polarization of human souls, groups, and values regularly occurs.* Most persons and groups who under normal conditions are neither too saintly nor too sinful, who render unto Caesar what is Caesar's and unto God what is God's, tend, in the conditions of catastrophe and crisis, to polarize. Some become more saintly, more religious, more ethical; others, more sinful, more atheistic, more cynical than before. The positive, religious-ethical polarization appears as a renaissance of religion and ethics, noted by Spengler and others. Factually, in the period of transition the full picture is growth not only of religiosity and morality but also of irreligiosity and demoralization. Only later on, when the new cultural supersystem emerges, does the positive polarization prevail and make the first phase of an emerging civilization ethically strong and noble.[21]

Notwithstanding the differences in the details and interpretations, almost all the writers considered agree on the revival of ethical movements in the last phase of the declining supersystem or civilization.

5

THE CRISIS OF OUR AGE AND THE COMING NEW CULTURE

All the writers are unanimous in viewing our times as the end of the Faustian (Spengler) or European (Danilevsky) or Western (Schweitzer) or hitherto dominant Heroic-Promethean cultural (Schubart) prototype; or of the Western Sensate supersystem (Sorokin) or as the Humanistic-Secular stage of Western culture (Berdyaev) or as the sharpest crisis of the Western theoretic culture (Northrop) or Western civilization (Toynbee and Kroeber). They all explicitly describe our times as the period of one of the greatest transitions from one civilization or cultural supersystem to another, different one.

As to the coming civilization or cultural prototype, most of the writers, with some reservations, prophesy that it will be Religiously-Ideational (Danilevsky, Spengler, Toynbee, Schubart, Berdyaev, to some extent myself) or Integral, as a synthesis of the Aesthetic-Theoretic (Northrop), of the Ideational-Sensate (Sorokin), of the Voluntaristically-Ethical and Rational (Schweitzer). In brief, the coming civilization or culture is going to be basically different from that which has been dominant during the last five or six centuries.

All the writers agree that with the end of the dominant old and the emergence of the dominant new culture, a shift is taking place from the geographical center of the dying culture to a new geographical center, and from the nation or nations that were the old supersystem's locale to a new nation or nations. Since Western Europe was the center of the dying cultural supersystem, the new civilization must emerge elsewhere. Danilevsky, Spengler, and Schubart believe it is going to be Eurasia and Russia, with the Slavic groups the center and chief instrument. I consider the vast region of the Pacific as the territorial center and the Americas, India, China, Japan, and Russia as the leading players in the coming drama of the emerging Integral or Ideational culture. If Europe is united it will have a leading role, but in no way as important a role as it has had in the last five centuries. If Europe is not unified, it will simply become one of the "provincial" theaters where nothing of great importance in the cosmic drama will be presented.[22]

6

THE DECISIVE ROLE OF IMMANENT FACTORS

As was briefly mentioned before, all the theories agree that the civilizations or cultural supersystems change, rise, decline, and follow one another mainly by virtue of the forces inherent in the cultural or civilizational systems themselves. Each cultural system or supersystem could not help changing incessantly, even if it were in an absolutely unchangeable milieu. Spenglerian "destiny," Toynbee's "suicide" as the reason for the disintegration and dissolution of his civilizations, the similar standpoint of Schubart, Berdyaev, and Kroeber, my extensively developed theory of the "immanent change and self-determination" of cultural systems—all these different terms convey the essentially similar idea of the immanent change and self-determination of the life-course of cultural systems. The cosmic or geographic, biological, and sociocultural forces external to the system accelerate or retard, facilitate or hinder, sometimes crush, a cultural system. These, however, are all the functions they perform. On this point the authors considered are fairly unanimous and differ sharply from the partisans of the "externalistic factors" as the main factors of change.

7

THE MOBILITY AND DIFFUSION OF CULTURAL PHENOMENA

Though most of the writers studied little the details of how the initial "germ" of a future civilization or supersystem develops into an enormous system, their cursory statements and incidental remarks contain a common core. The sound part of this common core seems to be summed up in the following propositions.[23]

(a) If a newly invented or discovered cultural system of great potentiality is destined to become an actual great system or supersystem, it must be transmitted from its author or authors to other persons and groups—must diffuse or socialize itself.

(b) It may diffuse only in its ideological form (for instance, an ideology of Communism or Buddhism known to millions of persons who do not practice either) or also in its behavioral and material forms (when Communism or Buddhism is not only theoretically learned and preached, but also practiced and incorporated into the buildings of Communist clubs, Communist newspapers, Buddhist temples, etc.).

(c) As a rule the ideological form of a cultural phenomenon diffuses faster and more easily over a vaster multitude of persons and groups, areas and cultures than its behavioral and material forms. Communism or Buddhism as ideologies are spread in the human universe to an incomparably greater degree than are their behavioral practice and material vehicles. Like millions of other persons, I know ideological forms of these cultural phenomena, but I neither practice them nor am surrounded to any great degree by a Communistic or Buddhistic material culture. This proposition, by the way, is opposite to the theories that claim earlier, easier, faster, and vaster diffusion of the so-called "material culture" compared with the "non-material." When tested, these theories are found to be untenable.

(d) Diffusion or mobility of cultural phenomena proceeds horizontally from persons and groups to other persons and groups of about the same social status and, vertically, from the lower to the higher strata (classes, castes, orders), and vice versa.

(e) Cultural phenomena diffuse or travel from their place of origin along all the existing lines of communications and routes—highways, railways, radio, airways, telephone, television, etc. These lines largely determine why a new fashion invented in Paris is more quickly transmitted to New York than to a little French village not too far from Paris; why the cities are more exposed to foreign cultural values than the rural parts; why foreign cultures are more diffused along seaports, big traffic centers, and so on. The proposition embraces also many special cases, including Kroeber's cases of the "insular cultures," and of the centripetal and centrifugal diffusions. (See above.)

(f) From the upper strata to the lower, from the big cities to the rural areas, from the so-called "civilized" to the "uncivilized" pre-literate groups, move mainly such cultural phenomena as enter the existing culture of the lower classes, rural populations, and pre-literate groups as a finished product. Whether it be an automobile or radio, a lipstick or a new hat, a new hit song or a creed, a new dance or a political ideology, they all enter these cultures and function there mainly as finished products, not as a raw material; mainly as systems, not as congeries. The cultural stream that moves in the opposite direction, from the lower to the higher strata, from the rural to the urban areas, from the pre-literate groups to the civilized populations carries mainly a "raw cultural material." No matter whether the given cultural phenomenon functions as a finished product in its native culture, it enters the cultures of the upper strata, of the cities or of the civilized groups, as a raw material to be manufactured, machine-made, and transformed into a finished product in these cultures. From agricultural products, iron ore, oil, and coal to a folk tune, folk dance, or fairy tale, these phenomena are taken as a raw material to be transformed into a finished product by these "upper-urban-civilized" cultures.

(g) Ordinarily, it is the upper and professional middle strata that initiate, create, or import a new cultural phenomenon into a given culture. Later on, with some lag, it moves into the culture of the lower strata. As a rule the stream of the new cultural phenomena—created or imported—moves mainly downward, from the upper to the lower classes. As a rule, the lower strata imitate the upper. However, in the periods of decay of upper strata culture, the stream reverses itself. In such periods the upper strata begin to imitate the lower; the cities begin to imitate the villages, and the "civilized" populations begin to ape the "savages." This statement in its developed form agrees with—but reveals a great deal more than—Toynbee's statement about the replacement of a creative minority, freely imitated by the "internal and external proletariat," by a dominant minority that begins to imitate the vices and manners of the lower classes. It also agrees with Spengler's "Caesarism"—the rude and cynical, but vigorous personal dictatorship (euphemistically called "charismatic" by Max Weber) of a leader and his faction that brings the traits of the lower classes into the top of a social pyramid, into a new "aristocracy" of the gang-leaders.

(h) Cultural phenomena travel or shift—horizontally and vertically—as congeries, as small and vast systems, as supersystems, and as total cultures. In the course of time the centers of creativity in various fields of culture, as well as the centers of human history itself, also shift from place to place, from group to group, from nation to nation. As mentioned before, we are witnessing at the present time a shift of the center of history from Europe to the Pacific (to Eurasia, according to Danilevsky, Schubart, and Spengler).

These propositions seem to sum up the somewhat cursory and fragmentary statements of Kroeber, Danilevsky, Spengler, Toynbee, and Schubart.

8

THE TRANSMISSIBILITY OF CULTURES OR CIVILIZATIONS

Overlooking the secondary differences, the main propositions of the theories about the transmissibility or non-transmissibility of each culture or civilization to other groups and peoples are concordant in their essential points. The differences between the propositions of, say, Danilevsky and Spengler or Kroeber are terminological rather than real. The common core of the sound views of our writers in this field are probably adequately expressed in the following generalized propositions.[24]

(a) When a cultural phenomenon passes from person to person, from group to group, it remains essentially unchanged if the culture of departure is identical with the culture of infiltration, and if the mechanical means of standardization are available.

(b) If the two cultures (of departure and infiltration) differ, the migrating cultural phenomenon changes, and the greater the difference of the two cultures, of persons or of groups, the more it changes.

(c) If the two cultures diverge fundamentally, then an important cultural part of one culture cannot pass into the other.

Two great mathematicians precisely understand, say, Einsteinian relativity; it can be passed from one to the other because their mathematical cultures are similar. If the attempt is made to pass the relativity theory to a person only moderately acquainted with mathematics, it can be passed only in a simplified, and somewhat distorted way. If the attempt is made to pass it to a person who does not know even arithmetic, it will fail. The same is true of any religious, philosophical, ethical, or other theory or cultural phenomenon.

(d) If we keep the difference between the cultures of the departure and of the infiltration constant, the extent of the transformation of the migrating cultural phenomenon depends upon its own nature. The more complex, refined, and intricate the phenomenon, and the greater the training required for its use, the more profoundly it changes in the culture of infiltration. Elementary mathematics can migrate from person to person, from group to group, more easily and with less distortion than a complex mathematical theory. A spade can pass into another culture, even into a pre-literate one, more easily and with less distortion of its operation than, say, a steam shovel. "Man came out of a monkey" diffuses more easily and with less distortion than a real Darwinian or biological theory of evolution.

(e) Other conditions being equal, among the cultural values of the same kind, price, and cultural milieu, the more refined and complex the value and the more special training it requires for its use, the less widely it spreads in comparison with a less complex value.

Arithmetic is more effectively spread than algebra or trigonometry, these more than calculus, and elementary calculus diffused more than the most complex problems of mathematics. Popularizations of philosophy, like Will Durant's *Story of Philosophy,* or of history, like H. G. Wells' *Outline of History,* are spread more widely than, say, Kant's *Critique of Pure Reason* or Mommsen's historical works. Elementary texts in any field are diffused more widely than more advanced texts. The simplest folk tunes or jazz are spread more than Beethoven or Bach. And so on. For this reason the best sellers and hits are as a rule fairly elementary and primitive. Only an insignificant portion of these are great works.

(f) Of the other factors influencing diffusion or socialization or transmission of a cultural phenomenon the following can be mentioned: (i) urgency and universality of the needs satisfied by it; (ii) congeniality of the receiving culture; (iii) force and coercion used for its imposition upon other persons and groups; (iv) advertising and the totality of the means of communication used.

(g) When two different cultures meet, in the form either of two persons or of two groups, their respective *congenial* elements tend to pass over from one to the other most easily, rapidly, and with a minimum of change. The less congenial they are, the more transformed they are in the process of passage. Their uncongenial elements cannot pass over at all, unless force and pressure are used.

Of the equally congenial elements the simplest ones tend to pass over more easily, faster, and more successfully than the more complex ones.[25]

(h) Contrary to the belief of many scholars, including Toynbee, the opinion that material, technological, and economic values penetrate another culture first, while the non-material, non-technological, or ideological values always lag in passage, this rule is neither invariable, universal, nor even prevalent. In some cases material values, in other cases non-material values, migrate and take root first. No uniformity whatsoever can be found on this point. Only one prevalent rule, already mentioned, seems to be correct—namely, that the ideological form of a cultural phenomenon tends to pass over earlier and diffuse faster and more easily than its behavioral and material forms.[26]

Such are the main uniformities in this field.

In the light of these statements, the contention of Danilevsky, Spengler, and in part Toynbee, that each civilization is untransmittable to persons and groups foreign to it, contains a particle of truth, if and when the culture of these persons and groups is quite uncongenial to the transmitted culture or civilization. However, if two cultures are somewhat congenial, they can exchange their parts, but each part becomes transformed in the process of passing over into and settling in the other civilization. Finally, the congenial parts of two civilizations can easily infiltrate into each other.

These and other propositions define more precisely and more validly the sound parts of the theories discussed in this respect. The propositions also point out the one-sidedness, exaggerations, and outright errors of these theories concerning the diffusion, transmissibility, transformation, migration, and mobility of cultural phenomena. All in all, our philosophers of history somewhat exaggerate the non-transmissibility of a given "civilizational" or cultural phenomenon to another culture and the impossibility of an adequate understanding of one civilization by persons and groups belonging to a different civilization. Such a statement is correct only in regard to basically uncongenial "civilizations" and only within these uncongenial limits. Beyond this, the parts of one civilization can pass over into another, changing in the process of passing, if these civilizations are somewhat different; and passing without any change and misunderstanding if the cultures are congenial.

9

THE SOCIOLOGY OF KNOWLEDGE

Since the major premises or prime symbols or philosophical presuppositions of each supersystem of civilization are different; since any cultural system is selective in what it ingests and what it rejects; and since any cultural phenomenon (be it science, philosophy, religion, literature, music, gadget, law or ethics, form of social, economic, or political organization) must undergo a change when it passes from one culture into another based upon a different premise—any "mental production" is thus conditioned, molded, and patterned by each civilization or supersystem in its own way. This "cultural conditioning" of all forms of "mental creativity," from science to the fine arts, assumes several forms.

(a) Eager ingestion by a given culture of those forms of science, philosophy, religion, fine arts, manners and mores, gadgets and forms of social institutions that are congenial to its major premise and to the central core of the supersystem or civilization.

(b) A successful diffusion, approval, and functioning of all such congenial "mental products" in such a culture-civilization.

(c) Rejection and absence in it of all forms of the "mental products" that are contradictory or uncongenial to a given supersystem.

(d) Hindering, disapproval, and a "poor existence" of all the uncongenial patterns of art, scientific, or religious theories, law norms or gadgets, and practically all uncongenial "mental products."

(e) Transformation and modification of these "products" according to the main character of a given culture or civilization: if it ingests something from a different culture, it patterns it in its own image.

(f) All this means that each basically different supersystem of culture or civilization has its own system of truth, beauty, and goodness; its own type of science, philosophy, painting or music, literature or architecture, ethics or politics, dissimilar from those of another, substantially different cultural supersystem. There have been and there are Apollinian, Faustian, or Magian mathematics or physics different from each other, according to Danilevsky or Spengler; Messianic or Heroic philosophies and world-views according to Schubart; Ideational, Sensate, and Idealistic systems of truth or law, fine arts or philosophy, economics or politics, according to my theory; the aesthetic and theoretic cognition, fine arts, philosophy, etc., according to Northrop; "Medieval" or "Secular-Humanistic" forms of these according to Berdyaev. These authors have demonstrated this cultural determination and molding of all "mental products" beyond a reasonable degree of doubt. In this sense they have contributed to the so-called "sociology of knowledge" or the *Wissenssoziologie* possibly more than any other philosophical or sociological school of recent decades.[27] Largely as a result of their labor we now know that even a mathematical number does not mean the same in essentially different cultures, not to mention sciences, philosophies, religious beliefs, ethical norms, even technological gadgets and what not. So far as they are ingested by a given cultural supersystem (and some forms are vigorously rejected) they all are modified and transformed in the image of the supersystem itself. The total discoveries of the writers in this field are by far more sound, fruitful, and important than all the noisy confusion of so-called "semantics," and other superficial fads and fashions in the field of cognition and creativity.

IO

INTEGRAL COGNITION AND EPISTEMIC CORRELATION

Danilevsky, Spengler, Schubart, Berdyaev, Northrop, myself, and possibly Toynbee and Kroeber are all in agreement in the field of cognition, knowledge and truth in a number of points: (a) that purely sensory or rational cognitions are not the only forms of cognition; (b) that they do not give a full cognition; (c) that besides these ways of knowing there is an additional "intuitive," "aesthetic," "mystic," "suprarational and suprasensory," "immediate" form of cognition quite different from the sensory and rational; (d) that this "third" way consists in a complete identification of the cognizing subject with the cognized object, in an elimination of any chasm between the subject and the object, in the subject ceasing to be an "observing outsider" in regard to the object and the subject-object becoming one. "When in opposing the subject and the object, philosophical theory abstracts them both from Being (reality), it makes the apprehension of Being impossible. To oppose knowledge and Being is to exclude knowledge from Being." [28] This third way of cognition is exceedingly important for a real understanding of sociocultural phenomena. A full cognition of these demands a proper integration or epistemic correlation of all three cognitions: sensory, logical, and intuitional; or, in Northrop's terms: "the aesthetic and theoretic"; or, in the terms of Spengler, Berdyaev and Schubart, the "immediate, intuitive" and "observational, intellectual, scientific."

We have seen how Spengler, especially, criticizes the inadequacy of a purely observational, intellectual science; in his opinion it can give only a mediated, "dead" knowledge about the "dead shells" of the living sociocultural, historical reality. Others, including myself, have demonstrated in many ways the utter inadequacy of a purely sensory or rational cognition of the sociocultural world especially, and the exceptionally important role of intuitional cognition and creativity. While approving the proper use of various empirical, quantitative, observational, experimental, and other logico-sensory methods of study of sociocultural phenomena; while confirming the use of various "objective" tests of human intelligence, emotionality, aptitudes, and other personality traits—still our authors have been the sharpest and most telling critics of an improper use of these procedures; of their limitations and pseudo-objectivity;

of the disease of "testophrenia" or "testomania" among many testers who really do not know what their tests test and what the results of testing mean; of a most unscientific imitation of various "operational," "instrumental," "functional," and other procedures of the natural sciences; of the mania of covering a perfectly arbitrary and incompetent procedure by an objective-looking use of this or that gadget, machine, or "experts' estimates," and so on. Especially strong criticism has been meted out by our writers to all investigators who, not distinguishing between a sociocultural system and a congeries, apply the same methods of atomistic and mechanistic, statistical and other procedures to both. As a result such investigators often make a living sociocultural system into mincemeat, cut into slices and cubes, each taken as a variable and each studied in its correlation with other slices and cubes of the mincemeat. On the other hand, they often unite into one variable a fantastic motley of the most heterogeneous and obviously unrelated phenomena and make out of this motley a unity, a variable. The variables of the "material" and "nonmaterial" culture can serve as a sample of this motley variable. Making a Yankee community into mincemeat, cut into six slices ("upper-upper, upper-lower, middle-upper," etc.) and then into more than two hundred cubes, with a subsequent study of the relationship between these cubes and slices, is an example of a senseless turning of a living system into dead mincemeat.[29] In various ways our philosophers of history demonstrate the inadequacy of these pseudo-scientific procedures and state that only the integral cognition or epistemic correlation of sensory, rational, and intuitional cognitions can give a full understanding of sociocultural phenomena.

On this point the writers considered assume the integralist standpoint that clearly sees (a) the enormous limitations of purely sensory-empirical and rationally-positivistic ways of cognition prevalent in the nineteenth century, (b) the paramount role of intuition in cognition and creativity, (c) the necessity of the unified epistemic correlation or integral cognition, truth, and creativity for knowing as well as for creating sociocultural reality. This new tide restores and recreates the

ancient "mystic" ways of cognition and creativity and blends
them with sensory and rational ways in one integral cognition
and truth. The mystic ways of cognition of Patanjali's Yoga,
of the great Buddhist logicians and philosophers (Gotama,
Dignaga, Vasubandhu, Nāgarjuna, Iśvarasena, Dharmakīrti
and others),[30] of practically all the religious and non-religious
mystic currents in Hinduism, Buddhism, Taoism, Jainism, in
the Suffist Islam, in Zoroastrianism, in Plato and Platonism,
Pythagoreanism, Plotinus, Dionysius the Areopagite, Gnostics,
and other mystic currents in the Graeco-Roman and Western
worlds; this intuitional-mystic current increasingly swells and
flows now in H. Bergson's and N. Lossky's "intuitional" knowledge and creativity; in Husserl's "intuition of essences"; in the
epistemological theories of Berdyaev, S. Frank, L. Shestov,
E. Heidegger, Soren Kierkegaard, K. Jaspers, J.-P. Sartre,
N. Hartmann, up to the theories of the "aesthetic" cognition
of Northrop, H. Margenau, E. Cassirer, Philipp Frank, and
many others.

Given its due, this intuitional cognition is now being unified
into one integral knowledge with sensory and rational cognitions. This integralist cognition now increasingly supplants
the one-sided, utterly inadequate theories of purely sensory
or purely rational cognitions prevalent in the nineteenth century, and still the dominant view of the rank and file of social
scientists, especially in the United States. Most of them seem
to be anemic epigoni of the earlier full-blooded "positivism"
and "empiricism." Trying to be "objectively observational,"
"objectively behavioristic," these epigoni are inimical towards
any intuition, any "arm-chair philosophy," any "integral" or
"mystic" theories of cognition and creativity. While their entire preoccupation with sensory, empirical "fact-finding" is
innocuous by itself, and once in a while it even delivers a
small fact of small significance, on the whole it has remained
sterile and unfruitful; has discovered very few, if any, really
significant facts, causal relationships or uniformities; has delivered mainly trainloads of chaotic facts, often dressed in the
quantitative and other forms of misleading preciseness; has
suffered from mechanical testomania or testophrenia. At best

it has been a painful elaboration of the obvious and a rediscovery of a table of multiplication, or of such uniformities as that "after the spring comes the summer, then the autumn, and then the winter," and the like. The very inadequacy of their cognitive theory is largely responsible for this sort of Alexandrian semi-erudition, technical virtuosity, and sterility, vs. the fruitful cognition and creativity of the "intuitional" age of Homer-Hesiod, or of the "integral" age of Plato-Phidias-Aristotle.

To sum up: Our philosophers of history are up-to-date leaders in the renaissance of the new integral cognition and creativity. This fact, perhaps, is responsible for the comparative significance of their works—for their real contributions as well as for their errors and mistakes.

I I

SIMILARITIES BETWEEN KROEBER'S AND SOROKIN'S FINDINGS

Passing to the more specific problems of cultural change, a series of similar results obtained by Kroeber and myself is to be noted.

(a) A total, national "civilization" displays a notable creativity in various cultural fields not necessarily once, but two or more times; in most historical total "civilizations" there have been two, three, or even more great creative blossomings. This result contradicts Spengler's and Toynbee's claim that each civilization has only one real florescence.

(b) Practically all great civilizations have been creative not alone in one specific field—e.g., the Hindu in religion, the Greek in the fine arts, etc.—but in several fields. In the course of such a civilization's existence, its creativity shifts from one field to another.

(c) None of the civilizations has, however, been encyclopedic in its creativity: each has been uncreative in one or more fields.

(d) The creativity of a given civilization or of its social group is neither continuous nor constant: it is intermittent and fluctuates erratically, now exploding, now declining.

(e) This intermittency is not periodic in the sense of a regular time interval in the duration of the creative and uncreative periods or in their alternation. The time duration of each wave varies and is hardly predictable.

(f) Similarly, the forms of creativity curves in any field also vary: in no way are they the same. Now creativity suddenly flares up and rises sharply, then slowly and gradually subsides; now it rises very gradually and slowly and declines rapidly and abruptly; now the curve is symmetrical. If we take several ups and downs of the creativity curve, each wave is different from the other, and the whole curves, when taken in their total length, differ from one another.

(g) The duration of the vaster cultural system tends to be longer than that of its sub-system.

(h) The rhythms of various creative processes are diverse. There are creative processes consisting of two-beat rhythms, three-beat rhythms, and still more complex rhythms. The same is to be said of the rhythms in the sequence of various cultural systems and supersystems. Kroeber does not give any theory of rhythms; but several casual remarks he makes seem to agree with the systematic theory of sociocultural rhythms given in my *Dynamics*.[31]

(i) As to the tempi of the cultural change or of the growth and decline of cultural supersystems, in the life-course of the supersystems *of the same kind*—say, Sensate in the past and in the modern time—the tempi tend to remain about the same. All the theories of a progressive acceleration of the tempi in the course of time are untenable. However, the tempo of the change of Sensate culture is generally faster than that of Ideational and Idealistic cultures; and in the overripe stage of Sensate culture its tempo becomes faster and more feverish than in its first phase. The tempi of the transitional periods from one supersystem to another are chaotic, noisy, unclear in their beats as well as in their velocity. The generalizations concerning faster tempi of Sensate than of Ideational or Idealistic culture and several other uniformities are my formulations, not found in Kroeber's work. However, in his work we find some casual observations of, for instance, a very slow tempo in a change of Hindu culture. As Hindu culture has been predominantly Ideational, its slow change is only one example of the uniform law of the comparatively slow tempo of the life-processes of Ideational cultures generally.[32]

(j) Contrary to prevalent Marxian and other claims that creativity and change appear first in the field of the "material culture" (technology, economics, means and instruments of production), while creativity and change in the field of the "non-material culture" appear only later, and that the material culture leads in the change while the non-material culture regularly lags behind the material culture, both Kroeber and I find that within the same national culture creativity appears first in religion, and in other fields of the non-material culture (statesmanship, literature), and only later does creativity develop in science, technology, and still later in business.

(k) Likewise my systematic, and Kroeber's somewhat casual, studies in this field contradict many other claims of the partisans of the leading role of the "material" (or "technological") culture and the lagging role of the "non-material" or "ideological" culture. Contrary to the contentions of these theorists, both "material" and "non-material" cultures are accumulative, both diffuse beyond the group in which a new cultural value is originated; neither regularly leads or lags behind the other in a change. The creativity in both is intermittent, but in the field of religion and statesmanship it starts earlier and is much less intermittent than in that of business; the creativity in the field of religion and business are negatively correlated.[33]

As to the relationships of creativity in other fields of culture —in science, philosophy, painting, sculpture, architecture, literature, music, drama, law, ethics, and politics—one must distinguish whether they are given in a little integrated, eclectic culture or in a highly integrated culture with a dominant Sensate, or Idealistic, or Ideational supersystem.

In eclectic culture the relationship of the foregoing classes of cultural phenomena—in regard to change and creativity—is mainly erratic, displaying no real uniformity. The relationships between two or more classes vary.

In the culture integrated into a dominant supersystem there is a tangible and broad uniformity in the relationship of these variables or subsystems in one supersystem. Its formula is as follows: Change and creativity in all main subsystems of the same supersystem—say, Sensate, or Ideational—tend to go together, as in organs of the same organism, though this causal togetherness does not mean a short-time synchronicity. The change or creativity in Sensate science, philosophy, fine arts, law, ethics, contractual relationship and finally, in Sensate business as the most conspicuous manifestation of Sensate culture, tend to be positively correlated in all these subsystems. And their change or creativity tend to be negatively associated with those in the subsystems of the Ideational supersystem. When Sensate philosophy—say, materialism—is on the rise, Ideational philosophy—say, theology and idealism—tends to decline; and vice versa.

Kroeber's study discloses an erratic relationship of creativity in various fields of culture. It does not show the basic positive relationship of creativity in all the subsystems of the same supersystem and the negative relationship between the creativity of Sensate and that of Ideational types. The reason for this is that Kroeber looks for creativity in the *total* field of a given national culture which, as has been shown, is an unintegrated dumping ground of a multitude of systems and congeries. Being eclectic in its nature, such a total culture can give only erratic relationships, devoid of any uniformity. If one takes instead a real unified system or supersystem, the situation becomes entirely different. As any real unity, a causal-meaningful supersystem grows and lives as one unified whole; all its main subsystems change and creatively grow or decline in togetherness, hand in hand, positively correlated and bound together. For the same reason the creativity in the opposite, and mutually competing, Ideational and Sensate supersystems must be and is negatively correlated: when one grows, the other declines. When one grows, its creativity in most of its main subsystems must grow: otherwise the supersystem would not grow. When it declines, the decline is largely due to a withering of the creativity in most or in all its compartments. The factual body of evidence well corroborates these generalizations.[34]

(1) When, however, we take an eclectic or little-integrated total culture or even various subsystems in a supersystem, there is no strictly uniform sequence of a manifestation of creativity or change among the various compartments of an eclectic culture or among the various subsystems of the same supersystem, whose change is now viewed from a shorter time period than when viewed for a change in togetherness. What in a change in togetherness appears to be synchronous (say one year), now appears to be non-synchronous if sub-system A changes five days earlier than subsystem B. Instead, for instance, of a universal sequence of a creative development first in science and second in philosophy, we find that in some cases (in eclectic cultures or even in supersystems) science develops first and then philosophy's creativity follows. But in other cases, the order is just reversed, and in still other cases the creativity in both bursts synchronously. The same is to be said about the temporal order of creativity's blossoming in science and the fine arts, or in philosophy and the fine arts, or in painting, sculpture, architecture, music, literature, or in science and law, or in the fine arts and ethics, or in politics and economics, and so on.

This diversity of time-sequences of creativity in eclectic cultures is comprehensible: its eclecticism means a crisscross of a multitude of various, chance forces yielding different results in different situations. The reasons for a diversity in the subsystems of the same supersystem are less comprehensible. However, even in subsystems there is a narrow margin for the activity of various chance forces, and each subsystem has a margin of autonomy. These determine now the growth of creativity of a whole Sensate supersystem, first in Sensate music, then in Sensate philosophy, and then in science and technology; in other cases they make the time-order different —for example, Sensate science, philosophy, technology and literature; and so forth.

Whatever the reason, the fact of diversity of the sequences remains certain, even for concrete mechanical and biological systems. Some human beings in their childhood begin first to walk and later learn to talk, while in others the order is reversed. Some azaleas first develop flowers and then leaves; in other azaleas leaves appear first. In some automobiles of the same make and year and model, trouble starts with one part, in others with other parts: even in such standardized mechanical systems there is a large margin for diversity of the sequence of the troubles. In a much more discrete sociocultural supersystem this diversity is to be expected much more than in biological organisms or in mechanical systems.

In my criticism of Northrop's uniform dependence of philosophy upon science, additional reasons have been given for this diversity. On this point the conclusions of Kroeber and my own seem to be in essential agreement.

(m) Our conclusions are also similar in regard to the relationship between economic or political creativity, on the one hand, and cultural florescence in other fields of culture. Contrary to Danilevsky's claim that political sovereignty and power are a necessary condition for any notable cultural florescence; contrary to Berdyaev's claim that the relationship between cultural creativity and real, especially politico-economic prosperity tends to be uniformly negative; contrary to Coste's contention that ideological creativity in religion, philosophy, and fine arts go on mainly in politically and economically weak countries and periods; and differing with Toynbee's view that the creative period of civilization's growth uniformly occurs when a certain group or nation is neither too prosperous nor too poor economically, when it is comparatively small and not a big political power, and that the periods of decline of civilizations are paralleled by their expansion, by growth of their political power and imperialism—contrary to these theories, each of which tends to claim a certain uniformity in the relationship of the economico-political and other cultural blossoming, neither Kroeber nor I find any such uniformity. Instead, we find four or five diversities of the relationship; namely, creativity occurs in poor and rich cultures and populations; in those that are politically powerful and weak, even dependent, but possessing the minimum of "cultural freedom" discussed. All theories that contend a uniform increase of creativity with a growth of material prosperity or political power are elevating a partial case to a universal rule. So do also those theories that contend a negative relationship between these variables.

If, however, a study of these relationships goes deeper into the distinction between Sensate, Idealistic, and Ideational kinds of creativity, there can be noted several rough uniformities as prevalent rules with exceptions. For instance, creativity in Ideational religion, theology, fine art and ethics tends to be negatively associated with economic prosperity (above the line of a minimal means of subsistence) and enormous secular political power. On the other hand, creativity in Sensate fine art, science, technology, philosophy, and ethics (utilitarian and hedonistic) tends (up to a certain limit) to be positively correlated with material affluence and enormous political power. Even here, however, beyond certain limits this positive relationship disappears and tends to become even negative in too prosperous and too politically powerful nations.[85]

Such are some of the main similarities between Kroeber's and my own findings. Our main disagreements have been noted before.

12

SIGNIFICANCE OF ETHICAL VALUES

In spite of the disagreements with Schweitzer that have been indicated, his reiteration of the old truth that without a minimum of what he calls "reverence for life" or love no real civilization is possible; and that without a strong revival of such an ethics (with a corresponding philosophy or religion) there is no chance for a creative renaissance of Western—and mankind's—civilization: these views I heartily share, as do, possibly, several others of the writers under discussion. It is my firm conclusion that without a notable altruization of individuals and groups, of social institutions and culture, neither can future wars be prevented nor a new, truly creative order be built, and it is for precisely this reason that there was created the Harvard Research Center in Altruistic Integration and Creativity. And further, like Schweitzer, I regard this ethical revival of love or reverence for life as the most urgent need of mankind at the present moment—more urgent than further scientific, technological, or other progress.[36]

Furthermore, Northrop, Schubart, Berdyaev, and I agree with Schweitzer that the revival of this ethic needs a corresponding "philosophy" or "world-view." Though I believe that several concrete philosophies can fill this order and serve as the presupposition of this ethic, we all agree with Schweitzer that such a philosophy is to be based not only upon a purely rational or sensory basis, but no less upon direct, primary, intuitive, suprarational, and suprasensory axiomatic self-evidence. In other words, it must be an Integralist philosophy (with Northrop's double and my triple "epistemic correlation") unifying in itself the intuitive, the rational, and the sensory "evidence" of its validity and practical effectiveness. Insofar as Schweitzer stresses the superrational, intuitive, and mystic will to live as the axiomatic and primordial datum and the superrational, mystic aspect of the needed world-view, insofar as he views it as opening up a far greater and deeper reality than a rational science, thus far is his thesis in agreement with the stress on intuition of Spengler, Schubart, Northrop, Berydaev, and myself. The concrete forms of such a philosophy are not necessarily to be limited to Schweitzer's somewhat desperate and solipsistic philosophy of voluntarism. There have been and are several other philosophical variations of the intuitive and superrational ethics of reverence for life or of love or of benevolence and reciprocity. But almost all the writers discussed in this volume share the view that any such philosophy is to be based upon the intuitive foundation, integrated with rational and sensory reason. None of them believes that purely rational or empirical ethical philosophy can fill the order. None of them considers that utilitarian or hedonistic calculations and empirical rationalizations can build an inspired and inspiring, powerfully effective ethics of love or reverence for life, not only preached on Sundays but practiced daily in human behavior, institutions, and culture. Only an integralist philosophy and ethics can successfully effect this end.

Finally, with the possible exception of Spengler, all the writers agree that the great crisis of our age is not necessarily tantamount to the fatal last act in the drama of human history. In spite of its apocalyptic character, its further development can be stopped and eventually replaced by a new constructive era. If humanity mobilizes all its wisdom, knowledge, beauty, and especially the all-giving and all-forgiving love or reverence for life and if a strenuous and sustaining effort of this kind is made by everyone—an effort deriving its strength from love and reverence for life—then the crisis will certainly be ended and a most magnificent new era of human history ushered in. It is up to mankind itself to decide what it will do with its future life-course.

13

SIGNIFICANCE OF ART-FORMS AND THEIR RHYTHMS

I have shown in Chapter II on "Aesthetic Interpretations of History" that in spite of many disagreements in the multitude of theories concerning art-phenomena, the best and most competent of these interpretations agree in their essentials: First, an endless variety of concrete art-phenomena can be reduced to a few main types of art. Second, these types, though variously named, are fairly similar. Third, dominant forms of art are closely connected with the dominant types of culture: in a predominantly "Archaic" culture the art is also "archaic"; in a preponderantly "Classic" culture, the art is also "classic"; in an unintegrated, eclectic culture, the art is also eclectic. In a predominantly Sensate or Ideational culture, the art is correspondingly Sensate or Ideational. When one dominant form of culture disintegrates and enters the stage of transition towards another culture, its art also disintegrates and assumes transitional forms (contemporary cubism, futurism, dadaism, surrealism, pointillism, and generally "modernism" in all fields of art). Fourth, in the life-history of the same culture the main art-forms incessantly fluctuate in their domination, and different forms of art are often dominant in different contemporaneous cultures. Fifth, specifically Graeco-Roman and Western fine art has, according to these theories, passed from one dominant form into another in about the same time: around the ninth and the eighth centuries B.C., around the fifth century B.C., around the fourth century A.D., around the thirteenth century A.D.; finally its Sensate form—dominant for the last five centuries—is ending now, and art is in a transitional stage. In these and several other points the theories discussed are in essential agreement. Their typology and approximate uniformities have thrown light upon the jungle of art-phenomena and upon even the how and why of sociocultural processes.

XV

The Importance of Social Philosophy in an Age of Crisis

In Chapter XIV we analyzed some of the important points on which modern social philosophers are in agreement. The extent of agreement is strong evidence in favor of the validity of these concordant results.

Taken as a whole, the group of "readers of historical events" we have considered is possibly as creative and fruitful in its contributions as any other group of social and humanistic scholars of our age. They deal with the basic problems of sociocultural life instead of pursuing "research" into its trivialities as many currents of social sciences do. They look straight at the sociocultural reality, no matter how terrible it is, instead of fooling themselves with its pleasant "streamlined" aspects only. They concentrate upon the difficult problems instead of wasting their efforts in a pseudo-scholastic preoccupation with various "techniques" of study, as most of the contemporary scholars do. They keep their skeptical judgment in regard to the doubtful and limited validity of a multitude of various "objective and mechanical tests" in this age of testophrenia and testomania. They possess a logical, epistemological, and philosophical background, as well as empirical knowledge and technical competence greater than that of most of the social and humanistic scholars. Finally, being graced by a spark of talent above the rank and file of social and humanistic "researchers" of our time, the group as a whole has re-created the old "philosophy of history" and re-established a most important "historico-sociological and philosophical school" in sociology and in the social and humanistic disciplines. Since the main problems of this school are on the agenda of history, there is no doubt that its explorations will increasingly continue in the future.

Whatever its mistakes are, the school does not dodge the truly crucial problems. For this reason even its errors are likely to be more fruitful than the correct trivialities or painfully accurate platitudes of the bulk of the precise "researches" of today's social and humanistic disciplines.

If the school decreases its impressionistic penchant and increases its empirical exploration and verification, if it still more systematically applies the integralist method of study with the integralist epistemic correlation and integralist understanding of the manifold sociocultural reality, then its fruitful results are bound to increase enormously. The present critical point of human history imperatively demands this deeper and more adequate integralist knowledge of man and man's sociocultural universe, not only for the sake of a more adequate comprehension of these most "mysterious" phenomena, but especially because the mortally dangerous crisis of mankind must be terminated and the way made clear for humanity's entrance into a new, creative, and harmonious era of history.

Notes

The following short titles are here used to refer to some of my own works:

Calamity   *Man and Society in Calamity* (New York, 1943)
Crisis   *The Crisis of Our Age* (New York, 1941)
Dynamics   *Social and Cultural Dynamics* (New York, 1937–1941); 4 vols.
Society   *Society, Culture, and Personality: Their Structure and Dynamics* (New York, 1947)
Theories   *Contemporary Sociological Theories* (New York, 1928)

CHAPTER I

MAN'S REFLECTION ON MAN'S DESTINY IN AN AGE OF CRISIS

[1] Cf. A. Erman, *The Literature of the Ancient Egyptians* (London, 1927); J. H. Breasted, *The Dawn of Conscience* (New York, 1933); J. Baikie, *A History of Egypt* (New York, 1929); Sorokin, *Calamity*, chaps. 10–12.

[2] Cf. J. H. Breasted, *op. cit.*, pp. 343 ff.; W. F. Albright, *From the Stone Age to Christianity* (Baltimore, 1940), pp. 269 ff.; *Calamity*, pp. 224 ff.

[3] Cf. Lî-kî, Book VII, in *The Sacred Books of the East* (Oxford, 1885), XXVII, 364 ff.

[4] Cf. excerpts and sources in *Dynamics*, II, 353 ff.; *The Vishnu Purana*, tr. by H. H. Wilson, 5 vols. (London, 1864–1877). See also *Calamity*, p. 214.

[5] See *Dynamics*, Vol. II, *passim*.

[6] *Ibid.*, Vol. II, chap. 10.

CHAPTER II

AESTHETIC INTERPRETATIONS OF HISTORY

[1] For a discussion of these theories, see *Dynamics*, Vol. I, chaps. 5, 6, 7. Practically the whole of this volume of *Dynamics* deals with the types, uniformities, and rhythms in art-phenomena: painting, sculpture, architecture, music, literature, and literary criticism.

[2] *The Revolutions of Civilization*, by W. M. F. Petrie, was published in London and New York in 1912.

[3] Petrie's article "History in Art" appeared in *Antiquity*, September, 1931.

[4] *Der Weg aus dem Chaos* was published in Munich in 1931.

[5] Petrie, "History in Art," pp. 288–289. See also O. G. S. Crawford, "Historical Cycles," *Antiquity*, March, 1931, pp. 5–21.

[6] Petrie, *The Revolutions of Civilization*, p. 97.

[7] *Ibid.* See also the summary table, pp. 104–105.

[8] For instance, the Marxist contention is that in any culture and at any period the means and instruments of production change first, and social relationships and ideological facts change later. In a diluted and much more primitive form this theory is now circulated under the guise of a postulate that the "immaterial" culture always lags behind the material culture in the process of social change. (See Ogburn, *Social Change* [New York, 1922] and most of the elementary texts in sociology.) On the other hand, writers like E. de Roberty contend that in the process of social change the material culture always lags behind the immaterial culture. At the first serious test these theories fall to pieces. Their general flaw is the assumption of a uniform sequence and a uniform and *invariable* order where, in fact, they do not exist.

[9] Petrie, *The Revolutions of Civilization*, pp. 94–95.

[10] W. R. Lethaby, "Mediaeval Architecture," and P. Vitry, "Medieval Sculpture," in *The Legacy of the Middle Ages*, ed. by G. C. Crump and D. F. Jacob (Oxford, 1926), pp. 60–91, 103 ff.

[11] Petrie, *The Revolutions of Civilization*, p. 96.

[12] See the data on scientific discoveries and inventions in *Dynamics*, Vol. I, pp. 202 ff.; Vol. II, chaps. 2, 3.

[13] Cf. *Dynamics*, I, 205–206.

[14] Petrie, *The Revolutions of Civilization*, p. 94. A variation of Ligeti's theory is given still more recently in C. Gray's *Predicaments: Music and the Future* (New York, 1936), which establishes this sequence: architecture, sculpture, painting, literature, music.

[15] Ligeti, *Der Weg aus dem Chaos*, p. 34; see also pp. 1–34 *et passim*.

[16] *Ibid.*, pp. 168 ff.

[17] *Ibid.*, pp. 51 ff.

[18] These are not based on my estimates. As in other works, I attempt to eliminate my personal tastes and judgments in such evaluations. This means also that I do not necessarily subscribe to these estimates. I merely confront one set of estimates with another. Cf. somewhat different data, pp. 240–241.

[19] Laprade's and Hegel's theories are those of recurrence in space as well as in time, and partly in both.

[20] See V. de Laprade, *Le sentiment de la nature avant le Christianisme* (Paris, 1866), pp. i–civ *et passim;* also his *Le sentiment de la nature chez les modernes* (Paris, 1868), *passim*.

[21] See G. W. F. Hegel, *The Philosophy of Fine Arts*, tr. by F. P. B. Osmaston (London, 1920), I, 125–147. This translation is the only complete one of Hegel's *Aesthetik*.

[22] *Ibid.*, I, 95–124; II, 1–5; III, 1–24; *et passim*.

[23] *Ibid.*, II, 3; I, 103–104.

[24] *Ibid.*, II, 3.

[25] *Ibid.*, I, 106–107.

[26] *Ibid.*, I, 110–124; III, 18 ff.; the last three volumes are mainly a development of this.

[27] See particularly *ibid.*, Vols. III and IV, which are devoted to a concrete analysis of the main forms of art—architecture, sculpture, painting, music, and poetry—from these standpoints.

[28] J. Combarieu, *Histoire de la musique* (Paris, 1913), I, 453–454.

[29] *Ibid.*, III, 8–9.

[30] A similar theory has been set forth by V. d'Indy in his *Course de*

composition musical (Paris, 1910), I, 216: "Music almost always lags behind the other arts because its domain is to be found in the depths of soul where, as in the depths of the ocean, the effects of the storms raging on the surface pass with retardation." See also Romain Rolland, *Jean Christophe,* No. 4, *Le revolte* (1906), p. 141. According to L. R. Farnell, in Greece "poetry attained a power of spiritual expression at a far earlier date than did painting and sculpture." *The Cults of the Greek States* (Oxford, 1896), I, 9–10. Cf. Charles Lalo, *Esquisse d'une esthetique musicale scientifique* (Paris, 1908), pp. 310–311.

[31] Combarieu, *op. cit.,* II, 270–271.

[32] See F. Brunetière, *Évolution de la poésie lyrique* (Paris, 1894), *ouverture lecture.*

[33] The term *malerisch* as it is used by Ligeti as well as by most of the German scholars in art (A. Riegl, H. Wolfflin, A. Schmarsow, O. Wulff, E. Panofsky, E. Utitz, H. Nohl, W. Worringer, M. Dvořak, E. Cohn-Wiener, L. Coellen, A. E. Brinckman, G. G. Weiszner, H. Schafer, K. Scheffler, and others) is almost untranslatable. It has a much more complex and deeper meaning than the term *pictorial* or *painterly.* For this reason I prefer to keep the German term.

[34] Ligeti, *op. cit.,* pp. 65–111, *et passim.*

[35] *Ibid.,* pp. 60–61.

[36] *Ibid.,* pp. 60 ff.

[37] G. W. F. Hegel, *op. cit.,* III, 5; C. Bayet, *Précis d'histoire de l'art* (Paris, 1905), pp. 11–13; C. Lalo, *op. cit.,* pp. 259 ff.; A. Venturi, *La Madonna* (Milan, 1900), p. v.

[38] *L'archéologie, sa valeur, ses méthodes,* by Waldemar Deonna, was published in Paris in 1912.

[39] W. Deonna, *op. cit.,* III, 6 ff. The many reproductions of these and other sculptures and paintings, though separated from one another by centuries and belonging to different art systems, indeed show a striking similarity in the whole as well as in technical details. See especially Vols. II and III, *passim.*

[40] *Ibid.,* III, 52, *et passim.* See the many reproductions printed in this work.

[41] *Ibid.,* III, 36–37. He intentionally omits the art of other cultures partly because he does not feel quite competent in those fields, partly because he prefers to demonstrate more substantially in fewer art systems than less substantially in many; but in passing note he indicates that the Egyptian, Chinese, Japanese, and other art systems display the same sequence of phases in their evolution.

[42] *Ibid.,* III, 41–52.

[43] *Ibid.,* Vol. III, chap. 5. See the many reproductions there and the detailed analysis by the author.

[44] *Ibid.,* Vol. III, chap. 6.

[45] *Ibid.,* Vol. III, chaps. 4, 8, 9, where the details and reproductions are given.

[46] Frank Chambers, *Cycles of Taste* (Cambridge, 1928), pp. 119–120, *et passim.*

[47] Frank Chambers, *The History of Taste* (New York, 1932), pp. 302–303, *et passim.*

[48] See particularly the Appendix in Chambers' *The History of Taste.*

[49] E. Bovet, *Lyrisme, Épopée, Drame: Une loi de l'histoire littéraire expliquée par l'évolution général* (Paris, 1911).

[50] *Ibid.*, pp. 139 ff.

[51] In *Esquisse d'une esthetique musicale scientifique,* quoted above.

[52] *Ibid.*, p. 261.

[53] *Ibid.*, pp. 262–320. My outline gives only a skeleton of the theory. Lalo fills the pages of his work with abundant factual material.

[54] *Ibid.*, p. 262. See also Deonna, *op. cit.*, Vol. II, chap. 7; Chambers, *The History of Taste*, pp. 269–270.

[55] For these theories, see *Dynamics,* Vols. I, II, and IV.

[56] J. L. Lowes, *Convention and Revolt in Poetry* (Boston, 1926).

[57] H. Wolfflin, *Principles of Art History* (New York, 1932).

[58] K. Scheffler, *Der Geist der Gothik* (Leipzig, 1919).

[59] A. Riegl, *Die spätromische Kunstindutrie* (Vienna, 1901); A. Schmarsow, *Grundbegrieffe der Kunstwissenschaft* (Leipzig-Berlin, 1905); M. Dvořak, *Kunstgeschichte als Geistesgeschichte* (Munich, 1924); W. Worringer, *Abstraktion und Einfühlung* (Munich, 1909); E. Panofsky, *Das Problem des Stils in der buildenden Kunst* (Leipzig, 1926); W. Passarge, *Die Philosophie der Kunstgeschichte in der Gegenwart* (Berlin, 1930); R. M. Wernaer, *Romanticism* (New York, 1910).

[60] See the typical traits of the art of agricultural peoples in P. Sorokin, C. Zimmermann, and C. Galpin, *A Systematic Source Book in Rural Sociology* (Minneapolis, 1931), Vol. II, chaps. 14 and 15.

[61] On these see *Dynamics,* Vol. I, *passim.*

[62] On this subject see E. von Sydow, *Die Kunst der Naturvolker und der Vorzeit,* 2d ed. (Berlin, 1927); F. Boas, *Primitive Art* (Oslo, 1927). See the appropriate remarks in R. Thurnwald's "Prinzipiengraden der ethnologischen Kunstforschung," in the *Zeitschrift fur Aesthetik,* XIX, 349–355.

[63] See the reproductions and analysis of paleolithic and neolithic art in the work of Von Sydow, pp. 66–67, 16–17, *et passim.* See also Max Verworn, *Zur Psychologie der Primitiven Kunst,* 2d ed. (Jena, 1917), and F. Boas, *op. cit.*

[64] See Sir E. Denison Ross (ed.), *The Art of Egypt through the Ages* (New York and London, 1931); J. Capart, *Lectures on Egyptian Art* (Chapel Hill, 1928); J. Capart, *L'art egyptien* (Bruxelles, 1924), Vol. I; J. Baikie, *A History of Egypt* (New York, 1929), I, 206 ff.

[65] See A. Waley, *An Introduction to the History of Chinese Painting* (London, 1923); O. Siren, *A History of Early Chinese Painting,* 2 vols. (London, 1933); W. Cohn, *Chinese Art* (London, 1930); J. C. Ferguson, *Chinese Painting* (Chicago, 1927).

[66] Siren, *op. cit.*, I, 1.

[67] Deonna, *op. cit.*, III, 52.

[68] See the sound criticism of these points of Deonna's work by V. Chapot, "Les methodes archéologiques," in *Revue de synthèse historique,* February, 1914, pp. 8–18. Compare J. Lagrange, *Mélangés d'histoire réligieuse* (Paris, 1915), pp. 227–279.

[69] For this see *Dynamics,* I, 195–730; a summary of it is given in *Crisis,* chap. 2, and in *Society,* chap. 40.

CHAPTER III

NIKOLAI DANILEVSKY

[1] See a full bibliography of Danilevsky's publications in N. Danilevsky, *Sbornik politi-tcheskykh i ekonomi-tcheskykh statey* (Political and Economic Essays) (St. Petersburg, 1890), pp. 673–676.

[2] *Rossia i Evropa* (Russia and Europe), in *Zaria* (1869), No. 1, p. 50. Throughout this chapter I shall refer to this first publication of Danilevsky's work in *Zaria*.

[3] *Ibid.*, No. 6, pp. 99–100.

[4] *Ibid.*, No. 1, p. 43. Toynbee has reiterated these observations made by Danilevsky. After surveying the history of Russo-European relations, Toynbee points out that the Russian Slavs were invaded by the West in the ninth century; "then again in the fourteenth century the best part of Russia's original domain was shorn . . . and annexed to Western Christendom"; in the seventeenth century Swedes, Lithuanians, and Poles invaded and even took possession of Moscow, an invasion which was repeated by the Swedes in the time of Peter the Great; in 1812 Napoleon led the European invasion of Russia; the Germans did it again in 1914 and 1941. "It is true that . . . Russian armies also marched and fought on Western ground, but they came in always as allies of one Western power against another" and for their part made a defensive counter-offensive. "In the annals of the centuries-long warfare between the two Christendoms, it would seem to be the fact that the Russians have been the victims of aggression, and the Westerners the aggressors, more often than not." A. J. Toynbee, *Civilization on Trial* (New York, 1948), pp. 166–169. The whole chapter on "Russia's Byzantine Heritage" (pp. 164–183) is very similar to Danilevsky's analysis of Russo-European relations.

[5] *Zaria*, No. 1, pp. 51–53.

[6] *Ibid.*, No. 1, pp. 51–53.

[7] *Ibid.*, No. 2, pp. 52–56.

[8] *Ibid.*, No. 2, pp. 58 ff.

[9] *Ibid.*, No. 2, pp. 79–81.

[10] *Ibid.*, No. 2, pp. 81 ff.

[11] *Ibid.*, No. 2, pp. 84–87.

[12] *Ibid.*, No. 2, pp. 88–89.

[13] *Ibid.*, No. 2, pp. 89–90.

[14] *Ibid.*, No. 2, pp. 89–91.

[15] *Ibid.*, No. 3, pp. 1–2.

[16] *Ibid.*, No. 3, pp. 2–3.

[17] *Ibid.*, No. 3, p. 5.

[18] *Ibid.*, No. 3, pp. 9–10.

[19] *Ibid.*, No. 3, pp. 10–11. In commenting on his laws Danilevsky offers several of the most important generalizations of contemporary sociology and anthropology concerning the diffusion, migration, expansion, and mobility of culture. Likewise he clearly sets forth the theory that technological or material culture tends to diffuse universally among all cultures, whereas non-neutral, non-material culture can diffuse only within its own area and cannot spread over various cultures except in its elements. This theory has been reiterated in the twentieth century by Alfred Weber, Louis

Weber, R. MacIver, and others. Apparently contemporary representatives of these theories hardly know of Danilevsky's work, for they never refer to it or to the work of several other predecessors. See *Dynamics*, IV, pp. 137 ff., 164 ff., *et passim*.

[20] *Zaria*, No. 3, pp. 11–13 ff., 41 ff.

[21] *Ibid.*, No. 3, pp. 15–16. Here Danilevsky clearly formulates the unit of historical study, culture-historical type or civilization, practically identical with Spengler's and Toynbee's units of historical study and with Toynbee's "operational" criterion of a civilization.

[22] (1) The stage of an "ethnographic material"; (2) the stage of a state or political federation; (3) the stage of civilization—such are the three main phases of the life-history of a culture-historical type. *Zaria*, No. 3, p. 27.

[23] It is to be noted that here Danilevsky uses the term "civilization" as meaning the last phase of the life-history of a cultural type—a meaning used by Spengler fifty years later. Danilevsky's terms "resting on their laurels," "petrifaction," "apathy of self-satisfaction and of despair," "insoluble contradictions renting the body and soul social," and so on, are again strikingly similar to the terms later used by Toynbee.

[24] *Zaria*, No. 3, pp. 21–28. Here we have a theory stating the specific creativity of each civilization in one or two fields only throughout its entire existence.

[25] *Zaria*, No. 3, pp. 19–20.

[26] *Ibid.*, No. 3, pp. 22–27. In a later part of his work Danilevsky divides all great civilizations into three main classes: (1) primary or autochthonous civilizations, which achieve religious, cultural (scientific-technical-aesthetic-industrial), political, and economic values in a preliminary form, without particularly developing any one of these values—such as the Egyptian, Chinese, Babylonian, Hindu, and Iranian civilizations; (2) civilizations that chiefly develop *one* of these main values—such as the Greek civilization (mainly aesthetic), the Hebrew (mainly religious), the Roman (mainly political); (3) civilizations that develop two or more of these main values; the European civilization is twofold in this respect, having developed both political and cultural (scientific-technological-aesthetic) values; the coming Slavic civilization may also belong to this complex, even quadruple, type, developing all four values, but mainly the socio-economic ones. *Zaria*, No. 9, pp. 92–114, 129.

[27] *Ibid.*, No. 4, p. 97. Here Danilevsky points out the "Indian summer" of civilization.

[28] *Zaria*, No. 4, p. 98. Here we have the idea of the lag and of the Indian summer similarly stressed by Spengler and Toynbee.

[29] See J. J. Maquet, *La sociologie de la connaissance* (Louvain, 1949). An English translation will be published under the title *The Sociology of Knowledge* (Boston, 1951).

[30] *Zaria*, No. 9, pp. 115, 121–122.

[31] *Ibid.*, No. 9, pp. 101–129.

[32] *Ibid.*, No. 8, pp. 8–23, 64. Of various nations, Danilevsky quite categorically regarded Turkey and Austria as already dead empires which had lost any reason for political existence. Again, these prognostications proved about to be true in the twentieth century.

[33] *Zaria*, No. 9, pp. 21–31, 55–63. Again, in 1869, Danilevsky outlined the two inimical camps, consisting of the Slavic federation, under the

leadership of Russia, and Europe, in a form that coincides with the contemporary division of Europe into the Eastern (Slavic) camp and the Western camp of Atlantic Pact Europe.

CHAPTER IV

OSWALD SPENGLER

[1] Whether or not Spengler knew of Danilevsky's work remains uncertain. He does not mention it in his writings. But he mentions and was acquainted with the works of S. and I. Aksakov, and those of other Slavophils of whom Danilevsky was one of the intellectual leaders. Professor Spet of Moscow University, who visited Spengler in 1921, has told me that at that time he saw Danilevsky's book in Spengler's library. If not in detail, Spengler could have known the work in outline form. On the other hand, the basic ideas of his work could have been suggested by such of Goethe's works as the little essays, *Geistesepochen, Orphische Urworte,* and so on. Of these Spengler says that they display "such a depth of insight that even today there is nothing to add . . . I would not have one single word changed," and that Goethe's "sentence [Spengler quotes] comprises my whole philosophy." (*Decline of the West* [New York, 1947], I, 49; II, 37.) Since organismic theories of culture and the cyclical interpretation of sociocultural processes similar to Danilevsky's and Spengler's theories go back to ancient Chinese, Hindu, Iranic, and Graeco-Roman thought, and since Spengler knew these theories, they could easily have been responsible for the formulation of his own version. On the history of organismic and cyclical theories of history and sociocultural processes, see *Theories,* chap. 4, and pp. 728–741; and *Dynamics,* Vol. IV, chaps. 8–13.

[2] *Decline of the West,* I, 94.

[3] *Ibid.,* I, 16–18.

[4] *Ibid.,* I, 8.

[5] "Everything that we grasp intellectually has a cause, everything that we live organically with inward certitude has a past." Science is on home ground when it tells us about "judgment," "perception," "awareness," and "recollection," but it remains silent when it comes to defining such words as "hope," "happiness," "despair," "repentance," and "consolation." Spengler, *op. cit.,* I, 117–118, 152.

[6] In natural science "the livingness and directedness and fated course of real Time is replaced by a figure which is only a *line,* measurable, divisible, reversible, and not a portrait of that which is incapable of being portrayed; it is replaced by a 'time' that can be mathematically expressed in such forms as $\sqrt{t}, t^2, -t$ from which the assumption of a time of zero magnitude or of negative times is not excluded. Obviously, this is something quite outside the domain of Life, Destiny, and living historical Time." "Causality has nothing whatever to do with Time." "Real history is heavy with fate but free of laws," "one can divine the future but one cannot reckon it." Spengler, *op. cit.,* I, 120–124.

Generally, historical, living reality has nothing to do with the "truths" of the natural "systematic." The real world of the living soul is the full-blooded world of forms, individualities, color, "physiognomy," in contrast to the lifeless, colorless, formless, quantitative concepts and scientific laws and truths.

[7] Spengler, *op. cit.,* I, 96.

[8] *Ibid.,* I, 4–8, 25, 29–31, 38 ff., 54 ff., 94 ff., 100–102, 121; II, 11 ff., 46 ff., *et passim.*

[9] *Ibid.,* I, 20–22.

[10] *Ibid.,* I, 106.

[11] *Ibid.,* I, 31 ff., 72 ff., 104 ff., 108, 129 ff.; II, 33 ff., 49, 433 ff., *et passim.*

[12] *Ibid.,* II, 440 ff.

[13] *Ibid.,* I, 16–18; II, 189 ff.

[14] Like Danilevsky, Spengler says that "the word 'Europe' ought to be struck out of history." Historically there is no European type of culture. There is only the Western or Faustian culture, utterly different from the Russian. "The Russian *instinct* has very truly and fundamentally divided 'Europe' from 'Mother Russia' with the hostility that we can see embodied in Tolstoi, Aksakov, or Dostoyevski. 'East' and 'West' are notions that contain real history, whereas 'Europe' is an empty sound." The Western culture came into existence between the Vistula and the Adriatic and the Guadalquivir. Even the Greece of today does not belong to it.

The profound difference between the Western and the not fully realized Russian Culture also emerges in their expressive and religious forms. According to Spengler the unfolding of Russian Culture has been hindered and distorted by the pressure and influence of other, older Cultures, particularly the Magian and Western ("pseudomorphosis"). Therefore the "prime symbol" of Russia—the "plane without limit"—has not been fully realized as yet either in Russian religion or Russian architecture. Russian Church architecture is a mixture of the Magian, Armenian-Iranian, and primitive styles. In both religion and architecture the existing style is only "the promise of a style that will awaken when the real Russian religion awakens."

The prime symbol of the "plane without limit" manifests itself in many forms, however: in the absence of any vertical tendency in Russian architecture, in life-feeling, in the Russian conception of God, and in their ideas on the state and property. The Russian epic hero, Ilya Murometz, sits as a peasant for thirty years. The Russian has a very remote relationship with a *Father*-God. His ethos is not a filial, but a *fraternal,* love. Even Christ is thought of as a *brother.* In these points the agreement between Danilevsky and Spengler is almost complete. Moreover, in several places Spengler hints that after the decline of the Western Culture "it is possible that . . . a Culture may arise somewhere in the planes between the Vistula and the Amur during the next millennium." *Decline of the West,* I, 201; II, 362 ff.; Spengler, *Man and Technics* (New York, 1932), p. 78.

[15] *Decline of the West,* I, 178–180. From this standpoint Spengler's work is one of the most important treatises in the *Wissensoziologie* or sociology of knowledge and of all mental articulations from the fine arts up to religion and cult. See J. J. Maquet, *op. cit.*

[16] *Decline of the West,* I, 183–184.

[17] *Ibid.,* I, 184–188.

[18] *Ibid.,* I, 188 ff.

[19] *Ibid.,* I, 183 ff., 201 ff.; II, 223 ff., 235 ff.

[20] *Ibid.,* I, 8–12.

[21] *Ibid.,* I, 59.
[22] *Ibid.,* I, 62 ff.
[23] *Ibid.,* I, 90.
[24] *Ibid.,* I, 302–303.
[25] *Ibid.,* I, 299–310.
[26] *Ibid.,* I, chaps. 7, 8.
[27] *Ibid.,* I, 341 ff. See there a detailed development of these ideas.
[28] *Ibid.,* I, 356.
[29] *Ibid.,* I, chap. 11.
[30] See *ibid.,* I, 420–428.
[31] *Ibid.,* Vol. II, chap. 4; *Man and Technics,* pp. 19 ff.
[32] *Decline of the West,* II, 87–107.
[33] *Man and Technics,* pp. 90–103.
[34] *Decline of the West,* Vol. II, pp. 448–465, chaps. 13, 14.
[35] *Ibid.,* I, 138 ff., 151–160.
[36] *Ibid.,* I, 152 ff.
[37] *Ibid.,* II, 31–38, 57 ff.
[38] *Decline of the West,* I, 178 ff., 213–214, 222, 303–304; II, 50 ff., 170 ff. Spengler, however, had to make some reservations to these categoric statements, for otherwise his own interpretations of the High Cultures would be regarded as misinterpretations that contradict his own statements. For this reason he admits in several places the possibility of intuitive poets' or thinkers' understanding an alien Culture to some extent. See Vol. I, pp. 159–160; Vol. II, pp. 171 ff. In other places, however, he frankly says that his interpretations of all the great Cultures are those of the Faustian man.
[39] *Ibid.,* I, 441 ff., 476 ff.; II, 49 ff., 170 ff.
[40] *Ibid.,* I, 104 ff., 356 ff., 424 ff.; II, 353–62, 429 ff., 445 ff., 471 ff., *et passim.*
[41] *Ibid.,* I, 109–110.
[42] *Ibid.,* I, 128, 224.
[43] *Ibid.,* II, 469 ff.
[44] *Ibid.,* II, 171 ff.

CHAPTER V

ARNOLD J. TOYNBEE

[1] Toynbee, *A Study of History,* I, 45.
[2] *Ibid.,* I, 129 ff.
[3] *Ibid.,* I, 132 ff.; IV, 1 ff.
[4] *Ibid.,* I, 183–338; Vol. II, *passim.*
[5] *Ibid.,* III, 128.
[6] *Ibid.,* III, 128 ff.
[7] *Ibid.,* III, 173–174.
[8] *Ibid.,* III, 128 ff., 182 ff.
[9] *Ibid.,* III, 248 ff.
[10] *Ibid.,* III, 128–390.
[11] *Ibid.,* IV, 1–2.
[12] *Ibid.,* IV, 120.
[13] *Ibid.,* IV, 6.

[14] *Ibid.*, IV, 62 ff.; V, 2 ff.
[15] *Ibid.*, VI, 321.
[16] Toynbee, *Civilization on Trial* (New York, 1948), 232 ff.
[17] *A Study of History*, VI, 171.
[18] *Ibid.*, VI, 324.
[19] *Ibid.*, VI, 235–236, 263.

CHAPTER VI

WALTER SCHUBART

[1] Walter Schubart, *Europa und die Seele des Ostens* (Lucerne, 1938), pp. 13 ff. A systematic and detailed history of rhythmic and cyclic theories of historical processes can be found in *Dynamics*, Vol. II, chap. 10; Vol. IV, chaps. 8–16.
[2] Schubart, *op. cit.*, pp. 13–16.
[3] *Ibid.*, pp. 16–27.
[4] *Ibid.*, pp. 37–38.
[5] *Ibid.*, pp. 53–85.
[6] *Ibid.*, pp. 95–211.
[7] *Ibid.*, pp. 313–318. See also Schubart's *Geistige Wandlung*, where he traces changes in this direction in contemporary culture, science, philosophy, and art.

CHAPTER VII

NIKOLAI BERDYAEV

[1] Nikolai Berdyaev, *Smysl istorii* (Berlin, 1923), pp. 30–34. There is an English translation, *The Meaning of History* (New York, 1936). See also his *Solitude and Society*, pp. 48 ff.
[2] These varieties of linear conception of historical process are discussed in *Dynamics*, Vol. I, chap. 4. Berdyaev, *Smysl istorii*, chap. 5, and pp. 145 ff.
[3] *Ibid.*, pp. 144 ff.
[4] See *Society*, chap. 34; and my "Lasting and Dying Factors in the World's Cultures," in *Ideological Differences and World Order*, ed. by F. S. C. Northrop (New Haven, 1949).
[5] *Smysl istorii*, pp. 166 ff.
[6] *Ibid.*, pp. 212–213.
[7] *Ibid.*, pp. 249–269.

CHAPTER VIII

F. S. C. NORTHROP

[1] F. S. C. Northrop, *The Meeting of East and West* (New York, 1946), pp. 14, 249, 437.
[2] *Ibid.*, pp. 288 ff. See also pp. 117, 163, 265–280, *et passim*. On this point Northrop's theory approaches quite closely the theory of E. de Roberty, who contended that in any culture at any period its scientific

(or analytical) thought directly determines its synthesizing (philosophical or religious) thought; this, in turn, conditions its aesthetic (symbolic) thought or its fine arts; and all three define its practical or applied (technological) thought in all fields of culture—from the "technology of gadgets" to that of the techniques of education, religious ritual, court procedure, and so on. Each of the preceding forms of thought leads, in time, all the subsequent forms of thought; each subsequent form lags, in time, in comparison with all the preceding forms. See *Theories,* pp. 438–463, and *Dynamics,* IV, 292 ff.

[3] Northrop, *op. cit.,* p. 15.

[4] *Ibid.,* pp. 17–28.

[5] *Ibid.,* pp. 66–164.

[6] *Ibid.,* pp. 176 ff.

[7] *Ibid.,* p. 190.

[8] *Ibid.,* chap. 5.

[9] *Ibid.,* p. 246, and chap. 6.

[10] *Ibid.,* chaps. 7, 12; pp. 442–43, 453–54.

CHAPTER IX

ALFRED L. KROEBER

[1] Alfred L. Kroeber, *Configurations of Culture Growth* (Berkeley and Los Angeles, 1944), pp. 826, 839, 7–16, 701.

[2] *Ibid.,* p. 23.

[3] *Ibid.,* p. 32. Cf. *Dynamics,* Vol. II, chaps. 1–10.

[4] Kroeber, *op. cit.,* pp. 36 ff.

[5] Cf. *Dynamics,* Vol. IV, pp. 155–196, chaps. 6, 7.

[6] *Ibid.,* chaps. 9, 10.

[7] Kroeber, *op. cit.,* pp. 75–92. Cf. *Dynamics,* Vol. IV, chaps. 12–15.

[8] Cf. *Dynamics,* Vol. I, *passim.*

[9] Kroeber, *op. cit.,* pp. 663–65, 668–70, 676, 690, 694, 697, 700–703, 710, 713, 805–808. Cf. *Dynamics,* Vol. IV, chap. 7; *Society,* chaps. 35–37.

[10] Kroeber, *op. cit.,* pp. 762–763, 828. Cf. *Society,* chaps. 35, 36.

[11] Kroeber, *op. cit.,* p. 763. Cf. *Society,* chaps. 34, 47.

[12] Kroeber, *op. cit.* pp. 769, 805 ff. Cf. *Dynamics,* IV, 374–388.

[13] Kroeber, *op. cit.,* pp. 763 ff., 664–67, 774. Cf. *Dynamics,* Vol. IV, chaps. 12–16.

[14] Kroeber, *op. cit.,* pp. 754, 622. Cf. *Dynamics,* Vol. I, chaps. 5–13.

[15] Kroeber, *op. cit.,* pp. 766 ff. Cf. *Dynamics,* all volumes, especially Vol. IV, chaps. 7–9; *Society,* chaps. 35–39.

[16] Kroeber, *op. cit.,* pp. 773–777. Cf. *Dynamics,* IV, 268–288.

[17] Kroeber, *op. cit.,* pp. 769–773. Cf. *Dynamics,* Vol. I, chaps. 1–3; Vol. IV, chaps. 1–3.

[18] Kroeber, *op. cit.,* p. 778. Cf. *Dynamics,* Vol. I, pp. 209 ff., Vol. II, *passim;* Vol. III, chap. 8; Vol. IV, pp. 234–252, chap. 7; *Society,* pp. 548 ff.

[19] Kroeber, *op. cit.,* pp. 778–79. Cf. *Dynamics,* Vol. I, chap. 1; Vol. IV, chaps. 3, 4, 6.

[20] Kroeber, *op. cit.,* pp. 782–790; also 77–78, 98, 136, 173, 190, 199–211. Cf. *Dynamics,* Vol. IV, chaps. 6–8.

[21] Kroeber, *op. cit.,* pp. 790–95, 811. Cf. *Dynamics,* Vol. III, chaps. 1–3, 8; Vol. IV, pp. 130 ff.; *Society,* pp. 544–546.

[22] Kroeber, *op. cit.,* pp. 665, 670, 676, 683–84, 690, 705, 714, 723, 736.

[23] *Ibid.,* pp. 723, 795.

[24] *Ibid.,* pp. 795–99; also 201, 672–73. Cf. *Dynamics,* IV, 230–252.

[25] Kroeber, *op. cit.,* pp. 803–804. Cf. *Dynamics,* Vol. IV, chaps. 6, 7.

[26] Kroeber, *op. cit.,* pp. 799–804. Cf. *Dynamics,* Vol. I, chaps. 5–13; Vol. II, *passim.*

[27] Kroeber, *op. cit.,* pp. 804, 808–810. Cf. *Dynamics,* Vol. IV, chap. 11.

[28] Kroeber, *op. cit.,* pp. 810–811. Cf. *Dynamics,* IV, 234 ff.

[29] Kroeber, *op. cit.,* pp. 812–13.

[30] Kroeber, *op. cit.,* pp. 813–18. Cf. *Dynamics,* Vol. IV, chap. 5.

[31] Kroeber, *op. cit.,* pp. 818 ff. Cf. *Dynamics,* IV, 82–95; *Society,* chap. 47.

[32] Kroeber, *op. cit.,* pp. 820–825.

[33] Kroeber, *op. cit.,* pp. 825–834. Cf. *Dynamics,* all volumes, *passim.*

CHAPTER X

ALBERT SCHWEITZER

[1] Albert Schweitzer, *The Philosophy of Civilization* (New York, 1949), pp. 22–23, 38, 39, 91.

[2] *Ibid.,* pp. 39, xii–xv, 2–6.

[3] *Ibid.,* p. xii, *et passim.*

[4] *Ibid.,* pp. xii–6, 78–79, 91–92, 103–104, 150–180, 282–83, 305 ff.

[5] *Ibid.,* pp. 4, xiv.

[6] *Ibid.,* pp. 9–20.

[7] *Ibid.,* pp. 85–93.

[8] *Ibid.,* pp. 76 ff., 92–93.

[9] *Ibid.,* pp. 281 ff., 78–79, 91 ff.

[10] *Ibid.,* p. 305 ff.

[11] *Ibid.,* pp. 80–81.

[12] *Ibid.,* p. 79.

[13] *Ibid.,* pp. 102–103.

[14] *Ibid.,* p. 289.

[15] *Ibid.,* chaps. 26–27.

[16] *Ibid.,* p. 104.

CHAPTER XI

BASES OF CRITICISM: CULTURAL SYSTEMS, SUPERSYSTEMS, AND CONGERIES

[1] For a systematic and detailed development of these concepts, see *Dynamics,* all four volumes; for an abbreviated one, see *Crisis* and *Society.*

[2] For a systematic and detailed analysis of the componential structure of sociocultural phenomena, see *Society,* chaps, 3, 4; *Dynamics,* Vol. IV, chaps. 1, 2.

[3] For details, see *Society,* chap. 17.

[4] For an analysis of organized groups, see *Society,* chap. 4.

[5] For the detailed development of this, see *Society,* chaps. 17, 18; *Dynamics,* Vol. I, chap 1; Vol. IV, chaps. 1–3.

[6] For the most detailed analysis of these supersystems, see *Dynamics,* Vol. I, chaps. 2, 3, 7; Vol. II, chaps. 1, 2; Vol. IV, chaps. 1–3; *et passim* in all volumes; also *Society,* pp. 317 ff.

[7] For the detailed analysis and classification of the main organized groups, see *Society,* chaps. 4–15.

[8] For a detailed analysis and demonstration of these propositions, see *Society,* chaps. 17–20; *Dynamics,* Vol. IV, chap. 3.

CHAPTER XII

CRITICAL EXAMINATION OF THE THEORIES OF DANILEVSKY, SPENGLER, AND TOYNBEE

[1] Toynbee, *A Study of History,* III, 380, 152; cf. I, 34 ff., 43 ff., 149 ff., 153 ff.

[2] Kroeber, *op. cit.,* pp. 826–827.

[3] See *Society* (pp. 548–554) for data showing in which of the creative fields (politics, economics, literature, science, sculpture, architecture, music, painting, religion, philosophy, law and ethics) and at which periods the various civilizations (Egypt, India, China, Japan, Greece, Rome, Arabic-Islamic world, France, Germany, England, Italy, Russia) have been creative. A mere glance at these data is sufficient to reveal the fallacy of a specificity of the creativeness of each culture or civilization.

[4] Toynbee, *A Study of History,* III, 154 ff.; IV, 40 ff., *et passim.*

[5] Toynbee, *Civilization on Trial,* pp. 222–23.

[6] Like the taxonomy of plants and animals in biology, the taxonomy of social groups is a fairly important part of sociology and occupies a considerable space there. Cf. *Society,* chaps. 9–16.

[7] Cf. *Theories,* chap. 4; and *Dynamics,* IV, 417 ff., 504 ff.

[8] Toynbee, *A Study of History,* IV, 1–2.

[9] For other data and for details, see *Society,* chap. 34.

[10] For a factual study of the fluctuation of these supersystems, see *Dynamics* and *Society.*

[11] See the details in *Society,* chaps. 35–38. The bulk of contemporary anthropological, sociological, and historical theories in this field are generally vague on the problems of the birth, death, growth, and decline of cultural phenomena. Even more so than Danilevsky, Spengler, and Toynbee, the bulk of sociologists and anthropologists who deal with these problems stop where real analysis should begin.

[12] Cf. *Society,* pp. 544–555. Kroeber arrives at similar conclusions.

[13] Some of Toynbee's "hard" environments other historians find "soft," and vice versa. Cf. Pieter Geyl, "Toynbee's System of Civilization," in *The Pattern of the Past* (Boston, 1949), pp. 18 ff. This book consists of essays by Geyl, Toynbee, and myself.

[14] For a detailed analysis and criticism of the theories of geographical factors of sociocultural phenomena, see *Theories,* chaps. 2, 3; and *Dynamics,* IV, 500 ff., 531 ff.

[15] In addition, taking the historical cases with which Toynbee illustrates these factors, Geyl finds that the cases are one-sidedly selected and interpreted; see *The Pattern of the Past,* pp. 16 ff. "To my ears this has a rather naïve sound," says Geyl about this challenge-response factor.

[16] See *Society,* chaps. 35–37; *Dynamics,* Vol. IV, chap. 16. Just as an increase of political power is not uniformly followed by an increase of creativity, so also progressively increasing economic prosperity is not always, nor even very frequently, followed by an increase of creativity.

[17] See the detailed data in *Dynamics,* Vol. III.

[18] See the figures of discoveries, inventions, and philosophical systems in *Dynamics,* Vol. II, chap. 3, *et passim.*

[19] See the data in *Dynamics,* Vols. II and III.

[20] See the data on discoveries and technological inventions in *Dynamics,* Vol. II, chap. 3.

[21] See the figures in *Dynamics,* Vol. II, chap. 3.

[22] See the data in *Dynamics,* Vol. III, chap. 3.

[23] Cf. *Society,* chaps. 39–42.

[24] Cf. *Society,* pp. 548–550; there are presented similar data for China, Japan, Rome, Arabic-Islamic World, Germany, Great Britain, Italy, and Russia.

[25] See the detailed data in *Society,* pp. 548–554, 570–572; *Dynamics,* II, 150 ff.; E. Fischer, *Passing of the European Age* (Cambridge, Mass., 1942).

[26] A study of sociocultural rhythms has been greatly neglected by the social sciences of the last century or so. Even the current texts of sociology, anthropology, philosophy of history, and political science devote almost no space to it. Economics deals with economic rhythms in its study of business cycles. Meanwhile the sociocultural rhythms are one of the basic problems of all generalizing social sciences. As such it must and will certainly be cultivated in the nearest future. See the systematic theory of sociocultural rhythms in *Dynamics,* Vol. IV, chaps. 8–11.

CHAPTER XIII

CRITICAL EXAMINATION OF THE THEORIES OF NORTHROP, KROEBER, SCHUBART, BERDYAEV, AND SCHWEITZER

[1] For a systematic development of all this, see *Dynamics,* Vol. II, chaps. 1–4 *et passim;* Vol. IV, chap. 16. For a detailed analysis of Ideational, Sensate, and Idealistic painting, sculpture, architecture, literature, music, drama, philosophy, law, ethics, forms of government and economics, see *Dynamics,* Vols. I–III.

[2] Cf. Northrop, *The Meeting of East and West,* pp. 117–119, 196, 263 ff., 279–280, 294, 348, 351, 377, 447, 450–460, *et passim.*

[3] *Ibid.,* pp. 447 ff.

[4] *Ibid.,* pp. 366, 471.

[5] *Ibid.,* pp. 348, 351, 366, 377, 411, 440, *et passim.*

[6] "The Shih King" and "The Hsiao King," in *The Sacred Books of the East* (Oxford, 1883), III, 291 ff., 481 ff. Exactly for this practical purpose Confucius made his collection of poetry and odes and his codes of the rituals as a means of social control.

[7] For a most detailed analysis of these problems based upon a systematic

study of some 150,000 pictures and sculptures, of the bulk of the Western and Eastern music, literature, and architecture, see *Dynamics*, I, 195–730.

[8] Cf. the names of Graeco-Roman and Western Christian mystics in religious and philosophical thought in *Dynamics*, II, 639 ff.

[9] *Ibid.*, Vol. II, chap. 1, *et passim*.

[10] For the movement of scientific discoveries and technological inventions in connection with the Ideational, Idealistic, and Sensate types of culture see *Dynamics*, Vol. II, chaps. 1, 2, *et passim*.

[11] For a detailed criticism of all the main theories of one-sided dependence and of one-sided lead and lag of scientific, philosophical, religious, aesthetic, and practical forms of thought and of the "material" and "non-material," "technological" and "ideological," "civilizational and cultural" forms of sociocultural phenomena (theories of E. de Roberty, A. Coste, K. Marx, W. Ogburn, T. Veblen, L. Weber, A. Weber, R. MacIver, and others) see *Dynamics*, Vol. IV, chaps. 6, 7, and pp. 167–196. The multiform relationship between philosophy and science is also Kroeber's conclusion.

[12] On all this confusion see *Dynamics*, Vol. I, chap. 1; Vol. IV, chaps. 1–3; *Society*, pp. 337 ff. My criticism of the existing conclusions and the offer of a constructive theory in this as well as in many other fields, such as social mobility, basic dynamic processes, and the crisis of our time, called forth, at the moment of the publication of my works (*Social Mobility, Social and Cultural Dynamics*, etc.) a violent denunciation of my efforts on the part of some noisy "functional," "psychoanalytic," "realistic," "operational," "naturalistic," and "integrative" social scientists. Sometimes this violent rejection went so far that it called forth protests against incompetent, biased, and unfair reviews of my works (for instance, the first review of my *Social Mobility* in the *American Journal of Sociology*) from such eminent sociologists as the late Charles H. Cooley (who sent a short protest to the editors of this *Journal*, after which they published another, quite different review of this work).

The humorous aspect of this matter is that, a few years after the sharpest denunciation of my theories, most of the noisy critics usually "discover" them, appropriate and begin to use them without any reference to my works and theories. Thus, at the present time they all use social mobility, vertical and horizontal, and all the other propositions of my work, sometimes lifting a whole chapter or part of it, without any reference to my *Social Mobility*. The same is true about my theories of the crisis of our time, and also about my conceptions of social and cultural congeries, systems, organized and unorganized groups, and so on. An ever-increasing number of the denunciators are already using the terms "cultural system," "social system," "congeries," "meaningful consistency," "ultimate major premise" or "ultimate value" as the basis of a system, "integration" (causal and meaningful), and so on, usually without any reference to my works.

I am glad that some of the ideas initiated by myself are thus spreading (often thinly veiled by different terms) and diffusing. It is unimportant whether my little contributions are mentioned or not. I can, however, demand one of two things: either I am not to be denounced for what is later appropriated and used as something valid and important; or, if I am denounced, then my theories are not to be subsequently appropriated and used as valid by the denunciators and critics. This demand does not seem to be excessive.

Kroeber, of course, in no way is guilty of these "machinations" of the noisy critics.

[13] Cf. R. K. Merton, *Social Theory and Social Structure* (Glencoe, 1949), chaps. 1–3, where an able analysis of the confusion covered by the terms "function," "functionalists," etc., is given.

[14] See the details in all volumes of *Dynamics*.

As a humorous curiosity: I have been criticized by some "statisticians" for a supposedly incorrect use of the statistical method. These "statisticians" seem not to have seen that almost no statistics except plain arithmetic were used in my work; and the arithmetical computations were quite correct. Even the statistical "universes" in my study were mostly not just representative samples but the entire universes—*all* the philosophers mentioned in the fullest histories of philosophy, almost *all* the pictures and sculptures known, *all* the scientific discoveries and inventions known, *all* the names of scientists and inventors known, etc. Only in regard to the magnitude of war and revolution were some—the simplest possible—estimates introduced. In their logical simplicity they are less objectionable than many complex estimates, arbitrary assumptions, and techniques made by statisticians when they actually apply their tools to empirical reality.

The rough soundness of even this part of my work was well corroborated by the fact of confirming all the main movements of my curves of wars by the curve of war movements obtained by Quincy Wright and others in their *Study of War* (Chicago, 1942). Eminent mathematical statisticians like Dr. Rashevsky well understood all this and did not hesitate to approve openly the rough soundness of my arithmetic or—if one prefers—statistics. Cf. N. Rashevsky, *Mathematical Theory of Human Relations*, p. v. The critics, most of whom have hardly gone beyond the freshman class in their study of epistemology, logic, mathematics, and even statistics, wanted to show their "high-brow" statistical "scientism"; instead, they succeeded only in displaying their logical, mathematical, historical, and even statistical, incompetence.

[15] As a further humorous illustration of the "competence and sincerity" of some of my critics, it is to be noted that they heartily approved this procedure in Kroeber's work whereas they disapproved it in mine.

[16] On the anonymity of Ideational cultures and on the individualistic self-advertising and publicity of Sensate cultures, see *Dynamics,* all volumes, *passim.*

[17] Cf. *Dynamics,* Vol. II, chap. 3.

[18] On this basic difference and polarity, see *Dynamics* (all volumes) and *Crisis;* also J. J. Maquet, *op. cit.*

[19] For a factual corroboration and a detailed analysis of this basic difference in the creativity of Ideational and Sensate cultures, see *Dynamics,* all volumes.

[20] The Copernican or Relativity viewpoint is explicitly assumed in my *Dynamics.* Most of the critics of this book, still having a Ptolemaic-Sensate viewpoint but being perfectly unaware of it, naturally failed to understand my more scientific position and accordingly decided that I was inimical to the "modern [Sensate] viewpoint and culture" and captivated by the "ignorant, superstitious, and bad culture of the 'Dark Ages' "; that from my standpoint everything Ideational was good and everything Sensate was bad, etc. An example of such a criticism is H. Speier's "The Sociological

Ideas of P. A. Sorokin: 'Integralist Sociology'" in H. E. Barnes (ed.) *An Introduction to the History of Sociology* (Chicago, 1948), chap. 46. The foregoing explains why these criticisms by the "Ptolemaic" social scientists hardly ever hit anything in my theories except some "bogeymen" created by the Ptolemaic critics themselves. Speier's article also supplies an example of such a bogeyman.

Fortunately, side by side with this sort of inept criticism there is a much larger body of thoughtful analysis and criticism of my theories. Most recent examples of this sort of literature are: J. J. Maquet, *Sociologie de la connaissance,* with a preface by F. S. C. Northrop; E. Smedes, "Een Amerikaans Cultureel Architect: P. A. Sorokin," *Mens en Maatschappij,* 24e Jaargang, Nov., 1949, 358–371; E. Smedes, "Over Periode, Rhythme en generatie inde Geschiedenis," *Tijdschrift voor Geschiedenis,* Nov., 1949, 36–83; L. von Wiese, "Pitirim A. Sorokin," *Kölner Zeitschrift für Soziologie,* 1948–49, Heft 2, 209–221; L. von Wiese, "Sorokins System der Allgemeinen Soziologie," *ibid.,* Heft 3, 111–123; Karl Olivecrona, "Is a Sociological Explanation of Law Possible," *Theoria: a Swedish Journal of Philosophy and Psychology,* Vol. XIV, No. 2 (1948), 167–207; L. Dechesne, "La nouvelle sociologie de Sorokin," *Academie Royale de Belgique: Bulletin de la classe des lettres,* 5e série, Tome XXXIII, 426–441; L. Dechesne, "La Reconstruction de l'humanité d'après Sorokin," *ibid.,* Tome XXXIV, 613–623; D. W. Soper, "Beyond Our Sensate Culture: A Study of P. A. Sorokin," *Theology Today,* Vol. V (1949), 501–516; "Man in Society," an editorial in the London *Times Literary Supplement,* Sept. 18, 1948; A. Maurois, "Journal Etat Unis," *Revue de Paris,* Sept., 1946; D. Bidney, "Meta-anthropology" in F. S. C. Northrop (ed.) *Ideological Differences and World Order* (New Haven, 1949); the Editor, "A Blueprint for a Positive Polarization," *PraBuddha Bharata,* October, 1948; Karl Pichl, "Soziologie der Zeitwende: Der Beitrag P. A. Sorokins," *Wort und Wahrheit,* Feb., 1950.

[21] Cf. *Dynamics,* Vol. II, chaps. 13–15; *Crisis,* chap. 4.

[22] For a detailed study of this, see *Dynamics,* vol. II, *passim; Crisis,* chap. 3.

[23] Cf. *Dynamics,* Vol. II, chaps. 14, 16; *Crisis,* chap. 4.

[24] Schweitzer, *Philosophy of Civilization,* pp. 76–77, 102–103, *et passim.*

[25] On this, see my "Manifoldness of Love" in P. Sorokin (ed.), *Explorations in Altruistic Love and Behavior: A Symposium* (Boston, 1950).

CHAPTER XIV

AREAS OF AGREEMENT AMONG MODERN SOCIAL PHILOSOPHIES

[1] Cf. *Dynamics,* IV, 701 ff.

[2] Cf. *Dynamics,* Vol. IV, chaps. 2, 12–14; *Society,* chap. 8.

[3] In Toynbee's *Civilization on Trial* there does appear an eschatological or linear notion that each of his civilizations existed to produce its own universal church and that in the course of time these religions have been becoming more and more nearly perfect, culminating in Christianity—particularly Anglican Christianity—as the terminal point of a spiritualization and etherialization of man. This trans-scientific or metaphysical belief is also

present but less noticeable in Toynbee's larger work, where the main meaning of a rise and fall of his civilization is seen in an incessant creativity that justifies itself at each moment of history. "The music that the rhythm of Yin and Yang beats out is the song of creation. . . . Creation would not be creative if it did not swallow up in itself all things in Heaven and Earth, including its own antithesis." *A Study of History,* VI, 324.

[4] Cf. *Dynamics,* Vol. II, chap. 9; Vol. IV, chaps. 8–10.

[5] On the four varieties of linear conceptions of sociocultural change, see *Dynamics,* Vol. I, chap. 4.

[6] On entropy, see R. Clausius, "Le second principe fondamental de la théorie mécanique de chaleur," *Revue des cours scientifique,* 1868, p. 158; P. Duhem, *L'évolution de la mécanique* (Paris, 1902); H. Poincaré, *Thermodynamique* (Paris, 1892).

[7] E. G. Conklin, *The Direction of Human Evolution* (New York, 1925), pp. 15, 17, 75, 78. Conklin's conception of bio-social evolution is quite typical of the prevalent conception of biological evolution in the nineteenth and to some extent in the twentieth century. In a similar linear manner though not so anthropomorphically, biological evolution was interpreted by the rank and file of biologists of the nineteenth century. The formulas of evolution of Milne-Edwards, K. von Baer, Herbert Spencer, and E. Heckel run along the same lines. The concepts of biological evolution of J. Arthur Thompson, J. S. Huxley, C. L. Morgan, Sir Arthur Smith Woodward, and many biologists of even the twentieth century are also similar. They not only are all linear but identify evolution with progress. Cf. E. Haeckel, *Prinzipen der generellen Morphologie* (Tuebingen, 1906); J. C. Smuts, *Holism and Evolution* (New York, 1925); and two symposia on evolution: *Creation by Evolution* (New York, 1928), and *Evolution in the Light of Modern Knowledge* (New York, 1925).

[8] Cf. Herder's *Outlines of a Philosophy of the History of Man,* tr. by T. Churchill (London, 1803); Kant's *The Idea of a Universal History on a Cosmo-Political Plan,* tr. by T. DeQuincey (Hanover, 1927).

[9] Cf. Fichte's *Characteristics of the Present Age* (1804) and Hegel's *Philosophy of History,* tr. by J. Sibree (New York and London, 1900).

[10] Cf. Auguste Comte, *Cours de philosophie positive* (Paris: 1877), I, 8 ff., and throughout all volumes. About the theories of his predecessors, cf. R. Mathis, *La loi des trois états* (Nancy: 1924). See also Herbert Spencer, *First Principles* (London: 1870), chap. 22 *et passim;* and his *Principles of Sociology* (London, 1885), 3 vols. Though the Spencerian formula of evolution-progress includes the opposite process of dissolution, Spencer fails to deal with the dissolution aspect in his study of sociocultural evolution-progress. Such a neglect of this opposite process is symptomatic of the preoccupation we have noted.

[11] For a bibliography of the works of all the authors mentioned see *Theories* and *Dynamics* (all four volumes). Space does not allow reproduction of this bibliography here.

[12] The *Cambridge Modern History* (New York and Cambridge, 1934), I, 4. Note that the work was first written in the nineteenth century. A contemporary example is H. Fischer's *History of Europe* (London, 1905), where an aversion to historical generalizations is contradicted by the statement that "the fact of progress is written plain and large in the pages of history" (Vol. I, p. vii).

[13] Thus in the *Cambridge Modern History* we read: "The practical applications of scientific knowledge will go on extending and . . . future ages will see no limit to the growth of man's power over the resources of nature, and of his intelligent use of them for the welfare of his race" (XII, 791).

[14] For a systematic analysis, see *Dynamics*, Vol. I, chap. 4; Vol. IV, chaps. 12–16; *et passim* throughout all volumes.

[15] Cf. *Theories, passim.*

[16] The fullest concise survey and analysis of the main studies of sociocultural rhythms, cycles, periodicities, and uniformities of tempo is probably given in *Dynamics*, Vol. IV, chaps. 6–11, *et passim* throughout all four volumes. Most sociologists have, as mentioned, lagged in the transfer of their attention and energy to the study of these phenomena.

[17] Cf. Kroeber, *Configurations*, pp. 801 ff.

[18] *Ibid.*, pp. 799–804.

[19] *Ibid.*, pp. 803–04.

[20] Cf. *Dynamics*, IV, 770 ff.

[21] On the law of polarization, see *Calamity*, chaps. 9–12.

[22] Cf. E. Fischer, *Passing of the European Age.*

[23] For a detailed demonstration of these summary propositions, see *Dynamics*, IV, 197–252; and *Society*, chap. 37.

[24] For a detailed analysis of these propositions see *Dynamics*, IV, 252–288; and *Society*, chap. 38.

[25] See the details, evidence, facts in *Society*, chap. 38; and *Dynamics*, IV, 252 ff.

[26] See above, page 300.

[27] Cf. J. J. Maquet, *op. cit.*

[28] N. Berdyaev, *Solitude and Society* (London, 1938), p. 48.

[29] For this criticism especially, see my *Sociocultural Causality, Space, Time* (Duke University Press, 1943); *Dynamics*, Vol. IV, *passim; Society*, chap. 43.

[30] The best work on this subject is T. Stcherbatsky, *Buddhist Logic* (Leningrad, 1932), 2 vols.

[31] Vol. IV, chaps. 8–10.

[32] *Dynamics*, chap. 11. Generally the problem of sociocultural rhythms and tempi has not as yet become one of the important problems of the social sciences. The mass of sociologists and anthropologists are still unaware of these important problems.

[33] *Ibid.*, Vol. IV, chaps. 4, 6, 7.

[34] *Ibid.*, Vol. IV, chap. 7; and all four volumes, *passim.*

[35] *Ibid.*, Vol. III, chap. 8; Vol. IV, chap. 7; *et passim;* also *Society*, pp. 175–177, 543–545.

[36] Cf. my *Reconstruction of Humanity* (Boston, 1948), and my *Altruistic Love* (Boston, 1950).

Index

Mozart, W. A., 14, 20, 22, 84, 94, 143
Myron, 15, 94

Napoleon I, 67, 100, 131
Neumann, 129
Newton, Sir Isaac, 84, 91, 149, 150, 228, 229, 234
Nicolaus Cusanus (Nicholas of Cusa), 90, 153, 255
Nietzsche, Friedrich Wilhelm, 72, 92, 122, 141
Northrop, F. S. C., 9, 138, 145–158, 178, 199, 207 f., 244 ff., 258 ff., 268 ff., 276 ff., 292 ff., 307 ff., 310, 316, 318 ff.
Novalis, 143
Novicow, 283

Ogburn, William F., 283
O'Keeffe, Georgia, 251
Origen, 86, 90
Orosco, José Clemente, 148
Orosius, 5

Palestrina, Giovanni, 14, 22, 37, 226
Panofsky, E., 40, 325 (n. 33)
Pascal, Blaise, 84, 91
Paul, St., 86, 109
Pericles, 15, 55, 100
Peter the Great, 133, 215
Petrie, W. F. M. (Sir Flinders), 11 ff., 17, 290
Phidias, 15, 67, 84, 94, 109, 171, 311
Philip the Fair, 56
Philo, 5, 255
Philostratus, 34
Pindar, 21
Plato, 5, 6, 28, 34, 67, 84, 85, 108, 133, 161, 188, 220, 225, 228, 229, 236, 255, 290, 310, 311
Plotinus, 34, 86, 90, 225, 255, 310
Plutarch, 5, 34
Polybius, 5, 236, 290
Polygnotus, 81
Praxiteles, 30, 67, 84, 109
Pseudo-Dionysius. See Dionysius the Areopagite
Pushkin, Aleksander Sergeevich, 133
Pythagoras, 84

Raphael, 171
Rembrandt van Rijn, 81, 94
Ricardo, David, 149
Richelieu, Cardinal, 56, 100
Rickert, Heinrich, 76
Riegl, Alois, 39, 40, 325 (n. 33)
Riemann, Georg Friedrich Bernhard, 84, 92
Rivera, Diego, 148
Roberty, E. de, 259, 283 f., 324 (n. 8), 332 (n. 2)
Rousseau, Jean-Jacques, 6, 91
Rückert, Friedrich, 129

Sankara, 225
Scarlatti, Alessandro and Domenico, 14
Schafer, Heinrich, 39, 40, 43, 325 (n. 33)
Scheler, Max, 148
Schelling, Friedrich, 143
Scheltemas, 40
Schiller, Johann Cristoph Friedrich von, 22, 143, 178
Schirazi, 86
Schleiermacher, Friedrich Ernst Daniel, 143
Schmarsow, A., 39, 40, 325 (n. 33)
Schopenhauer, Arthur, 22, 92, 129, 143
Schubart, Walter, 9, 121–136, 144, 178, 206, 230, 234, 242, 244, 266, 276 ff., 292 ff., 299, 302, 307 ff., 318 ff.
Schumann, Robert, 21, 22
Schweitzer, Albert, 9, 176–183, 206, 244, 266 ff., 276 ff., 318
Settignano, Desiderio da, 30
Shakespeare, William, 35, 270, 278
Simonides of Ceos, 21
Skovoroda, 134
Smith, Adam, 7, 68, 112, 149, 150, 269
Sophocles, 21, 220, 226
Spencer, Herbert, 7, 38, 92, 141, 282, 340 (n. 7)
Spengler, Oswald, 6, 9, 50, 69, 72–112, 121, 122, 125, 126, 132, 133, 138, 139, 144, 164, 170, 174, 176, 182, 183, 206 ff., 209 ff., 218 ff.,

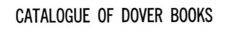

CATALOGUE OF DOVER BOOKS

Social Sciences

SOCIAL THOUGHT FROM LORE TO SCIENCE, H. E. Barnes and H. Becker. An immense survey of sociological thought and ways of viewing, studying, planning, and reforming society from earliest times to the present. Includes thought on society of preliterate peoples, ancient non-Western cultures, and every great movement in Europe, America, and modern Japan. Analyzes hundreds of great thinkers: Plato, Augustine, Bodin, Vico, Montesquieu, Herder, Comte, Marx, etc. Weighs the contributions of utopians, sophists, fascists and communists; economists, jurists, philosophers, ecclesiastics, and every 19th and 20th century school of scientific sociology, anthropology, and social psychology throughout the world. Combines topical, chronological, and regional approaches, treating the evolution of social thought as a process rather than as a series of mere topics. "Impressive accuracy, competence, and discrimination . . . easily the best single survey," Nation. Thoroughly revised, with new material up to 1960. 2 indexes. Over 2200 bibliographical notes. Three volume set. Total of 1586pp. 5⅜ x 8.

T901 Vol I   Paperbound **$2.50**
T902 Vol II   Paperbound **$2.50**
T903 Vol III   Paperbound **$2.35**
The set **$7.35**

FOLKWAYS, William Graham Sumner. A classic of sociology, a searching and thorough examination of patterns of behaviour from primitive, ancient Greek and Judaic, Medieval Christian, African, Oriental, Melanesian, Australian, Islamic, to modern Western societies. Thousands of illustrations of social, sexual, and religious customs, mores, laws, and institutions. Hundreds of categories: Labor, Wealth, Abortion, Primitive Justice, Life Policy, Slavery, Cannibalism, Uncleanness and the Evil Eye, etc. Will extend the horizon of every reader by showing the relativism of his own culture. Prefatory note by A. G. Keller. Introduction by William Lyon Phelps. Bibliography. Index. xiii + 692pp. 5⅜ x 8.   T508 Paperbound **$2.49**

PRIMITIVE RELIGION, P. Radin. A thorough treatment by a noted anthropologist of the nature and origin of man's belief in the supernatural and the influences that have shaped religious expression in primitive societies. Ranging from the Arunta, Ashanti, Aztec, Bushman, Crow, Fijian, etc., of Africa, Australia, Pacific Islands, the Arctic, North and South America, Prof. Radin integrates modern psychology, comparative religion, and economic thought with first-hand accounts gathered by himself and other scholars of primitive initiations, training of the shaman, and other fascinating topics. "Excellent," NATURE (London). Unabridged reissue of 1st edition. New author's preface. Bibliographic notes. Index. x + 322pp. 5⅜ x 8.

T393 Paperbound **$1.85**

PRIMITIVE MAN AS PHILOSOPHER, P. Radin. A standard anthropological work covering primitive thought on such topics as the purpose of life, marital relations, freedom of thought, symbolism, death, resignation, the nature of reality, personality, gods, and many others. Drawn from factual material gathered from the Winnebago, Oglala Sioux, Maori, Baganda, Batak, Zuni, among others, it does not distort ideas by removing them from context but interprets strictly within the original framework. Extensive selections of original primitive documents. Bibliography. Index. xviii + 402pp. 5⅜ x 8.   T392 Paperbound **$2.25**

A TREATISE ON SOCIOLOGY, THE MIND AND SOCIETY, Vilfredo Pareto. This treatise on human society is one of the great classics of modern sociology. First published in 1916, its careful catalogue of the innumerable manifestations of non-logical human conduct (Book One); the theory of "residues," leading to the premise that sentiment not logic determines human behavior (Book Two), and of "derivations," beliefs derived from desires (Book Three); and the general description of society made up of non-elite and elite, consisting of "foxes" who live by cunning and "lions" who live by force, stirred great controversy. But Pareto's passion for isolation and classification of elements and factors, and his allegiance to scientific method as the key tool for scrutinizing the human situation made his a truly twentieth-century mind and his work a catalytic influence on certain later social commentators. These four volumes (bound as two) require no special training to be appreciated and any reader who wishes to gain a complete understanding of modern sociological theory, regardless of special field of interest, will find them a must. Reprint of revised (corrected) printing of original edition. Translated by Andrew Bongiorno and Arthur Livingston. Index. Bibliography. Appendix containing index-summary of theorems. 48 diagrams. Four volumes bound as two. Total of 2063pp. 5⅜ x 8½.   The set Clothbound **$15.00**

THE POLISH PEASANT IN EUROPE AND AMERICA, William I. Thomas, Florian Znaniecki. A seminal sociological study of peasant primary groups (family and community) and the disruptions produced by a new industrial system and immigration to America. The peasant's family, class system, religious and aesthetic attitudes, and economic life are minutely examined and analyzed in hundreds of pages of primary documentation, particularly letters between family members. The disorientation caused by new environments is scrutinized in detail (a 312-page autobiography of an immigrant is especially valuable and revealing) in an attempt to find common experiences and reactions. The famous "Methodological Note" sets forth the principles which guided the authors. When out of print this set has sold for as much as $50. 2nd revised edition. 2 vols. Vol. 1: xv + 1115pp. Vol. 2: 1135pp. Index. 6 x 9.   T478 Clothbound 2 vol. set **$12.50**

Psychology

YOGA: A SCIENTIFIC EVALUATION, Kovoor T. Behanan. A complete reprinting of the book that for the first time gave Western readers a sane, scientific explanation and analysis of yoga. The author draws on controlled laboratory experiments and personal records of a year as a disciple of a yoga, to investigate yoga psychology, concepts of knowledge, physiology, "supernatural" phenomena, and the ability to tap the deepest human powers. In this study under the auspices of Yale University Institute of Human Relations, the strictest principles of physiological and psychological inquiry are followed throughout. Foreword by W. A. Miles, Yale University. 17 photographs. Glossary. Index. xx + 270pp. 5⅜ x 8. T505 Paperbound **$1.75**

CONDITIONED REFLEXES: AN INVESTIGATION OF THE PHYSIOLOGICAL ACTIVITIES OF THE CEREBRAL CORTEX, I. P. Pavlov. Full, authorized translation of Pavlov's own survey of his work in experimental psychology reviews entire course of experiments, summarizes conclusions, outlines psychological system based on famous "conditioned reflex" concept. Details of technical means used in experiments, observations on formation of conditioned reflexes, function of cerebral hemispheres, results of damage, nature of sleep, typology of nervous system, significance of experiments for human psychology. Trans. by Dr. G. V. Anrep, Cambridge Univ. 235-item bibliography. 18 figures. 445pp. 5⅜ x 8. S614 Paperbound **$2.35**

EXPLANATION OF HUMAN BEHAVIOUR, F. V. Smith. A major intermediate-level introduction to and criticism of 8 complete systems of the psychology of human behavior, with unusual emphasis on theory of investigation and methodology. Part I is an illuminating analysis of the problems involved in the explanation of observed phenomena, and the differing viewpoints on the nature of causality. Parts II and III are a closely detailed survey of the systems of McDougall, Gordon Allport, Lewin, the Gestalt group, Freud, Watson, Hull, and Tolman. Biographical notes. Bibliography of over 800 items. 2 Indexes. 38 figures. xii + 460pp. 5½ x 8¾. T253 Clothbound **$6.00**

SEX IN PSYCHO-ANALYSIS (formerly CONTRIBUTIONS TO PSYCHO-ANALYSIS), S. Ferenczi. Written by an associate of Freud, this volume presents countless insights on such topics as impotence, transference, analysis and children, dreams, symbols, obscene words, masturbation and male homosexuality, paranoia and psycho-analysis, the sense of reality, hypnotism and therapy, and many others. Also includes full text of THE DEVELOPMENT OF PSYCHO-ANALYSIS by Ferenczi and Otto Rank. Two books bound as one. Total of 406pp. 5⅜ x 8. T324 Paperbound **$1.85**

BEYOND PSYCHOLOGY, Otto Rank. One of Rank's most mature contributions, focussing on the irrational basis of human behavior as a basic fact of our lives. The psychoanalytic techniques of myth analysis trace to their source the ultimates of human existence: fear of death, personality, the social organization, the need for love and creativity, etc. Dr. Rank finds them stemming from a common irrational source, man's fear of final destruction. A seminal work in modern psychology, this work sheds light on areas ranging from the concept of immortal soul to the sources of state power. 291pp. 5⅜ x 8. T485 Paperbound **$2.00**

ILLUSIONS AND DELUSIONS OF THE SUPERNATURAL AND THE OCCULT, D. H. Rawcliffe. Holds up to rational examination hundreds of persistent delusions including crystal gazing, automatic writing, table turning, mediumistic trances, mental healing, stigmata, lycanthropy, live burial, the Indian Rope Trick, spiritualism, dowsing, telepathy, clairvoyance, ghosts, ESP, etc. The author explains and exposes the mental and physical deceptions involved, making this not only an exposé of supernatural phenomena, but a valuable exposition of characteristic types of abnormal psychology. Originally titled "The Psychology of the Occult." 14 illustrations. Index. 551pp. 5⅜ x 8. T503 Paperbound **$2.00**

THE PRINCIPLES OF PSYCHOLOGY, William James. The full long-course, unabridged, of one of the great classics of Western literature and science. Wonderfully lucid descriptions of human mental activity, the stream of thought, consciousness, time perception, memory, imagination, emotions, reason, abnormal phenomena, and similar topics. Original contributions are integrated with the work of such men as Berkeley, Binet, Mills, Darwin, Hume, Kant, Royce, Schopenhauer, Spinoza, Locke, Descartes, Galton, Wundt, Lotze, Herbart, Fechner, and scores of others. All contrasting interpretations of mental phenomena are examined in detail — introspective analysis, philosophical interpretation, and experimental research. "A classic," JOURNAL OF CONSULTING PSYCHOLOGY. "The main lines are as valid as ever," PSYCHO-ANALYTICAL QUARTERLY. "Standard reading . . . a classic of interpretation," PSYCHIATRIC QUARTERLY. 94 illustrations. 1408pp. 2 volumes. 5⅜ x 8. Vol. 1, T381 Paperbound **$2.50** Vol. 2, T382 Paperbound **$2.50**

THE DYNAMICS OF THERAPY IN A CONTROLLED RELATIONSHIP, Jessie Taft. One of the most important works in literature of child psychology, out of print for 25 years. Outstanding disciple of Rank describes all aspects of relationship or Rankian therapy through concise, simple elucidation of theory underlying her actual contacts with two seven-year olds. Therapists, social caseworkers, psychologists, counselors, and laymen who work with children will all find this important work an invaluable summation of method, theory of child psychology. xix + 296pp. 5⅜ x 8. T325 Paperbound **$1.75**

Books Explaining Science and Mathematics

WHAT IS SCIENCE?, N. Campbell. The role of experiment and measurement, the function of mathematics, the nature of scientific laws, the difference between laws and theories, the limitations of science, and many similarly provocative topics are treated clearly and without technicalities by an eminent scientist. "Still an excellent introduction to scientific philosophy," H. Margenau in PHYSICS TODAY. "A first-rate primer . . . deserves a wide audience," SCIENTIFIC AMERICAN. 192pp. 5⅜ x 8.   S43 Paperbound **$1.25**

THE NATURE OF PHYSICAL THEORY, P. W. Bridgman. A Nobel Laureate's clear, non-technical lectures on difficulties and paradoxes connected with frontier research on the physical sciences. Concerned with such central concepts as thought, logic, mathematics, relativity, probability, wave mechanics, etc. he analyzes the contributions of such men as Newton, Einstein, Bohr, Heisenberg, and many others. "Lucid and entertaining . . . recommended to anyone who wants to get some insight into current philosophies of science," THE NEW PHILOSOPHY. Index. xi + 138pp. 5⅜ x 8.   S33 Paperbound **$1.25**

EXPERIMENT AND THEORY IN PHYSICS, Max Born. A Nobel Laureate examines the nature of experiment and theory in theoretical physics and analyzes the advances made by the great physicists of our day: Heisenberg, Einstein, Bohr, Planck, Dirac, and others. The actual process of creation is detailed step-by-step by one who participated. A fine examination of the scientific method at work. 44pp. 5⅜ x 8.   S308 Paperbound **75¢**

THE PSYCHOLOGY OF INVENTION IN THE MATHEMATICAL FIELD, J. Hadamard. The reports of such men as Descartes, Pascal, Einstein, Poincaré, and others are considered in this investigation of the method of idea-creation in mathematics and other sciences and the thinking process in general. How do ideas originate? What is the role of the unconscious? What is Poincaré's forgetting hypothesis? are some of the fascinating questions treated. A penetrating analysis of Einstein's thought processes concludes the book. xiii + 145pp. 5⅜ x 8.   T107 Paperbound **$1.25**

THE NATURE OF LIGHT AND COLOUR IN THE OPEN AIR, M. Minnaert. Why are shadows sometimes blue, sometimes green, or other colors depending on the light and surroundings? What causes mirages? Why do multiple suns and moons appear in the sky? Professor Minnaert explains these unusual phenomena and hundreds of others in simple, easy-to-understand terms based on optical laws and the properties of light and color. No mathematics is required but artists, scientists, students, and everyone fascinated by these "tricks" of nature will find thousands of useful and amazing pieces of information. Hundreds of observational experiments are suggested which require no special equipment. 200 illustrations; 42 photos. xvi + 362pp. 5⅜ x 8.   T196 Paperbound **$2.00**

THE UNIVERSE OF LIGHT, W. Bragg. Sir William Bragg, Nobel Laureate and great modern physicist, is also well known for his powers of clear exposition. Here he analyzes all aspects of light for the layman: lenses, reflection, refraction, the optics of vision, x-rays, the photoelectric effect, etc. He tells you what causes the color of spectra, rainbows, and soap bubbles, how magic mirrors work, and much more. Dozens of simple experiments are described. Preface. Index. 199 line drawings and photographs, including 2 full-page color plates. x + 283pp. 5⅜ x 8.   T538 Paperbound **$1.85**

SOAP-BUBBLES: THEIR COLOURS AND THE FORCES THAT MOULD THEM, C. V. Boys. For continuing popularity and validity as scientific primer, few books can match this volume of easily-followed experiments, explanations. Lucid exposition of complexities of liquid films, surface tension and related phenomena, bubbles' reaction to heat, motion, music, magnetic fields. Experiments with capillary attraction, soap bubbles on frames, composite bubbles, liquid cylinders and jets, bubbles other than soap, etc. Wonderful introduction to scientific method, natural laws that have many ramifications in areas of modern physics. Only complete edition in print. New Introduction by S. Z. Lewin, New York University. 83 illustrations; 1 full-page color plate. xii + 190pp. 5⅜ x 8½.   T542 Paperbound **95¢**

Classics of Science

THE DIDEROT PICTORIAL ENCYCLOPEDIA OF TRADES AND INDUSTRY, MANUFACTURING AND THE TECHNICAL ARTS IN PLATES SELECTED FROM "L'ENCYCLOPEDIE OU DICTIONNAIRE RAISONNE DES SCIENCES, DES ARTS, ET DES METIERS" OF DENIS DIDEROT, edited with text by C. Gillispie. The first modern selection of plates from the high point of 18th century French engraving, Diderot's famous Encyclopedia. Over 2000 illustrations on 485 full page plates, most of them original size, illustrating the trades and industries of one of the most fascinating periods of modern history, 18th century France. These magnificent engravings provide an invaluable glimpse into the past for the student of early technology, a lively and accurate social document to students of cultures, an outstanding find to the lover of fine engravings. The plates teem with life, with men, women, and children performing all of the thousands of operations necessary to the trades before and during the early stages of the industrial revolution. Plates are in sequence, and show general operations, closeups of difficult operations, and details of complex machinery. Such important and interesting trades and industries are illustrated as sowing, harvesting, beekeeping, cheesemaking, operating windmills, milling flour, charcoal burning, tobacco processing, indigo, fishing, arts of war, salt extraction, mining, smelting iron, casting iron, steel, extracting mercury, zinc, sulphur, copper, etc., slating, tinning, silverplating, gilding, making gunpowder, cannons, bells, shoeing horses, tanning, papermaking, printing, dying, and more than 40 other categories. 920pp. 9 x 12. Heavy library cloth. T421 Two volume set **$18.50**

THE PRINCIPLES OF SCIENCE, A TREATISE ON LOGIC AND THE SCIENTIFIC METHOD, W. Stanley Jevons. Treating such topics as Inductive and Deductive Logic, the Theory of Number, Probability, and the Limits of Scientific Method, this milestone in the development of symbolic logic remains a stimulating contribution to the investigation of inferential validity in the natural and social sciences. It significantly advances Boole's logic, and describes a machine which is a foundation of modern electronic calculators. In his introduction, Ernest Nagel of Columbia University says, "(Jevons) . . . continues to be of interest as an attempt to articulate the logic of scientific inquiry." Index. liii + 786pp. 5⅜ x 8. S446 Paperbound **$2.98**

*DIALOGUES CONCERNING TWO NEW SCIENCES, Galileo Galilei. A classic of experimental science which has had a profound and enduring influence on the entire history of mechanics and engineering. Galileo based this, his finest work, on 30 years of experimentation. It offers a fascinating and vivid exposition of dynamics, elasticity, sound, ballistics, strength of materials, and the scientific method. Translated by H. Crew and A. de Salvio. 126 diagrams. Index. xxi + 288pp. 5⅜ x 8. S99 Paperbound **$1.75**

DE MAGNETE, William Gilbert. This classic work on magnetism founded a new science. Gilbert was the first to use the word "electricity," to recognize mass as distinct from weight, to discover the effect of heat on magnetic bodies; invented an electroscope, differentiated between static electricity and magnetism, conceived of the earth as a magnet. Written by the first great experimental scientist, this lively work is valuable not only as an historical landmark, but as the delightfully easy-to-follow record of a perpetually searching, ingenious mind. Translated by P. F. Mottelay. 25 page biographical memoir. 90 fix. lix + 368pp. 5⅜ x 8. S470 Paperbound **$2.00**

*OPTICKS, Sir Isaac Newton. An enormous storehouse of insights and discoveries on light, reflection, color, refraction, theories of wave and corpuscular propagation of light, optical apparatus, and mathematical devices which have recently been reevaluated in terms of modern physics and placed in the top-most ranks of Newton's work! Foreword by Albert Einstein. Preface by I. B. Cohen of Harvard U. 7 pages of portraits, facsimile pages, letters, etc. cxvi + 412pp. 5⅜ x 8. S205 Paperbound **$2.25**

A SURVEY OF PHYSICAL THEORY, M. Planck. Lucid essays on modern physics for the general reader by the Nobel Laureate and creator of the quantum revolution. Planck explains how the new concepts came into being; explores the clash between theories of mechanics, electrodynamics, and thermodynamics; and traces the evolution of the concept of light through Newton, Huygens, Maxwell, and his own quantum theory, providing unparalleled insights into his development of this momentous modern concept. Bibliography. Index. vii + 121pp. 5⅜ x 8. S650 Paperbound **$1.15**

A SOURCE BOOK IN MATHEMATICS, D. E. Smith. English translations of the original papers that announced the great discoveries in mathematics from the Renaissance to the end of the 19th century: succinct selections from 125 different treatises and articles, most of them unavailable elsewhere in English—Newton, Leibniz, Pascal, Riemann, Bernoulli, etc. 24 articles trace developments in the field of number, 18 cover algebra, 36 are on geometry, and 13 on calculus. Biographical-historical introductions to each article. Two volume set. Index in each. Total of 115 illustrations. Total of xxviii + 742pp. 5⅜ x 8. S552 Vol I Paperbound **$1.85**
S553 Vol II Paperbound **$1.85**
The set, boxed **$3.50**

*THE THIRTEEN BOOKS OF EUCLID'S ELEMENTS, edited by T. L. Heath. This is the complete EUCLID — the definitive edition of one of the greatest classics of the western world. Complete English translation of the Heiberg text with spurious Book XIV. Detailed 150-page introduction discusses aspects of Greek and medieval mathematics: Euclid, texts, commentators, etc. Paralleling the text is an elaborate critical exposition analyzing each definition, proposition, postulate, etc., and covering textual matters, mathematical analyses, refutations, extensions, etc. Unabridged reproduction of the Cambridge 2nd edition. 3 volumes. Total of 995 figures, 1426pp. 5⅜ x 8.   S88, 89, 90 — 3 vol. set, Paperbound **$6.75**

*THE GEOMETRY OF RENE DESCARTES. The great work which founded analytic geometry. The renowned Smith-Latham translation faced with the original French text containing all of Descartes' own diagrams! Contains: Problems the Construction of Which Requires Only Straight Lines and Circles; On the Nature of Curved Lines; On the Construction of Solid or Supersolid Problems. Notes. Diagrams. 258pp.   S68 Paperbound **$1.60**

*A PHILOSOPHICAL ESSAY ON PROBABILITIES, P. Laplace. Without recourse to any mathematics above grammar school, Laplace develops a philosophically, mathematically and historically classical exposition of the nature of probability: its functions and limitations, operations in practical affairs, calculations in games of chance, insurance, government, astronomy, and countless other fields. New introduction by E. T. Bell. viii + 196pp. S166 Paperbound **$1.35**

DE RE METALLICA, Georgius Agricola. Written over 400 years ago, for 200 years the most authoritative first-hand account of the production of metals, translated in 1912 by former President Herbert Hoover and his wife, and today still one of the most beautiful and fascinating volumes ever produced in the history of science! 12 books, exhaustively annotated, give a wonderfully lucid and vivid picture of the history of mining, selection of sites, types of deposits, excavating pits, sinking shafts, ventilating, pumps, crushing machinery, assaying, smelting, refining metals, making salt, alum, nitre, glass, and many other topics. This definitive edition contains all 289 of the 16th century woodcuts which made the original an artistic masterpiece. It makes a superb gift for geologists, engineers, libraries, artists, historians, and everyone interested in science and early illustrative art. Biographical, historical introductions. Bibliography, survey of ancient authors. Indices. 289 illustrations. 672pp. 6¾ x 10¾. Deluxe library edition.   S6 Clothbound **$10.00**

GEOGRAPHICAL ESSAYS, W. M. Davis. Modern geography and geomorphology rest on the fundamental work of this scientist. His new concepts of earth-processes revolutionized science and his broad interpretation of the scope of geography created a deeper understanding of the interrelation of the landscape and the forces that mold it. This first inexpensive unabridged edition covers theory of geography, methods of advanced geographic teaching, descriptions of geographic areas, analyses of land-shaping processes, and much besides. Not only a factual and historical classic, it is still widely read for its reflections of modern scientific thought. Introduction. 130 figures. Index. vi + 777pp. 5⅜ x 8.
                                                    S383 Paperbound **$2.95**

CHARLES BABBAGE AND HIS CALCULATING ENGINES, edited by P. Morrison and E. Morrison. Friend of Darwin, Humboldt, and Laplace, Babbage was a leading pioneer in large-scale mathematical machines and a prophetic herald of modern operational research—true father of Harvard's relay computer Mark I. His Difference Engine and Analytical Engine were the first successful machines in the field. This volume contains a valuable introduction on his ·life and work; major excerpts from his fascinating autobiography, revealing his eccentric and unusual personality; and extensive selections from "Babbage's Calculating Engines," a compilation of hard-to-find journal articles, both by Babbage and by such eminent contributors as the Countess of Lovelace, L. F. Menabrea, and Dionysius Lardner. 11 illustrations. Appendix of miscellaneous papers. Index. Bibliography. xxxviii + 400pp. 5⅜ x 8.   T12 Paperbound **$2.00**

*THE WORKS OF ARCHIMEDES WITH THE METHOD OF ARCHIMEDES, edited by T. L. Heath. All the known works of the greatest mathematician of antiquity including the recently discovered METHOD OF ARCHIMEDES. This last is the only work we have which shows exactly how early mathematicians discovered their proofs before setting them down in their final perfection. A 186 page study by the eminent scholar Heath discusses Archimedes and the history of Greek mathematics. Bibliography. 563pp. 5⅜ x 8.   S9 Paperbound **$2.25**

Medicine

CLASSICS OF MEDICINE AND SURGERY, edited by C. N. B. Camac. 12 greatest papers in medical history, 11 in full: Lister's "Antiseptic Principle;" Harvey's "Motion in the Heart and Blood;" Auenbrugger's "Percussion of the Chest;" Laënnec's "Auscultation and the Stethoscope;" Jenner's "Inquiry into Smallpox Vaccine," 2 related papers; Morton's "Administering Sulphuric Ether," letters to Warren, "Physiology of Ether;" Simpson's "A New Anaesthetic Agent;" Holmes' "Puerperal Fever." Biographies, portraits of authors, bibliographies. Formerly "Epoch-making Contributions to Medicine, Surgery, and the Allied Sciences." Introduction. 14 illus. 445pp. 5⅜ x 8. S539 Paperbound **$2.25**

A WAY OF LIFE, Sir William Osler. The complete essay, stating his philosophy of life, as given at Yale University by this great physician and teacher. 30 pages. Copies limited, no more than 1 to a customer. Free.

SOURCE BOOK OF MEDICAL HISTORY, compiled, annotated by Logan Clendening, M.D. Unequalled collection of 139 greatest papers in medical history, by 120 authors, covers almost every area: pathology, asepsis, preventive medicine, bacteriology, physiology, etc. Hippocrates, Gain, Vesalius, Malpighi, Morgagni, Boerhave, Pasteur, Walter Reed, Florence Nightingale, Lavoisier, Claude Bernard, 109 others, give view of medicine unequalled for immediacy. Careful selections give heart of each paper save you reading time. Selections from non-medical literature show lay-views of medicine: Aristophanes, Plato, Arabian Nights, Chaucer, Molière, Dickens, Thackeray, others. "Notable . . . useful to teacher and student alike," Amer. Historical Review. Bibliography. Index. 699pp. 5⅜ x 8. T621 Paperbound **$2.75**

EXPERIMENTS AND OBSERVATIONS ON THE GASTRIC JUICE AND THE PHYSIOLOGY OF DIGESTION, William Beaumont. A gunshot wound which left a man with a 2½ inch hole through his abdomen into his stomach (1822) enabled Beaumont to perform the remarkable experiments set down here. The first comprehensive, thorough study of motions and processes of the stomach, "his work remains a model of patient, persevering investigation. . . . Beaumont is the pioneer physiologist of this country." (Sir William Osler, in his introduction.) 4 illustrations. xi + 280pp. 5⅜ x 8. S527 Paperbound **$1.50**

AN INTRODUCTION TO THE STUDY OF EXPERIMENTAL MEDICINE, Claude Bernard. 90-year-old classic of medical science, only major work of Bernard available in English, records his efforts to transform physiology into exact science. Principles of scientific research illustrated by specific case histories from his work; roles of chance, error, preliminary false conclusions, in leading eventually to scientific truth; use of hypothesis. Much of modern application of mathematics to biology rests on the foundation set down here. New foreword by Professor I. B. Cohen, Harvard Univ. xxv + 266pp. 5⅜ x 8. T400 Paperbound **$1.50**

A WAY OF LIFE, AND OTHER SELECTED WRITINGS, Sir William Osler, Physician and humanist, Osler discourses brilliantly in thought provoking essays and on the history of medicine. He discusses Thomas Browne, Gui Patin, Robert Burton, Michael Servetus, William Beaumont, Laënnec. Includes such favorite writings as the title essay, "The Old Humanities and the New Science," "Creators, Transmitters, and Transmuters," "Books and Men," "The Student Life," and five more of his best discussions of philosophy, religion and literature. 5 photographs. Introduction by G. L. Keynes, M.D., F.R.C.S. Index. xx + 278pp. 5⅜ x 8. T488 Paperbound **$1.50**

THE HISTORY OF SURGICAL ANESTHESIA, Thomas E. Keys. Concise, but thorough and always engrossing account of the long struggle to find effective methods of eliminating pain during surgery, tracing the remarkable story through the centuries to the eventual successes by dedicated researchers, the acceptance of ether, the work of men such as Priestley, Morton, Lundy, and many, many others. Discussions of the developments in local, regional, and spinal anesthesia, etc. "The general reader as well as the medical historian will find material to interest him in this fascinating story," U.S. QUARTERLY BOOKLIST. Revised, enlarged publication of original edition. Introductory essay by C. D. Leake. Concluding chapter by N. A. Gillespie. Appendix by J. F. Fulton. 46 illustrations. New preface by the author. Chronology of events. Extensive bibliographies. Index. xxx + 193pp. 5⅜ x 8½. T1122 Paperbound **$2.00**

A SHORT HISTORY OF ANATOMY AND PHYSIOLOGY FROM THE GREEKS TO HARVEY, Charles Singer. Corrected edition of THE EVOLUTION OF ANATOMY, classic work tracing evolution of anatomy and physiology from prescientific times through Greek & Roman periods, Dark Ages, Renaissance, to age of Harvey and beginning of modern concepts. Centered on individuals, movements, periods that definitely advanced anatomical knowledge: Plato, Diocles, Aristotle, Theophrastus, Herophilus, Erasistratus, the Alexandrians, Galen, Mondino, da Vinci, Linacre, Sylvius, others. Special section on Vesalius; Vesalian atlas of nudes, skeletons, muscle tabulae. Index of names, 20 plates. 270 extremely interesting illustrations of ancient, medieval, Renaissance, Oriental origin. xii + 209pp. 5⅜ x 8. T389 Paperbound **$1.75**

Philosophy, Religion

GUIDE TO PHILOSOPHY, C. E. M. Joad. A modern classic which examines many crucial problems which man has pondered through the ages: Does free will exist? Is there plan in the universe? How do we know and validate our knowledge? Such opposed solutions as subjective idealism and realism, chance and teleology, vitalism and logical positivism, are evaluated and the contributions of the great philosophers from the Greeks to moderns like Russell, Whitehead, and others, are considered in the context of each problem. "The finest introduction," BOSTON TRANSCRIPT. Index. Classified bibliography. 592pp. 5⅜ x 8.
T297 Paperbound **$2.00**

HISTORY OF ANCIENT PHILOSOPHY, W. Windelband. One of the clearest, most accurate comprehensive surveys of Greek and Roman philosophy. Discusses ancient philosophy in general, intellectual life in Greece in the 7th and 6th centuries B.C., Thales, Anaximander, Anaximenes, Heraclitus, the Eleatics, Empedocles, Anaxagoras, Leucippus, the Pythagoreans, the Sophists, Socrates, Democritus (20 pages), Plato (50 pages), Aristotle (70 pages), the Peripatetics, Stoics, Epicureans, Sceptics, Neo-platonists, Christian Apologists, etc. 2nd German edition translated by H. E. Cushman. xv + 393pp. 5⅜ x 8. T357 Paperbound **$1.85**

ILLUSTRATIONS OF THE HISTORY OF MEDIEVAL THOUGHT AND LEARNING, R. L. Poole. Basic analysis of the thought and lives of the leading philosophers and ecclesiastics from the 8th to the 14th century—Abailard, Ockham, Wycliffe, Marsiglio of Padua, and many other great thinkers who carried the torch of Western culture and learning through the "Dark Ages": political, religious, and metaphysical views. Long a standard work for scholars and one of the best introductions to medieval thought for beginners. Index. 10 Appendices. xiii + 327pp. 5⅜ x 8. T674 Paperbound **$2.00**

PHILOSOPHY AND CIVILIZATION IN THE MIDDLE AGES, M. de Wulf. This semi-popular survey covers aspects of medieval intellectual life such as religion, philosophy, science, the arts, etc. It also covers feudalism vs. Catholicism, rise of the universities, mendicant orders, monastic centers, and similar topics. Unabridged. Bibliography. Index. viii + 320pp. 5⅜ x 8. T284 Paperbound **$1.85**

AN INTRODUCTION TO SCHOLASTIC PHILOSOPHY, Prof. M. de Wulf. Formerly entitled SCHOLASTICISM OLD AND NEW, this volume examines the central scholastic tradition from St. Anselm, Albertus Magnus, Thomas Aquinas, up to Suarez in the 17th century. The relation of scholasticism to ancient and medieval philosophy and science in general is clear and easily followed. The second part of the book considers the modern revival of scholasticism, the Louvain position, relations with Kantianism and Positivism. Unabridged. xvi + 271pp. 5⅜ x 8.
T296 Clothbound **$3.50**
T283 Paperbound **$1.75**

A HISTORY OF MODERN PHILOSOPHY, H. Höffding. An exceptionally clear and detailed coverage of western philosophy from the Renaissance to the end of the 19th century. Major and minor men such as Pomponazzi, Bodin, Boehme, Telesius, Bruno, Copernicus, da Vinci, Kepler, Galileo, Bacon, Descartes, Hobbes, Spinoza, Leibniz, Wolff, Locke, Newton, Berkeley, Hume, Erasmus, Montesquieu, Voltaire, Diderot, Rousseau, Lessing, Kant, Herder, Fichte, Schelling, Hegel, Schopenhauer, Comte, Mill, Darwin, Spencer, Hartmann, Lange, and many others, are discussed in terms of theory of knowledge, logic, cosmology, and psychology. Index. 2 volumes, total of 1159pp. 5⅜ x 8.
T117 Vol. 1, Paperbound **$2.25**
T118 Vol. 2, Paperbound **$2.25**

ARISTOTLE, A. E. Taylor. A brilliant, searching non-technical account of Aristotle and his thought written by a foremost Platonist. It covers the life and works of Aristotle; classification of the sciences; logic; first philosophy; matter and form; causes; motion and eternity; God; physics; metaphysics; and similar topics. Bibliography. New Index compiled for this edition. 128pp. 5⅜ x 8. T280 Paperbound **$1.00**

THE SYSTEM OF THOMAS AQUINAS, M. de Wulf. Leading Neo-Thomist, one of founders of University of Louvain, gives concise exposition to central doctrines of Aquinas, as a means toward determining his value to modern philosophy, religion. Formerly "Medieval Philosophy Illustrated from the System of Thomas Aquinas." Trans. by E. Messenger. Introduction. 151pp. 5⅜ x 8. T568 Paperbound **$1.25**

LEIBNIZ, H. W. Carr. Most stimulating middle-level coverage of basic philosophical thought of Leibniz. Easily understood discussion, analysis of major works: "Theodicy," "Principles of Nature and Grace," "Monadology"; Leibniz's influence; intellectual growth; correspondence; disputes with Bayle, Malebranche, Newton; importance of his thought today, with reinterpretation in modern terminology. "Power and mastery," London Times. Bibliography. Index. 226pp. 5⅜ x 8. T624 Paperbound **$1.35**

Dover Classical Records

Now available directly to the public exclusively from Dover: top-quality recordings of fine classical music for only $2 per record! Almost all were released by major record companies to sell for $5 and $6. These recordings were issued under our imprint only after they had passed a severe critical test. We insisted upon:

First-rate music that is enjoyable, musically important and culturally significant.

First-rate performances, where the artists have carried out the composer's intentions, in which the music is alive, vigorous, played with understanding and sensitivity.

First-rate sound—clear, sonorous, fully balanced, crackle-free, whir-free.

Have in your home music by major composers, performed by such gifted musicians as Elsner, Gitlis, Wührer, Beveridge Webster, the Barchet Quartet, Gimpel, etc. Enthusiastically received when first released, many of these performances are definitive. The records are not seconds or remainders, but brand new pressings made on pure vinyl from carefully chosen master tapes. "All purpose" 12″ monaural 33⅓ rpm records, they play equally well on hi-fi and stereo equipment. Fine music for discriminating music lovers, superlatively played, flawlessly recorded: there is no better way to build your library of recorded classical music at remarkable savings. There are no strings; this is not a come-on, not a club, forcing you to buy records you may not want in order to get a few at a lower price. Buy whatever records you want in any quantity, and never pay more than $2 each. Your obligation ends with your first purchase. And that's when ours begins. Dover's money-back guarantee allows you to return any record for any reason, even if you don't like the music, for a full, immediate refund—no questions asked.

MOZART: STRING QUARTETS: IN A (K. 464) AND C ("DISSONANT") (K. 465), Barchet Quartet. The final two of the famous Haydn Quartets, high-points in the history of music. The A Major was accepted with delight by Mozart's contemporaries, but the C Major, with its dissonant opening, aroused strong protest. Today, of course, the remarkable resolutions of the dissonances are recognized as major musical achievements. "Beautiful warm playing," MUSICAL AMERICA. "Two of Mozart's loveliest quartets in a distinguished performance," REV. OF RECORDED MUSIC. (Playing time 58 mins.) HCR 5200 **$2.00**

MOZART: STRING QUARTETS: IN G (K. 80), D (K. 156), and C (K. 157), Barchet Quartet. The early chamber music of Mozart receives unfortunately little attention. First-rate music of the Italian school, it contains all the lightness and charm that belongs only to the youthful Mozart. This is currently the only separate source for the composer's work of this period. "Excellent," HIGH FIDELITY. "Filled with sunshine and youthful joy; played with verve, recorded sound live and brilliant," CHRISTIAN SCI. MONITOR. (playing time 51 mins.) HCR 5201 **$2.00**

MOZART: SERENADES: #9 IN D ("POSTHORN") (K. 320), #6 IN D ("SERENATA NOTTURNA") (K. 239), Pro Musica Orch. of Stuttgart, under Edouard van Remoortel. For Mozart, the serenade was a highly effective form, since he could bring to it the immediacy and intimacy of chamber music as well as the free fantasy of larger group music. Both these serenades are distinguished by a playful, mischievous quality, a spirit perfectly captured in this fine performance. "A triumph, polished playing from the orchestra," HI FI MUSIC AT HOME. "Sound is rich and resonant, fidelity is wonderful," REV. OF RECORDED MUSIC. (Playing time 51 mins.) HCR 5202 **$2.00**

MOZART: DIVERTIMENTO FOR VIOLIN, VIOLA AND CELLO IN E FLAT (K. 563); ADAGIO AND FUGUE IN F MINOR (K. 404a), Kehr Trio. The divertimento is one of Mozart's most beloved pieces, called by Einstein "the finest and most perfect trio ever heard." It is difficult to imagine a music lover who will not be delighted by it. This is the only recording of the lesser known Adagio and Fugue, written in 1782 and influenced by Bach's Well-Tempered Clavichord. "Extremely beautiful recording, strongly recommended," THE OBSERVER. "Superior to rival editions," HIGH FIDELITY. (Playing time 51 mins.) HCR 5203 **$2.00**

SCHUMANN: KREISLERIANA (OPUS 16) AND FANTASIA IN C (OPUS 17), Vlado Perlemuter, Piano. The vigorous Romantic imagination and the remarkable emotional qualities of Schumann's piano music raise it to a special eminence in 19th-century creativity. Both these pieces are rooted to the composer's tortuous romance with his future wife, Clara, and both receive brilliant treatment at the hands of Vlado Perlemuter, Paris Conservatory, proclaimed by Alfred Cortot "not only a great virtuoso but also a great musician." "The best Kreisleriana to date," BILLBOARD. (Playing time 55 mins.) HCR 5204 **$2.00**

J. S. BACH: PARTITAS FOR UNACCOMPANIED VIOLIN: #2 in D Minor and #3 in E, Bronislav Gimpel. Bach's works for unaccompanied violin fall within the same area that produced the Brandenburg Concerti, the Orchestral Suites, and the first part of the Well-Tempered Clavichord. The D Minor is considered one of Bach's masterpieces; the E Major is a buoyant work with exceptionally interesting bariolage effects. This is the first release of a truly memorable recording by Bronislav Gimpel, "as a violinist, the equal of the greatest" (P. Leron, in OPERA, Paris). (Playing time 53 mins.)   HCR 5212 **$2.00**

ROSSINI: QUARTETS FOR WOODWINDS: #1 IN F, #4 IN B FLAT, #5 IN D, AND #6 IN F, N. Y. Woodwind Quartet Members: S. Baron, Flute, J. Barrows, French Horn; B. Garfield, Bassoon; D. Glazer, Clarinet. Rossini's great genius was centered in the opera, but he also wrote a small amount of first-rate non-vocal music. Among these instrumental works, first place is usually given to the very interesting quartets. Of the three different surviving arrangements, this wind group version is the original, and this is the first recording of these works. "Each member of the group displays wonderful virtuosity when the music calls for it, at other times blending sensitively into the ensemble," HIGH FIDELITY. "Sheer delight," Philip Miller. (Playing time 45 mins.)   HCR 5214 **$2.00**

TELEMANN: THE GERMAN FANTASIAS FOR HARPSICHORD (#1-12), Helma Elsner. Until recently, Georg Philip Telemann (1681-1767) was one of the mysteriously neglected great men of music. Recently he has received the attention he deserved. He created music that delights modern listeners with its freshness and originality. These fantasias are free in form and reveal the intricacy of thorough bass music, the harmonic wealth of the "new music," and a distinctive melodic beauty. "This is another blessing of the contemporary LP output. Miss Elsner plays with considerable sensitivity and a great deal of understanding," REV. OF RECORDED MUSIC. "Fine recorded sound," Harold Schonberg. "Recommended warmly, very high quality," DISQUES. (Playing time 50 mins.)   HCR 5210 **$2.00**

Nova Recordings

In addition to our reprints of outstanding out-of-print records and American releases of first-rate foreign recordings, we have established our own new records. In order to keep every phase of their production under our own control, we have engaged musicians of world renown to play important music (for the most part unavailable elsewhere), have made use of the finest recording studios in New York, and have produced tapes equal to anything on the market, we believe. The first of these entirely new records are now available.

RAVEL: GASPARD DE LA NUIT, LE TOMBEAU DE COUPERIN, JEUX D'EAU, Beveridge Webster, Piano. Webster studied under Ravel and played his works in European recitals, often with Ravel's personal participation in the program. This record offers examples of the three major periods of Ravel's pianistic work, and is a must for any serious collector or music lover. (Playing time about 50 minutes).   Monaural HCR 5213 **$2.00**
                                  Stereo HCR ST 7000 **$2.00**

EIGHTEENTH CENTURY FRENCH FLUTE MUSIC, Jean-Pierre Rampal, Flute, and Robert Veyron-Lacroix, Harpsichord. Contains Concerts Royaux #7 for Flute and Harpsichord in G Minor, Francois Couperin; Sonata dite l'Inconnue in G for Flute and Harpsichord, Michel de la Barre; Sonata #6 in A Minor, Michel Blavet; and Sonata in D Minor, Anne Danican-Philidor. In the opinion of many Rampal is the world's premier flutist. (Playing time about 45 minutes)   Monaural HCR 5238 **$2.00**
                                  Stereo HCR ST 7001 **$2.00**

SCHUMANN: NOVELLETTEN (Opus 21), Beveridge Webster, Piano. Brilliantly played in this original recording by one of America's foremost keyboard performers. Connected Romantic pieces. Long a piano favorite. (Playing time about 45 minutes)   Monaural HCR 5239 **$2.00**
                                  Stereo HCR ST 7002 **$2.00**

Music

A GENERAL HISTORY OF MUSIC, Charles Burney. A detailed coverage of music from the Greeks up to 1789, with full information on all .types of music: sacred and secular, vocal and instrumental, operatic and symphonic. Theory, notation, forms, instruments, innovators, composers, performers, typical and important works, and much more in an easy, entertaining style. Burney covered much of Europe and spoke with hundreds of authorities and composers so that this work is more than a compilation of records . . . it is a living work of careful and first-hand scholarship. Its account of thoroughbass (18th century) Italian music is probably still the best introduction on the subject. A recent NEW YORK TIMES review said, "Surprisingly few of Burney's statements have been invalidated by modern research . . . still of great value." Edited and corrected by Frank Mercer. 35 figures. Indices. 1915pp. 5⅜ x 8. 2 volumes. **T36 The Set, Clothbound $12.50**

A DICTIONARY OF HYMNOLOGY, John Julian. This exhaustive and scholarly work has become known as an invaluable source of hundreds of thousands of important and often difficult to obtain facts on the history and use of hymns in the western world. Everyone interested in hymns will be fascinated by the accounts of famous hymns and hymn writers and amazed by the amount of practical information he will find. More than 30,000 entries on individual hymns, giving authorship, date and circumstances of composition, publication, textual variations, translations, denominational and ritual usage, etc. Biographies of more than 9,000 hymn writers, and essays on important topics such as Christmas carols and children's hymns, and much other unusual and valuable information. A 200 page double-columned index of first lines — the largest in print. Total of 1786 pages in two reinforced clothbound volumes. 6¼ x 9¼. The set, **T333 Clothbound $17.50**

MUSIC IN MEDIEVAL BRITAIN, F. Ll. Harrison. The most thorough, up-to-date, and accurate treatment of the subject ever published, beautifully illustrated. Complete account of institutions and choirs; carols, masses, and motets; liturgy and plainsong; and polyphonic music from the Norman Conquest to the Reformation. Discusses the various schools of music and their reciprocal influences; the origin and development of new ritual forms; development and use of instruments; and new evidence on many problems of the period. Reproductions of scores, over 200 excerpts from medieval melodies. Rules of harmony and dissonance; influence of Continental styles; great composers (Dunstable, Cornysh, Fairfax, etc.); and much more. Register and index of more than 400 musicians. Index of titles. General Index. 225-item bibliography. 6 Appendices. xix + 491pp. 5⅝ x 8¾. **T705 Clothbound $10.00**

THE MUSIC OF SPAIN, Gilbert Chase. Only book in English to give concise, comprehensive account of Iberian music; new Chapter covers music since 1941. Victoria, Albéniz, Cabezón, Pedrell, Turina, hundreds of other composers; popular and folk music; the Gypsies; the guitar; dance, theatre, opera, with only extensive discussion in English of the Zarzuela; virtuosi such as Casals; much more. "Distinguished . . . readable," Saturday Review. 400-item bibliography. Index. 27 photos. 383pp. 5⅜ x 8. **T549 Paperbound $2.00**

ON STUDYING SINGING, Sergius Kagen. An intelligent method of voice-training, which leads you around pitfalls that waste your time, money, and effort. Exposes rigid, mechanical systems, baseless theories, deleterious exercises. "Logical, clear, convincing . . . dead right," Virgil Thomson, N.Y. Herald Tribune. "I recommend this volume highly," Maggie Teyte, Saturday Review. 119pp. 5⅜ x 8. **T622 Paperbound $1.25**

WILLIAM LAWES, M. Lefkowitz. This is the definitive work on Lawes, the versatile, prolific, and highly original "King's musician" of 17th century England. His life is reconstructed from original documents, and nearly every piece he ever wrote is examined and evaluated: his fantasias, pavans, violin "sonatas," lyra viol and bass viol suites, and music for harp and theorbo; and his songs, masques, and theater music to words by Herrick ("Gather Ye Rosebuds"), Jonson, Suckling, Shirley, and others. The author shows the innovations of dissonance, augmented triad, and other Italian influences Lawes helped introduce to England. List of Lawes' complete works and several complete scores by this major precursor of Purcell and the 18th century developments. Index. 5 Appendices. 52 musical excerpts, many never before in print. Bibliography. x + 320pp. 5⅜ x 8. **T706 Clothbound $10.00**

THE FUGUE IN BEETHOVEN'S PIANO MUSIC, J. V. Cockshoot. The first study of a neglected aspect of Beethoven's genius: his ability as a writer of fugues. Analyses of early studies and published works demonstrate his original and powerful contributions to composition. 34 works are examined, with 143 musical excerpts. For all pianists, teachers, students, and music-minded readers with a serious interest in Beethoven. Index. 93-item bibliography. Illustration of original score for "Fugue in C." xv + 212pp. 5⅝ x 8⅜. **T704 Clothbound $6.00**

Literature, History of Literature

ARISTOTLE'S THEORY OF POETRY AND THE FINE ARTS, edited by S. H. Butcher. The celebrated Butcher translation of this great classic faced, page by page, with the complete Greek text. A 300 page introduction discussing Aristotle's ideas and their influence in the history of thought and literature, and covering art and nature, imitation as an aesthetic form, poetic truth, art and morality, tragedy, comedy, and similar topics. Modern Aristotelian criticism discussed by John Gassner. lxxvi + 421pp. 5⅜ x 8.   T42 Paperbound **$2.00**

INTRODUCTIONS TO ENGLISH LITERATURE, edited by B. Dobrée. Goes far beyond ordinary histories, ranging from the 7th century up to 1914 (to the 1940's in some cases.) The first half of each volume is a specific detailed study of historical and economic background of the period and a general survey of poetry and prose, including trends of thought, influences, etc. The second and larger half is devoted to a detailed study of more than 5000 poets, novelists, dramatists; also economists, historians, biographers, religious writers, philosophers, travellers, and scientists of literary stature, with dates, lists of major works and their dates, keypoint critical bibliography, and evaluating comments. The most compendious bibliographic and literary aid within its price range.

Vol. I. THE BEGINNINGS OF ENGLISH LITERATURE TO SKELTON, (1509), W. L. Renwick, H. Orton. 450pp. 5⅛ x 7⅞.   T75 Clothbound **$4.50**

Vol. II. THE ENGLISH RENAISSANCE, 1510-1688, V. de Sola Pinto. 381pp. 5⅛ x 7⅞.   T76 Clothbound **$4.50**

Vol. III. AUGUSTANS AND ROMANTICS, 1689-1830, H. Dyson, J. Butt. 320pp. 5⅛ x 7⅞.   T77 Clothbound **$4.50**

Vol. IV. THE VICTORIANS AND AFTER, 1830-1940's, E. Batho, B. Dobrée. 360pp. 5⅛ x 7⅞.   T78 Clothbound **$4.50**

EPIC AND ROMANCE, W. P. Ker. Written by one of the foremost authorities on medieval literature, this is the standard survey of medieval epic and romance. It covers Teutonic epics, Icelandic sagas, Beowulf, French chansons de geste, the Roman de Troie, and many other important works of literature. It is an excellent account for a body of literature whose beauty and value has only recently come to be recognized. Index. xxiv + 398pp. 5⅜ x 8.   T355 Paperbound **$2.00**

THE POPULAR BALLAD, F. B. Gummere. Most useful factual introduction; fund of descriptive material; quotes, cites over 260 ballads. Examines, from folkloristic view, structure; choral, ritual elements; meter, diction, fusion; effects of tradition, editors; almost every other aspect of border, riddle, kinship, sea, ribald, supernatural, etc., ballads. Bibliography. 2 indexes. 374pp. 5⅜ x 8.   T548 Paperbound **$1.85**

MASTERS OF THE DRAMA, John Gassner. The most comprehensive history of the drama in print, covering drama in every important tradition from the Greeks to the Near East, China, Japan, Medieval Europe, England, Russia, Italy, Spain, Germany, and dozens of other drama producing nations. This unsurpassed reading and reference work encompasses more than 800 dramatists and over 2000 plays, with biographical material, plot summaries, theatre history, etc. "Has no competitors in its field," THEATRE ARTS. "Best of its kind in English," NEW REPUBLIC. Exhaustive 35 page bibliography. 77 photographs and drawings. Deluxe edition with reinforced cloth binding, headbands, stained top. xxii + 890pp. 5⅜ x 8.   T100 Clothbound **$6.95**

THE DEVELOPMENT OF DRAMATIC ART, D. C. Stuart. The basic work on the growth of Western drama from primitive beginnings to Eugene O'Neill, covering over 2500 years. Not a mere listing or survey, but a thorough analysis of changes, origins of style, and influences in each period; dramatic conventions, social pressures, choice of material, plot devices, stock situations, etc.; secular and religious works of all nations and epochs. "Generous and thoroughly documented researches," Outlook. "Solid studies of influences and playwrights and periods," London Times. Index. Bibliography. xi + 679pp. 5⅜ x 8.
            T693 Paperbound **$2.75**

A SOURCE BOOK IN THEATRICAL HISTORY (SOURCES OF THEATRICAL HISTORY), A. M. Nagler. Over 2000 years of actors, directors, designers, critics, and spectators speak for themselves in this potpourri of writings selected from the great and formative periods of western drama. On-the-spot descriptions of masks, costumes, makeup, rehearsals, special effects, acting methods, backstage squabbles, theatres, etc. Contemporary glimpses of Molière rehearsing his company, an exhortation to a Roman audience to buy refreshments and keep quiet, Goethe's rules for actors, Belasco telling of $6500 he spent building a river, Restoration actors being told to avoid "lewd, obscene, or indecent postures," and much more. Each selection has an introduction by Prof. Nagler. This extraordinary, lively collection is ideal as a source of otherwise difficult to obtain material, as well as a fine book for browsing. Over 80 illustrations. 10 diagrams. xxiii + 611pp. 5⅜ x 8.   T515 Paperbound **$3.00**

CATALOGUE OF DOVER BOOKS

WORLD DRAMA, B. H. Clark. The dramatic creativity of a score of ages and eras — all in two handy compact volumes. Over ⅓ of this material is unavailable in any other current edition! 46 plays from Ancient Greece, Rome, Medieval Europe, France, Germany, Italy, England, Russia, Scandinavia, India, China, Japan, etc. — including classic authors like Aeschylus, Sophocles, Euripides, Aristophanes, Plautus, Marlowe, Jonson, Farquhar, Goldsmith, Cervantes, Molière, Dumas, Goethe, Schiller, Ibsen, and many others. This creative collection avoids hackneyed material and includes only completely first-rate works which are relatively little known or difficult to obtain. "The most comprehensive collection of important plays from all literature available in English," SAT. REV. OF LITERATURE. Introduction. Reading lists. 2 volumes. 1364pp. 5⅜ x 8.   Vol. 1, T57 Paperbound **$2.25**
                                                                Vol. 2, T59 Paperbound **$2.50**

MASTERPIECES OF THE RUSSIAN DRAMA, edited with introduction by G. R. Noyes. This only comprehensive anthology of Russian drama ever published in English offers complete texts, in 1st-rate modern translations, of 12 plays covering 200 years. Vol. 1: "The Young Hopeful," Fonvisin; "Wit Works Woe," Griboyedov; "The Inspector General," Gogol; "A Month in the Country," Turgenev; "The Poor Bride," Ostrovsky; "A Bitter Fate," Pisemsky. Vol. 2: "The Death of Ivan the Terrible," Alexey Tolstoy "The Power of Darkness," Lev Tolstoy; "The Lower Depths," Gorky; "The Cherry Orchard," Chekhov; "Professor Storitsyn," Andreyev; "Mystery Bouffe," Mayakovsky. Bibliography. Total of 902pp. 5⅜ x 8.
                                                                Vol. 1 T647 Paperbound **$2.00**
                                                                Vol. 2 T648 Paperbound **$2.00**

EUGENE O'NEILL: THE MAN AND HIS PLAYS, B. H. Clark. Introduction to O'Neill's life and work. Clark analyzes each play from the early THE WEB to the recently produced MOON FOR THE MISBEGOTTEN and THE ICEMAN COMETH revealing the environmental and dramatic influences necessary for a complete understanding of these important works. Bibliography. Appendices. Index. ix + 182pp. 5⅜ x 8.   T379 Paperbound **$1.35**

THE HEART OF THOREAU'S JOURNALS, edited by O. Shepard. The best general selection from Thoreau's voluminous (and rare) journals. This intimate record of thoughts and observations reveals the full Thoreau and his intellectual development more accurately than any of his published works: self-conflict between the scientific observer and the poet, reflections on transcendental philosophy, involvement in the tragedies of neighbors and national causes, etc. New preface, notes, introductions. xii + 228pp. 5⅜ x 8.   T741 Paperbound **$1.50**

H. D. THOREAU: A WRITER'S JOURNAL, edited by L. Stapleton. A unique new selection from the Journals concentrating on Thoreau's growth as a conscious literary artist, the ideals and purposes of his art. Most of the material has never before appeared outside of the complete 14-volume edition. Contains vital insights on Thoreau's projected book on Concord, thoughts on the nature of men and government, indignation with slavery, sources of inspiration, goals in life. Index. xxxiii + 234pp. 5⅜ x 8.   T678 Paperbound **$1.65**

THE HEART OF EMERSON'S JOURNALS, edited by Bliss Perry. Best of these revealing Journals, originally 10 volumes, presented in a one volume edition. Talks with Channing, Hawthorne, Thoreau, and Bronson Alcott; impressions of Webster, Everett, John Brown, and Lincoln; records of moments of sudden understanding, vision, and solitary ecstasy. "The essays do not reveal the power of Emerson's mind . . . as do these hasty and informal writings," N.Y. Times. Preface by Bliss Perry. Index. xiii + 357pp. 5⅜ x 8.   T477 Paperbound **$1.85**

FOUNDERS OF THE MIDDLE AGES, E. K. Rand. This is the best non-technical discussion of the transformation of Latin pagan culture into medieval civilization. Covering such figures as Tertullian, Gregory, Jerome, Boethius, Augustine, the Neoplatonists, and many other literary men, educators, classicists, and humanists, this book is a storehouse of information presented clearly and simply for the intelligent non-specialist. "Thoughtful, beautifully written," AMERICAN HISTORICAL REVIEW. "Extraordinarily accurate," Richard McKeon, THE NATION. ix + 365pp. 5⅜ x 8.   T369 Paperbound **$2.00**

PLAY-MAKING: A MANUAL OF CRAFTSMANSHIP, William Archer. With an extensive, new introduction by John Gassner, Yale Univ. The permanently essential requirements of solid play construction are set down in clear, practical language: theme, exposition, foreshadowing, tension, obligatory scene, peripety, dialogue, character, psychology, other topics. This book has been one of the most influential elements in the modern theatre, and almost everything said on the subject since is contained explicitly or implicitly within its covers. Bibliography. Index. xlii + 277pp. 5⅜ x 8.   T651 Paperbound **$1.75**

HAMBURG DRAMATURGY, G. E. Lessing. One of the most brilliant of German playwrights of the eighteenth-century age of criticism analyzes the complex of theory and tradition that constitutes the world of theater. These 104 essays on aesthetic theory helped demolish the regime of French classicism, opening the door to psychological and social realism, romanticism. Subjects include the original functions of tragedy; drama as the rational world; the meaning of pity and fear, pity and fear as means for purgation and other Aristotelian concepts; genius and creative force; interdependence of poet's language and actor's interpretation; truth and authenticity; etc. A basic and enlightening study for anyone interested in aesthetics and ideas, from the philosopher to the theatergoer. Introduction by Prof. Victor Lange. xxii + 265pp. 4½ x 6⅜.   T32 Paperbound **$1.45**

Americana

THE EYES OF DISCOVERY, J. Bakeless. A vivid reconstruction of how unspoiled America appeared to the first white men. Authentic and enlightening accounts of Hudson's landing in New York, Coronado's trek through the Southwest; scores of explorers, settlers, trappers, soldiers. America's pristine flora, fauna, and Indians in every region and state in fresh and unusual new aspects. "A fascinating view of what the land was like before the first highway went through," Time. 68 contemporary illustrations, 39 newly added in this edition. Index. Bibliography. x + 500pp. 5⅜ x 8.   T761 Paperbound **$2.00**

AUDUBON AND HIS JOURNALS, J. J. Audubon. A collection of fascinating accounts of Europe and America in the early 1800's through Audubon's own eyes. Includes the Missouri River Journals —an eventful trip through America's untouched heartland, the Labrador Journals, the European Journals, the famous "Episodes", and other rare Audubon material, including the descriptive chapters from the original letterpress edition of the "Ornithological Studies", omitted in all later editions. Indispensable for ornithologists, naturalists, and all lovers of Americana and adventure. 70-page biography by Audubon's granddaughter. 38 illustrations. Index. Total of 1106pp. 5⅜ x 8.   T675 Vol I Paperbound **$2.25**
T676 Vol II Paperbound **$2.25**
The set **$4.50**

TRAVELS OF WILLIAM BARTRAM, edited by Mark Van Doren. The first inexpensive illustrated edition of one of the 18th century's most delightful books is an excellent source of first-hand material on American geography, anthropology, and natural history. Many descriptions of early Indian tribes are our only source of information on them prior to the infiltration of the white man. "The mind of a scientist with the soul of a poet," John Livingston Lowes. 13 original illustrations and maps. Edited with an introduction by Mark Van Doren. 448pp. 5⅜ x 8.
T13 Paperbound **$2.00**

GARRETS AND PRETENDERS: A HISTORY OF BOHEMIANISM IN AMERICA, A. Parry. The colorful and fantastic history of American Bohemianism from Poe to Kerouac. This is the only complete record of hoboes, cranks, starving poets, and suicides. Here are Pfaff, Whitman, Crane, Bierce, Pound, and many others. New chapters by the author and by H. T. Moore bring this thorough and well-documented history down to the Beatniks. "An excellent account," N. Y. Times. Scores of cartoons, drawings, and caricatures. Bibliography. Index. xxviii + 421pp. 5⅝ x 8⅜.   T708 Paperbound **$1.95**

THE EXPLORATION OF THE COLORADO RIVER AND ITS CANYONS, J. W. Powell. The thrilling first-hand account of the expedition that filled in the last white space on the map of the United States. Rapids, famine, hostile Indians, and mutiny are among the perils encountered as the unknown Colorado Valley reveals its secrets. This is the only uncut version of Major Powell's classic of exploration that has been printed in the last 60 years. Includes later reflections and subsequent expedition. 250 illustrations, new map. 400pp. 5⅝ x 8⅜.
T94 Paperbound **$2.25**

THE JOURNAL OF HENRY D. THOREAU, Edited by Bradford Torrey and Francis H. Allen. Henry Thoreau is not only one of the most important figures in American literature and social thought; his voluminous journals (from which his books emerged as selections and crystalliza-tions) constitute both the longest, most sensitive record of personal internal development and a most penetrating description of a historical moment in American culture. This present set, which was first issued in fourteen volumes, contains Thoreau's entire journals from 1837 to 1862, with the exception of the lost years which were found only recently. We are reissuing it, complete and unabridged, with a new introduction by Walter Harding, Secretary of the Thoreau Society. Fourteen volumes reissued in two volumes. Foreword by Henry Seidel Canby. Total of 1888pp. 8⅜ x 12¼.   T312-3 Two volume set, Clothbound **$20.00**

GAMES AND SONGS OF AMERICAN CHILDREN, collected by William Wells Newell. A remarkable collection of 190 games with songs that accompany many of them; cross references to show similarities, differences among them; variations; musical notation for 38 songs. Textual dis-cussions show relations with folk-drama and other aspects of folk tradition. Grouped into categories for ready comparative study: Love-games, histories, playing at work, human life, bird and beast, mythology, guessing-games, etc. New introduction covers relations of songs and dances to timeless heritage of folklore, biographical sketch of Newell, other pertinent data. A good source of inspiration for those in charge of groups of children and a valuable reference for anthropologists, sociologists, psychiatrists. Introduction by Carl Withers. New indexes of first lines, games. 5⅜ x 8½. xii + 242pp.   T354 Paperbound **$1.75**

CATALOGUE OF DOVER BOOKS

GARDNER'S PHOTOGRAPHIC SKETCH BOOK OF THE CIVIL WAR, Alexander Gardner. The first published collection of Civil War photographs, by one of the two or three most famous photographers of the era, outstandingly reproduced from the original positives. Scenes of crucial battles: Appomattox, Manassas, Mechanicsville, Bull Run, Yorktown, Fredericksburg, etc. Gettysburg immediately after retirement of forces. Battle ruins at Richmond, Petersburg, Gaines'Mill. Prisons, arsenals, a slave pen, fortifications, headquarters, pontoon bridges, soldiers, a field hospital. A unique glimpse into the realities of one of the bloodiest wars in history, with an introductory text to each picture by Gardner himself. Until this edition, there were only five known copies in libraries, and fewer in private hands, one of which sold at auction in 1952 for $425. Introduction by E. F. Bleiler. 100 full page 7 x 10 photographs (original size). 224pp. 8½ x 10¾. T476 Clothbound **$6.00**

A BIBLIOGRAPHY OF NORTH AMERICAN FOLKLORE AND FOLKSONG, Charles Haywood, Ph.D. The only book that brings together bibliographic information on so wide a range of folklore material. Lists practically everything published about American folksongs, ballads, dances, folk beliefs and practices, popular music, tales, similar material—more than 35,000 titles of books, articles, periodicals, monographs, music publications, phonograph records. Each entry complete with author, title, date and place of publication, arranger and performer of particular examples of folk music, many with Dr. Haywood's valuable criticism, evaluation. Volume I, "The American People," is complete listing of general and regional studies, titles of tales and songs of Negro and non-English speaking groups and where to find them, Occupational Bibliography including sections listing sources of information, folk material on cowboys, riverboat men, 49ers, American characters like Mike Fink, Frankie and Johnnie, John Henry, many more. Volume II, "The American Indian," tells where to find information on dances, myths, songs, ritual of more than 250 tribes in U.S., Canada. A monumental product of 10 years' labor, carefully classified for easy use. "All students of this subject . . . will find themselves in debt to Professor Haywood," Stith Thompson, in American Anthropologist. ". . . a most useful and excellent work," Duncan Emrich, Chief Folklore Section, Library of Congress, in "Notes." Corrected, enlarged republication of 1951 edition. New Preface. New index of composers, arrangers, performers. General index of more than 15,000 items. Two volumes. Total of 1301pp. 6⅛ x 9¼. T797-798 Clothbound **$12.50**

INCIDENTS OF TRAVEL IN YUCATAN, John L. Stephens. One of first white men to penetrate interior of Yucatan tells the thrilling story of his discoveries of 44 cities, remains of once-powerful Maya civilization. Compelling text combines narrative power with historical significance as it takes you through heat, dust, storms of Yucatan; native festivals with brutal bull fights; great ruined temples atop man-made mounds. Countless idols, sculptures, tombs, examples of Mayan taste for rich ornamentation, from gateways to personal trinkets, accurately illustrated, discussed in text. Will appeal to those interested in ancient civilizations, and those who like stories of exploration, discovery, adventure. Republication of last (1843) edition. 124 illustrations by English artist, F. Catherwood. Appendix on Mayan architecture, chronology. Two volume set. Total of xxviii + 927pp.

Vol I T926 Paperbound **$2.00**
Vol II T927 Paperbound **$2.00**
The set **$4.00**

A GENIUS IN THE FAMILY, Hiram Percy Maxim. Sir Hiram Stevens Maxim was known to the public as the inventive genius who created the Maxim gun, automatic sprinkler, and a heavier-than-air plane that got off the ground in 1894. Here, his son reminisces—this is by no means a formal biography—about the exciting and often downright scandalous private life of his brilliant, eccentric father. A warm and winning portrait of a prankish, mischievous, impious personality, a genuine character. The style is fresh and direct, the effect is unadulterated pleasure. "A book of charm and lasting humor . . . belongs on the 'must read' list of all fathers," New York Times. "A truly gorgeous affair," New Statesman and Nation. 17 illustrations, 16 specially for this edition. viii + 108pp. 5⅜ x 8½.

T948 Paperbound **$1.00**

HORSELESS CARRIAGE DAYS, Hiram P. Maxim. The best account of an important technological revolution by one of its leading figures. The delightful and rewarding story of the author's experiments with the exact combustibility of gasoline, stopping and starting mechanisms, carriage design, and engines. Captures remarkably well the flavor of an age of scoffers and rival inventors not above sabotage; of noisy, uncontrollable gasoline vehicles and incredible mobile steam kettles. ". . . historic information and light humor are combined to furnish highly entertaining reading," New York Times. 56 photographs, 12 specially for this edition. xi + 175pp. 5⅜ x 8½. T964 Paperbound **$1.35**

BODY, BOOTS AND BRITCHES: FOLKTALES, BALLADS AND SPEECH FROM COUNTRY NEW YORK, Harold W. Thompson. A unique collection, discussion of songs, stories, anecdotes, proverbs handed down orally from Scotch-Irish grandfathers, German nurse-maids, Negro workmen, gathered from all over Upper New York State. Tall tales by and about lumbermen and pirates, canalers and injun-fighters, tragic and comic ballads, scores of sayings and proverbs all tied together by an informative, delightful narrative by former president of New York Historical Society. ". . . a sparkling homespun tapestry that every lover of Americana will want to have around the house," Carl Carmer, New York Times. Republication of 1939 edition. 20 line-drawings. Index. Appendix (Sources of material, bibliography). 530pp. 5⅜ x 8½. T411 Paperbound **$2.00**

Art, History of Art, Antiques, Graphic Arts, Handcrafts

ART STUDENTS' ANATOMY, E. J. Farris. Outstanding art anatomy that uses chiefly living objects for its illustrations. 71 photos of undraped men, women, children are accompanied by carefully labeled matching sketches to illustrate the skeletal system, articulations and movements, bony landmarks, the muscular system, skin, fasciae, fat, etc. 9 x-ray photos show movement of joints. Undraped models are shown in such actions as serving in tennis, drawing a bow in archery, playing football, dancing, preparing to spring and to dive. Also discussed and illustrated are proportions, age and sex differences, the anatomy of the smile, etc. 8 plates by the great early 18th century anatomic illustrator Siegfried Albinus are also included. Glossary. 158 figures, 7 in color. x + 159pp. 5⅝ x 8⅜. T744 Paperbound **$1.50**

AN ATLAS OF ANATOMY FOR ARTISTS, F Schider. A new 3rd edition of this standard text enlarged by 52 new illustrations of hands, anatomical studies by Cloquet, and expressive life studies of the body by Barcsay. 189 clear, detailed plates offer you precise information of impeccable accuracy. 29 plates show all aspects of the skeleton, with closeups of special areas, while 54 full-page plates, mostly in two colors, give human musculature as seen from four different points of view, with cutaways for important portions of the body. 14 full-page plates provide photographs of hand forms, eyelids, female breasts, and indicate the location of muscles upon models. 59 additional plates show how great artists of the past utilized human anatomy. They reproduce sketches and finished work by such artists as Michelangelo, Leonardo da Vinci, Goya, and 15 others. This is a lifetime reference work which will be one of the most important books in any artist's library. "The standard reference tool," AMERICAN LIBRARY ASSOCIATION. "Excellent," AMERICAN ARTIST. Third enlarged edition. 189 plates, 647 illustrations. xxvi + 192pp. 7⅞ x 10⅝. T241 Clothbound **$6.00**

AN ATLAS OF ANIMAL ANATOMY FOR ARTISTS, W. Ellenberger, H. Baum, H. Dittrich. The largest, richest animal anatomy for artists available in English. 99 detailed anatomical plates of such animals as the horse, dog, cat, lion, deer, seal, kangaroo, flying squirrel, cow, bull, goat, monkey, hare, and bat. Surface features are clearly indicated, while progressive beneath-the-skin pictures show musculature, tendons, and bone structure. Rest and action are exhibited in terms of musculature and skeletal structure and detailed cross-sections are given for heads and important features. The animals chosen are representative of specific families so that a study of these anatomies will provide knowledge of hundreds of related species. "Highly recommended as one of the very few books on the subject worthy of being used as an authoritative guide," DESIGN. "Gives a fundamental knowledge," AMERICAN ARTIST. Second revised, enlarged edition with new plates from Cuvier, Stubbs, etc. 288 illustrations. 153pp. 11⅜ x 9. T82 Clothbound **$6.00**

THE HUMAN FIGURE IN MOTION, Eadweard Muybridge. The largest selection in print of Muybridge's famous high-speed action photos of the human figure in motion. 4789 photographs illustrate 162 different actions: men, women, children—mostly undraped—are shown walking, running, carrying various objects, sitting, lying down, climbing, throwing, arising, and performing over 150 other actions. Some actions are shown in as many as 150 photographs each. All in all there are more than 500 action strips in this enormous volume, series shots taken at shutter speeds as high as 1/6000th of a second! These are not posed shots, but true stopped motion. They show bone and muscle in situations that the human eye is not fast enough to capture. Earlier, smaller editions of these prints have brought $40 and more on the out-of-print market. "A must for artists," ART IN FOCUS. "An unparalleled dictionary of action for all artists," AMERICAN ARTIST. 390 full-page plates, with 4789 photographs. Printed on heavy glossy stock. Reinforced binding with headbands. xxi + 390pp. 7⅞ x 10⅝. T204 Clothbound **$10.00**

ANIMALS IN MOTION, Eadweard Muybridge. This is the largest collection of animal action photos in print. 34 different animals (horses, mules, oxen, goats, camels, pigs, cats, guanacos, lions, gnus, deer, monkeys, eagles—and 21 others) in 132 characteristic actions. The horse alone is shown in more than 40 different actions. All 3919 photographs are taken in series at speeds up to 1/6000th of a second. The secrets of leg motion, spinal patterns, head movements, strains and contortions shown nowhere else are captured. You will see exactly how a lion sets his foot down; how an elephant's knees are like a human's—and how they differ; the position of a kangaroo's legs in mid-leap; how an ostrich's head bobs; details of the flight of birds—and thousands of facets of motion only the fastest cameras can catch. Photographed from domestic animals and animals in the Philadelphia zoo, it contains neither semiposed artificial shots nor distorted telephoto shots taken under adverse conditions. Artists, biologists, decorators, cartoonists, will find this book indispensable for understanding animals in motion. "A really marvelous series of plates," NATURE (London). "The dry plate's most spectacular early use was by Eadweard Muybridge," LIFE. 3919 photographs; 380 full pages of plates. 440pp. Printed on heavy glossy paper. Deluxe binding with headbands. 7⅞ x 10⅝. T203 Clothbound **$10.00**

CATALOGUE OF DOVER BOOKS

ART ANATOMY, William Rimmer, M.D. Often called one of America's foremost contributions to art instruction, a work of art in its own right. More than 700 line drawings by the author, first-rate anatomist and dissector as well as artist, with a non-technical anatomical text. Impeccably accurate drawings of muscles, skeletal structure, surface features, other aspects of males and females, children, adults and aged persons show not only form, size, insertion and articulation but personality and emotion as reflected by physical features usually ignored in modern anatomical works. Complete unabridged reproduction of 1876 edition slightly rearranged. Introduction by Robert Hutchinson. 722 illustrations. xiii + 153pp. 7¾ x 10¾.
T908 Paperbound **$2.00**

ANIMAL DRAWING: ANATOMY AND ACTION FOR ARTISTS, C. R. Knight. The author and illustrator of this work was "the most distinguished painter of animal life." This extensive course in animal drawing discusses musculature, bone structure, animal psychology, movements, habits, habitats. Innumerable tips on proportions, light and shadow play, coloring, hair formation, feather arrangement, scales, how animals lie down, animal expressions, etc., from great apes to birds. Pointers on avoiding gracelessness in horses, deer; on introducing proper power and bulk to heavier animals; on giving proper grace and subtle expression to members of the cat family. Originally titled "Animal Anatomy and Psychology for the Artist and Layman." Over 123 illustrations. 149pp. 8¼ x 10½.
T426 Paperbound **$2.00**

DESIGN FOR ARTISTS AND CRAFTSMEN, L. Wolchonok. The most thorough course ever prepared on the creation of art motifs and designs. It teaches you to create your own designs out of things around you — from geometric patterns, plants, birds, animals, humans, landscapes, and man-made objects. It leads you step by step through the creation of more than 1300 designs, and shows you how to create design that is fresh, well-founded, and original. Mr. Wolchonok, whose text is used by scores of art schools, shows you how the same idea can be developed into many different forms, ranging from near representationalism to the most advanced forms of abstraction. The material in this book is entirely new, and combines full awareness of traditional design with the work of such men as Miro, Léger, Picasso, Moore, and others. 113 detailed exercises, with instruction hints, diagrams, and details to enable you to apply Wolchonok's methods to your own work. "A great contribution to the field of design and crafts," N. Y. SOCIETY OF CRAFTSMEN. More than 1300 illustrations. xv + 207pp. 7⅞ x 10¾.
T274 Clothbound **$4.95**

HAWTHORNE ON PAINTING. A vivid recreation, from students' notes, of instruction by Charles W. Hawthorne, given for over 31 years at his famous Cape Cod School of Art. Divided into sections on the outdoor model, still life, landscape, the indoor model, and water color, each section begins with a concise essay, followed by epigrammatic comments on color, form, seeing, etc. Not a formal course, but comments of a great teacher-painter on specific student works, which will solve problems in your own painting and understanding of art. "An excellent introduction for laymen and students alike," Time. Introduction. 100pp. 5⅜ x 8.
T653 Paperbound **$1.00**

THE ENJOYMENT AND USE OF COLOR, Walter Sargent. This book explains fascinating relations among colors, between colors in nature and art; describes experiments that you can perform to understand these relations more thoroughly; points out hundreds of little known facts about color values, intensities, effects of high and low illumination, complementary colors, color harmonies. Practical hints for painters, references to techniques of masters, questions at chapter ends for self-testing all make this a valuable book for artists, professional and amateur, and for general readers interested in world of color. Republication of 1923 edition. 35 illustrations, 6 full-page plates. New color frontispiece. Index. xii + 274pp. 5⅜ x 8.
T944 Paperbound **$2.25**

DECORATIVE ALPHABETS AND INITIALS, ed. by Alexander Nesbitt. No payment, no permission needed to reproduce any one of these 3924 different letters, covering 1000 years. Crisp, clear letters all in line, from Anglo-Saxon mss., Luebeck Cathedral, 15th century Augsburg; the work of Dürer, Holbein, Cresci, Beardsley, Rossing Wadsworth, John Moylin, etc. Every imaginable style. 91 complete alphabets. 123 full-page plates. 192pp. 7¾ x 10¾.
T544 Paperbound **$2.25**

THREE CLASSICS OF ITALIAN CALLIGRAPHY, edited by Oscar Ogg. Here, combined in a single volume, are complete reproductions of three famous calligraphic works written by the greatest writing masters of the Renaissance: Arrighi's OPERINA and IL MODO, Tagliente's LO PRESENTE LIBRO, and Palatino's LIBRO NUOVO. These books present more than 200 complete alphabets and thousands of lettered specimens. The basic hand is Papal Chancery, but scores of other alphabets are also given: European and Asiatic local alphabets, foliated and art alphabets, scrolls, cartouches, borders, etc. Text is in Italian. Introduction. 245 plates. x + 272pp. 6⅛ x 9¼.
T212 Paperbound **$2.25**

CALLIGRAPHY, J. G. Schwandner. One of the legendary books in the graphic arts, copies of which brought $500 each on the rare book market, now reprinted for the first time in over 200 years. A beautiful plate book of graceful calligraphy, and an inexhaustible source of first-rate material copyright-free, for artists, and directors, craftsmen, commercial artists, etc. More than 300 ornamental initials forming 12 complete alphabets, over 150 ornate frames and panels, over 200 flourishes, over 75 calligraphic pictures including a temple, cherubs, cocks, dodos, stags, chamois, foliated lions, greyhounds, etc. Thousand of calligraphic elements to be used for suggestions of quality, sophistication, antiquity, and sheer beauty. Historical introduction. 158 full-page plates. 368pp. 9 x 13.
T475 Clothbound **$10.00**

Miscellaneous

THE COMPLETE KANO JIU-JITSU (JUDO), H. I. Hancock and K. Higashi. Most comprehensive guide to judo, referred to as outstanding work by Encyclopaedia Britannica. Complete authentic Japanese system of 160 holds and throws, including the most spectacular, fully illustrated with 487 photos. Full text explains leverage, weight centers, pressure points, special tricks, etc.; shows how to protect yourself from almost any manner of attack though your attacker may have the initial advantage of strength and surprise. This authentic Kano system should not be confused with the many American imitations. xii + 500pp. 5⅜ x 8.
T639 Paperbound **$2.00**

THE MEMOIRS OF JACQUES CASANOVA. Splendid self-revelation by history's most engaging scoundrel—utterly dishonest with women and money, yet highly intelligent and observant. Here are all the famous duels, scandals, amours, banishments, thefts, treacheries, and imprisonments all over Europe: a life lived to the fullest and recounted with gusto in one of the greatest autobiographies of all time. What is more, these Memoirs are also one of the most trustworthy and valuable documents we have on the society and culture of the extravagant 18th century. Here are Voltaire, Louis XV, Catherine the Great, cardinals, castrati, pimps, and pawnbrokers—an entire glittering civilization unfolding before you with an unparalleled sense of actuality. Translated by Arthur Machen. Edited by F. A. Blossom. Introduction by Arthur Symons. Illustrated by Rockwell Kent. Total of xlviii + 2216pp. 5⅜ x 8.
T338 Vol I Paperbound **$2.00**
T339 Vol II Paperbound **$2.00**
T340 Vol III Paperbound **$2.00**
The set **$6.00**

BARNUM'S OWN STORY, P. T. Barnum. The astonishingly frank and gratifyingly well-written autobiography of the master showman and pioneer publicity man reveals the truth about his early career, his famous hoaxes (such as the Fejee Mermaid and the Woolly Horse), his amazing commercial ventures, his fling in politics, his feuds and friendships, his failures and surprising comebacks. A vast panorama of 19th century America's mores, amusements, and vitality. 66 new illustrations in this edition. xii + 500pp. 5⅜ x 8.
T764 Paperbound **$1.65**

THE STORY OF THE TITANIC AS TOLD BY ITS SURVIVORS, ed. by Jack Winocour. Most significant accounts of most overpowering naval disaster of modern times: all 4 authors were survivors. Includes 2 full-length, unabridged books: "The Loss of the S.S. Titanic," by Laurence Beesley, "The Truth about the Titanic," by Col. Archibald Gracie; 6 pertinent chapters from "Titanic and Other Ships," autobiography of only officer to survive, Second Officer Charles Lightoller; and a short, dramatic account by the Titanic's wireless operator, Harold Bride. 26 illus. 368pp. 5⅜ x 8.
T610 Paperbound **$1.50**

THE PHYSIOLOGY OF TASTE, Jean Anthelme Brillat-Savarin. Humorous, satirical, witty, and personal classic on joys of food and drink by 18th century French politician, litterateur. Treats the science of gastronomy, erotic value of truffles, Parisian restaurants, drinking contests; gives recipes for tunny omelette, pheasant, Swiss fondue, etc. Only modern translation of original French edition. Introduction. 41 illus. 346pp. 5⅜ x 8⅜.
T591 Paperbound **$1.50**

THE ART OF THE STORY-TELLER, M. L. Shedlock. This classic in the field of effective story-telling is regarded by librarians, story-tellers, and educators as the finest and most lucid book on the subject. The author considers the nature of the story, the difficulties of communicating stories to children, the artifices used in story-telling, how to obtain and maintain the effect of the story, and, of extreme importance, the elements to seek and those to avoid in selecting material. A 99-page selection of Miss Shedlock's most effective stories and an extensive bibliography of further material by Eulalie Steinmetz enhance the book's usefulness. xxi + 320pp. 5⅜ x 8.
T635 Paperbound **$1.50**

CREATIVE POWER: THE EDUCATION OF YOUTH IN THE CREATIVE ARTS, Hughes Mearns. In first printing considered revolutionary in its dynamic, progressive approach to teaching the creative arts; now accepted as one of the most effective and valuable approaches yet formulated. Based on the belief that every child has something to contribute, it provides in a stimulating manner invaluable and inspired teaching insights, to stimulate children's latent powers of creative expression in drama, poetry, music, writing, etc. Mearns's methods were developed in his famous experimental classes in creative education at the Lincoln School of Teachers College, Columbia Univ. Named one of the 20 foremost books on education in recent times by National Education Association. New enlarged revised 2nd edition. Introduction. 272pp. 5⅜ x 8.
T490 Paperbound **$1.75**

FREE AND INEXPENSIVE EDUCATIONAL AIDS, T. J. Pepe, Superintendent of Schools, Southbury, Connecticut. An up-to-date listing of over 1500 booklets, films, charts, etc. 5% costs less than 25¢; 1% costs more; 94% is yours for the asking. Use this material privately, or in schools from elementary to college, for discussion, vocational guidance, projects. 59 categories include health, trucking, textiles, language, weather, the blood, office practice, wild life, atomic energy, other important topics. Each item described according to contents, number of pages or running time, level. All material is educationally sound, and without political or company bias. 1st publication. Second, revised edition. Index. 244pp. 5⅜ x 8.
T663 Paperbound **$1.50**

CATALOGUE OF DOVER BOOKS

CHRONICLES OF THE HOUSE OF BORGIA, Frederick Baron Corvo (Frederick W. Rolfe). In the opinion of many this is the major work of that strange Edwardian literary figure, "Baron Corvo." It was Corvo's intention to investigate the notorious Borgias, from their first emergence in Spain to the Borgia saint in the 16th century and discover their true nature, disregarding both their apologists and their enemies. How well Corvo succeeded is questionable in a historical sense, but as a literary achievement and as a stylistic triumph the "Chronicles" has been a treasured favorite for generations. All the fabulous intrigues and devious currents and countercurrents of the Renaissance come vividly to life in Corvo's work, which is peopled with the notorious and notable personages of Italy and packed with fascinating lore. This is the first complete reprinting of this work, with all the appendices and illustrations. xxi + 375pp. 5⅝ x 8½. T275 Paperbound **$2.00**

ERROR AND ECCENTRICITY IN HUMAN BELIEF, Joseph Jastrow. A thoroughly enjoyable exposé, by a noted psychologist, of the ineradicable gullibility of man. Episodes throughout history —180 A.D. to 1930—that will shock and amuse by revelations of our tendency to fashion belief from desire not reason: the case of "Patience Worth," Ozark woman taking down novels from dictation of 17th-century girl from Devon; "Taxil," perhaps greatest hoaxer of all time; the odic force of Baron Reichenbach; Charles Richet, Nobel Laureate, accepting brazen trickeries of Eusapia Palladino; dozens of other lunacies, crank theories, public tricksters and frauds. For anyone who likes to read about the aberrations of his race. Formerly "Wish and Wisdom." 58 illustrations; 22 full-page plates. Index. xiv + 394pp. 5⅜ x 8½. T986 Paperbound **$1.85**

FADS AND FALLACIES IN THE NAME OF SCIENCE, Martin Gardner. Formerly entitled IN THE NAME OF SCIENCE, this is the standard account of various cults, quack systems, and delusions which have masqueraded as science: hollow earth fanatics, Reich and orgone sex energy, dianetics, Atlantis, multiple moons, Forteanism, flying saucers, medical fallacies like iridiagnosis, zone therapy, etc. A new chapter has been added on Bridey Murphy, psionics, and other recent manifestations in this field. This is a fair, reasoned appraisal of eccentric theory which provides excellent inoculation against cleverly masked nonsense. "Should be read by everyone, scientist and non-scientist alike," R. T. Birge, Prof. Emeritus of Physics, Univ. of California; Former President, American Physical Society. Index. x + 365pp. 5⅜ x 8. T394 Paperbound **$1.50**

MONEY CONVERTER AND TIPPING GUIDE FOR EUROPEAN TRAVEL, C. Vomacka. A small, convenient handbook crammed with information on currency regulations and tipping for every European country including the Iron Curtain countries, plus Israel, Egypt, and Turkey. Currency conversion tables for every country from U.S. to foreign and vice versa. The only source of such information as phone rates, postal rates, clothing sizes, what and when to tip, duty-free imports, and dozens of other valuable topics. Always kept up to date. 128 pp. 3½ x 5¼. T260 Paperbound **75¢**

HOW ADVERTISING IS WRITTEN—AND WHY, Aesop Glim. The best material from the famous "Aesop Glim" column in Printer's Ink. Specific, practical, constructive comments and criticisms on such matters as the aims of advertising, importance of copy, art of the headline, adjusting "tone of voice," creating conviction, etc. Timely, effective, useful. Written for the person interested in advertising profession, yet it has few equals as a manual for effective writing of any kind. Revised edition. 150pp. 5⅜ x 8. T782 Paperbound **$1.25**

THE WORLD'S GREAT SPEECHES, edited by Lewis Copeland and Lawrence Lamm. 255 speeches ranging over scores of topics and moods (including a special section of "Informal Speeches" and a fine collection of historically important speeches of the U.S.A. and other western hemisphere countries), present the greatest speakers of all time from Pericles of Athens to Churchill, Roosevelt, and Dylan Thomas. Invaluable as a guide to speakers, fascinating as history both past and contemporary, much material here is available elsewhere only with great difficulty. 3 indices: Topic, Author, Nation. xx + 745pp. 5⅜ x 8. T468 Paperbound **$2.75**

Pets

CARE AND FEEDING OF BUDGIES (SHELL PARRAKEETS), C. H. Rogers. Sources of information and supply. Index. 40 illustrations. 93pp. 5 x 7¼. T937 Paperbound **65¢**

THE CARE AND BREEDING OF GOLDFISH, Anthony Evans. Hundreds of important details about indoor and outdoor pools and aquariums; the history, physical features and varieties of goldfish; selection, care, feeding, health and breeding—with a special appendix that shows you how to build your own goldfish pond. Enlarged edition, newly revised. Bibliography. 22 full-page plates; 4 figures. 129pp. 5 x 7¼. T935 Paperbound **75¢**

OBEDIENCE TRAINING FOR YOUR DOG, C. Wimhurst. You can teach your dog to heel, retrieve, sit, jump, track, climb, refuse food, etc. Covers house training, developing a watchdog, obedience tests, working trials, police dogs. "Proud to recommend this book to every dog owner who is attempting to train his dog," says Blanche Saunders, noted American trainer, in her Introduction. Index. 34 photographs. 122pp. 5 x 7¼. T938 Paperbound **75¢**

Language Books and Records

GERMAN: HOW TO SPEAK AND WRITE IT. AN INFORMAL CONVERSATIONAL METHOD FOR SELF STUDY, Joseph Rosenberg. Eminently useful for self study because of concentration on elementary stages of learning. Also provides teachers with remarkable variety of aids: 28 full- and double-page sketches with pertinent items numbered and identified in German and English; German proverbs, jokes; grammar, idiom studies; extensive practice exercises. The most interesting introduction to German available, full of amusing illustrations, photographs of cities and landmarks in German-speaking cities, cultural information subtly woven into conversational material. Includes summary of grammar, guide to letter writing, study guide to German literature by Dr. Richard Friedenthal. Index. 400 illustrations. 384pp. 5⅜ x 8½.
T271 Paperbound **$2.00**

FRENCH: HOW TO SPEAK AND WRITE IT. AN INFORMAL CONVERSATIONAL METHOD FOR SELF STUDY, Joseph Lemaitre. Even the absolute beginner can acquire a solid foundation for further study from this delightful elementary course. Photographs, sketches and drawings, sparkling colloquial conversations on a wide variety of topics (including French culture and custom), French sayings and quips, are some of aids used to demonstrate rather than merely describe the language. Thorough yet surprisingly entertaining approach, excellent for teaching and for self study. Comprehensive analysis of pronunciation, practice exercises and appendices of verb tables, additional vocabulary, other useful material. Index. Appendix. 400 illustrations. 416pp. 5⅜ x 8½. T268 Paperbound **$2.00**

DICTIONARY OF SPOKEN SPANISH, Spanish-English, English-Spanish. Compiled from spoken Spanish, emphasizing idiom and colloquial usage in both Castilian and Latin-American. More than 16,000 entries containing over 25,000 idioms—the largest list of idiomatic constructions ever published. Complete sentences given, indexed under single words—language in immediately useable form, for travellers, businessmen, students, etc. 25 page introduction provides rapid survey of sounds, grammar, syntax, with full consideration of irregular verbs. Especially apt in modern treatment of phrases and structure. 17 page glossary gives translations of geographical names, money values, numbers, national holidays, important street signs, useful expressions of high frequency, plus unique 7 page glossary of Spanish and Spanish-American foods and dishes. Originally published as War Department Technical Manual TM 30-900. iv + 513pp. 5⅜ x 8. T495 Paperbound **$1.75**

SPEAK MY LANGUAGE: SPANISH FOR YOUNG BEGINNERS, M. Ahlman, Z. Gilbert. Records provide one of the best, and most entertaining, methods of introducing a foreign language to children. Within the framework of a train trip from Portugal to Spain, an English-speaking child is introduced to Spanish by a native companion. (Adapted from a successful radio program of the N. Y. State Educational Department.) Though a continuous story, there are a dozen specific categories of expressions, including greetings, numbers, time, weather, food, clothes, family members, etc. Drill is combined with poetry and contextual use. Authentic background music is heard. An accompanying book enables a reader to follow the records, and includes a vocabulary of over 350 recorded expressions. Two 10″ 33⅓ records, total of 40 minutes. Book. 40 illustrations. 69pp. 5¼ x 10½. T890 The set **$4.95**

AN ENGLISH-FRENCH-GERMAN-SPANISH WORD FREQUENCY DICTIONARY, H. S. Eaton. An indispensable language study aid, this is a semantic frequency list of the 6000 most frequently used words in 4 languages—24,000 words in all. The lists, based on concepts rather than words alone, and containing all modern, exact, and idiomatic vocabulary, are arranged side by side to form a unique 4-language dictionary. A simple key indicates the importance of the individual words within each language. Over 200 pages of separate indexes for each language enable you to locate individual words at a glance. Will help language teachers and students, authors of textbooks, grammars, and language tests to compare concepts in the various languages and to concentrate on basic vocabulary, avoiding uncommon and obsolete words. 2 Appendixes. xxi + 441pp. 6½ x 9¼. T738 Paperbound **$2.45**

NEW RUSSIAN-ENGLISH AND ENGLISH-RUSSIAN DICTIONARY, M. A. O'Brien. Over 70,000 entries in the new orthography! Many idiomatic uses and colloquialisms which form the basis of actual speech. Irregular verbs, perfective and imperfective aspects, regular and irregular sound changes, and other features. One of the few dictionaries where accent changes within the conjugation of verbs and the declension of nouns are fully indicated. "One of the best," Prof. E. J. Simmons, Cornell. First names, geographical terms, bibliography, etc. 738pp. 4½ x 6¼. T208 Paperbound **$2.00**

96 MOST USEFUL PHRASES FOR TOURISTS AND STUDENTS in English, French, Spanish, German, Italian. A handy folder you'll want to carry with you. How to say "Excuse me," "How much is it?", "Write it down, please," etc., in four foreign languages. Copies limited, no more than 1 to a customer. **FREE**

CATALOGUE OF DOVER BOOKS

INVITATION TO GERMAN POETRY record. Spoken by Lotte Lenya. Edited by Gustave Mathieu, Guy Stern. 42 poems of Walther von der Vogelweide, Goethe, Hölderlin, Heine, Hofmannsthal, George, Werfel, Brecht, other great poets from 13th to middle of 20th century, spoken with superb artistry. Use this set to improve your diction, build vocabulary, improve aural comprehension, learn German literary history, as well as for sheer delight in listening. 165-page book contains full German text of each poem; English translations; biographical, critical information on each poet; textual information; portraits of each poet, many never before available in this country. 1 12" 33⅓ record; 165-page book; album. **The set $4.95**

ESSENTIALS OF RUSSIAN record, A von Gronicka, H. Bates-Yakobson. 50 minutes of spoken Russian based on leading grammar will improve comprehension, pronunciation, increase vocabulary painlessly. Complete aural review of phonetics, phonemics—words contrasted to highlight sound differences. Wide range of material: talk between family members, friends; sightseeing; adaptation of Tolstoy's "The Shark;" history of Academy of Sciences; proverbs, epigrams; Pushkin, Lermontov, Fet, Blok, Maikov poems. Conversation passages spoken twice, fast and slow, let you anticipate answers, hear all sounds but understand normal speed. 12" 33⅓ record, album sleeve. 44-page manual with entire record text. Translation on facing pages, phonetic instructions. **The set $4.95**

Note: For students wishing to use a grammar as well, set is available with grammar-text on which record is based, Gronicka and Bates-Yakobson's "Essentials of Russian" (400pp., 6 x 9, clothbound; Prentice Hall), an excellent, standard text used in scores of colleges, institutions. Augmented set: book, record, manual, sleeve **$10.70**

DICTIONARY OF SPOKEN RUSSIAN, English-Russian, Russian-English. Based on phrases and complete sentences, rather than isolated words; recognized as one of the best methods of learning the idiomatic speech of a country. Over 11,500 entries, indexed by single words, with more than 32,000 English and Russian sentences and phrases, in immediately useable form. Probably the largest list ever published. Shows accent changes in conjugation and declension; irregular forms listed in both alphabetical place and under main form of word. 15,000 word introduction covering Russian sounds, writing, grammar, syntax. 15-page appendix of geographical names, money, important signs, given names, foods, special Soviet terms, etc. Travellers, businessmen, students, government employees have found this their best source for Russian expressions. Originally published as War Department Technical Manual TM 30-944. iv + 573pp. 5⅝ x 8⅜. **T496 Paperbound $2.75**

THE GIFT OF LANGUAGE, M. Schlauch. Formerly titled THE GIFT OF TONGUES, this is a middle-level survey that avoids both superficiality and pedantry. It covers such topics as linguistic families, word histories, grammatical processes in such foreign languages as Aztec, Ewe, and Bantu, semantics, language taboos, and dozens of other fascinating and important topics. Especially interesting is an analysis of the word-coinings of Joyce, Cummings, Stein and others in terms of linguistics. 232 bibliographic notes. Index. viii + 342pp. 5⅜ x 8. **T243 Paperbound $1.85**

Prices subject to change without notice.

Dover publishes books on art, music, philosophy, literature, languages, history, social sciences, psychology, handcrafts, orientalia, puzzles and entertainments, chess, pets and gardens, books explaining science, intermediate and higher mathematics, mathematical physics, engineering, biological sciences, earth sciences, classics of science, etc. Write to:

Dept. catrr.
Dover Publications, Inc.
180 Varick Street, N.Y. 14, N.Y.

DATE DUE